SUPER-FAST
Recipes & Tips!

If you're like other family cooks around the country, your daily schedule is jam-packed with errands, activities, chores—you name it. That means you don't have lots of time to prepare the scrumptious, wholesome, home-style meals you want. What's a busy cook to do? The answer is right here in **2011 QUICK COOKING ANNUAL RECIPES!**

The thirteenth edition in our ever-popular *Quick Cooking Annual Recipes* series, this brand-new cookbook features every single dish that appeared in *Simple & Delicious* magazine during 2010. Plus, you get dozens of helpful hints and how-to's. It all adds up to more than 600 recipes and tips—right here in one convenient resource!

With gorgeous full-color photos and more, this must-have collection makes it as easy as ever for you to serve delectable, family-pleasing foods every day of the week.

■ IT'S ALL HERE FOR TIME-CRUNCHED COOKS! ■

CHAPTERS THAT MEET YOUR NEEDS
Choose from 20 convenient chapters, from "Swift Snacks & Appetizers" to "Delectable Desserts." Just turn to page 3 for a complete chapter list, and you're sure to find one that perfectly suits your menu plan and schedule.

For instance, when you have only 10 minutes to spare, whip up Pronto Chicken Fajitas, Sauteed Orange Shrimp with Rice, Raspberry-Walnut Brie, Roasted Red Pepper Spread, Peanut Butter Banana Smoothies or any of the 15 other fast-as-can-be foods in "10 Minutes to the Table."

Or, on weeknights when the kids are hungry and the clock is ticking, rely on the "30 Minutes to Mealtime" chapter for 20 family-pleasing menus—all ready in half an hour or less!

SIX-WEEK MENU PLANNER
The home economists in our Test Kitchen used their best recipes to put together 6 full weeks of Monday-through-Friday entrees, complete with a shopping list for each week. Simply follow these meal plans for weeks of stress-free suppers.

CONTEST-WINNING DISHES
You get all of the standout specialties that earned honors in the five national recipe contests held last year: Easy-as-Pie Pizza, Sensational Spuds, Berry Bonanza, Five-Ingredient Favorites and Super Stovetop Entrees. Turn to page 4 to "meet" the Grand Prize winners and see where each winning recipe is located in this book.

SPECIAL SECTIONS BUILT FOR YOU
In two handy chapters—"Easy Odds & Ends" and "Test Kitchen Secrets"—we've grouped recipes by theme. Featuring grilled fare, leftover makeovers, cooking for two and more, these special sections give you even more options to fit your lifestyle.

TWO HELPFUL INDEXES
See the General Recipe Index on page 314 to locate any recipe by category and/or major ingredient...or check the Alphabetical Index on page 331 when you're looking for a specific dish by name. In both indexes, you'll find a red checkmark (✓) next to recipes that include Nutrition Facts.

Our Test Kitchen pros selected every time-saving recipe and kitchen tip in this collection with on-the-go cooks in mind. So no matter how hectic your schedule may be, you and your family can enjoy this indispensable cookbook now and for years to come.

taste of home
quick
COOKING
2011

p. 12

p. 8

p. 88

VICE PRESIDENT, EDITOR IN CHIEF: Catherine Cassidy
VICE PRESIDENT, EXECUTIVE EDITOR/BOOKS: Heidi Reuter Lloyd
CREATIVE DIRECTOR: Howard Greenberg
FOOD DIRECTOR: Diane Werner, RD
SENIOR EDITOR/BOOKS: Mark Hagen
EDITOR: Michelle Rozumalski
ASSOCIATE CREATIVE DIRECTOR: Edwin Robles, Jr.
ART DIRECTOR: Gretchen Trautman
FOOD EDITOR: Amy Welk-Thieding, RD
CONTENT PRODUCTION SUPERVISOR: Julie Wagner
DESIGN LAYOUT ARTISTS: Kathy Crawford, Nancy Novak
PROOFREADER: Linne Bruskewitz
RECIPE ASSET SYSTEM MANAGER: Coleen Martin
PREMEDIA SUPERVISOR: Scott Berger
RECIPE TESTING AND EDITING: Taste of Home Test Kitchen
FOOD PHOTOGRAPHY: Taste of Home Photo Studio
ADMINISTRATIVE ASSISTANT: Barb Czysz
COVER PHOTOGRAPHER: Rob Hagen
COVER FOOD STYLIST: Diane Armstrong
COVER SET STYLIST: Stephanie Marchese

NORTH AMERICAN CHIEF MARKETING OFFICER: Lisa Karpinski
VICE PRESIDENT/BOOK MARKETING: Dan Fink
CREATIVE DIRECTOR/CREATIVE MARKETING: Jim Palmen

THE READER'S DIGEST ASSOCIATION, INC.
PRESIDENT AND CHIEF EXECUTIVE OFFICER: Mary G. Berner
PRESIDENT, NORTH AMERICAN AFFINITIES: Suzanne M. Grimes

© 2011 Reiman Media Group, LLC
5400 S. 60th St., Greendale WI 53129
All rights reserved.

Taste of Home is a registered trademark of
The Reader's Digest Association, Inc.

INTERNATIONAL STANDARD BOOK NUMBER (10): 0-89821-841-1
INTERNATIONAL STANDARD BOOK NUMBER (13): 978-0-89821-841-1
LIBRARY OF CONGRESS CONTROL NUMBER: 1522-6603

Printed in U.S.A.
1 3 5 7 9 10 8 6 4 2

For other Taste of Home books and products,
visit **ShopTasteofHome.com**

PICTURED ON FRONT COVER:
Country-Style Ribs (p. 171), Spirals and Cheese (p. 72),
Orange-Maple Vegetable Ribbons (p. 55), Cranberry-Cherry Nut Pie (p. 45)
and Italian Cloverleaf Rolls (p. 32).

PICTURED ON BACK COVER:
Bacon-Chicken Sandwiches and Easy Sweet Slaw (p. 12), Frozen Strawberry
Delight (p. 240), Pepperoni Pizza Pasta (p. 74), Heirloom Tomato Salad (p. 135),
Chicken Artichoke Casserole (p. 251) and Gooey Chocolate-Peanut Bars (p. 97).

Contents

RECIPE CONTESTS YIELD QUICK WINNERS

Busy cooks responded in droves whenever *Simple & Delicious* magazine announced a national recipe contest during the past year. They sent thousands of their very best family recipes in hopes they would be named winners.

Want to know which scrumptious, speedy dishes were deemed tops in those contests? Find out by checking the special section here.

On these two pages, we've featured the five cooks who won the Grand Prize in a 2010 contest. We've also let you know where you can find their first-place creations in this book, so you can turn to those celebrated dishes right away...and even make them for your family tonight.

Plus, we've highlighted all of the other recipes that were honored in each contest. You get a complete listing of all 72 contest-winning dishes!

The contest topics yielded a wide range of reader recipes, but all of the winners have one thing in common—they're quick-to-fix and fabulous.

In the "Easy-as-Pie Pizza" contest, we received ideas for sensational slices. Potatoes were at the root of "Sensational Spuds," and our judges picked only the juicy best from "Berry Bonanza."

The next competition, "Five-Ingredient Favorites," brought in so many entries that our judges selected 12 extra runners-up! And "Super Stovetop Entrees" gave family cooks great suppertime solutions.

Simply choose your favorites from this exciting array. Your family is sure to love them! ■

EASY-AS-PIE PIZZA CONTEST

Most nights, Pam Brooks doesn't have much more than 30 minutes to put dinner on the table for husband Dean, an ironworker, and whichever of their two sons happens to be home.

"I always need a plan," says this busy physician services coding supervisor from South Berwick, Maine. She also needs satisfying recipes like her Stuffed-Crust Chicken Pizza, the Grand Prize winner of the "Easy-as-Pie Pizza" contest.

"I've been making the stuffed crust for years, but the chicken version is relatively new. I developed it myself," Pam says. "My kids love it. Sometimes I use rotisserie chicken to streamline preparation even more."

SENSATIONAL SPUDS CONTEST

Our judges considered more than 1,000 recipes submitted in the "Sensational Spuds" contest, but they had no trouble agreeing on Au Gratin Potato Pancakes from Grand Prize winner Cathy Hall of Phoenix, Arizona.

Cathy grew up on her mother's potato cakes, made with leftover mashed potatoes, flour and eggs. And today, in Cathy's own kitchen, you just can't make too many mashed potatoes. Extras are set aside for her crispy pancakes the next night.

"My kids and husband love the gooey cheese in this recipe," she says. "Most people are pleasantly surprised and say they've never tasted anything like it before."

BERRY BONANZA CONTEST

Marilyn Haynes has blueberry bushes right outside her kitchen door in Sylacauga, Alabama. "But we have to fight the birds and our pony, Daisy, to get enough for this recipe in summer," she says of her Over-the-Top Blueberry Bread Pudding. It received highest honors in the "Berry Bonanza" contest.

Marilyn strives to use fresh, seasonal produce when cooking for husband Ben and her three daughters. "But I still make my bread pudding off-season," she says.

"The rest of the year, I prepare it about once a month with frozen berries. We can't go too long without this dessert because we like it too much!"

FIVE-INGREDIENT FAVORITES CONTEST

Juggling a full-time job and college classes, Shawn Singleton of Beaumont, Texas doesn't have a lot of time to spare. So he's learned to appreciate recipes that come together with just a few items.

His Chipotle Sliders, the top winner in the "Five-Ingredient Favorites" contest, really fill the bill. "Most people can't believe the punch of flavor they pack," Shawn says.

SUPER STOVETOP ENTREES CONTEST

Like many of us with beat-the-clock schedules, Yvonne Starlin of Hermitage, Tennessee struggles to satisfy a hungry family on weeknights.

"Most of the recipes I make are quick because I'd rather spend time with my family than cook," says the Grand Prize winner of our "Super Stovetop Entrees" contest.

Everyday ingredients in her scrumptious Bacon & Rosemary Chicken come together in minutes for a taste that wowed our judges.

"I like to see what's available in my pantry and do a little experimenting," Yvonne says. "My dad gets tired of chicken, but he says this recipe redeems it for him."

CHAPTER 1

Readers' Favorite Fast Meals

Clever cooks always have their "go-to" menus—the ones they turn to again and again when time is especially tight. In this chapter, you'll find 10 of those speedy spreads so you can whip them up for your own family.

Try Salsa Sloppy Joes, Ranch Pasta Salad and cool Strawberry Spritzer...Italian Bread Salad, Chicken Marinara and Lemon Ice...Cider Pork Chops, sauteed Asparagus with Mushrooms and Broiled Blueberry Dessert...and much more.

These guaranteed-to-please meals go beyond great taste. Each complete dinner can be put together from start to finish in just 30 minutes—or less! ■

COOK'S CHOICE. Bacon-Chicken Sandwiches and Easy Sweet Slaw (both recipes on p. 12).

SUPPERTIME IN THE SOUTHWEST

With just a few handy fixings, Jennifer Villarreal can treat friends and family in Texas City, Texas to a fabulous and filling three-course feast in a snap.

"I don't have a lot of spare time for cooking, but we want to eat healthy," she says. "That often means bypassing restaurants and making food at home instead."

Determined to cut prep work without sacrificing taste, Jennifer frequently gets meals on the table with the help of her freezer.

"In winter, I stock up on turkey," she says. "Once a month, I cook an entire bird and shred the meat. Then I freeze it for whenever I need it."

Jennifer pops the turkey out of the freezer to use in everything from salads and sandwiches to tacos—as well as the south-of-the-border supper here.

"When I serve Taco Soup at parties, everyone asks for the recipe," she says. "It makes a lot, so if I'm not feeding a crowd, I freeze the leftovers."

The hearty soup is easy to stir up because it relies on ground beef and a few canned goods.

While the soup is simmering, she tosses together Jalapeno Avocado Salad. "Its tangy dressing will have everyone asking for seconds," Jennifer says. "Guests like it because it's different, and I like the fact that I can add whatever vegetables I have."

For a swift yet scrumptious dessert, four-ingredient Cinnamon Graham Sundaes are hard to beat.

"Many Mexican restaurants serve ice cream in deep-fried shells," she says. "I decided to combine cinnamon graham crackers and honey to get a similar taste. You can replace the honey with caramel or chocolate syrup with good results." ■

Taco Soup

Prep/Total Time: 25 min.

1-1/2 pounds ground beef
  1 envelope taco seasoning
  2 cans (15-1/4 ounces *each*) whole kernel corn, undrained
  2 cans (15 ounces *each*) Ranch Style beans (pinto beans in seasoned tomato sauce)
  2 cans (14-1/2 ounces *each*) diced tomatoes, undrained
Crushed tortilla chips and shredded cheddar cheese
Flour tortillas, warmed

In a Dutch oven, cook the beef over medium heat until no longer pink; drain. Stir in taco seasoning, corn, beans and tomatoes. Cover and simmer for 15 minutes or until heated through, stirring occasionally.

Place tortilla chips in soup bowls; ladle soup over top. Sprinkle with cheddar cheese. Serve with tortillas. **Yield:** 8 servings (about 2 quarts).

Jalapeno Avocado Salad

Prep/Total Time: 20 min.

  2 medium ripe avocados, peeled and cubed
  2 medium tomatoes, chopped
  1 medium onion, chopped
  2 jalapeno peppers, seeded and chopped
  1 cup lime juice
1-1/2 teaspoons sugar
  8 cups torn salad greens

In a large bowl, combine avocados, tomatoes, onion, jalapeno peppers and lime juice; let stand for 5 minutes. Drain, reserving 1/3 cup juice. Stir sugar into reserved juice; add to the avocado mixture. Place the greens in a salad bowl; add the avocado mixture and toss to coat. **Yield:** 10 servings.

Editor's Note: When cutting hot peppers, disposable gloves are recommended. Avoid touching your face.

Cinnamon Graham Sundaes

Prep/Total Time: 10 min.

 10 whole cinnamon graham crackers
1/2 gallon vanilla ice cream
  3 tablespoons honey
  2 teaspoons ground cinnamon

For each serving, place two graham cracker squares on a plate. Top with a scoop of ice cream and drizzle with honey. Sprinkle with cinnamon. **Yield:** 10 servings.

FAVORITES FOR LUNCH OR LATER

Sometimes dinner isn't the main meal of the day. For Tammy Griffin's family in Frankston, Texas, lunch happens to trump dinner in importance.

"My husband, Mike, is a pastor who goes to church early and then stops home for lunch," Tammy says. "I'm a teacher and homeschool my son, Caleb. This lets us all sit down together around noon."

When she's not spending time with her family, Tammy enjoys growing tomatoes, zucchini and other veggies. She also likes to review books on her blog.

In spite of her full schedule, she always finds time to serve a special lunch, such as the one featured here. Each easy recipe works just as well for dinner.

Topped with a zippy dressing, Southwestern Steak Salads provide plenty of wholesome flavor. They're complemented by Garlic Cheese Bread Slices.

"People really love the topping," Tammy says. "Sometimes I switch it up for my son by combining cinnamon, sugar and butter, spreading it on and then broiling the bread."

A glass of sweet Almond Tea always rounds out the menu in a wonderful way. "I received the recipe from a friend and make it about twice a week," Tammy says. "It's such a refreshing drink." ■

Almond Tea

Prep/Total Time: 10 min.

    6 cups water
  3/4 cup sugar
  3/4 cup thawed limeade concentrate
4-1/2 teaspoons unsweetened instant tea
  1/2 teaspoon almond extract
  1/2 teaspoon vanilla extract
    1 medium orange, sliced
    1 medium lemon, sliced
    1 medium lime, sliced
Ice cubes

In a 2-qt. pitcher, combine the water, sugar, limeade concentrate, unsweetened instant tea and the almond and vanilla extracts. Add the fruit slices. Serve over ice. **Yield:** 7 servings.

Southwestern Steak Salads

Prep/Total Time: 25 min.

    1 pound beef top sirloin steak (1 inch thick)
  1/4 teaspoon salt
  1/8 teaspoon pepper
    2 packages (6 ounces *each*) fresh baby spinach
    1 cup chopped sweet red pepper
  3/4 cup chopped tomatoes
  1/3 cup chopped red onion
  1/3 cup ranch salad dressing
    2 tablespoons picante sauce
    1 teaspoon taco seasoning

Sprinkle steak with salt and pepper. Grill steak, covered, over medium heat for 8-10 minutes on each side or until the meat reaches desired doneness (for medium-rare, a meat thermometer should read 145°; medium, 160°; well-done, 170°).

Meanwhile, combine the spinach, sweet red pepper, tomatoes and onion; divide among four serving plates. In a small bowl, combine ranch salad dressing, picante sauce and taco seasoning. Slice steak against the grain; arrange over the salads. Drizzle with the salad dressing. **Yield:** 4 servings.

Garlic Cheese Bread Slices

Prep/Total Time: 10 min.

1/2 cup grated Parmesan cheese
1/2 cup shredded cheddar cheese
1/2 cup mayonnaise
1/4 teaspoon garlic powder
  1 loaf (8 ounces) French bread, halved
    lengthwise

In a small bowl, combine the cheeses, mayonnaise and garlic powder. Spread over cut sides of bread. Place on an ungreased baking sheet.

Broil bread 4 in. from the heat for 2-3 minutes or until lightly browned. Cut each piece in half. Serve warm. **Yield:** 4 servings.

GREAT FLAVOR WITHOUT A FUSS

Although Agnes Ward of Stratford, Ontario lives alone, she often finds herself cooking for more than one.

"There are six units in my apartment building, and we all look after each other," she says. "So it's not unusual for me to share my soups, pies or other foods with neighbors."

After years of feeding her family, Agnes has quick cooking down to a science. "Even though it's just me now, I still do things to make meals easier," she says. "For instance, I'll make big batches and freeze them as single servings."

Thanks to her speedy outlook, the complete menu she shares here comes together in a snap yet delivers loads of appeal.

"Everyone likes my Bacon-Chicken Sandwiches," she says. "Flattening the chicken helps it cook faster, and the mango chutney makes it memorable."

The sandwiches pair well with Agnes' Easy Sweet Slaw. "It was a church cookbook recipe I tweaked," she says. "It's the only coleslaw I make."

Blueberry Shortcake Sundaes offer a refreshing conclusion to the meal. "I fix this yummy dessert quite often," she says. "If you need to save even more time in the kitchen, just buy blueberry pie filling and thin it out with a little orange juice." ∎

Bacon-Chicken Sandwiches

Prep/Total Time: 25 min.

    4 boneless skinless chicken breast halves
      (5 ounces *each*)
1/2 teaspoon salt
1/2 teaspoon pepper
    2 teaspoons canola oil
    4 tomato slices
    4 slices process Swiss cheese
1/4 cup mango chutney
    3 tablespoons mayonnaise
    4 kaiser rolls, split and toasted
    1 cup fresh baby spinach
    8 slices ready-to-serve fully cooked bacon,
      warmed

Flatten chicken to 1/2-in. thickness; sprinkle with salt and pepper. In a large skillet over medium heat, cook the chicken in oil for 4-5 minutes on each side or until chicken juices run clear. Top each chicken breast half with a tomato and cheese slice; cover and cook for 2-3 minutes or until cheese is melted.

Combine chutney and mayonnaise; spread over the roll bottoms. Layer with the spinach, chicken and bacon; replace tops. **Yield:** 4 servings.

Easy Sweet Slaw

Prep/Total Time: 15 min.

    4 cups coleslaw mix
1/2 cup finely chopped onion
1/4 cup finely chopped celery
1/4 cup finely chopped green pepper
DRESSING:
1/2 cup mayonnaise
1/4 cup canned unsweetened crushed pineapple,
      drained
    2 tablespoons unsweetened pineapple juice
    2 tablespoons cider vinegar
    2 to 4 teaspoons sugar
1/2 teaspoon salt
1/4 teaspoon pepper

In a serving bowl, combine coleslaw mix, onion, celery and green pepper. Combine dressing ingredients; pour over cabbage mixture and toss to coat. Chill until serving. **Yield:** 4 servings.

Blueberry Shortcake Sundaes

Prep/Total Time: 20 min.

    1/3 cup sugar
1-1/2 teaspoons cornstarch
    1/4 teaspoon ground cinnamon
      3 tablespoons water
1-1/2 cups fresh *or* frozen blueberries
      4 slices pound cake
      4 scoops vanilla ice cream

In a small saucepan, combine the sugar, cornstarch and cinnamon. Stir in water and blueberries until blended. Bring mixture to a boil; cook and stir for 2-4 minutes or until thickened.

Place cake slices on four dessert plates. Top each with ice cream and blueberry sauce. **Yield:** 4 servings.

TASTY PORK DINNER PRONTO

When it comes to special but speedy food, this restaurant-quality dinner from Betty Jean Nichols of Eugene, Oregon really shines.

"I love spending time in the kitchen and have been coming up with recipes for years," she shares. "Since retiring from the University of Oregon's Business Office, I've been cooking even more than before."

While Betty Jean also likes to paint and write, her culinary talents have garnered the most recognition. She has received top prizes in both state and national recipe contests.

Whether she's fixing a meal for herself or for her three grown children and their families, Betty Jean serves no-fuss dishes with flair. She shares one of her favorite menus here.

Moist Cider Pork Chops get mouthwatering flavor from garlic, green onions, celery, dried thyme and apple cider. "If you have fresh thyme in your garden, use that," Betty Jean says. "And boneless pork chops cook even faster."

To complement the entree, she frequently chooses Asparagus with Mushrooms. "This side dish isn't complicated but looks and tastes that way," she says. "People always say it's delicious."

Presented in individual dishes, Broiled Blueberry Dessert makes a yummy and memorable ending. "My daughter and her husband grow blueberries," Betty Jean says. "So I enjoy the challenge of trying to create new ways to prepare them." ■

Cider Pork Chops

Prep/Total Time: 25 min.

- 2 tablespoons all-purpose flour
- 1/2 teaspoon salt
- 1/4 teaspoon pepper
- 4 bone-in pork loin chops (7 ounces *each*)
- 1 tablespoon canola oil
- 1 cup sliced celery
- 4 green onions, sliced
- 2 garlic cloves, minced
- 1/4 teaspoon dried thyme
- 1 cup apple cider *or* juice

In a large resealable plastic bag, combine the flour, salt and pepper. Add pork chops and toss to coat. In a large skillet, brown chops in oil. Remove and keep warm.

In the same skillet, saute celery, green onions, garlic and thyme for 2-3 minutes or until crisp-tender. Return the pork to the pan. Add the apple cider. Bring to a boil. Reduce heat; cover and simmer for 7-8 minutes or until a meat thermometer reads 160°. Serve with a slotted spoon. **Yield:** 4 servings.

Asparagus with Mushrooms

Prep/Total Time: 15 min.

- 1 pound fresh asparagus, trimmed and cut into 2-inch pieces
- 2 teaspoons ground ginger
- 2 tablespoons canola oil
- 3 cups sliced fresh mushrooms
- 1 teaspoon salt
- 1/8 teaspoon sugar
- 1/8 teaspoon pepper

In a large skillet, saute the asparagus and ginger in oil for 2-3 minutes or until the asparagus is crisp-tender. Add the mushrooms, salt, sugar and pepper. Cook and stir 2-3 minutes longer or until mushrooms are tender. **Yield:** 4 servings.

Broiled Blueberry Dessert

Prep/Total Time: 10 min.

- 3 cups fresh blueberries
- 1/2 cup sour cream
- 2 tablespoons brown sugar

Divide blueberries among four ovenproof 8-oz. custard cups. Spread with sour cream; sprinkle with brown sugar. Place on a baking sheet.

Broil 4-6 in. from the heat for 3-4 minutes or until bubbly and sugar is melted. **Yield:** 4 servings.

LAMB FOR A LITTLE VARIETY

When you have a taste for something different, consider this change-of-pace fare from Ruth Lee of Troy, Ontario.

"My parents raised sheep for more than 30 years, so I've built up a good collection of lamb recipes," Ruth says. "They're great to have on hand when I'm in the mood for something other than the usual chicken, beef or pork."

Her main course of Lamb with Sauteed Veggies takes a mere 20 minutes to prepare. "I can count on these chops to come out tender and delicious every time," Ruth says.

While the lamb broils, Ruth sautes red pepper and zucchini to accompany it. "People always comment on this great combination," she says.

Partner that entree with tasty Seasoned Couscous for a nicely filled dinner plate. Flecked with basil and parsley, the speedy side dish goes together easily on the stovetop.

Ruth caps it all off with Brownie Sundaes. "Using convenient prepared brownies, I can assemble this sweet treat in a flash," she says.

"For extra flair, I roll the ice cream in pecans before placing them on top of the brownies. It's a perfect finish to a mouthwatering meal." ■

Lamb with Sauteed Veggies

Prep/Total Time: 20 min.

- 3 tablespoons olive oil, *divided*
- 2 tablespoons Dijon mustard
- 2 tablespoons balsamic vinegar
- 2 teaspoons dried thyme
- 2 garlic cloves, minced
- 1/4 teaspoon salt
- 1/4 teaspoon pepper
- 12 lamb loin chops (1 inch thick and 3 ounces *each*)
- 1 medium sweet red pepper, thinly sliced
- 2 small zucchini, thinly sliced
- 1 medium sweet onion, thinly sliced

In a small bowl, combine 2 tablespoons oil, mustard, balsamic vinegar, thyme, garlic, salt and pepper; set aside 1 tablespoon. Place the lamb chops on a broiler pan. Spread remaining mustard mixture over both sides of chops. Broil 4-6 in. from the heat for 4-6 minutes on each side or until meat reaches desired doneness (for medium-rare, a meat thermometer should read 145°; medium, 160°; well-done, 170°).

Meanwhile, in a large skillet, saute the red pepper, zucchini and onion in remaining oil until crisp-tender. Stir in reserved mustard mixture; toss to coat. Serve with lamb chops. **Yield:** 6 servings.

Seasoned Couscous

Prep/Total Time: 15 min.

- 2 cups water
- 1 tablespoon butter
- 1 tablespoon dried parsley flakes
- 2 teaspoons chicken bouillon granules
- 1/2 teaspoon dried minced onion
- 1/2 teaspoon dried basil
- 1/4 teaspoon pepper
- 1/8 teaspoon garlic powder
- 1 package (10 ounces) couscous

In a large saucepan, combine the first eight ingredients; bring to a boil. Remove from the heat; stir in couscous. Cover and let stand for 5 minutes or until the liquid is absorbed. Fluff with a fork. **Yield:** 6 servings.

Brownie Sundaes

Prep/Total Time: 10 min.

- 3/4 cup semisweet chocolate chips
- 1/2 cup evaporated milk
- 2 tablespoons brown sugar
- 2 teaspoons butter
- 1/2 teaspoon vanilla extract
- 6 prepared brownies (3 inches square)
- 6 scoops vanilla *or* chocolate fudge ice cream
- 1/2 cup chopped pecans

In a large saucepan, combine the semisweet chocolate chips, milk and brown sugar. Cook and stir over medium heat for 5 minutes or until chocolate is melted and sugar is dissolved. Remove from the heat; stir in the butter and vanilla until smooth.

Spoon about 2 tablespoons warm chocolate sauce onto each dessert plate. Top with a brownie and a scoop of ice cream. Drizzle with additional chocolate sauce if desired. Sprinkle with pecans. **Yield:** 6 servings.

TRIO WITH AN ITALIAN ACCENT

Nothing brings 'em running to the table quite like a homemade Italian supper featuring pasta, salad and a delicious dessert. And this memorable menu shared by Kathleen Williams of St. Albans, West Virginia delivers all of that in just half an hour.

"When I retired, I realized that retirement doesn't necessarily mean you have more time to devote to food preparation," she says. "I keep busy with lots of activities, including volunteering."

Still, Kathleen fixes a home-cooked dinner almost every night. "When time is tight, I fall back on the fast-to-fix dishes that were mainstays when I was working, like this Italian meal," she says.

Garlic and basil flavor the tomato sauce that coats tender Chicken Marinara. "A friend gave me this skillet recipe years ago," Kathleen says. "It's easy to make using pre-sliced mushrooms, purchased sauce and quick-cooking pasta."

For a fresh-tasting side, Kathleen serves up Italian Bread Salad. "This pretty medley is a snap to prepare," she says. "For variety, add different veggies, such as peppers, zucchini, summer squash or olives."

Kathleen takes advantage of convenient pantry items to dress up Lemon Ice. "I concocted this when I wanted to turn ordinary lemon ice into something more satisfying," she says. "Raspberry preserves and chocolate syrup really reduce the prep work." ■

Chicken Marinara

Prep/Total Time: 30 min.

- 4 boneless skinless chicken breast halves (4 ounces *each*)
- 2 cups sliced fresh mushrooms
- 3 garlic cloves, minced
- 1 teaspoon dried basil
- 1/2 teaspoon Italian seasoning
- 1 jar (26 ounces) meatless spaghetti sauce
- 1/2 cup dry red wine *or* chicken broth
- Hot cooked angel hair pasta *or* spaghetti

In a large nonstick skillet coated with cooking spray, cook chicken over medium heat for 4-6 minutes on each side or until a meat thermometer reads 170°; remove and keep warm.

In the same skillet, saute the mushrooms, garlic, basil and Italian seasoning until mushrooms are tender. Stir in spaghetti sauce and wine.

Add the chicken; cover and simmer for 10 minutes or until heated through. Serve with angel hair pasta. **Yield:** 4 servings.

Italian Bread Salad

Prep/Total Time: 25 min.

- 4 slices Italian *or* French bread (1 inch thick)
- 2 tablespoons olive oil, *divided*
- 2 plum tomatoes, halved lengthwise and sliced
- 1 medium cucumber, seeded and chopped
- 2 to 3 green onions, sliced
- 2 tablespoons shredded Parmesan cheese
- Lettuce leaves
- 3 tablespoons red wine vinegar
- 1 garlic clove, minced
- 1/4 teaspoon dried basil

Brush both sides of Italian bread with 1 tablespoon oil. Place on a baking sheet. Broil 4 in. from the heat for 1-2 minutes on each side or until lightly browned. Cut into 1-in. cubes.

In a large bowl, toss the Italian bread cubes, tomatoes, cucumber, green onions and Parmesan cheese. Divide the mixture among four lettuce-lined salad plates. In a small bowl, whisk the red wine vinegar, garlic, basil and remaining oil. Drizzle over salads. Serve immediately. **Yield:** 4 servings.

Lemon Ice

Prep/Total Time: 10 min.

- 1/4 cup raspberry preserves
- 2 tablespoons orange juice
- 1 pint lemon ice *or* sherbet
- Chocolate syrup

In a small bowl, combine the preserves and orange juice. Spoon into four dessert dishes. Top each with a scoop of lemon ice. Drizzle with chocolate syrup. Serve immediately. **Yield:** 4 servings.

SUPER SANDWICH FOR SUPPER

Thanks to Krista Collins of Concord, North Carolina, the words "effortless" and "mouthwatering" will be the best ones to describe your next gathering. The spread she shares here is ideal for a casual get-together...and great for a busy weeknight, too.

"When I'm planning menus for my family, I have to keep several things in mind," Krista says. "My kids can be picky eaters, so whatever I cook must appeal to them. We're also on a budget, and it's much more economical to prepare our meals at home than to eat at a restaurant."

This 25-minute dinner is inexpensive and pleases everyone at the table. Krista puts together the pasta salad first, the sandwiches next and the punch last so it retains its fizz.

"I've made Ranch Pasta Salad for years—the recipe came from a high school friend's mother," she says. "It's satisfying and wholesome because of the variety of vegetables it calls for. You can use low-fat dressing or substitute vegetables of your choice to suit tastes or dietary needs."

To make the filling for popular Salsa Sloppy Joes, Krista needs just four convenient ingredients that are usually in her pantry.

"I created these sandwiches in a pinch one night when I realized I was out of canned sloppy joe sauce," she says. "The sweet brown sugar really complements the tangy salsa."

For a great thirst-quencher to round out supper, Krista stirs up refreshing Strawberry Spritzers. "My grandma, Naomi Beller, served this in a punch bowl every year at Christmas, and we all looked forward to that tradition," she says.

"This beverage is also wonderful on hot summer days when the grill is fired up. Plus, it's an easy way to get my children to eat their fruit!" ■

Salsa Sloppy Joes

Prep/Total Time: 20 min.

1 pound ground beef
1-1/3 cups salsa
1 can (10-3/4 ounces) condensed tomato soup, undiluted
1 tablespoon brown sugar
8 hamburger buns, split

In a large skillet, cook the beef over medium heat until no longer pink; drain. Stir in the salsa, tomato soup and brown sugar. Cover and simmer for 10 minutes or until heated through. Spoon 1/2 cup onto each hamburger bun. **Yield:** 8 servings.

Ranch Pasta Salad

Prep/Total Time: 25 min.

3 cups uncooked tricolor spiral pasta
1 cup chopped fresh broccoli florets
3/4 cup chopped seeded peeled cucumber
1/2 cup chopped seeded tomato
1 bottle (8 ounces) ranch salad dressing
1/2 cup shredded Parmesan cheese

Cook spiral pasta according to the package directions; drain and rinse in cold water. In a large bowl, combine the pasta, broccoli, cucumber and tomato. Drizzle with ranch salad dressing; toss to coat. Sprinkle with cheese. **Yield:** 8 servings.

Strawberry Spritzer

Prep/Total Time: 10 min.

1 package (10 ounces) frozen sweetened sliced strawberries, thawed
2 liters lemon-lime soda, chilled
1 can (12 ounces) frozen pink lemonade concentrate, thawed

Place the strawberries in a blender; cover and process until pureed. Pour into a pitcher; stir in the lemon-lime soda and pink lemonade concentrate. Serve immediately. **Yield:** 2-1/2 quarts.

Believe it or not, fresh vegetables can be a time-crunched cook's friend. Just ask Trisha Kruse of Eagle, Idaho.

She counts on produce to get food on the table quickly, despite a packed schedule. "I use fresh items as much as possible," she says. "Our home sits on an acre with a garden, fruit trees and raspberries. I love cooking what I grow. But I'll admit, on hectic days, frozen veggies can be a big help!"

An accountant who volunteers, takes dance classes and regularly exercises, Trisha fits a lot into her daily routine...and her husband, David, is just as busy.

"We always seem to be on the go," she says, "but good nutrition and sit-down meals are a priority for us. I accomplish this by being organized, planning ahead and using lots of shortcuts. I assemble freezable dinners, take advantage of my slow cooker and focus on efficiency when shopping, prepping or baking. But I still try to keep it fun!"

To prepare homemade dinners for herself and her husband most nights of the week, Trisha came up with a strategy. "I map out a week's worth of menus, shop with a list and use seasonal ingredients and coupons. I also prep a lot in advance, and I spend a lot of time in the kitchen on Sundays."

Here, Trisha shares a satisfying supper featuring delicious Ham and Swiss Biscuits. "It's an easy main dish I serve often," she says.

"Even people who don't care for cauliflower love Creamy Cauliflower Soup. And Curry-Cranberry Spinach Salad is so versatile—sometimes I switch things up a bit by using dried apricots or pineapple, as well as arugula or other sturdy greens." ■

Curry-Cranberry Spinach Salad

Prep/Total Time: 10 min.

5 cups fresh baby spinach
1/4 cup pine nuts
3 tablespoons dried cranberries
1 tablespoon sesame seeds
1/4 cup packed brown sugar
1/4 cup rice vinegar
1/4 cup olive oil
1 tablespoon soy sauce
2 teaspoons dried minced onion
1/2 teaspoon curry powder
1/4 teaspoon salt

In a large salad bowl, combine the spinach, pine nuts, cranberries and sesame seeds. In a small bowl, whisk the remaining ingredients. Drizzle over the salad and toss to coat. **Yield:** 5 servings.

Creamy Cauliflower Soup

Prep/Total Time: 25 min.

1 package (16 ounces) frozen cauliflower
1 cup frozen sliced carrots
3 tablespoons dried minced onion
1 tablespoon chicken bouillon granules
2-1/4 cups water, *divided*
2 cups 2% milk
1 can (10-3/4 ounces) condensed cream of potato soup, undiluted
1/2 teaspoon garlic powder
1/8 teaspoon ground nutmeg
4 teaspoons cornstarch
1 cup (4 ounces) shredded cheddar cheese

In a large saucepan, combine cauliflower, carrots, dried onion, chicken bouillon and 2 cups water. Bring to a boil. Reduce heat; cover and simmer for 4-6 minutes or until vegetables are tender.

Stir in the milk, soup, garlic powder and nutmeg. Combine cornstarch and remaining water until smooth; gradually stir into soup. Bring to a boil; cook and stir for 2 minutes or until slightly thickened. Stir in cheese until melted. **Yield:** 5 servings.

Ham and Swiss Biscuits

Prep/Total Time: 20 min.

2 cups biscuit/baking mix
1/4 pound fully cooked ham, finely chopped
1/2 cup shredded Swiss cheese
2/3 cup 2% milk
1 egg
1 tablespoon honey mustard
2 teaspoons dried minced onion

In a small bowl, combine biscuit mix, ham and cheese. Combine the milk, egg, mustard and onion. Stir into biscuit mixture just until moistened. Drop by 1/4 cupfuls 2 in. apart onto a greased baking sheet.

Bake at 425° for 10-12 minutes or until golden brown. Serve warm. **Yield:** 10 biscuits.

With 10 grandkids, frequent company on Sundays and a husband who is often traveling, Lee Deneau of Lansing, Michigan faces a few challenges when serving dinner.

"My husband preaches at different churches, so our schedules can really get hectic," Lee says. "I often use my slow cooker so we have a hot meal when we do get home. I also plan ahead and use some premade items in my otherwise 'from-scratch' dishes."

Despite her busy lifestyle, Lee lends her culinary skills wherever she can. "I oversee a lot of cooking for church functions and like to make contributions for potlucks, too," she says.

Thanks to all of that kitchen time, Lee has learned some time-saving tricks. "When preparing hamburger, I make extra—sometimes with celery and onions—and freeze it for casseroles or chili," she shares. "I do the same with chicken and diced veggies."

To keep crowd-size cooking within her budget, Lee shops sales, buys fruits and vegetables in season, uses coupons and cans produce in fall. The result is always economical but good food, including the tasty menu she shares here.

"Chili Mac combines my chili recipe with a pasta recipe I have," she says. "I serve it to guests and take it to gatherings. Sometimes I add taco seasoning or use beanless chili and add black beans."

Lee tweaked In a Snap Pepperoni Salad by replacing bacon with pepperoni. "I just snip it with a kitchen shears and sprinkle it on," she says. "This salad is a good way for kids to get their vegetables."

For a special finale, she relies on Peanut Butter Pie. "It's a favorite, so I fix it every chance I get," Lee says. "My youngest son wanted pies around his wedding cake, and this was one of his requests!" ■

Chili Mac

Prep/Total Time: 20 min.

1 cup uncooked elbow macaroni
1 pound ground beef
1 small green pepper, chopped
1 small onion, chopped
2 cans (15 ounces *each*) chili with beans
1 can (11 ounces) whole kernel corn, drained
1 cup (4 ounces) shredded cheddar cheese

Cook the macaroni according to package directions.
   Meanwhile, in a large skillet, cook the beef, green pepper and onion over medium heat until meat is no longer pink; drain. Stir in chili and corn. Drain macaroni; add to the skillet and heat through. Sprinkle with cheese. **Yield:** 6 servings.

In a Snap Pepperoni Salad

Prep/Total Time: 15 min.

24 slices pepperoni
 4 green onions, chopped
 2 cups fresh broccoli florets
 1 cup fresh cauliflowerets
1/2 cup chopped celery
1/2 cup golden raisins
DRESSING:
 2/3 cup mayonnaise
 1/3 cup sugar
 4 teaspoons cider vinegar

In a large serving bowl, combine the first six ingredients. For the dressing, in a small bowl, whisk together the mayonnaise, sugar and vinegar. Pour over salad; toss to coat. **Yield:** 6 servings.

Peanut Butter Pie

Prep/Total: 10 min.

3/4 cup peanut butter
 4 ounces cream cheese, softened
 1 cup confectioners' sugar
 1 carton (8 ounces) frozen whipped topping, thawed
 1 graham cracker crust (9 inches)
Salted chopped peanuts

In a large bowl, beat the peanut butter, cream cheese and confectioners' sugar until smooth. Fold in whipped topping; pour into the graham cracker crust. Sprinkle with peanuts. Chill until serving. Refrigerate leftovers. **Yield:** 8 servings.

HOME COOKING IN A HURRY

Mix a practical attitude with creativity and a love of food, and you've got Margaret Wilson's kitchen philosophy. "I don't care for time-consuming or complex recipes," says the Sun City, California cook. "I'd rather come up with a scrumptious, satisfying meal by being inventive with what I have on hand."

With a husband who's frequently on the road, Margaret's got good reason to put together delicious, welcoming dishes.

"Tracy's a truck driver and really appreciates home cooking on his days off," she explains. "We value our time together when he's here, so I rely on quick fare to avoid being preoccupied in the kitchen."

Margaret's strategy for serving tempting, fast-to-fix suppers not only leaves minutes to spare, but also saves money. "I plan my menus by concentrating on ingredients I already have in the pantry," she says. "At the grocery store, I cut costs with coupons and by shopping sales."

The tasty dinner featured here perfectly illustrates her no-nonsense approach to cooking. For example, Turkey Cutlets with Pan Gravy takes just 20 minutes and delivers lots of appeal.

"Using cutlets or any boneless meat will speed up cooking," Margaret says. "If you prefer, replace the turkey with thin boneless, skinless chicken breast."

To savor all of the gravy from that entree, she fixes Crunchy Mashed Potatoes. "Stirring up the instant kind is convenient, but you can use leftover mashed potatoes, too," she shares. "I sometimes try different flavors of onion rings or add garlic."

Italian Vegetable Medley finishes filling up plates while lending an eye-catching pop of color. "People are always surprised at how simple this is," she says. "And it's a great way to use leftover veggies." ■

GOOD GRAVY

- To avoid lumpy gravy, first make a roux (pronounced "roo"), which is a mixture of flour and fat (in this case, butter) that's cooked over low heat and used to thicken sauces. A roux can be white, blond or brown, depending on how long it's allowed to cook and what fat the flour is mixed with.
- Make sure the butter is completely melted before adding the flour. Test it by sprinkling in a pinch of flour. If it slowly starts to bubble, whisk in the rest of the flour. Whisk the butter and flour constantly until the mixture is blended and smooth.
- Gradually whisk or stir in the chicken broth. Bring the mixture to a boil, whisking constantly until the gravy is thickened, about 2 minutes.

Turkey Cutlets with Pan Gravy

Prep/Total Time: 20 min.

- 1 teaspoon poultry seasoning
- 1/2 teaspoon seasoned salt
- 1/4 teaspoon pepper, *divided*
- 1 package (17.6 ounces) turkey breast cutlets
- 2 tablespoons canola oil
- 2 tablespoons butter
- 1/4 cup all-purpose flour
- 2 cups chicken broth

Combine the poultry seasoning, salt and 1/8 teaspoon pepper. Sprinkle over the turkey. In a large skillet, cook cutlets in batches in oil for 2-3 minutes on each side or until turkey juices run clear. Remove meat to a serving platter and keep warm.

In the same skillet, melt the butter and stir in the flour until smooth. Gradually stir in the chicken broth. Bring to a boil; cook and stir for 2 minutes or until thickened. Remove from the heat; season with remaining pepper. Serve with turkey. **Yield:** 4 servings.

Italian Vegetable Medley

Prep/Total Time: 15 min.

- 1 package (16 ounces) broccoli stir-fry vegetables
- 1 tablespoon butter
- 2 tablespoons grated Parmesan cheese
- 1 tablespoon seasoned bread crumbs
- 1/8 teaspoon garlic powder
- 1/8 teaspoon seasoned salt
- 1/8 teaspoon pepper

Microwave the stir-fry vegetables according to package directions; drain. Stir in the butter. Meanwhile, in a small bowl, combine the Parmesan cheese, seasoned bread crumbs, garlic powder, salt and pepper; sprinkle over vegetables. **Yield:** 4 servings.

Crunchy Mashed Potatoes

Prep/Total Time: 15 min.

- 3 cups chicken broth
- 1 cup 2% milk
- 1 garlic clove, minced
- 1/4 teaspoon pepper
- 3 cups mashed potato flakes
- 1/4 cup sour cream
- 1-1/2 cups cheddar french-fried onions
- 1/4 cup grated Parmesan cheese

In a large saucepan, bring the chicken broth to a boil. Remove from the heat. Add the milk, garlic and pepper. Whisk in the mashed potato flakes and sour cream until mixture is smooth.

Spoon potato mixture into a greased 9-in. square baking pan. Sprinkle with onions and cheese. Broil 4-6 in. from heat for 20-30 seconds or until golden brown. **Yield:** 5 servings.

CHAPTER 2

Holiday & Seasonal Pleasers

Celebrate every special time of year with the sparkling treats in this fun-filled chapter. They're not only sure to delight family and friends, but also a cinch to put together.

Say "I love you" on February 14 with Valentine Heart Cakes... conjure up a yummy Cauldron Cheese Ball for Halloween... and spread lots of good cheer at Christmastime with a batch of Double-Decker Fudge.

The excitement keeps going when you fix the festive recipes we've featured for Easter, the Fourth of July and Thanksgiving, from All-American Hamburgers to Company's Coming Turkey.

It's all here—unforgettable foods for every occasion! ■

BOO-TIFUL BUFFET. Spiderweb Brownie Trifle (p. 38), Halloween Cutout Cookies (p. 37), Cauldron Cheese Ball (p. 39) and Caramel Corn Treats (p. 38).

BEYOND A BOX OF CHOCOLATES

Talk about love at first sight...or first bite! With its incomparable taste and luxurious richness, chocolate is always the perfect choice as a Valentine's Day gift. Instead of giving loved ones the kind that comes in a box, why not try the easy, decadent recipes here? Don't forget to indulge yourself, too! ■

Valentine Heart Cakes
(Pictured below and below right)

Prep: 30 min.

Show that special someone how much you care by serving up one of these adorable cakes from our Test Kitchen staff. The no-bake treats are a cinch to put together.

10 individual cream-filled sponge cakes
1/4 cup corn syrup
1/4 cup pink sprinkles
3/4 cup canned vanilla frosting, *divided*
1/2 cup canned chocolate frosting
Pink paste food coloring
Coarse sugar

Slice five sponge cakes diagonally in half widthwise in the same direction. Slice the remaining cakes diagonally in the opposite direction.

On each of four dessert plates, place two oppositely cut cake halves together to form a heart. In a microwave, heat the corn syrup for 15 seconds or just until thinned; brush over tops and sides of cakes. Gently press sprinkles over cakes to coat.

Assemble the remaining cake halves into heart shapes on a wire rack over waxed paper. Place 1/2 cup vanilla frosting in a small microwave-safe bowl; tint pink. Place chocolate frosting in a separate small microwave-safe

bowl. Microwave frostings on high for 10 seconds; stir. Microwave in 5-second intervals until slightly thinned.

Spoon frosting evenly over tops and sides of cakes, letting excess drip off. Let stand until set. Repeat. Gently transfer cakes to dessert plates. Tint remaining vanilla frosting pink if desired. Pipe onto cakes and decorate with coarse sugar as desired. **Yield:** 10 servings.

Fudgy Brownies

Prep: 15 min. + chilling **Bake:** 25 min. + cooling

These irresistible brownies are finished off with not one luscious topping, but two—a peanut butter pudding and fudgy frosting. All you have to add is a glass of milk!
—Amy Crook, Syracuse, Utah

1 package fudge brownie mix (13-inch x 9-inch pan size)
1-1/2 cups confectioners' sugar
1/2 cup butter, softened
2 to 3 tablespoons peanut butter
2 tablespoons cold 2% milk
4-1/2 teaspoons instant vanilla pudding mix
1 can (16 ounces) chocolate fudge frosting

Prepare and bake the brownies according to the package directions. Cool on a wire rack.

Meanwhile, in a small bowl, beat the confectioners' sugar, butter, peanut butter, milk and pudding mix until smooth. Spread over the brownies. Cover and refrigerate for 30 minutes or until firm. Frost with chocolate fudge frosting just before cutting. **Yield:** 2-1/2 dozen.

Editor's Note: This recipe was tested with creamy-style frosting. Whipped frosting is not recommended for this recipe.

Chocolate-Frosted Heart Cookies
(Pictured above)

Prep: 45 min. + chilling **Bake:** 15 min./batch + cooling

Mmmm—these cutouts have a hint of orange flavor and are spread with melted chocolate. For a faster set, place them in the fridge after frosting. They'll be ready to enjoy in moments. —Jackie Messina, Chardon, Ohio

    3/4 cup butter, softened
    1/2 cup sugar
      1 egg
      4 teaspoons grated orange peel
    1/2 teaspoon vanilla extract
      2 cups all-purpose flour
    3/4 teaspoon salt
    1/4 cup semisweet chocolate chips
      2 ounces white baking chocolate, chopped
Chocolate, red and pink sprinkles

In a large bowl, cream butter and sugar until light and fluffy. Beat in the egg, orange peel and vanilla. Combine the flour and salt; gradually add to the creamed mixture and mix well.

Divide dough in half. Shape into a ball, then flatten into a disk. Wrap each in plastic wrap and refrigerate for 1 hour or until firm.

On a lightly floured surface, roll the dough to 1/8-in. thickness. Cut with a floured 3-in. heart-shaped cookie cutter. Place 1 in. apart on ungreased baking sheets. Bake at 325° for 13-15 minutes or until edges are golden brown. Remove to wire racks to cool completely.

In a microwave, melt the chocolate chips; stir until smooth. Repeat with white chocolate. Frost half of the cookies with semisweet chocolate and the remaining half with white chocolate. Immediately decorate cookies as desired with sprinkles. Let stand until set. Store in an airtight container. **Yield:** 3 dozen.

Peanut Butter Cheesecake Pizza
(Pictured below)

Prep: 25 min. **Bake:** 15 min. + cooling

My grandkids love to help me make this yummy dessert by pressing the dough into the pan and sprinkling on the chips and nuts. Most of all, they love eating the results! —Fancheon Resler, Bluffton, Indiana

      1 tube (16-1/2 ounces) refrigerated sugar
        cookie dough
      1 package (8 ounces) cream cheese, softened
      2 eggs
    1/2 cup sugar
      1 cup peanut butter chips
      1 cup chopped unsalted peanuts
      1 cup milk chocolate chips
      1 teaspoon shortening

Press dough onto an ungreased 14-in. pizza pan. Bake at 350° for 15-18 minutes or until deep golden brown.

In a small bowl, beat cream cheese until fluffy. Add eggs and sugar; beat until combined. Spread over crust. Sprinkle with peanut butter chips and peanuts.

Bake for 15-18 minutes or until center is set. Cool for 15 minutes. Meanwhile, in a microwave, melt chocolate chips and shortening; stir until smooth. Drizzle over the pizza. Refrigerate leftovers. **Yield:** 16 slices.

Celebrate the annual visit of Peter Cottontail—and the first hints of spring—with this simplified menu. Your get-together will be hoppin' in no time!

From a main course of Ham with Spiced-Cherry Sauce to buttery Italian Cloverleaf Rolls and Green Beans with Lemon and Pine Nuts, this plate-filling meal is sure to delight your guests on Easter Sunday. And everyone at the table will want to save room for an extra-fun dessert—Colorful Easter Cake. ∎

Italian Cloverleaf Rolls
(Pictured below and at far right)

Prep: 20 min. + rising **Bake:** 15 min.

A sprinkling of seasonings on top gives these dressed-up rolls an eye-appealing look and fantastic taste.
—Heidi Hall, North St. Paul, Minnesota

    1 package (16 ounces) hot roll mix
    2 tablespoons butter, melted
    3 tablespoons grated Parmesan cheese
    1 tablespoon sesame seeds
    3/4 teaspoon dill weed
    3/4 teaspoon dried basil
    1/2 teaspoon garlic salt

Prepare roll mix according to package directions. Divide dough into 12 portions; divide each into three pieces. Shape each into a ball; place three balls in each greased muffin cup. Brush with butter.

Combine Parmesan cheese, sesame seeds, dill, basil and garlic salt; sprinkle over tops. Cover and let rise in a warm place until doubled, about 20 minutes.

Bake at 375° for 15-20 minutes or until golden brown. Remove rolls from the pan to a wire rack. Serve warm.
Yield: 1 dozen.

Colorful Easter Cake
(Pictured above)

Prep: 30 min. **Bake:** 25 min. + cooling

Easter dessert just doesn't get much easier—or prettier—than this beautified cake from a mix. To make it, our Test Kitchen home economists decorated the frosted, two-layer treat with brightly colored jelly beans and Fruit Roll-Ups. If you like, try different candies such as chocolate eggs.

    1 package (18-1/4 ounces) white cake mix
    1 can (16 ounces) vanilla frosting
Fruit Roll-Ups
Jelly beans
Decorating icing of your choice

Prepare and bake white cake according to the package directions, using two greased 9-in. round baking pans. Cool for 10 minutes before removing from pans to wire racks to cool completely.

Spread frosting between layers and over the top and sides of cake. Cut the Fruit Roll-Ups into strips of desired widths. Lightly press onto the sides of cake. Arrange jelly beans around the edges of cake. Decorate with icing as desired. **Yield:** 12 servings.

Ham with Spiced-Cherry Sauce
(Pictured above)

Prep: 15 min. **Bake:** 2 hours 20 min. + standing

This showstopping entree will have everyone coming back for another slice and another spoonful of sauce. The recipe lends a tantalizing sweet-tart flair to tender ham.
—Sherry Thompson, Seneca, South Carolina

1 boneless fully cooked ham (6 pounds)
2 jars (12 ounces *each*) cherry preserves
1/2 cup cider vinegar
1/4 cup packed brown sugar
1/4 cup water
1/2 teaspoon *each* ground cinnamon, nutmeg and allspice

Place ham on a rack in a shallow roasting pan. Score the surface of ham, making diamond shapes 1/2 in. deep. Bake, uncovered, at 325° for 2 hours.

Meanwhile, in a small saucepan, combine the cherry preserves, vinegar, brown sugar, water and spices. Bring to a boil. Reduce heat; cover and simmer for 3-4 minutes or until sugar is dissolved.

Pour 3/4 cup sauce mixture over ham. Bake 20-30 minutes longer or until a meat thermometer reads 140°. Let stand for 10 minutes before slicing. Serve with the remaining sauce. **Yield:** 18 servings.

Green Beans with Lemon and Pine Nuts
(Pictured above)

Prep/Total Time: 20 min.

With only six other ingredients, these green beans really shine for a holiday dinner. The grated lemon peel, fresh parsley and toasted pine nuts create a wonderful balance of flavors your loved ones are sure to remember.
—Cittie, Taste of Home Online Community

1-1/2 pounds fresh green beans, trimmed and cut into 2-inch pieces
2 tablespoons minced fresh parsley
4 teaspoons olive oil
1-1/2 teaspoons grated lemon peel
1/2 teaspoon salt
1/4 teaspoon pepper
1/4 cup pine nuts, toasted

Place the green beans in a large saucepan and cover with water. Bring to a boil. Cover and cook for 5 minutes. Drain and immediately place beans in ice water. Drain and pat dry.

Meanwhile, in a small bowl, combine the parsley, olive oil, lemon peel, salt and pepper. Pour over the beans; sprinkle with the pine nuts. Toss to coat. **Yield:** 8 servings.

In the good old U.S.A., nothing says summer more than a traditional backyard barbecue. So celebrate the most patriotic day of the season with an outdoor spread of All-American Hamburgers, Basil Corn on the Cob, Three-Pepper Coleslaw and Delightful Apple Pie. Your party will truly sparkle! ▪

Delightful Apple Pie
(Pictured below)

Prep: 25 min. **Bake:** 45 min. + cooling

What makes eyes light up more than fresh-baked apple pie? With a yummy nut topping, this is one you can hang your hat on. —Amy Wood, Wichita, Kansas

- 1 sheet refrigerated pie pastry
- 6 cups thinly sliced peeled tart apples (about 5 medium)
- 1/4 cup apple butter
- 3 tablespoons all-purpose flour
- 2 tablespoons plus 1-1/2 teaspoons sugar
- 1-1/2 teaspoons apple pie spice
- 1 teaspoon ground cinnamon

TOPPING:
- 1/2 cup all-purpose flour
- 1/4 cup sugar
- 1/4 cup packed brown sugar
- 1/2 teaspoon apple pie spice
- 1/2 teaspoon ground cinnamon
- 3 tablespoons cold butter
- 1/2 cup chopped walnuts

Vanilla ice cream, optional

Unroll pastry into a 9-in. pie plate; flute edges. In a large bowl, toss apples with apple butter. Combine the flour,

sugar, pie spice and cinnamon; add to the apple mixture and toss to coat. Transfer to crust.

In a small bowl, combine flour, sugar, brown sugar, pie spice and cinnamon. Cut in the butter until mixture resembles coarse crumbs. Add nuts; sprinkle over filling.

Bake at 375° for 45-50 minutes or until the filling is bubbly and topping is browned. Cover edges with foil during the last 15 minutes to prevent overbrowning if necessary. Cool on a wire rack. Serve with ice cream if desired. **Yield:** 8 servings.

Editor's Note: This recipe was tested with commercially prepared apple butter.

Basil Corn on the Cob
(Pictured above)

Prep: 25 min. + soaking **Grill:** 25 min.

Steaming the basil under the husks adds lots of flavor to these fantastic ears of corn. Lime makes their sweet taste pop even more. —Diane Eaton, Campbell, California

- 6 large ears sweet corn in husks
- 6 tablespoons butter, softened
- 1/2 teaspoon dried basil
- 1/4 teaspoon sugar

Dash salt
Dash garlic salt
- 1 cup fresh basil leaves

Lime wedges

Carefully peel back corn husks to within 1 in. of bottoms; remove silk. In a small bowl, combine the butter, dried basil, sugar, salt and garlic salt; spread over corn. Place basil leaves over butter mixture. Rewrap corn in husks and secure with kitchen string. Place in a stockpot; cover with cold water. Soak for 20 minutes; drain.

Grill corn in husks, covered, over medium heat for 25-30 minutes or until tender, turning often. Serve with lime wedges. **Yield:** 6 servings.

All-American Hamburgers
(Pictured above)

Prep/Total Time: 30 min.

On a hot summer's day full of fresh-air fun, nothing can beat these juicy, stacked-high bacon cheeseburgers.
—*Jackie Burns, Silverdale, Washington*

  2 tablespoons finely chopped onion
  2 tablespoons ketchup
  1 garlic clove, minced
  1 teaspoon sugar
  1 teaspoon Worcestershire sauce
  1 teaspoon steak sauce
  1/4 teaspoon cider vinegar
  1 pound ground beef
  4 slices process American cheese
  4 hamburger buns, split
  8 cooked bacon strips
Optional toppings: lettuce leaves and tomato
  and onion slices

In a large bowl, combine the first seven ingredients. Crumble beef over the mixture and mix well. Shape into four patties.

  Grill the burgers, covered, over medium heat or broil 4 in. from the heat for 5-7 minutes on each side or until a meat thermometer reads 160° and juices run clear. Top with cheese. Grill 1 minute longer or until the cheese is melted. Serve on buns with bacon and toppings of your choice. **Yield:** 4 servings.

Three-Pepper Coleslaw
(Pictured above)

Prep: 20 min. + chilling

There are never any leftovers when I take this to a picnic, barbecue or other get-together. The recipe begins with a convenient packaged coleslaw mix. To jazz it up, I simply add three kinds of peppers, green onions and a fast-to-fix dressing. The jalapenos provide a bit of a kick.
—*Priscilla Gilbert, Indian Harbour Beach, Florida*

  1 package (10 ounces) angel hair coleslaw mix
  1 medium sweet red pepper, finely chopped
  1 medium green pepper, finely chopped
  1 to 2 jalapeno peppers, seeded and finely
    chopped
  3 green onions, chopped
  1/4 cup white wine vinegar
  2 tablespoons lime juice
  2 teaspoons canola oil
  1 teaspoon sugar
  1/2 teaspoon salt
  1/4 teaspoon pepper

Place the first five ingredients in a large serving bowl. In a small bowl, whisk remaining ingredients. Pour over the coleslaw mixture; toss to coat. Cover and refrigerate the coleslaw for at least 30 minutes before serving. **Yield:** 8 servings.

  Editor's Note: When cutting hot peppers, disposable gloves are recommended. Avoid touching your face.

Does the thought of hosting a Halloween party give you more chills than thrills? Never fear! The recipes here use purchased convenience foods. All you have to do is dress them up for the occasion.

Using products such as biscuit dough and pudding mix, you'll soon have treats galore for every ghost, witch or goblin who appears on Halloween. ■

Halloween Pretzel Treats

(Pictured below)

Prep: 35 min. + standing

Sweet-salty snack sticks—what's not to love? The crafty cooks in our Test Kitchen dipped plain pretzel rods, then decorated them with jimmies in festive colors.

    8 ounces white baking chocolate, chopped
    1 package (10 ounces) pretzel rods
    1 cup orange candy coating disks
Yellow, orange and brown jimmies

In a microwave, melt baking chocolate; stir until smooth. Dip each pretzel halfway into chocolate allowing excess to drip off. Place on waxed paper; let stand until set.

In a microwave, melt candy coating disks; stir until smooth. Dip pretzel tips into coating allowing excess to drip off; sprinkle with jimmies. Let stand until set. Store in an airtight container. **Yield:** about 2 dozen.

Trick-or-Treat Biscuit Pizzas

(Pictured above)

Prep: 25 min. **Bake:** 15 min.

These cute pizza pockets are simple to make. The hardest part is keeping little hands away before guests arrive!
—Jody Tanner, Milwaukie, Oregon

    1 tube (16.3 ounces) large refrigerated flaky
      biscuits
    3 tablespoons pizza sauce
   16 slices pepperoni
  1/4 cup pineapple tidbits, drained
  1/4 cup sliced ripe olives, drained
  1/2 cup shredded pizza cheese blend
    1 egg yolk, beaten
Assorted food coloring

On a lightly floured surface, roll each biscuit into a 4-in. circle. Transfer four biscuits to an ungreased baking sheet; spread pizza sauce to 1/2 in. of edges. Top each with pepperoni, pineapple, olives and cheese.

With Halloween cookie cutters, lightly press a different design into each of the remaining biscuits. Place over filling; pinch seams to seal.

Divide egg yolk among three custard cups; tint each portion with a different color. Brush over the Halloween shapes. Bake at 350° for 15-20 minutes or until golden brown. **Yield:** 4 servings.

Halloween Cutout Cookies
(Pictured above and page 28)

Prep: 30 min. **Bake:** 10 min./batch + cooling

Take advantage of your Christmas cookie cutters to create these fun-filled Halloween goodies from our Test Kitchen staff. Trick-or-treaters are sure to go batty for them!

    1 tube (16-1/2 ounces) **refrigerated sugar**
       cookie dough
  2/3 cup **all-purpose flour**
    1 can (16 ounces) **vanilla frosting**
Green paste food coloring
    1 can (16 ounces) **chocolate frosting**
Chocolate wafers, crushed Shredded Wheat,
    M&M's miniature baking bits, miniature
    semisweet chocolate chips and Fruit Roll-Ups

Let the cookie dough stand at room temperature for 5 minutes to soften. In a small bowl, beat cookie dough and flour until combined.

On a lightly floured surface, roll the cookie dough to 1/8-in. thickness. Cut with a floured 4-1/2-in. Christmas tree-shaped cookie cutter, a 3-in. candy cane-shaped cookie cutter and a 3-in. star-shaped cookie cutter. Cut each star in half. Place shapes 2 in. apart on ungreased baking sheets.

Bake at 350° for 6-8 minutes or until edges are lightly browned. Remove to wire racks to cool completely.

For witches: Tint a portion of vanilla frosting green. Frost the bottom two-thirds of a tree cookie green; frost the top third with chocolate frosting.

For witches' hats, microwave the chocolate wafers for a few seconds to slightly soften as needed. Use a serrated knife to cut a triangle out of one chocolate wafer. Cut another wafer in half, forming two hat brims. Place a triangle over chocolate frosting; add a brim.

Add Shredded Wheat for the hair. Add facial features with baking bits, chocolate chips and cut up pieces of Fruit Roll-Ups.

For snakes: Frost the candy cane cookies as desired. Cut Fruit Roll-Ups into triangles; attach to cookies. Add facial features.

For bats: Frost the halved star cookies with chocolate frosting. For ears, microwave chocolate wafers for a few seconds to slightly soften as needed. Use a serrated knife to cut small triangles; attach to the cookies. Add facial features as desired. **Yield:** about 2 dozen.

Caramel Corn Treats

(Pictured above and on page 28)

Prep/Total Time: 15 min.

Caramel corn, cheese crackers and peanut butter candies give a fall twist to traditional Rice Krispie treats. They're a cinch to make and guaranteed to thrill kids.
—Cathy Tang, Redmond, Washington

    5 cups caramel corn
    2 cups miniature pretzels
    1 cup miniature cheddar cheese fish-shaped
      crackers
1-1/4 cups Reese's pieces, *divided*
    1 package (10-1/2 ounces) miniature
      marshmallows
  1/4 cup butter, cubed
  1/4 teaspoon vanilla extract

In a large bowl, combine caramel corn, pretzels, crackers and 1 cup Reese's pieces. In a large microwave-safe bowl, melt the marshmallows and butter; add vanilla and stir until smooth. Pour over the pretzel mixture; stir until well coated.

    Press into a greased 13-in. x 9-in. pan. Sprinkle with remaining Reese's pieces; press lightly. Let stand until set. Cut into bars. **Yield:** 2 dozen.

Spiderweb Brownie Trifle

(Pictured above and on page 28)

Prep: 35 min. + chilling **Bake:** 25 min. + cooling

I created this layered dessert for my husband because he's a fan of Butterfinger candy bars. Everyone loves it.
—Gloria Wilbanks, Baldwin, Georgia

    1 package caramel swirl brownie mix (8-inch
      square pan size)
    2 packages (8 ounces *each*) cream cheese,
      softened
    2 cups confectioners' sugar
    1 carton (16 ounces) frozen whipped topping,
      thawed, *divided*
    3 cups 2% milk
    1 package (5.9 ounces) instant chocolate
      pudding mix
    1 package (3.4 ounces) instant French vanilla
      pudding mix
1-1/2 cups finely chopped pecans
    3 Butterfinger candy bars (2.1 ounces *each*),
      finely chopped, *divided*
    3 tablespoons chocolate syrup

Prepare and bake brownie mix according to the package directions. Cool on a wire rack. Cut into 1-in. cubes.

In a large bowl, beat the cream cheese until fluffy. Gradually add confectioners' sugar; beat until smooth. Fold in 2 cups whipped topping. Place half of brownie cubes in a 4-qt. trifle bowl or glass serving dish; layer with half of the cream cheese mixture.

In another bowl, whisk the milk and pudding mixes for 2 minutes. Let stand for 2 minutes or until soft-set. Set aside half of pudding mixture. Stir the pecans and 1 cup chopped candy bars into the remaining pudding mixture; spread over the cream cheese layer. Layer with remaining brownies and cream cheese mixture.

Fold 2 cups whipped topping into reserved pudding mixture; spread over the cream cheese layer. Spread the remaining whipped topping over top.

Place chocolate syrup in a heavy-duty resealable plastic bag; cut a small hole in a corner of bag. Pipe eight thin concentric circles 1/2 in. apart on the whipped topping. Beginning with center circle, gently pull a knife through circles toward the outer edge. Wipe knife clean. Repeat to complete the spiderweb pattern. Sprinkle the remaining crushed candy bars in the center of web. Refrigerate until chilled. **Yield:** 21 servings (3/4 cup each).

Cauldron Cheese Ball
(Pictured at left and on page 29)

Prep/Total Time: 25 min.

Strips of red and yellow pepper make the perfect "flames" for this easily constructed cauldron from our Test Kitchen cooks. Taco seasoning gives it great taste, too.

- 3 packages (8 ounces *each*) cream cheese, softened
- 2 cups (8 ounces) shredded cheddar cheese
- 1 envelope taco seasoning
- 1 bunch green onions, chopped, *divided*
- 1 slice process American cheese
- 3/4 cup crushed blue tortilla chips
Sweet red and yellow pepper strips, carrot sticks, pretzel rods and additional tortilla chips

In a large bowl, combine cream cheese, cheddar cheese, taco seasoning and 2/3 cup onions. Shape into a cauldron; wrap in plastic wrap. Refrigerate until serving.

Just before serving, cut face shapes out of American cheese as desired; press onto cauldron. Press crushed chips onto cauldron to coat. Place remaining onions on top.

Garnish with pepper strips, carrot sticks and pretzels. Serve with additional tortilla chips. **Yield:** 4 cups.

Pumpkin Chip Cream Pie

Prep: 20 min. + chilling

This yummy, no-bake pie is perfect for Halloween or any fall occasion. I use a store-bought graham cracker crust.
—Maria Regakis, Somerville, Massachusetts

- 3/4 cup cold 2% milk
- 1 package (3.4 ounces) instant vanilla pudding mix
- 2/3 cup miniature semisweet chocolate chips

- 1/2 cup canned pumpkin
- 3/4 teaspoon pumpkin pie spice
- 1 carton (8 ounces) frozen whipped topping, thawed, *divided*
- 1 graham cracker crust (9 inches)
Slivered almonds and chocolate curls, optional

In a large bowl, whisk milk and vanilla pudding mix for 2 minutes. Let stand for 2 minutes or until soft-set. Stir in the chocolate chips, pumpkin and pie spice. Fold in 2 cups whipped topping. Spoon into crust. Refrigerate for 4 hours or until set.

Spread with remaining whipped topping; garnish with almonds and chocolate if desired. **Yield:** 8 servings.

Orange Pineapple Smoothies
(Pictured below)

Prep/Total Time: 10 min.

Apricot nectar is the secret ingredient in these delightfully light smoothies. You'll find it in small cans in your store's juice aisle. —*Sean Scales, Waukesha, Wisconsin*

- 1 package (16 ounces) frozen pineapple chunks
- 1 cup thawed orange juice concentrate
- 2 cans (5-1/2 ounces *each*) apricot nectar
- 2 cups ice cubes
- 1 envelope (.15 ounce) unsweetened orange soft drink mix

Place half of each ingredient in a blender. Cover; process until smooth. Pour into chilled glasses. Repeat. Serve immediately. **Yield:** 6 servings.

An abundance of family-pleasing fare will grace your holiday table when you turn to the recipes here. Each memorable dish is a tried-and-true favorite for special occasions or anytime.

For the main course, you just can't beat Company's Coming Turkey paired with Seasoned Turkey Gravy. Add delectable Bacon-Almond Broccoli Medley and Apple Cranberry Relish, and you'll have the makings of a feast loved ones won't soon forget.

Want to include a standout stuffing or pie? Choose from the impressive options on pages 42-45. ∎

Company's Coming Turkey
(Pictured below)

Prep: 20 min. **Bake:** 3-1/2 hours + standing

Here is every cook's Thanksgiving dinner dream—a bird that delivers the bountiful flavors of fresh herbs and more in every bite. It's a mouthwatering centerpiece for your celebration, and best of all, it isn't difficult to prepare.
—Caroline Wamelink, Cleveland Heights, Ohio

- 8 tablespoons butter, softened, *divided*
- 3 garlic cloves, minced
- 1 tablespoon poultry seasoning

- 1 tablespoon minced fresh rosemary
- 1 tablespoon minced fresh thyme
- 1 turkey (14 to 16 pounds)
- 3/4 teaspoon salt
- 3/4 teaspoon pepper
- 3 large onions, quartered, *divided*
- 3 garlic cloves
- 2 fresh rosemary sprigs
- 2 fresh thyme sprigs
- 2 cans (14-1/2 ounces *each*) chicken broth
- 3 cups white wine *or* additional chicken broth
- 3 celery ribs, cut into 2-inch pieces
- 3 medium carrots, cut into 2-inch pieces

In a small bowl, combine 5 tablespoons butter, minced garlic, poultry seasoning, minced rosemary and minced thyme. With your fingers, carefully loosen the skin from the turkey breast; rub the butter mixture under loosened skin. Rub remaining butter over skin of turkey. Sprinkle salt and pepper over turkey and inside cavity.

Place two onions, the garlic cloves and the rosemary and thyme sprigs inside the cavity. Place the turkey on a rack in a large shallow roasting pan. Pour the chicken broth and wine into the pan. Add the celery, carrots and remaining onion.

Bake, uncovered, at 325° for 3-1/2 to 4 hours or until a meat thermometer reads 180°, basting occasionally. Cover loosely with foil if the turkey browns too quickly. Cover the turkey and let stand for 20 minutes before slicing. If desired, thicken the pan drippings for gravy. **Yield:** 14 servings.

Seasoned Turkey Gravy
(Pictured at left)

Prep/Total Time: 20 min.

This tasty, don't-miss-a-drop gravy is the kind that makes a great turkey even better. If your family prefers a darker color, simply let the flour brown slightly when you mix it into the saucepan with the seasonings and reserved fat.
—Terri McKitrick, Delafield, Wisconsin

Roasted turkey drippings
Chicken broth *or* water
- 1/4 cup all-purpose flour
- 1/4 teaspoon onion powder
- 1/4 teaspoon rubbed sage
- 1/4 teaspoon pepper
- 1/8 teaspoon garlic powder

Pour the turkey drippings and loosened browned bits into a measuring cup. Skim the fat, reserving 1/4 cup; set aside. Add enough chicken broth to the drippings to measure 2 cups.

In a small saucepan, heat reserved fat. Stir in the flour and seasonings until smooth. Gradually stir in the broth mixture. Bring to a boil; cook and stir for 2 minutes or until thickened. **Yield:** 2 cups.

Bacon-Almond Broccoli Medley

(Pictured above)

Prep/Total Time: 20 min.

Our Test Kitchen staff combined broccoli, yellow pepper and bacon bits in a sweet, buttery sauce for this colorful veggie side. Sliced almonds give it a nice crunch.

1-1/2 pounds fresh broccoli spears
1/4 cup water
  1 medium sweet yellow pepper, cut into strips
1/4 cup butter, cubed
1/4 cup packed brown sugar
  2 teaspoons balsamic vinegar
  1 teaspoon Worcestershire sauce
1/4 cup bacon bits
1/4 cup sliced almonds, toasted

Place the broccoli in a 2-qt. microwave-safe dish; add the water. Cover and microwave on high for 4-5 minutes or until tender.

Meanwhile, in a small skillet, saute pepper in butter until tender. Stir in the sugar, vinegar and Worcestershire sauce. Cook for 1 minute or until sugar is dissolved.

Drain broccoli; place in a serving bowl. Add pepper mixture, bacon and almonds; toss to coat. Serve with a slotted spoon. **Yield:** 8 servings.

Apple Cranberry Relish

(Pictured above)

Prep/Total Time: 25 min.

With five basic ingredients, this refreshing accompaniment will dress up poultry or any other meat entree.
      —*Macey Allen, Green Forest, Arkansas*

  4 cups fresh *or* frozen cranberries, thawed
  2 medium apples, peeled and chopped
2/3 cup thawed apple juice concentrate
1/2 cup raisins
1/4 cup packed brown sugar

In a large saucepan, combine all ingredients. Cook, uncovered, over medium heat, stirring occasionally, until the berries pop and the mixture thickens, about 15 minutes. Serve the relish warm or chilled. Refrigerate leftovers. **Yield:** 3 cups.

If you're like many folks around the country, stuffing is a must-have dish for a Thanksgiving feast. Want to get a taste of recipes from other regions? Here, you'll find traditional stuffing variations from the Midwest, West Coast, East Coast and South.

So go ahead—try something different this year. You just might discover a new family favorite! ■

Sourdough Almond Stuffing
(Pictured below)

Prep: 25 min. **Bake:** 30 min.

Rosemary, artichoke hearts and sun-dried tomatoes give this scrumptious, West Coast-style stuffing a sophisticated feel. It's perfect for an elegant get-together.
—*Hannah Thompson, Scotts Valley, California*

    2 cups sliced baby portobello mushrooms
    1 medium onion, chopped
    4 garlic cloves, minced
  3/4 cup butter, cubed
    1 teaspoon salt
    1 teaspoon dried rosemary, crushed
  1/2 teaspoon pepper
   11 cups cubed day-old sourdough bread
    1 can (14 ounces) water-packed artichoke
      hearts, rinsed, drained and chopped
  3/4 cup slivered almonds
  3/4 cup oil-packed sun-dried tomatoes, chopped
  1/2 cup minced fresh basil
    2 eggs
    1 can (14-1/2 ounces) chicken broth

In a large skillet, saute the mushrooms, onion and garlic in butter until tender. Stir in salt, rosemary and pepper.

In a large bowl, combine the bread cubes, artichokes, almonds, tomatoes, basil and mushroom mixture. In another bowl, whisk eggs and broth. Pour over bread mixture; stir until moistened.

Transfer the mixture to a greased 13-in. x 9-in. baking dish. Cover and bake at 350° for 25 minutes. Uncover; bake 5-10 minutes longer or until lightly browned and a thermometer reads 160°. **Yield:** 17 servings.

Fruited Sausage Stuffing
(Pictured below)

Prep: 25 min. **Bake:** 25 min.

How good is this dish? My family often begs me to make it all by itself as our supper! The sweet, savory and rich ingredients balance each other out wonderfully.
—*Aysha Schurman, Ammon, Idaho*

    1 package (16 ounces) bulk pork sausage
    2 celery ribs, chopped
    1 medium red onion, chopped
    5 green onions, chopped
    2 tablespoons butter
    4 cups seasoned stuffing cubes
    2 cups chicken broth
    1 cup chopped walnuts
    1 cup dried cranberries
  3/4 cup chopped dried apricots
    2 tablespoons minced fresh parsley
  1/2 teaspoon minced fresh rosemary *or*
      1/8 teaspoon dried rosemary, crushed
  1/2 teaspoon pepper

In a large skillet, cook the sausage over medium heat until no longer pink; drain the sausage and set aside. In

the same skillet, saute the celery and onions in the butter until tender.

In a large bowl, combine the stuffing cubes, broth, walnuts, cranberries, apricots, parsley, rosemary, pepper, sausage and onion mixture. Transfer to a greased 13-in. x 9-in. baking dish. Bake, uncovered, at 375° for 25-30 minutes until lightly browned. **Yield:** 13 servings.

Bacon & Oyster Stuffing
(Pictured below)

Prep: 25 min. **Bake:** 30 min.

Crumbled bacon adds mouthwatering flavor to this East Coast-inspired stuffing. The other star attractions are the oysters! If you really like them, add an extra can.
—Sherry Thompson, Seneca, South Carolina

    2 celery ribs, chopped
    1 bunch green onions, chopped
    3 garlic cloves, minced
 1/2 cup butter, cubed
 1/4 cup minced fresh parsley
1-1/2 teaspoons minced fresh sage *or*
      1/2 teaspoon rubbed sage
1-1/2 teaspoons minced fresh thyme *or*
      1/2 teaspoon dried thyme
 1/2 teaspoon poultry seasoning
 1/8 teaspoon pepper
   12 cups cubed day-old French bread
 1/2 pound bacon strips, cooked and crumbled
    2 eggs
    1 cup chicken broth
    1 can (8 ounces) whole oysters, drained and chopped
 1/4 cup white wine *or* additional chicken broth

In a large skillet, saute celery, green onions and garlic in the butter until tender. Add the parsley, sage, thyme, poultry seasoning and pepper.

Place bread cubes in a large bowl; add celery mixture and bacon. In another bowl, whisk the eggs, chicken broth, oysters and wine. Add to bread mixture; stir just until moistened.

Transfer the mixture to a greased 3-qt. baking dish. Cover and bake at 350° for 20 minutes. Uncover; bake 10-15 minutes longer or until lightly browned and a thermometer reads 160°. **Yield:** 12 servings.

Southern Corn Bread Dressing
(Pictured below)

Prep: 20 min. **Bake:** 40 min.

When I was growing up in Mississippi, money was tight, and we learned to stretch what food we had. This recipe makes a rather large batch because of the big families it had to feed. For me, it's still a can't-miss holiday side.
—Margaret Kendall, McConnelsville, Ohio

    8 cups coarsely crumbled corn bread
    4 hard-cooked eggs, chopped
    1 medium green pepper, finely chopped
    1 medium onion, finely chopped
    2 celery ribs, finely chopped
Turkey giblets, finely chopped
    2 garlic cloves, minced
 1-1/2 teaspoons poultry seasoning
  1/2 teaspoon salt
  1/2 teaspoon pepper
    3 eggs, beaten
    3 cups chicken broth

In a large bowl, combine the first 10 ingredients. In another bowl, whisk the eggs and broth. Add to bread mixture; stir until moistened.

Transfer the mixture to a greased 13-in. x 9-in. baking dish. Bake, uncovered, at 350° for 40-45 minutes or until lightly browned and a thermometer reads 160°. **Yield:** 10 servings.

On Christmas, Thanksgiving and other extra-special occasions, everyone at the dinner table saves room for dessert. And nothing makes eyes light up more than a fresh-from-the-oven, homemade pie.

Any way you slice it, the favorites here are sure to be the stars of your menus. If you like, use the recipe on page 45 to make your own Basic Pie Pastry. ■

Mayan Chocolate Pecan Pie
(Pictured below)

Prep: 20 min. **Bake:** 55 min. + cooling

Dark chocolate, coffee liqueur and ancho chili pepper will take your holiday pecan dessert to a whole new level.
—Chris Michalowski, Dallas, Texas

    1/2 cup chopped pecans
    1/2 cup dark chocolate chips
      1 unbaked deep-dish pastry shell (9 inches)
      3 eggs
      1 cup sugar
      1 cup dark corn syrup
      2 tablespoons butter, melted
      1 tablespoon coffee liqueur
      1 teaspoon ground ancho chili pepper
      1 teaspoon vanilla extract
      1 cup pecan halves

Sprinkle chopped pecans and chocolate chips into the pastry shell. In a small bowl, whisk the eggs, sugar, corn syrup, butter, coffee liqueur, pepper and vanilla. Pour into pastry; arrange pecan halves over filling.

Bake at 350° for 55-60 minutes or until set. Cool on a wire rack. Refrigerate leftovers. **Yield:** 8 servings.

Caramel Sweet Potato Pie
(Pictured above)

Prep: 25 min. **Bake:** 50 min. + cooling

I give traditional sweet potato pie a whimsical twist with apple butter and caramel ice cream topping. Serve pieces with whipped topping and a caramel drizzle.
—Heidi Hall, North St. Paul, Minnesota

Pastry for single-crust pie (9 inches)
    1/2 cup chopped walnuts
    1/4 cup caramel ice cream topping, warmed
      3 eggs
      1 cup mashed sweet potato
      1 cup apple butter
    3/4 cup packed brown sugar
      1 cup evaporated milk
      1 teaspoon vanilla extract
    1/2 teaspoon salt
    1/2 teaspoon ground cinnamon
    1/4 teaspoon ground ginger
    1/8 teaspoon ground allspice
Whipped cream and additional caramel ice cream topping

Line a 9-in. pie plate with pastry; trim and flute edges. Sprinkle with walnuts and drizzle with ice cream topping. In a large bowl, beat eggs, sweet potato, apple butter, brown sugar, milk, vanilla, salt and spices until blended. Pour into pastry.

Bake at 400° for 50-55 minutes or until a knife inserted near the center comes out clean. Cover the edges with foil during the last 15 minutes to prevent overbrowning if necessary. Cool on a wire rack. Garnish with whipped cream and additional ice cream topping. Refrigerate leftovers. **Yield:** 8 servings.

Cranberry-Cherry Nut Pie

(Pictured below)

Prep: 20 min. **Bake:** 40 min. + cooling

This showstopper from our Test Kitchen home economists has gorgeous ruby-red color, ideal for Christmastime. To add a festive accent, use cookie cutters to cut small stars or other shapes from the top pastry. A pretty sprinkling of coarse sugar provides the perfect finishing touch.

Pastry for double-crust pie (9 inches)
- 1 can (21 ounces) cherry pie filling
- 2 cups fresh *or* frozen cranberries, thawed
- 3/4 cup sugar
- 1/2 cup chopped walnuts
- 2 tablespoons cornstarch
- 1 teaspoon vanilla extract
- 1/2 teaspoon ground cinnamon
- 1/8 teaspoon ground allspice
- 2 tablespoons butter
- 1 teaspoon 2% milk
- 1 tablespoon coarse sugar

Line a 9-in. pie plate with bottom pastry; trim to 1 in. beyond edge of plate. In a large bowl, combine the pie filling, cranberries, sugar, walnuts, cornstarch, vanilla, cinnamon and allspice. Spoon into the crust. Dot with the butter.

Roll out remaining pastry to fit top of pie. Cut vents using decorative cookie cutters. Place pastry over filling; trim, seal and flute edges. Brush with milk; sprinkle with coarse sugar.

Bake at 375° for 40-45 minutes or until crust is golden brown and filling is bubbly. Cover edges with foil during the last 30 minutes to prevent overbrowning if necessary. Cool on a wire rack. **Yield:** 8 servings.

PASTRY POINTERS

A food processor makes the first step in creating Basic Pie Pastry (recipe below) a cinch. Simply pulse the shortening mixture for coarse crumbs.

The key to making a flaky crust is to avoid overmixing when adding lemon-lime soda to the flour and shortening mixture. Process just until the mixture comes together.

To flute the pie's edges, position your index finger or thumb on the inside of the crust. Place your other hand's thumb and index finger on the outside edge and pinch around your index finger to form a V-shape.

Basic Pie Pastry

Prep: 20 min. + chilling

This pastry is so easy! Try it for the pies on pages 44-45 or anywhere you'd use a regular or deep-dish pie crust.
—Susan Westerfield, Albuquerque, New Mexico

- 2-1/4 cups all-purpose flour
- 3/4 teaspoon salt
- 3/4 cup plus 3 tablespoons shortening
- 6 to 7 tablespoons lemon-lime soda, chilled

In a food processor, combine the flour and salt. Add the shortening; cover and pulse until the mixture resembles coarse crumbs. While processing, gradually add soda until the dough forms a ball. Cover and refrigerate for 1 hour or until easy to handle.

For two single crust pies, on a lightly floured surface, roll out half of the pastry to fit a 9-in. pie plate. Transfer pastry to pie plate. Trim pastry to 1/2 in. beyond edge of plate; flute edges. Repeat with remaining pastry. Fill or bake according to recipe directions.

For a double crust pie, divide dough in half so that one portion is slightly larger than the other. On a lightly floured surface, roll out larger portion to fit a 9-in. pie plate. Transfer pastry to pie plate. Trim pastry to 1 in. beyond edge of plate. Add filling.

Roll out remaining pastry to fit top of pie; place over filling. Trim, seal and flute edges. Cut slits in pastry. Bake according to recipe directions. **Yield:** 2 pastry shells.

Editor's Note: To make without a food processor, in a large bowl, combine flour and salt; cut in the shortening until crumbly. Gradually add soda, tossing with a fork until dough forms a ball. Proceed as directed.

Make merry in December with these yummy Yuletide sensations. They're perfect for giving as gifts, topping off special meals or treating drop-in guests.

Cool slices of Creamy Raspberry Dessert...luscious Double-Decker Fudge...Cookie Pretzel Peanut Bark... fudgy Mint Brownies...whichever delectable delight you choose, you just can't go wrong! ■

Double-Decker Fudge

(Pictured below)

Prep: 15 min. + chilling

Microwave-quick and peanut buttery, this two-layer fudge is just the thing to have on hand for holiday visitors.
—*Sherri Melotik, Oak Creek, Wisconsin*

  1 teaspoon butter
  1 cup peanut butter chips
  1 can (14 ounces) sweetened condensed milk,
    divided
  1 teaspoon vanilla extract, *divided*
  1 cup (6 ounces) semisweet chocolate chips

Line an 8-in. square pan with foil; butter the foil and set aside. In a microwave-safe bowl, combine peanut butter chips and 2/3 cup milk. Microwave on high for 1 minute; stir. Microwave at additional 15-second intervals, stirring

until smooth. Stir in 1/2 teaspoon vanilla. Pour into the prepared pan. Refrigerate for 10 minutes.

Meanwhile, in a microwave-safe bowl, combine the chocolate chips and remaining milk. Microwave on high for 1 minute; stir. Microwave at additional 15-seconds intervals, stirring until smooth. Stir in remaining vanilla. Spread over peanut butter layer.

Refrigerate for 1 hour or until firm. Using foil, remove the fudge from the pan. Cut into 1-in. squares. **Yield:** about 1-1/2 pounds.

Creamy Raspberry Dessert

(Pictured above)

Prep: 25 min. + freezing

This smooth dessert has become a family favorite. With a beautiful color and delightful raspberry-chocolate flavor combination, it gets smiles from everyone at the table.
—*Karen Wirth, Tavistock, Ontario*

  1 cup chocolate wafer crumbs
  2 tablespoons butter, melted
  1 can (11-1/2 ounces) frozen white
    grape-raspberry juice concentrate, thawed
  1 package (8 ounces) cream cheese, cubed
  2 tablespoons confectioners' sugar
  4 cups whipped topping
Chocolate curls *or* grated chocolate, optional

In a small bowl, combine wafer crumbs and butter. Press onto the bottom of a greased 9-in. springform pan. Refrigerate for 30 minutes.

Meanwhile, in a food processor, combine concentrate, cream cheese and sugar. Cover; process until smooth. Pour into a large bowl and fold in the whipped topping. Pour over crust. Cover and freeze for 4 hours or until firm. Remove from the freezer 10 minutes before slicing. Garnish with chocolate if desired. **Yield:** 10 servings.

Mint Brownies
(Pictured above)

Prep: 10 min. **Bake:** 30 min. + cooling

It's amazing that so few ingredients—just two—can add up to brownies that are so decadent. You'll love 'em!
—Kelly Ward-Hartman, Cape Coral, Florida

- 1 package fudge brownie mix (13-inch x 9-inch pan size)
- 2 packages (4.67 ounces *each*) mint Andes candies

Prepare and bake the fudge brownie mix according to the package directions.

Chop five candies; set aside. Arrange the remaining candies in a single layer over the warm brownies. Bake 20-25 seconds longer or until candy is softened; spread over the top. Cool on a wire rack. Sprinkle with chopped candies. **Yield:** 2 dozen.

Cookie Pretzel Peanut Bark

Prep: 15 min. + standing

Looking for a last-minute treat? This sweet-salty candy comes together so easily and pleases everyone.
—Peggy Detjen, Lakeville, Minnesota

- 1-1/4 pounds white candy coating, coarsely chopped
- 3 cups pretzel sticks, broken into pieces
- 1-1/2 cups dry roasted peanuts
- 14 chocolate cream-filled sandwich cookies, broken into chunks

In a microwave, melt candy coating; stir until smooth. Stir in the pretzels, peanuts and cookies.

Drop by tablespoonfuls into miniature paper liners or onto waxed paper. Let stand until set. Store in an airtight container. **Yield:** 8 dozen.

CHAPTER 3

30 Minutes to Mealtime

Imagine...arriving home after a non-stop day and having the recipes for an easy, delicious 30-minute dinner right at your fingertips. You'll have just that, thanks to this chapter packed with 20 meals—all of which can be fixed in half an hour or less!

That means a whole month of weeknight suppers you can serve in a snap. Choose from a wide variety of main courses, each paired with the perfect side or dessert.

Cilantro-Lime Salmon and Squash Saute...Buffalo Chicken and Sweet Cucumber Salad... Open-Faced Texas Burgers and Seasoned Corn with Bacon... these menus are sure to please time-crunched cooks just as much as their families. ■

HALF-AN-HOUR EASE. Turkey Piccata and Colorful Rosemary Rice (both recipes on p. 61).

FLAVOR FROM THE FAR EAST

Let Asian inspiration hit the table tonight. Your meal will cost less than takeout and taste just as good!

For a little over $1.50 a plate, the menu here will deliver a restaurant-quality meal. It features a main dish of Chicken Fried Rice from Taryn Kuebelbeck of Plymouth, Minnesota.

Incredibly easy Broccoli in Hoisin Sauce is sure to surprise even confirmed broccoli-haters with its great flavor. This side dish rounds out a meal you'll be proud to serve to your family.

With some of the money you save, why not grab a bag of fortune cookies for dessert? ■

Chicken Fried Rice

Prep/Total Time: 25 min.

1 small carrot, finely chopped
1 celery rib, chopped
3 tablespoons canola oil
4 cups cold cooked instant rice
3 eggs, beaten
2 cups cubed cooked chicken
1/4 cup chopped green onions
2 tablespoons soy sauce
1/4 teaspoon pepper

In a large skillet or wok, stir-fry carrot and celery in oil for 5 minutes or until crisp-tender. Add rice; stir-fry for 3 minutes or until heated through.

Make a well in the center of the rice mixture; add the eggs. Stir-fry for 2-3 minutes or until eggs are completely set. Add the remaining ingredients; stir-fry until heated through. **Yield:** 4 servings.

Broccoli in Hoisin Sauce

Prep/Total Time: 15 min.

1 package (16 ounces) frozen broccoli florets, thawed
3 garlic cloves, minced
2 teaspoons minced fresh gingerroot
1 teaspoon canola oil
2 tablespoons water
4-1/2 teaspoons hoisin sauce
1/4 teaspoon salt

In a large skillet or wok, stir-fry the broccoli, garlic and ginger in the oil for 2-3 minutes or until the broccoli is crisp-tender. Add the water, hoisin sauce and salt. Cook and stir until sauce is thickened. **Yield:** 4 servings.

SIMPLE BUT SPECIAL SEAFOOD

Here's a menu that's guaranteed to net compliments! Plus, it proves that scrumptious meals don't have to be complicated.

The heartwarming supper comes together in no time and is likely to become one of those versatile standbys—quick enough for weeknights but special enough to serve company at a moment's notice.

To welcome your dinner guests, start the menu with a main course of Glazed Salmon from Angela Lively of Baxter, Tennessee. That dish pairs perfectly with colorful Creamy Spinach Noodle Toss shared by Josie Smith of Winamac, Indiana. ■

Glazed Salmon

Prep/Total Time: 20 min.

    4 salmon fillets (6 ounces *each*)
1/4 teaspoon salt
1/8 teaspoon pepper
    2 tablespoons brown sugar
    2 tablespoons lemon juice
    2 tablespoons Dijon mustard
    1 teaspoon ground cumin

Place the salmon in a greased 11-in. x 7-in. baking dish; sprinkle with salt and pepper. Combine the remaining ingredients; spoon over fillets.

Bake, uncovered, at 400° for 10-15 minutes or until fish flakes easily with a fork. **Yield:** 4 servings.

Creamy Spinach Noodle Toss

Prep/Total Time: 30 min.

1-1/2 cups uncooked egg noodles
    2 bacon strips, diced
    2 teaspoons finely chopped onion
6-1/2 teaspoons all-purpose flour
    3/4 teaspoon salt-free seasoning blend
    1/8 teaspoon salt
Dash pepper
1-1/4 cups 2% milk
    1 package (9 ounces) fresh baby spinach
    3/4 cup grated Parmesan cheese

Cook the noodles according to the package directions. Meanwhile, in a large skillet, cook bacon and onion over medium heat until bacon is crisp. Using a slotted spoon, remove to paper towels to drain.

Stir the flour, seasoning blend, salt and pepper into drippings until blended; gradually add milk. Bring to a boil; cook and stir for 2 minutes or until thickened. Add spinach, cook and stir until spinach is wilted.

Drain noodles; transfer to a serving bowl. Add spinach mixture and cheese; toss to combine. Sprinkle with the bacon mixture. **Yield:** 4 servings.

TASTE OF THE LONE STAR STATE

Have an appetite as big as Texas? This hearty meal is for you! The amazing dishes pack huge flavor into two special servings.

Dig into Open-Faced Texas Burgers from Willie DeWaard of Coralville, Iowa. And don't slow down until you've devoured Seasoned Corn with Bacon from Melissa Just of Minneapolis, Minnesota. ■

Open-Faced Texas Burgers

Prep/Total Time: 30 min.

- 2 tablespoons chopped onion
- 1 small garlic clove, minced
- 1/8 teaspoon dried thyme
- 2/3 cup shredded Colby-Monterey Jack cheese, *divided*
- 2/3 pound ground beef
- 2 slices frozen garlic Texas toast
- 1/2 cup tomato sauce
- 1-1/2 teaspoons packed brown sugar
- 1/2 teaspoon Worcestershire sauce
- 1/2 teaspoon A.1. steak sauce

In a large bowl, combine the onion, garlic, thyme and 1/2 cup cheese. Crumble beef over mixture and mix well. Shape into two oval patties.

In a large skillet, cook the burgers over medium heat for 5-6 minutes on each side or until meat is no longer pink. Meanwhile, prepare Texas toast according to the package directions.

Drain the burgers; set aside and keep warm. Add the tomato sauce, brown sugar, Worcestershire sauce and steak sauce to the skillet. Bring to a boil; cook and stir for 1 to 2 minutes or until slightly thickened. Return the burgers to skillet; turn to coat. Sprinkle with remaining cheese. Serve burgers on toast. **Yield:** 2 servings.

Seasoned Corn with Bacon

Prep/Total Time: 20 min.

- 2 bacon strips, diced
- 1-2/3 cups frozen corn, thawed
- 1 tablespoon finely chopped onion
- 1/8 teaspoon garlic powder
- 1/8 teaspoon lemon-pepper seasoning
- 1/8 teaspoon dried basil

In a large skillet, cook bacon over medium heat until crisp. Using a slotted the spoon, remove to paper towels; drain, reserving 1/2 teaspoon drippings.

Saute the corn, onion, garlic powder, lemon-pepper and basil in reserved drippings until corn is tender. Stir in bacon. **Yield:** 2 servings.

A LINE ON A FISH DINNER

Savor a special meal without spending a lot of time or money. Half an hour and about $3 per plate are all you'll need! Your family will love Parmesan-Crusted Tilapia from Christi McElroy of Neenah, Wisconsin and Dilled Brussels Sprout Medley shared by Priscilla Gilbert of Indian Harbour Beach, Florida. ■

Parmesan-Crusted Tilapia

Prep/Total Time: 25 min.

1/2 cup all-purpose flour
1 egg, beaten
1/2 cup crushed butter-flavored crackers (about 10 crackers)
1/4 cup grated Parmesan cheese
1/2 teaspoon salt
4 tilapia fillets (5 ounces *each*)
2 tablespoons olive oil
Lemon wedges

Place flour and egg in separate shallow bowls. In another shallow bowl, combine the butter-flavored crackers, Parmesan cheese and salt. Dip fillets in the flour, egg, then cracker mixture.

In a large skillet, cook fillets in oil over medium heat for 4-5 minutes on each side or until golden brown and fish flakes easily with a fork. Serve with lemon wedges. **Yield:** 4 servings.

Dilled Brussels Sprout Medley

Prep/Total Time: 30 min.

2-1/4 cups fresh *or* frozen brussels sprouts, thawed and halved
1-1/4 cups fresh baby carrots
1 tablespoon butter
3 teaspoons snipped fresh dill *or* 1 teaspoon dill weed
1-1/2 teaspoons olive oil
1-1/2 teaspoons balsamic vinegar
1/4 teaspoon salt
1/8 teaspoon pepper

Place 1 in. of water in a large saucepan; add the brussels sprouts and carrots. Bring to a boil. Reduce the heat; cover and simmer for 8-12 minutes or until crisp-tender. Drain. Stir in remaining ingredients. **Yield:** 4 servings.

FAST FAMILY FARE FOR BUSY DAYS

Transform a hectic weekday into a stress-free night with this simple spread. It can help you work around your gang's schedule—and empty stomachs!

When school, sports events and extra-curricular activities have your family on the run, full-flavored Beef & Broccoli Skillet will bring them to the table and satisfy hearty appetites in a hurry. "This dish is also wonderful with venison," says Jackie Hannahs of Fountain, Michigan.

For a complete meal you can all find time for, add a dessert of yummy Pear Sundaes from Mary Ann Shoemaker of Loveland, Colorado. ■

Beef & Broccoli Skillet

Prep/Total Time: 30 min.

1 pound boneless beef sirloin steak, cut into thin strips
1 tablespoon canola oil
3 cups fresh broccoli florets
1 can (10-3/4 ounces) condensed tomato soup, undiluted
3 tablespoons soy sauce
1 tablespoon cider vinegar
1 teaspoon garlic powder
Hot cooked rice, optional

In a large skillet, saute beef in oil until no longer pink; drain. Remove and keep warm. In same skillet, combine the broccoli, tomato soup, soy sauce, cider vinegar and garlic powder. Bring to a boil. Reduce heat; cover and simmer for 3-4 minutes or until broccoli is crisp-tender. Stir in the beef; heat through. Serve with rice if desired. **Yield:** 4 servings.

Pear Sundaes

Prep/Total Time: 5 min.

1 can (29 ounces) pear halves, drained
1 quart vanilla ice cream
1/2 cup chocolate syrup
1/2 cup sliced almonds, toasted

Place the pear halves, flat side up, in individual dessert dishes. Top with a scoop of vanilla ice cream. Drizzle with the chocolate syrup; sprinkle with sliced almonds. **Yield:** 6 servings.

FINE DINING ON SHORT NOTICE

Have drop-in guests at dinnertime? You'll reel in raves with this quick-fixing seafood supper that's as pretty as a picture.

Crispy Potato-Crusted Snapper is so tender and tasty—and a favorite with Athena Russell and her family in Florence, South Carolina. "The fillets are great with steamed green beans, rice pilaf...just about any side at all," she says.

To round out a company-worthy meal that couldn't be easier on the cook, we paired Athena's entree with the sweet, citrusy flavor of Orange-Maple Vegetable Ribbons from our Test Kitchen. ■

Potato-Crusted Snapper

Prep/Total Time: 30 min.

- 2 eggs, beaten
- 1-1/2 cups mashed potato flakes
- 2 teaspoons dried thyme
- 4 red snapper fillets (6 ounces *each*)
- 1/2 teaspoon salt
- 1/4 teaspoon pepper
- 1/4 cup olive oil

Place eggs in a shallow bowl. In another shallow bowl, combine the potato flakes and thyme. Sprinkle the fillets with salt and pepper. Dip in the eggs and coat with the potato mixture.

In a large skillet, cook the fillets in oil in batches over medium heat for 4-5 minutes on each side or until fish flakes easily with a fork. **Yield:** 4 servings.

Orange-Maple Vegetable Ribbons

Prep/Total Time: 20 min.

- 1 large zucchini
- 1 large yellow summer squash
- 2 medium carrots
- 1 tablespoon butter
- 1/4 cup maple syrup
- 1 tablespoon orange juice
- 1/2 teaspoon grated orange peel
- 1/4 teaspoon salt
- 1/8 teaspoon pepper
- 1/4 cup chopped pecans, toasted

Using a vegetable peeler, cut the vegetables into very thin lengthwise strips.

In a large skillet, saute the vegetable strips in butter until tender; remove and set aside. In the same skillet, combine the syrup, orange juice, peel, salt and pepper. Bring to a boil; cook for 2-3 minutes or until most of the liquid is evaporated. Return the vegetables to pan; toss to coat and sprinkle with pecans. Serve with a slotted spoon. **Yield:** 4 servings.

PORK FOR A CHANGE OF PACE

Try something new tonight with a mouthwatering dinner the whole family will love. It starts out with a sure winner—our Test Kitchen's sweet and tangy Maple Pork Chops. Crispy on the outside, they're wonderfully tender inside.

Lime Carrots from Steve Foy of Kirkwood, Missouri go wonderfully with the juicy chops. Best of all, this simple side comes together in a snap. ■

Maple Pork Chops

Prep/Total Time: 30 min.

    4 boneless pork loin chops (6 ounces *each*)
1/4 teaspoon salt
1/4 teaspoon pepper
    1 egg
1/4 teaspoon ground ginger
1/2 cup dry bread crumbs
    3 tablespoons butter
SAUCE:
1/2 cup maple syrup
    1 tablespoon Dijon mustard
    2 teaspoons cider vinegar
1/8 teaspoon ground ginger

Sprinkle pork chops with salt and pepper. In a shallow bowl, beat the egg and ginger. Place bread crumbs in another shallow bowl. Dip chops in egg mixture, then coat with crumbs.

In a large skillet, cook pork in butter over medium heat for 5-7 minutes on each side or until a meat thermometer reads 160°. Remove and keep warm. Add the remaining ingredients to the skillet; cook and stir for 1-2 minutes or until slightly thickened. Serve with chops. **Yield:** 4 servings.

Lime Carrots

Prep/Total Time: 15 min.

    1 pound fresh baby carrots
    2 tablespoons water
    1 tablespoon brown sugar
    1 tablespoon butter
    1 tablespoon lime juice
1/2 teaspoon grated lime peel
1/4 teaspoon onion powder
1/4 teaspoon dill weed

Place the carrots and water in a microwave-safe bowl. Cover and microwave on high for 4-6 minutes or until crisp-tender; drain and keep warm.

Place brown sugar and butter in another microwave-safe bowl; cover and cook on high for 30-45 seconds or until sugar is dissolved. Stir in the remaining ingredients. Pour over carrots; toss to coat. **Yield:** 4 servings.

Editor's Note: This recipe was tested in a 1,100-watt microwave.

SPREAD FROM THE SOUTHWEST

Even when winter winds are blowing, you can warm your family right down to their toes with this quick, delicious supper full of Southwestern flavor. And they're sure to request it time and again, no matter what the weather!

Three-Bean Taco Chili from Wanda Lee of Yakima, Washington is packed with ground beef and topped off with cheese. The recipe takes just 30 minutes to fix but tastes like it simmered all day.

"Depending on the size of your family, you just might want to freeze some for an even faster meal later on," Wanda says. "You can freeze extra chili for up to three months. Then thaw it in the fridge, heat it in a saucepan and enjoy."

Spiced-up Mexican Cheese Corn Bread makes an ideal side. Not only is it scrumptious all by itself, but it's also great for soaking up every last bit of goodness in your bowl. Susan Westerfield whips up the golden squares often in Albuquerque, New Mexico. ∎

Three-Bean Taco Chili

Prep/Total Time: 30 min.

- 2 pounds ground beef
- 2 cups water
- 1 can (16 ounces) refried beans
- 1 can (16 ounces) kidney beans, rinsed and drained
- 1 can (16 ounces) chili beans, undrained
- 1 can (15-1/4 ounces) whole kernel corn, drained
- 1 can (14-1/2 ounces) stewed tomatoes
- 1 can (8 ounces) tomato sauce
- 1 cup chunky salsa
- 1 envelope taco seasoning
- 1 can (2-1/4 ounces) sliced ripe olives, drained
- 1 cup (4 ounces) shredded cheddar cheese

In a Dutch oven, cook ground beef over medium heat until no longer pink; drain. Stir in the water, beans, corn, stewed tomatoes, tomato sauce, salsa, taco seasoning and olives.

Bring to a boil. Reduce heat; simmer, uncovered, for 10 minutes. Garnish with cheese. **Yield:** 9 servings.

Mexican Cheese Corn Bread

Prep/Total Time: 30 min.

- 1 package (8-1/2 ounces) corn bread/muffin mix
- 1 teaspoon dried minced onion
- 1/2 teaspoon ground cumin
- 2 eggs
- 1/3 cup 2% milk
- 2 tablespoons butter, melted, *divided*
- 3/4 cup shredded Mexican cheese blend, *divided*

In a small bowl, combine muffin mix, onion and cumin. In another bowl, whisk the eggs, milk and 1 tablespoon butter; stir into the dry ingredients just until moistened. Fold in 1/2 cup cheese.

Transfer dough to a greased 8-in. square baking dish. Bake at 400° for 15 minutes. Brush with the remaining butter and sprinkle with the remaining cheese. Bake 2-4 minutes longer or until cheese is melted and a toothpick inserted near the center comes out clean. Serve warm. **Yield:** 9 servings.

BETTER BREAD

To make jazzed-up corn bread, I use a small box mix that calls for one egg and 1/3 cup milk. But instead of the milk, I stir in 3/4 cup of purchased French onion dip. It's an easy way to boost the flavor.
—*Donna Frederick, Topeka, Kansas*

EASY BUT ELEGANT MEAL

Looking for a fantastic but budget-friendly supper for the end of a busy week? With a delectable sauce, Down-Home Pork Chops shared by Denise Hruz of Germantown, Wisconsin is company-special fare. Fill plates by adding Roasted Asparagus with Orange Juice from Donna Bardocz of Howell, Michigan. ■

Down-Home Pork Chops

Prep/Total Time: 25 min.

- 4 boneless pork loin chops (4 ounces *each*)
- 1 tablespoon canola oil
- 1 garlic clove, minced
- 1/2 cup beef broth
- 2 tablespoons brown sugar
- 1 tablespoon soy sauce
- 1/4 teaspoon crushed red pepper flakes
- 2 teaspoons cornstarch
- 2 tablespoons cold water

In a large skillet over medium-high heat, brown pork chops on both sides in oil; remove and set aside. Add garlic to the pan; saute for 1 minute. Stir in the broth, brown sugar, soy sauce and pepper flakes. Return chops to the pan; cover and simmer for 8-10 minutes or until a meat thermometer reads 160°.

Remove chops and keep warm. Combine cornstarch and water until smooth; stir into broth mixture. Bring to a boil; cook and stir for 1 minute or until thickened. Serve with chops. **Yield:** 4 servings.

Roasted Asparagus with Orange Juice

Prep/Total Time: 30 min.

- 1 pound fresh asparagus, trimmed
- 1 tablespoon olive oil
- 1/2 cup orange juice
- 2 garlic cloves, minced
- 1 teaspoon poppy seeds
- 1/4 teaspoon salt

Place asparagus in an ungreased 15-in. x 10-in. x 1-in. baking pan; drizzle with the oil. Combine the remaining ingredients. Pour over asparagus; toss to coat.

Bake at 400° for 18-22 minutes or until tender, stirring occasionally. **Yield:** 4 servings.

CLASSIC ITALIAN AT ITS BEST

When you and your family aren't hungry for a heavy meal, look to this lighter, lickety-split chicken dinner. It's wholesome, delicious and comes together in a mere 20 minutes.

Moist, savory Tuscan Chicken from Debra LeGrand of Port Orchard, Washington is an unbelievably fast entree. From Elizabeth, Pennsylvania, Debbie Balta shares Vegetable Medley for a colorful, tasty side. ■

Tuscan Chicken

Prep/Total Time: 15 min.

    4 boneless skinless chicken breast halves
       (5 ounces *each*)
1/2 teaspoon salt
1/2 teaspoon pepper
    2 garlic cloves, sliced
    2 teaspoons dried rosemary, crushed
1/2 teaspoon rubbed sage
1/2 teaspoon dried thyme
    2 tablespoons olive oil

Flatten the chicken breast halves to 1/2-in. thickness; sprinkle with salt and pepper.

In a large skillet over medium heat, cook and stir the garlic, rosemary, sage and thyme in oil for 1 minute. Add chicken; cook for 5-7 minutes on each side or until chicken juices run clear. **Yield:** 4 servings.

Vegetable Medley

Prep/Total Time: 20 min.

    1 cup uncooked medium pasta shells
    1 package (16 ounces) frozen cut green beans
    1 tablespoon cornstarch
3/4 cup chicken broth
    3 tablespoons butter
1-1/2 teaspoons Dijon mustard
1/2 teaspoon dried basil
1/4 teaspoon garlic powder
    1 can (4-1/2 ounces) whole mushrooms,
       drained
    1 small tomato, chopped

In a Dutch oven, cook the pasta according to package directions, adding the beans during the last 5 minutes of cooking.

Meanwhile, combine cornstarch and chicken broth until smooth; set aside. In a large saucepan, melt butter; add the mustard, basil and garlic powder. Gradually stir in the broth mixture. Bring to a boil; cook and stir for 2 minutes or until thickened.

Drain pasta and beans; return to the Dutch oven. Add the mustard sauce and mushrooms; toss to coat. Stir in tomato. **Yield:** 6 servings.

FAMILY-FRIENDLY SKILLET AND SIDE

Looking for a speedy menu that'll please young and old alike? Comforting and hearty Sausage Macaroni Skillet from Phyllis Schmalz of Kansas City, Kansas is just the ticket. Evaporated milk and chili sauce add a bit of creamy sweetness kids will really go for.

To serve a nutritious veggie side, add a few simple herbs to microwave-quick Seasoned Broccoli Spears from Melissa Just of Minneapolis, Minnesota. ■

Sausage Macaroni Skillet

Prep/Total Time: 30 min.

- 1 pound bulk Italian sausage
- 1/4 cup chopped onion
- 2 tablespoons chopped green pepper
- 2 tablespoons chopped sweet red pepper
- 2 cups uncooked elbow macaroni
- 2 cups water
- 1 cup chili sauce
- 1 can (5 ounces) evaporated milk
- 1/2 cup shredded cheddar cheese

In a large skillet, cook sausage, onion and peppers over medium heat until meat is no longer pink; drain. Add the macaroni and water. Bring to a boil. Reduce heat; cover and simmer for 7-8 minutes or until the macaroni is tender.

Stir in chili sauce and evaporated milk. Bring to a boil. Reduce heat; simmer, uncovered, for 3-4 minutes or until heated through.

Remove from the heat. Sprinkle with cheese. Cover and let stand for 5 minutes or until the cheese is melted. **Yield:** 5 servings.

Seasoned Broccoli Spears

Prep/Total Time: 15 min.

- 5 cups frozen broccoli florets, thawed
- 1 tablespoon butter, melted
- 2 garlic cloves, minced
- 1/4 teaspoon onion salt
- 1/4 teaspoon dried basil
- 1/4 teaspoon dried thyme
- 1/8 teaspoon pepper

Place broccoli in a large microwave-safe bowl. Combine the remaining ingredients. Pour over broccoli; toss to coat. Cover and microwave on high for 3-4 minutes or until tender. **Yield:** 5 servings.

Editor's Note: This recipe was tested in a 1,100-watt microwave.

ENTERTAINING WITH EASE

Planning to have friends over for dinner? Keep the evening light and relaxed with this flavorful menu.

In El Cajon, California, Leslie Rodriguez adds a buttery sauce with capers and a hint of lemon to her Turkey Piccata. Pair that elegant entree with our Test Kitchen's veggie-filled Colorful Rosemary Rice. ■

Turkey Piccata

Prep/Total Time: 25 min.

- 1/4 cup all-purpose flour
- 1/2 teaspoon salt
- 1/4 teaspoon pepper
- 1 package (17.6 ounces) turkey breast cutlets
- 2 tablespoons olive oil
- 1/2 cup chicken broth
- 3 tablespoons butter
- 1 tablespoon lemon juice
- 1 tablespoon minced fresh parsley
- 1 tablespoon capers, drained

In a shallow bowl, combine flour, salt and pepper. Add turkey slices, one at a time, and turn to coat.

In a large skillet, cook turkey in oil in batches for 2-3 minutes on each side or until juices run clear. Remove to a serving platter and keep warm.

In the same skillet, add chicken broth. Bring to a boil; cook until the liquid is reduced by half. Stir in butter and lemon juice; cook and stir for 30 seconds or until butter is melted. Add the parsley and capers; pour over turkey. **Yield:** 4 servings.

Colorful Rosemary Rice

Prep/Total Time: 15 min.

- 1-1/2 cups water
- 1/3 cup finely chopped sweet yellow pepper
- 1/4 cup shredded carrots
- 2 green onions, thinly sliced
- 2 teaspoons butter
- 1/2 teaspoon dried rosemary, crushed
- 1/4 teaspoon salt
- 1/4 teaspoon pepper
- 1-1/2 cups uncooked instant rice

In a large saucepan, combine the first eight ingredients; bring to a boil. Stir in the rice. Cover and remove from the heat; let stand for 5 minutes. Fluff with a fork. **Yield:** 4 servings.

CASUAL BUT FILLING COMBO

"I'm hungry—what's for dinner?" Sometimes, the answer can be as simple as a hearty and satisfying sandwich. Shared by Terri McCarty of Oro Grande, California, Rotisserie Chicken Panini is packed with bacon, ooey-gooey cheese, chicken and just enough lemon to tickle your taste buds. Pair it with awesome Chili Potato Wedges shared by Peggy Key of Grant, Alabama, and supper is served! ■

Chili Potato Wedges

Prep/Total Time: 30 min.

- 1 teaspoon chili powder
- 1/4 teaspoon garlic powder
- 1/8 teaspoon salt
- 1 large baking potato
- Cooking spray

In a small bowl, combine the chili powder, garlic powder and salt. Cut the potato lengthwise into eight wedges. Spray the wedges with cooking spray, then coat with seasoning mixture.

Place in a single layer on a baking sheet coated with cooking spray. Bake, uncovered, at 450° for 25-30 minutes or until golden brown. **Yield:** 2 servings.

Rotisserie Chicken Panini

Prep/Total Time: 20 min.

- 3 tablespoons mayonnaise
- 1 1/2 teaspoons grated Parmesan cheese
- 1 teaspoon lemon juice
- 1/2 teaspoon prepared pesto
- 1/4 teaspoon grated lemon peel
- Dash pepper
- 4 slices sourdough bread
- 1/4 pound sliced rotisserie chicken
- 4 slices ready-to-serve fully cooked bacon
- 2 slices smoked part-skim mozzarella cheese
- 2 slices red onion, separated into rings
- 4 slices tomato
- 2 tablespoons butter, melted

In a small bowl, combine the first six ingredients; spread half over two sourdough bread slices. Layer with chicken, bacon, mozzarella cheese, onion and tomato. Spread the remaining mayonnaise mixture over the remaining bread slices; place over top. Brush outsides of sandwiches with butter.

Cook on a panini maker or indoor grill for 3-4 minutes or until bread is browned and cheese is melted. **Yield:** 2 servings.

TWO TASTES, ONE GREAT MEAL

They say opposites attract, and that certainly applies when you pair spice with fresh vegetables. It's what makes this menu such an unbeatable combination.

Topped with melted cheese and sauce, quick and easy Buffalo Chicken from Jeanne Collins of Cary, North Carolina is an appealing dish everyone loves. Cool it off with a side of refreshing Sweet Cucumber Salad from Marlene Kroll of Chicago, Illinois. ■

Buffalo Chicken

Prep/Total Time: 30 min.

    4 boneless skinless chicken breast halves
       (5 ounces *each*)
1/4 teaspoon salt
1/4 teaspoon pepper
    2 eggs
1/2 cup seasoned bread crumbs
    3 tablespoons canola oil
1/4 cup buffalo wing sauce
1/4 cup shredded provolone cheese
1/4 cup shredded part-skim mozzarella cheese

Flatten the chicken to 1/2-in. thickness. Sprinkle with salt and pepper. In a shallow bowl, whisk the eggs. Place the seasoned bread crumbs in another shallow bowl. Dip the chicken in the eggs, then coat with the seasoned bread crumbs.

In a large skillet over medium heat, cook the chicken in oil for 7-10 minutes on each side or until chicken juices run clear, adding the buffalo wing sauce during the last 2 minutes. Turn to coat chicken. Sprinkle with the cheeses. Cover and cook until the cheese is melted. **Yield:** 4 servings.

Sweet Cucumber Salad

Prep/Total Time: 15 min.

    3 cups thinly sliced quartered cucumber
    2 teaspoons minced fresh cilantro
DRESSING:
1/4 cup sugar
    2 tablespoons water
    2 tablespoons white wine vinegar
    2 tablespoons lime juice
    1 green onion, thinly sliced
1/2 teaspoon salt

In a salad bowl, combine the cucumber and cilantro. In a small bowl, whisk the dressing ingredients. Drizzle over salad and toss to coat. Serve with a slotted spoon. **Yield:** 4 servings.

BREAKFAST THAT CAN'T BE BEAT

Rise and shine for a satisfying family meal. You'll love it in the morning—or any time of day at all!

Featuring the creamiest and richest scrambled eggs you'll likely ever try served alongside crispy, buttery cinnamon breadsticks, this is a decadent spread no matter when you put it on the table.

From Gladstone, Oregon, Suzy Horvath shares her special recipe for Creamy Scrambled Eggs with Ham. Cinnamon Crescent Twists are a favorite from Ruth Vineyard's kitchen in Plano, Texas. ■

Creamy Scrambled Eggs with Ham

Prep/Total Time: 20 min.

     8 eggs
 1/3 cup heavy whipping cream
 2/3 cup cubed fully cooked ham
     1 green onion, chopped
Dash salt
Dash pepper
     4 teaspoons butter
     4 ounces cream cheese, cubed

In a large bowl, whisk eggs and cream; stir in the ham, onion, salt and pepper. In a large skillet, heat butter over medium heat. Add the egg mixture; cook and stir until almost set. Stir in the cream cheese. Cook and stir until completely set. **Yield:** 4 servings.

Cinnamon Crescent Twists

Prep/Total Time: 20 min.

     1 package (8 ounces) refrigerated crescent rolls
 1/4 cup packed brown sugar
     2 tablespoons butter, softened
 1-1/2 teaspoons ground cinnamon
GLAZE:
 1/4 cup confectioners' sugar
     1 tablespoon butter, melted
 1-1/2 teaspoons hot water
 1/8 teaspoon almond extract

Separate crescent roll dough into four rectangles; press seams to seal. In a small bowl, combine brown sugar, butter and cinnamon; spread over two rectangles. Top with the remaining two rectangles. Starting from a long side, cut each rectangle into eight strips. Twist each strip several times; seal ends together.

Place twists on greased baking sheets. Bake at 375° for 10-12 minutes or until golden brown. Immediately remove to wire racks. Combine glaze ingredients; brush over warm twists. **Yield:** 16 servings.

THE CATCH OF THE DAY

This memorable meal is so easy to fix, you'll wonder why you don't serve seafood more often!

From Karen Conklin of Supply, North Carolina, Zesty Baked Catfish combines common seasonings for a taste that's anything but basic. While it's in the oven, you can focus on delicious Lemon Snap Peas from Marguerite Shaeffer of Sewell, New Jersey. ■

Lemon Snap Peas

Prep/Total Time: 15 min.

1-1/3 cups fresh *or* frozen sugar snap peas
1/2 teaspoon grated lemon peel
1/2 teaspoon minced fresh thyme *or*
    1/8 teaspoon dried thyme
2 teaspoons butter
Dash salt
Dash pepper

In a large saucepan, bring 1 in. of water to a boil. Add the sugar snap peas; cover and boil for 3 minutes. Drain and immediately place the peas in ice water. Drain and pat dry.

In a large skillet, saute peas, lemon peel and thyme in butter until crisp-tender. Sprinkle with salt and pepper. **Yield:** 2 servings.

Zesty Baked Catfish

Prep/Total Time: 20 min.

1 teaspoon canola oil
1 teaspoon lemon juice
2 catfish fillets (6 ounces *each*)
1-1/2 teaspoons paprika
1/2 teaspoon dried tarragon
1/2 teaspoon dried basil
1/2 teaspoon pepper
1/4 teaspoon salt
1/8 teaspoon cayenne pepper

Combine the oil and lemon juice; brush over both sides of fillets. Combine remaining ingredients; rub over both sides of fillets. Place in an ungreased 15-in. x 10-in. x 1-in. baking pan.

Bake, uncovered, at 350° for 10-15 minutes or until fish flakes easily with a fork. **Yield:** 2 servings.

IMPRESSIVE AND EASY MENU

The aroma alone will have your crew running to the table to enjoy this special meal. Lemon-Mustard Pork Chops from Kathy Specht of Clinton, Montana blend colorful, flavorful ingredients for a standout main course. Prepare our Test Kitchen's Squash and Veggie Couscous as a great accompaniment. ■

Lemon-Mustard Pork Chops

Prep/Total Time: 20 min.

4 boneless pork loin chops (1 inch thick and 6 ounces *each*)
2 tablespoons lemon juice
2 tablespoons minced fresh parsley
2 tablespoons Dijon mustard
1 garlic clove, minced
1 teaspoon grated lemon peel
1/2 teaspoon dried rosemary, crushed
1/4 teaspoon salt
Lemon wedges

Drizzle the pork chops with lemon juice. Combine the parsley, mustard, garlic, lemon peel, rosemary and salt; brush over both sides of chops.

Place pork on a greased broiler pan. Broil 3-4 in. from the heat for 4-6 minutes on each side or until a meat thermometer reads 160°. Serve with lemon wedges. **Yield:** 4 servings.

Squash and Veggie Couscous

Prep/Total Time: 20 min.

1 cup chicken broth
3/4 cup uncooked couscous
1 medium yellow summer squash, chopped
3/4 cup chopped carrot
1/2 cup chopped green pepper
1/4 cup chopped sweet onion
2 tablespoons butter
1/2 teaspoon Italian seasoning
1/2 teaspoon salt-free lemon-pepper seasoning

In a small saucepan, bring the broth to a boil. Stir in the couscous. Remove from the heat; cover and let stand for 5-10 minutes or until broth is absorbed.

Meanwhile, in a large skillet, saute the squash, carrot, green pepper and onion in butter until tender. Stir in seasonings. Fluff couscous with a fork; toss with vegetable mixture. **Yield:** 4 servings.

QUICK BUT TASTY TWOSOME

When it's just the two of you at the table, consider this sized-right dinner of fish and veggies. It's ready in minutes and sure to satisfy.

Fresh lime brightens the flavor of Cilantro-Lime Salmon from Lillian Julow of Gainesville, Florida. Served alongside Squash Saute from Vicki Shurk of Hamden, Connecticut and some cold lemonade, it's an entree you'll want to have time and again. ■

Squash Saute

Prep/Total Time: 15 min.

1 cup sliced zucchini
1 cup sliced yellow summer squash
2 tablespoons finely chopped onion
1/2 teaspoon olive oil
1/4 teaspoon dried basil
1/4 teaspoon dried oregano
1/8 teaspoon salt
Dash garlic powder
Dash pepper

In a large skillet, saute zucchini, yellow summer squash and onion in oil for 4-6 minutes or until crisp-tender. Add the remaining ingredients; cook 1 minute longer. **Yield:** 2 servings.

Cilantro-Lime Salmon

Prep/Total Time: 20 min.

2 tablespoons sour cream
1 green onion, chopped
1 tablespoon minced fresh cilantro
1 garlic clove, minced
1/4 teaspoon minced fresh gingerroot
1/4 teaspoon grated lime peel
1/8 teaspoon salt
Dash ground cumin
Dash pepper
Dash crushed red pepper flakes
2 salmon fillets (6 ounces *each*)
Lime wedges

In a small bowl, combine the first 10 ingredients. Place the salmon fillets skin side down in a greased 1-1/2-qt. microwave-safe dish; top with sour cream mixture.

Cover and microwave on high for 4-6 minutes or until fish flakes easily with a fork. Serve with lime wedges. **Yield:** 2 servings.

Editor's Note: This recipe was tested in a 1,100-watt microwave oven.

SPICY MAKEOVER FOR MAINSTAYS

With a kick from taco seasoning, this mouthwatering meal will make your everyday routine take a backseat to something new and exciting.

You're sure to like Fay Baswell's dressed-up version of a weeknight staple. In her Lodi, California kitchen, she prepares Taco Pork Chops that are tender, saucy and just right for kids.

From Willie DeWaard of Coralville, Iowa, Green Chili Rice will round out your meal...and guarantee requests for second helpings. ■

Taco Pork Chops

Prep/Total Time: 30 min.

4 boneless pork loin chops (6 ounces *each*)
1 tablespoon canola oil
1 can (8 ounces) tomato sauce
1 cup water, *divided*
1 medium onion, chopped
1 envelope taco seasoning
2 tablespoons all-purpose flour

In a large skillet, brown the pork chops in oil. In a small bowl, combine the tomato sauce, 3/4 cup water, onion and taco seasoning. Pour over pork and bring to a boil. Reduce heat; cover and simmer for 15-20 minutes or until meat is tender.

Remove the pork to a serving plate and keep warm. Combine the flour and remaining water until smooth. Stir into skillet. Bring to a boil; cook and stir for 2 minutes or until the sauce is thickened. Serve with pork chops. **Yield:** 4 servings.

Green Chili Rice

Prep/Total Time: 25 min.

1 cup water
1/2 cup frozen corn, thawed
1/2 cup chopped sweet orange pepper
1/2 cup black beans, rinsed and drained
1 can (4 ounces) chopped green chilies
2 tablespoons butter
1 garlic clove, minced
1/4 teaspoon salt
1/4 teaspoon ground cumin
1/8 teaspoon ground turmeric
1 cup uncooked instant rice

In a large saucepan, combine first 10 ingredients; bring to a boil. Stir in rice. Cover and remove from heat; let stand for 5 minutes. Fluff with a fork. **Yield:** 4 servings.

FAMILY PLEASERS, PRONTO!

Sit down to a hearty skillet supper that's ready in no time flat. Everyone will love Simple Sloppy Joes from Karen Anderson of Cuyahoga Falls, Ohio. Try it spooned over corn bread if you don't have buns.

For a filling meal your family won't soon forget, toss together Peppered Corn Salad from Pat Lovdahl of Falcon Heights, Minnesota. ■

Simple Sloppy Joes

Prep/Total Time: 30 min.

1-1/2 pounds ground beef
  1 can (10 ounces) diced tomatoes and green chilies, undrained
  1 can (6 ounces) tomato paste
1/4 cup ketchup
  2 tablespoons brown sugar
  1 tablespoon spicy brown mustard
1/4 teaspoon salt
  6 sandwich buns, split

In a large skillet, cook beef over medium heat until meat is no longer pink; drain. Stir in tomatoes, tomato paste, ketchup, brown sugar, mustard and salt. Bring to a boil. Reduce heat; simmer, uncovered, for 5 minutes or until heated through. Serve on buns. **Yield:** 6 servings.

Peppered Corn Salad

Prep/Total Time: 20 min.

  1 package (16 ounces) frozen corn
  2 medium tomatoes, chopped
  4 green onions, chopped
1/2 cup chopped green pepper
  2 tablespoons canola oil
  1 tablespoon white vinegar
  2 teaspoons minced fresh parsley
1/2 teaspoon salt
1/2 teaspoon lemon juice
1/4 teaspoon sugar
1/4 teaspoon dried basil
1/8 teaspoon crushed red pepper flakes

Prepare corn according to package directions; drain and set aside. In a large bowl, combine the tomatoes, onions and green pepper; stir in corn.

In a small bowl, combine the remaining ingredients; pour over the salad and toss to coat. Chill until serving. **Yield:** 6 servings.

CHAPTER 4

Cooking for Kids

It's child's play to serve kids wholesome, home-cooked food they'll *want* to eat. Just turn to the time-saving yet tot-pleasing recipes in this chapter.

After a long day at school, children will love sitting down to a main dish of Southwestern Wagon Wheels, Pepperoni Pizza Pasta or biscuit-wrapped Bacon Cheeseburger Roll-Ups.

Choose from plenty of sweet treats, too! Whip up a batch of chocolaty Marshmallow Pops for the classroom, or delight the birthday girl or boy with an adorable Circus Cake.

You'll also find an easy idea for just-for-play dough that youngsters can help you create. Imagine the fun they'll have playing with it, and the money you'll save making it! ■

YOUTH-FRIENDLY FARE. Taco Biscuit Bake (p. 74).

Spirals and Cheese
(Pictured below)

Prep: 15 min. **Bake:** 20 min.

What kid doesn't like macaroni and cheese? My grandkids simply love it, especially this version. The crumb-topped, oven-baked dish is so yummy and comforting on chilly evenings. It's sure to be a favorite with your gang, too!
—Flo Burtnett, Gage, Oklahoma

3-1/2 cups uncooked spiral pasta
    4 tablespoons butter, *divided*
    3 tablespoons all-purpose flour
    3 cups 2% milk
2-1/2 cups (10 ounces) shredded cheddar cheese, *divided*
  3/4 cup grated Parmesan cheese, *divided*
  1/2 teaspoon salt
  1/2 teaspoon pepper
  1/2 cup dry bread crumbs

Cook the spiral pasta according to package directions. Meanwhile, in a Dutch oven, melt 3 tablespoons butter. Stir in the flour until smooth; gradually add milk. Bring to a boil; cook and stir for 2 minutes or until thickened. Add 2 cups cheddar cheese, 1/2 cup Parmesan cheese, salt and pepper.

Drain spiral pasta. Add to the cheese mixture; toss gently to coat. Transfer to a greased 11-in. x 7-in. baking dish. Melt the remaining butter; add the bread crumbs and remaining cheddar and Parmesan cheeses. Sprinkle over the top.

Bake, uncovered, at 400° for 20-25 minutes or until golden brown. **Yield:** 6 servings.

On-the-Go Granola Bars
(Pictured above)

Prep: 20 min. + chilling

These homemade bars have store-bought ones beat by a mile. They're terrific for kids' lunch bags or to grab as an on-the-go snack when you're headed out the door.
—Suzanne McKinley, Lyons, Georgia

    7 tablespoons butter, softened, *divided*
1-1/2 cups miniature marshmallows
  1/2 cup apricot *or* peach preserves
  1/4 cup packed brown sugar
    4 cups reduced-fat granola with raisins
1-1/3 cups diced dried mixed fruit

Line an 8-in. square pan with waxed paper. Grease the paper with 1 tablespoon butter; set aside. In a large heavy saucepan, combine the marshmallows, preserves, brown sugar and remaining butter; cook and stir over medium heat until blended. Remove from the heat.

Stir in the granola and mixed fruit; toss to coat. Press firmly into prepared pan. Cover and refrigerate for 1-1/2 hours or until firm. Invert and remove waxed paper. Cut into bars. **Yield:** 16 bars.

MAC MAKEOVER

For a tasty next-day dish, I jazz up leftover macaroni and cheese by adding ground beef, chili powder, cumin, garlic powder and frozen or canned corn. Then I sprinkle cheddar cheese on top and bake.
—Kathy Ramirez, Yakima, Washington

Bacon Cheeseburger Roll-Ups
(Pictured above)

Prep: 25 min. **Bake:** 20 min.

Here's a fun twist on hamburgers—the ground beef and toppings are all wrapped up in biscuit dough. The recipe won a first place prize at the Iowa State Fair.
—*Jessica Cain, Des Moines, Iowa*

- 1 pound ground beef
- 6 bacon strips, diced
- 1/2 cup chopped onion
- 1 package (8 ounces) process cheese (Velveeta), cubed
- 1 tube (16.3 ounces) large refrigerated buttermilk biscuits
- 1/2 cup ketchup
- 1/4 cup yellow mustard

In a large skillet, cook the beef, bacon and onion over medium heat until meat is no longer pink; drain. Add cheese; cook and stir until melted. Remove from heat.

Flatten each biscuit into a 5-in. circle; spoon 1/3 cup beef mixture onto each biscuit. Fold sides and ends over filling and roll up. Place seam side down on a greased baking sheet.

Bake at 400° for 18-20 minutes or until golden brown. In a small bowl, combine ketchup and mustard; serve with roll-ups. **Yield:** 8 servings.

Pepperoni Pizza Pasta

(Pictured above)

Prep: 20 min. **Bake:** 20 min. + standing

Pizza taste, pronto—without takeout? Believe it! Loaded with pepperoni and ooey-gooey mozzarella cheese, this recipe gives you a great alternative to delivery.
—Mary Shivers, Ada, Oklahoma

  1-1/2 cups uncooked elbow macaroni
      2 eggs, lightly beaten
    1/3 cup grated Parmesan cheese
    1/4 cup sour cream
    1/2 teaspoon Italian seasoning
  1-1/2 cups pizza sauce
      2 cups (8 ounces) shredded part-skim
          mozzarella cheese
     30 slices pepperoni
      1 can (2-1/4 ounces) sliced ripe olives, drained

Cook macaroni according to package directions; drain. Stir in the eggs, Parmesan cheese, sour cream and Italian seasoning. Transfer to a greased 11-in. x 7-in. baking dish. Bake at 375° for 10 minutes.

Spread with the pizza sauce. Sprinkle with mozzarella cheese; top with the pepperoni and olives. Bake 10-15 minutes longer or until cheese is melted. Let stand for 10 minutes before serving. **Yield:** 6 servings.

Chocolate Chip Toffee Bars

Prep: 20 min. **Bake:** 35 min. + cooling

For a chocolate lover like myself, this is a quick and easy way to satisfy cravings. No one can resist these crumbly, nutty bars. —Kimberly Post, Colwich, Kansas

  2-1/2 cups all-purpose flour
    2/3 cup packed brown sugar
    3/4 cup cold butter
      1 egg
      1 cup chopped almonds
      2 cups (12 ounces) semisweet chocolate chips,
          divided
      1 can (14 ounces) sweetened condensed milk
  1-3/4 cups toffee bits, *divided*

In a large bowl, combine flour and brown sugar; cut in butter until mixture resembles coarse crumbs. Add egg; mix well. Stir in the almonds and 1-1/2 cups chocolate chips. Set aside 1-1/2 cups for topping. Press remaining mixture into a greased 13-in. x 9-in. baking pan.

Bake at 350° for 10 minutes. Pour the sweetened condensed milk over the crust; sprinkle with 1-1/2 cups toffee bits, reserved topping and remaining chips. Bake 25-30 minutes longer or until lightly browned. Sprinkle with remaining toffee bits. Cool on a wire rack. Cut into bars. **Yield:** 3 dozen.

Taco Biscuit Bake

(Pictured below and on page 70)

Prep: 20 min. **Bake:** 25 min.

Your whole gang will enjoy this Mexican bake. It's a tasty new take on tacos…and less messy for little ones to eat.
—Sara Martin, Whitefish, Montana

      1 pound lean ground beef (90% lean)
    2/3 cup water
      1 envelope taco seasoning
      2 tubes (12 ounces *each*) refrigerated
          buttermilk biscuits
      1 can (15 ounces) chili con carne
      1 cup (4 ounces) shredded reduced-fat
          cheddar cheese
Salsa and sour cream, optional

In a large skillet, cook ground beef over medium heat until no longer pink; drain. Stir in the water and taco seasoning. Bring to a boil; cook and stir for 2 minutes or until thickened.

Meanwhile, quarter the biscuits; place in a greased 13-in. x 9-in. baking dish. Layer with the ground beef mixture, chili and cheddar cheese. Bake, uncovered, at 375° for 25-30 minutes or until the cheese is melted and the biscuits are golden brown. Serve with salsa and sour cream if desired. **Yield:** 8 servings.

Back to School Cupcakes
(Pictured above)

Prep: 1 hour

This adorable bus from our Test Kitchen staff will make kids want to "get on board" for the first day of school! The treat is a cinch to make for the big event and fun for all ages. See our handy how-to's in the tip box at right.

    22 cupcakes of your choice
     2 cans (16 ounces *each*) vanilla frosting
Yellow, black and red paste food coloring
Chocolate wafers, miniature cream-filled chocolate
    sandwich cookies and vanilla wafers
Other paste food coloring of your choice
Coarse sugar

On a covered cake board, place a row of five cupcakes for top of bus. Arrange six cupcakes each in the second and third rows. Follow with a row of five cupcakes.

Tint 2-1/2 cups vanilla frosting yellow; carefully spread over the cupcakes. Spread vanilla frosting over cupcakes as desired for windows. Place a chocolate wafer on bus for each tire; attach a miniature sandwich cookie hubcap to each tire with frosting.

Tint a small amount of vanilla frosting black and a small amount red; set aside. Pipe outlines and desired details onto bus with black frosting.

Place a vanilla wafer in each window. Tint remaining frosting as desired. Pipe faces on vanilla wafers; pipe hair, hats and shirts as desired.

Spread red frosting onto the cupcakes for stop sign and taillights. Fill in the headlights with coarse sugar.
Yield: 22 cupcakes.

SCHOOL BUS HOW-TO'S

1. Arrange a total of 22 cupcakes next to each other in the shape of a school bus in the center of a covered cake board.

2. Tint 2-1/2 cups vanilla frosting yellow; carefully spread yellow frosting over the tops of the cupcakes.

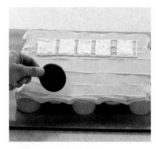

3. Spread vanilla frosting over the cupcakes to form five bus windows. Place two chocolate wafers along bottom of bus for tires.

4. Tint a small amount of vanilla frosting black. Pipe outlines, words and desired details on bus.

5. Place a vanilla wafer in each window. Tint the remaining frosting the desired colors for students. Pipe faces on the wafers; pipe hair, hats and shirts on students as desired.

6. Spread tinted red frosting onto bus for the stop sign and taillights. Fill in the headlights with coarse sugar.

Marshmallow Pops
(Pictured above)

Prep/Total Time: 30 min.

Decorated with colorful sprinkles, coconut or nuts, these chocolate-dipped goodies are ideal for school classrooms or birthdays. —Marcia Porch, Winter Park, Florida

    2 cups (12 ounces) semisweet chocolate chips
4-1/2 teaspoons canola oil
   40 large marshmallows
   20 Popsicle sticks
Toppings: assorted sprinkles, flaked coconut and
   ground walnuts

In a microwave, melt the semisweet chocolate chips and oil. Stir until smooth.

Thread two marshmallows onto each wooden stick. Roll marshmallows in melted chocolate, turning to coat. Allow excess to drip off. Roll in toppings of your choice. Place on waxed paper-lined baking sheets. Chill until firm. **Yield:** 20 servings.

Curveball Cupcakes

Prep: 50 min. **Bake:** 20 min. + cooling

If you have little-leaguers in the family, they're bound to think these are a home run! I simply use white frosting to frost cupcakes made from a mix, then pipe on the stitch marks with red icing so they look like baseballs.
—Cathy Runyon, Allendale, Michigan

1 package (18-1/4 ounces) yellow cake mix
1 can (16 ounces) vanilla frosting
1 tube red decorating frosting

Prepare the cake batter according to package directions. Fill paper-lined muffin cups two-thirds full. Bake at 350° for 20-22 minutes or until a toothpick inserted near the center comes out clean. Cool cupcakes for 10 minutes before removing from the muffin pans to wire racks to cool completely.

Frost the cupcakes with vanilla frosting. Use the red decorating frosting to pipe stitch marks to resemble baseballs. **Yield:** 2 dozen.

Monkey Cupcakes
(Pictured below)

Prep: 30 min. **Bake:** 20 min. + cooling

These funny monkeys make my kids smile and are a hit at bake sales. Try them for a zoo- or jungle-theme party.
—Sandra Seaman, Greensburg, Pennsylvania

  1 package (18-1/4 ounces) chocolate cake mix
  1 can (16 ounces) chocolate frosting
 24 vanilla wafers
Black and red decorating gel
 48 pastel blue *and/or* green milk chocolate M&M's
 12 peanut butter cream-filled sandwich cookies

Prepare and bake the cake batter according to package directions for cupcakes; cool completely.

Set aside 1/4 cup frosting. Frost the cupcakes with the remaining frosting. With a serrated knife, cut off and discard a fourth from each vanilla wafer. Place a wafer on each cupcake, with the rounded edge of wafer near edge of cupcake, for the face. Add dots of black gel for nostrils. With red gel, pipe a mouth on each.

Place M&M's above wafers for the eyes; add dots of black gel for the pupils. Using reserved frosting and a #16 star tip, pipe the hair. Carefully separate sandwich cookies; cut each in half. Position one on each side of cupcakes for ears. **Yield:** 2 dozen.

Cherry Chocolate Floats
(Pictured above)

Prep/Total Time: 30 min.

Old-time ice cream parlors have all but disappeared, but these fabulous floats from our Test Kitchen will pass that memorable taste on to new generations. Plus, these treats are such fun to make, everyone will want to help.

  1 cup water
3/4 cup sugar
  2 cups carbonated water, chilled
  3 tablespoons maraschino cherry juice
Chocolate syrup
 14 scoops chocolate ice cream
Whipped cream in a can
  7 maraschino cherries

In a large saucepan, bring the water and sugar to a boil. Reduce heat; simmer for 5 minutes. Cool. Stir in the carbonated water and cherry juice.

Drizzle chocolate syrup in each of seven chilled glasses. Place two scoops of ice cream in each glass. Pour carbonated water mixture over ice cream; top each with whipped cream and a cherry. Serve immediately. **Yield:** 7 servings.

Crisp Button Cookies
(Pictured below)

Prep: 20 min. + chilling **Bake:** 10 min./batch

Almost too cute to eat but too sweet to resist, these clever cookies take only minutes to make. And they'll disappear just as quickly!—Bonnie Buckley, Kansas City, Missouri

    3/4 cup butter, softened
      1 cup confectioners' sugar
      1 egg
      1 teaspoon vanilla extract
  2-1/2 cups all-purpose flour
    1/4 teaspoon salt
    1/4 teaspoon ground cardamom
Multi-colored pull-and-peel licorice

In a large bowl, cream butter and sugar. Beat in egg and vanilla. Combine the flour, salt and cardamom; gradually add to the creamed mixture. Cover and refrigerate for 2 hours or until easy to handle.

On a lightly floured surface, roll out the cookie dough to 1/4-in. thickness. Cut with a 2-1/2-in. round cookie cutter dipped in flour. Place 1 in. apart on ungreased baking sheets. With the top of a 1/4-cup measuring cup dipped in flour, press an indented edge into each cookie. Using a plastic straw, cut out four holes near the center of the cookie.

Bake at 350° for 10-15 minutes or until the edges are lightly browned. Remove to wire racks to cool. Lace licorice through the holes in each button; trim licorice. **Yield:** about 3 dozen.

Circus Cake
(Pictured above)

Prep: 30 min. **Bake:** 25 min. + cooling

Make a birthday child's eyes light up with this whimsical cake from our Test Kitchen cooks. It steals the show with a topping of cotton candy and lollipops.

    1 package (18-1/4 ounces) white cake mix
    1 can (16 ounces) vanilla frosting
Nerds candies
Miniature chocolate cream-filled chocolate
  sandwich cookies
Frosted animal crackers
Miniature marshmallows
Cotton candy
Lollipops

Prepare and bake the cake according to the package directions, using two greased 9-in. round baking pans. Cool for 10 minutes before removing from pans to wire racks to cool completely.

Spread frosting between layers and over the top and sides of cake. Lightly press the Nerds, sandwich cookies and animal crackers onto the sides of cake. Arrange marshmallows along edge of cake. Just before serving, arrange the cotton candy and lollipops on top of cake. **Yield:** 12 servings.

Tie-Dyed Kite Cookies
(Pictured above)

Prep: 30 min. **Bake:** 10 min.

The bakers in our Test Kitchen really had their heads in the clouds when they created these crispy treats! They "tie-dyed" refrigerated dough with food coloring to give the kites a multi-colored look, then turned licorice ropes and Life Savers candies into tails.

 1 tube (16-1/2 ounces) refrigerated sugar
   cookie dough
 1 to 2 tablespoons all-purpose flour
Pink, green and blue gel food coloring
 24 to 28 pieces multi-colored pull-and-peel
   licorice (9-1/2 inches *each*)
 48 to 56 Life Savers candies
 1/2 cup vanilla frosting

Cut cookie dough in half widthwise; let one half stand at room temperature for 5-10 minutes to soften (save the other half for another use). On a lightly floured surface, knead enough flour into softened dough until dough is stiff. Press into a 5-in. circle. Top with one dot of each color food coloring; knead 5-10 times or until color just begins to swirl.

Roll out the dough to 1/8-in. thickness. Cut out with a floured 3-in. diamond-shaped cookie cutter. Place 1 in. apart on ungreased baking sheets. Bake at 350° for 10-13 minutes or until edges are lightly browned. Cool for 2 minutes before removing from pans to wire racks.

Turn cookies bottom side up. For each cookie, lace one piece of licorice through one Life Saver; loop the licorice through the Life Saver again to hold the candy in place. Repeat with second Life Saver. Attach kite tails to the back of each cookie with frosting. Let stand until set. **Yield:** about 2 dozen.

Child's Play

Cook up some fun in the kitchen with this just-for-play dough from Kelly Kirby of Westville, Nova Scotia. She used basic pantry items to create colored balls kids can mold into all sorts of shapes, such as a burger and fries (shown below).

You'll need only 25 minutes to whip up your own dough. Store it in airtight containers or resealable plastic bags. ∎

Play Dough
(Pictured below)

Prep/Total Time: 25 min.

 2 cups all-purpose flour
 2 tablespoons cream of tartar
 1/2 cup salt
 2 cups water
 2 tablespoons canola oil
Food coloring

In a large saucepan, combine the flour, cream of tarter and salt. Gradually add the water and oil. Cook and stir over medium heat for 3-5 minutes or until a ball forms.

Cool. Divide dough and knead in colors as desired. Store in airtight containers or resealable plastic bags. **Yield:** 2-1/2 cups.

ABC Melt

(Pictured above)

Prep/Total Time: 10 min.

The alphabet-inspired name will please children, but the taste of these sandwiches will appeal to the whole family. It's a terrific recipe when you need something quick.
—Barbara Nowakowski, North Tonawanda, New York

- 2 English muffins, split and toasted
- 2 teaspoons prepared mustard
- 4 slices Canadian bacon
- 1 medium apple, thinly sliced
- 4 slices Swiss cheese

Place muffin halves, cut side up, on an ungreased baking sheet. Spread with mustard; layer with Canadian bacon, apple slices and cheese. Bake at 350° for 5-6 minutes or until cheese is melted. **Yield:** 2 servings.

Chewy Energy Bars

Prep: 20 min. + cooling

We like to pack these yummy goodies for lunch, but they also make a great portable breakfast or snack. The oats, peanut butter and cereal give me an energy boost.
—Sharon Rast, Show Low, Arizona

- 2-1/2 cups crisp rice cereal
- 2 cups old-fashioned oats
- 1/4 cup toasted wheat germ
- 1 cup corn syrup
- 1 cup peanut butter
- 1/2 cup packed brown sugar
- 1 teaspoon vanilla extract

In a large bowl, combine the cereal, oats and wheat germ. In a small saucepan, combine the corn syrup, peanut butter and brown sugar. Cook over medium heat until peanut butter is melted, stirring occasionally. Remove from the heat. Stir in vanilla. Pour over cereal mixture; mix well.

Transfer to a greased 9-in. square pan. Gently press cereal mixture evenly into pan. Cool completely. Cut into bars. **Yield:** 3 dozen.

Southwestern Wagon Wheels
(Pictured below)

Prep/Total Time: 20 min.

This kid-friendly recipe comes together with convenience products such as canned tomato soup and jarred salsa. The result is a satisfying dinner in just 20 minutes.
—Ramona Rasas-Satinskas, Hockessin, Delaware

- 4 cups uncooked wagon wheel pasta
- 1 pound lean ground beef (90% lean)
- 2 cans (10-3/4 ounces *each*) condensed tomato soup, undiluted
- 1 cup medium salsa
- 1 jar (4-1/2 ounces) sliced mushrooms, drained
- 1 teaspoon dried oregano
- 1/2 cup sour cream
- 1/3 cup shredded Monterey Jack cheese

Cook the pasta according to the package directions. Meanwhile, in a large skillet, cook beef over medium heat until no longer pink; drain. Stir in the soup, salsa,

mushrooms and oregano. Bring to a boil. Reduce heat; simmer, uncovered, for 5 minutes. Stir in the sour cream; heat through. Drain pasta; serve with the sauce mixture. Sprinkle with cheese. **Yield:** 5 servings.

Sunshine Cupcakes
(Pictured above)

Prep: 20 min. **Bake:** 20 min. + cooling

Cute and easy to make, these cheerful lemon cakes from our Test Kitchen will bring lots of smiles. Candy corn, chocolate chips and licorice form the sunny faces.

- 1 package (18-1/4 ounces) lemon cake mix
- 1 can (16 ounces) vanilla frosting

Yellow food coloring
Miniature semisweet chocolate chips, red shoestring licorice and candy corn

Prepare and bake the cake batter according to package directions for cupcakes; cool completely.

In a small bowl, tint frosting yellow. Frost cupcakes. Press two chocolate chips into each cupcake for eyes. For mouths, cut licorice into 1-in. pieces; bend slightly to curve. Press one licorice piece into each cupcake. Add candy corn around edges of cupcakes. **Yield:** 2 dozen.

FROST IT FAST

To quickly frost cupcakes, place frosting that has a soft, spreadable consistency in a bowl. If the frosting is too stiff, add milk a teaspoon at a time until it reaches the desired consistency. Dip the top of the cupcake into the frosting, twist slightly and lift up.

CHAPTER 5

Give Me 5 or Fewer

When the clock is ticking and everyone is famished, the last thing busy cooks want to do is spend time searching their pantry for endless ingredients— or make a special trip to the grocery store to pick up missing products for a recipe.

Just turn to this chapter! Each delectable dish comes together with only five items (excluding the kitchen staples of water, salt and pepper). So you'll get food on the table much faster.

After trying scrumptious fare such as Pesto-Olive Chicken, Southwest Stuffed Peppers, Big Kahuna Pizza, Smoky Apricot Tarts and Peach Crisp Delight, your family will never guess that it was so simple to fix. ■

TAKE FIVE. Dreamy S'more Pie (p. 91).

Pistachio Baked Salmon
(Pictured above)

Prep/Total Time: 25 min.

Next time you're clueless about what to make for drop-in guests, try this fancy, flavorful salmon. With pistachios, brown sugar and dill, it's a guaranteed hit.
—Cathy Hudak, Wadsworth, Ohio

    6 salmon fillets (6 ounces *each*)
    1 cup pistachios, chopped
1/2 cup packed brown sugar
    3 tablespoons lemon juice
    1 teaspoon dill weed
    1 teaspoon pepper

Place the salmon in a greased 13-in. x 9-in. baking dish. Combine the remaining ingredients; spoon over salmon. Bake, uncovered, at 425° for 12-15 minutes or until fish flakes easily with a fork. **Yield:** 6 servings.

Italian-Style Green Beans
(Pictured above)

Prep/Total Time: 25 min.

Using bottled dressing, this simple recipe turns ho-hum green beans into a side dish worthy of special occasions.
—Jeannie Klugh, Lancaster, Pennsylvania

1-1/2 pounds fresh green beans, trimmed
    2 plum tomatoes, chopped
    1 small red onion, thinly sliced
    1 can (3.8 ounces) sliced ripe olives, drained
1/2 cup prepared Italian salad dressing
Dash *each* salt and pepper

Place the green beans in a Dutch oven and cover with water. Bring to a boil. Cover and cook for 4-6 minutes or until crisp-tender; drain.

Add the remaining ingredients and heat through. **Yield:** 8 servings.

Grilled Steak Appetizers With Stilton Sauce

(Pictured below)

Prep: 25 min. **Grill:** 10 min.

Here's a sensational start to any party. The rich, creamy sauce complements the steak perfectly. If you can't find Stilton cheese, substitute 1/3 cup crumbled blue cheese.
—Radelle Knappenberger, Oviedo, Florida

    2 boneless beef top loin steaks (8 ounces *each*)
1/4 teaspoon salt
1/4 teaspoon pepper
1/2 cup white wine *or* chicken broth
1/3 cup heavy whipping cream
    3 tablespoons sour cream
    2 ounces Stilton cheese, cubed

Sprinkle steaks with salt and pepper. Grill steaks, covered, over medium heat for 4-6 minutes on each side or until meat reaches the desired doneness (for medium-rare, a meat thermometer should read 145°; medium, 160°; well-done, 170°). Remove meat to a cutting board and keep warm.

In a small saucepan, bring wine to a boil; cook until reduced by half. Add whipping cream. Bring to a gentle boil. Reduce heat; simmer, uncovered, until thickened, stirring occasionally. Remove from the heat. Add sour cream and cheese; stir until cheese is melted. Cut steaks into 1-in. cubes; skewer with toothpicks. Serve with the sauce. **Yield:** 20 appetizers (3/4 cup sauce).

Editor's Notes: Top loin steak may be labeled as strip steak, Kansas City steak, New York strip steak, ambassador steak or boneless club steak in your region. You may substitute 1/3 cup crumbled blue cheese for the Stilton cheese.

Elegant Weeknight Chicken

(Pictured above)

Prep: 10 min. **Bake:** 40 min.

While this tasty chicken is in the oven, I toss together a salad with arugula, basil, red onion, plum tomatoes and a lemon vinaigrette.   —Iliana Davila, Bear, Delaware

    1 pound fresh asparagus, trimmed
1/4 teaspoon salt, *divided*
1/8 teaspoon pepper, *divided*
1/4 cup white wine *or* chicken broth
    2 tablespoons butter, melted
    4 boneless skinless chicken breast halves
        (5 ounces *each*)
    1 cup (4 ounces) shredded part-skim
        mozzarella cheese

Place the asparagus in a greased 11-in. x 7-in. baking dish. Sprinkle with 1/8 teaspoon salt and a dash pepper. In a small bowl, combine white wine and butter; pour over asparagus.

Arrange the chicken over asparagus; sprinkle with the remaining salt and pepper. Bake, uncovered, at 350° for 35 minutes. Sprinkle with the mozzarella cheese; bake 5-10 minutes longer or until chicken juices run clear and cheese is melted. **Yield:** 4 servings.

▌ FRESH AS A FLOWER ▐

In order to keep asparagus fresh longer, I place the cut stems in a container of cold water—similar to flowers in a vase. I keep the asparagus in the fridge, changing the water at least once every 3 days.
—Mary Stewart, Council Bluffs, Iowa

Southwest Stuffed Peppers

(Pictured below)

Prep: 25 min. **Bake:** 30 min.

This special yet economical supper makes the most of my garden-grown peppers. For even more south-of-the-border flavor, I top off each serving with a dollop of sour cream and include a side of tortilla chips and salsa.
—Kimberly Coleman, Columbia, South Carolina

- 8 medium green peppers
- 1 pound lean ground beef (90% lean)
- 1 can (14-1/2 ounces) diced tomatoes and green chilies, undrained
- 1-1/2 cups water
- 1 envelope (5.4 ounces) Mexican-style rice and pasta mix
- 2 cups (8 ounces) shredded Mexican cheese blend

Cut the tops off peppers and remove seeds. In a Dutch oven, cook peppers in boiling water for 3-5 minutes. Drain and rinse in cold water; set aside.

In a large skillet, cook beef over medium heat until no longer pink; drain. Add the diced tomatoes, water and pasta mix. Bring to a boil. Reduce heat; cover and simmer for 6-8 minutes or until liquid is absorbed.

Place 1/3 cup rice mixture in each pepper; sprinkle each with 2 tablespoons cheese. Top with the remaining rice mixture. Place in a greased 13-in. x 9-in. baking dish. Cover and bake at 375° for 25 minutes. Sprinkle with the remaining cheese; bake 5-10 minutes longer or until the cheese is melted and the peppers are tender. **Yield:** 8 servings.

Orange-Glazed Salmon

(Pictured above)

Prep/Total Time: 20 min.

The first time I prepared this, my husband declared it to be his favorite dinner ever. That's saying a lot—normally his favorite meals involve a plateful of beef!
—Tammy Hayden, Quincy, Michigan

- 2 tablespoons Cajun seasoning
- 1 teaspoon brown sugar
- 4 salmon fillets (6 ounces *each*), skin removed
- 1/2 cup orange marmalade
- 1/4 cup lime juice

Combine Cajun seasoning and brown sugar; rub over the salmon fillets. In a large nonstick skillet coated with cooking spray, cook the fillets over medium heat for 3-4 minutes on each side or until the fish flakes easily with a fork. Add marmalade and lime juice to the skillet; heat through. **Yield:** 4 servings.

Coconut Joys

Prep: 20 min. + chilling

Like coconut? You're sure to love these no-bake, no-fuss chocolate candies. Keep a batch in the refrigerator for the kids after school and for late-night snacking.
—Flo Burtnett, North Gage, Oklahoma

- 1-1/2 cups flaked coconut
- 1 cup confectioners' sugar
- 1/4 cup butter, melted
- 1 ounce milk chocolate, melted
- 2 tablespoons chopped pecans

In a large bowl, combine coconut, confectioners' sugar and butter. Form into 1-in. balls.

Using the end of a wooden spoon handle, make an indentation in the center of each ball. Fill with chocolate. Sprinkle with the pecans. Place on a waxed paper-lined baking sheet. Chill until chocolate is firm. Store in the refrigerator. **Yield:** 1-1/2 dozen.

Summer Squash Saute

(Pictured below)

Prep/Total Time: 20 min.

Here's a quick and delicious way to enjoy yellow summer squash—just saute it with some garlic and sweet onion. The result is a terrific addition to just about any menu.
—*Christie Wethington, Lexington, Kentucky*

    6 small yellow summer squash, cut into
      1/2-inch slices
    1 large sweet onion, chopped
    1 garlic clove, minced
    1 tablespoon olive oil
    1 tablespoon butter
  1/2 teaspoon salt
  1/2 teaspoon pepper

In a large skillet, saute the squash, onion and garlic in oil and butter for 10-12 minutes or until tender. Sprinkle with salt and pepper. **Yield:** 8 servings.

Puff Pastry Chicken Bundles

(Pictured above)

Prep: 15 min. **Bake:** 20 min.

It's hard to believe that a main dish this impressive comes from only a handful of ingredients. But it's true!
—*Gina Hobbs, Tifton, Georgia*

    4 chicken tenderloins
  1/8 teaspoon salt
  1/8 teaspoon pepper
    1 sheet frozen puff pastry, thawed
  1/2 cup spinach and artichoke cream cheese
      spread
    4 slices Muenster cheese, halved
    1 egg
    1 tablespoon water

Sprinkle the chicken with salt and pepper; set aside. On a lightly floured surface, roll the puff pastry into a 14-in. square. Cut into four squares. Spoon 2 tablespoons cream cheese into the center of each square; top with Muenster cheese and chicken.

Whisk the egg and water; lightly brush over edges. Bring the opposite corners of pastry over each bundle; pinch the seams to seal. Place seam side down on a greased baking sheet; brush with remaining egg mixture. Bake at 400° for 18-22 minutes or until golden brown. **Yield:** 4 servings.

▮ SQUASH SECRET ▮

I fit yellow squash into our menus by pureeing the squash and stirring it into prepared macaroni and cheese. My family doesn't notice, and I feel better about including more veggies in our meals.
—*Angela Zwart, Maple Grove, Minnesota*

Chicken in Wine Sauce
(Pictured above)

Prep/Total Time: 25 min.

A splash of plum wine and lots of mushrooms transform this chicken into a sophisticated main dish. It's the ideal choice not only for dinner guests, but also for weeknights when time is tight but you want something special.
—Kathleen Valle, Philadelphia, Pennsylvania

4 boneless skinless chicken breast halves
   (5 ounces *each*)
1 egg
1 tablespoon water
3/4 cup all-purpose flour
1/2 teaspoon salt
1/2 teaspoon pepper
3/4 pound sliced fresh mushrooms
2/3 cup plum wine

Flatten chicken to 1/4-in. thickness. In a shallow bowl, whisk egg and water. In another shallow bowl, combine the flour, salt and pepper. Dip chicken in egg mixture, then coat with flour mixture.

In a large nonstick skillet coated with cooking spray, cook chicken over medium heat for 4-5 minutes on each side or until juices run clear. Remove and keep warm.

In the same skillet, saute the mushrooms until tender. Add the wine, stirring to loosen browned bits from pan. Bring to a boil; cook until liquid is reduced by half. Serve with chicken. **Yield:** 4 servings

Peanut Butter Oatmeal Cookies
(Pictured below)

Prep/Total Time: 20 min.

Serve a plate of these nutty goodies with glasses of milk, and you'll see smiles all around. The recipe gives you two dozen homemade cookies in just 20 minutes.
—Marilyn Blankschien, Clintonville, Wisconsin

1/2 cup chunky peanut butter
1/2 cup packed brown sugar
   1 egg
1-1/4 cups quick-cooking oats
1/2 teaspoon baking soda

In a small bowl, cream peanut butter and brown sugar until fluffy. Beat in the egg. Add oats and baking soda to creamed mixture; mix well.

Drop the dough by tablespoonfuls 2 in. apart onto greased baking sheets; flatten slightly. Bake at 350° for 6-8 minutes. Remove to wire racks to cool. Store in an airtight container. **Yield:** 2 dozen.

▮ MUSHROOM METHOD ▮

To gently remove dirt from fresh mushrooms, rub them with a mushroom brush or wipe them with a damp paper towel. Or, quickly rinse mushrooms under cold water, drain them and pat them dry with paper towels. Do not peel mushrooms.

Chipotle Sliders
(Pictured above)

Prep/Total Time: 30 min.

When it comes to mini burgers, these are the ultimate. The flavor the beef patties get from just a handful of ingredients is incredible! Mayonnaise, Hawaiian sweet rolls and pepper Jack cheese help balance the heat from the chipotle peppers.
—Shawn Singleton, Vidor, Texas

  1 package (12 ounces) Hawaiian sweet rolls
  1 teaspoon salt
1/2 teaspoon pepper
  8 teaspoons minced chipotle peppers in adobo sauce, *divided*
1-1/2 pounds ground beef

10 slices pepper Jack cheese
1/2 cup mayonnaise

Place 2 Hawaiian sweet rolls in a food processor; process until crumbly.

Transfer processed rolls to a large bowl; add the salt, pepper and 6 teaspoons chipotle peppers. Crumble the beef over mixture and mix well. Shape into 10 patties.

Grill the burgers, covered, over medium heat for 3-4 minutes on each side or until a meat thermometer reads 160° and juices run clear. Top with cheese. Grill 1 minute longer or until cheese is melted.

Split the remaining Hawaiian rolls and grill, cut side down, over medium heat for 30-60 seconds or until toasted. Combine mayonnaise and remaining chipotle peppers; spread over the roll bottoms. Top each with a burger. Replace roll tops. **Yield:** 10 sliders.

Editor's Note: Look for Hawaiian sweet rolls in your grocer's deli section.

Smoky Grilled Shrimp
(Pictured below)

Prep/Total Time: 25 min.

Grill up these bacon-wrapped hors d'oeuvres, then watch them disappear! They taste just as good as they look, and the reserved sauce is wonderful for dipping.
—Debbie Taylor, White Bluff, Tennessee

- 1 package (1 pound) sliced bacon
- 1-1/4 cups honey Dijon salad dressing
- 4 teaspoons prepared horseradish
- 1 garlic clove, minced
- 1 pound uncooked large shrimp, peeled and deveined

Cut bacon strips in half widthwise. In a large skillet, cook bacon over medium heat until partially cooked but not crisp. Remove to paper towels to drain.

In a small bowl, combine the Dijon salad dressing, horseradish and garlic; set aside 3/4 cup. Brush remaining dressing mixture over both sides of shrimp. Wrap a piece of bacon around each shrimp; thread onto four metal or soaked wooden skewers.

Using long-handled tongs, moisten a paper towel with cooking oil and lightly coat grill rack. Grill shrimp, covered, over medium heat or broil 4 in. from the heat for 5-8 minutes or until shrimp turn pink, turning once. Serve shrimp with reserved sauce. **Yield:** 2-1/2 dozen (3/4 cup sauce).

Maple Pretzel Chicken
(Pictured above)

Prep/Total Time: 20 min.

This unexpected combination of maple syrup and crushed pretzels is a really yummy coating for chicken. The finer the pretzel crumb, the better—large pieces don't coat.
—Tara Szlag, Columbus, Ohio

- 4 boneless skinless chicken breast halves (5 ounces *each*)
- 1 egg
- 1/2 cup maple syrup
- 1-1/2 cups crushed pretzels
- 1/4 cup canola oil

Flatten chicken breasts to 1/2-in. thickness. In a shallow bowl, whisk egg and syrup. Place pretzels in a separate shallow bowl. Dip the chicken in egg mixture and coat with pretzels.

In a large skillet, cook chicken in oil over medium heat for 5-6 minutes on each side or until juices run clear. **Yield:** 4 servings.

FLAT-OUT FAST

Flattening or pounding meat can serve several purposes. It is typically done for quicker, more even cooking and to produce an attractive appearance.

To flatten chicken breasts for Maple Pretzel Chicken (recipe above), place the chicken breasts between two pieces of waxed paper on a cutting board. Using a meat mallet, rolling pin or soup can, pound evenly to the desired thickness. Afterward, discard the waxed paper and sanitize all surfaces.

Big Kahuna Pizza

Prep/Total Time: 30 min.

With a prebaked crust and refrigerated barbecued pork, this meaty pizza is super-easy. Cut it into bite-size pieces, and it makes a great last-minute appetizer, too.
—Joni Hilton, Rocklin, California

1 prebaked 12-inch pizza crust
1 carton (18 ounces) refrigerated fully cooked barbecued shredded pork
1 can (20 ounces) pineapple chunks, drained
1/3 cup chopped red onion
2 cups (8 ounces) shredded part-skim mozzarella cheese

Place the pizza crust on an ungreased 12-in. pizza pan. Spread the shredded pork over crust; top with pineapple and onion. Sprinkle with cheese.

Bake at 350° for 20-25 minutes or until the cheese is melted. **Yield:** 6 servings.

Spinach Cheese Dip

(Pictured below)

Prep/Total Time: 30 min.

I've had so many compliments on this creamy, cheesy dip recipe and have shared it with a number of friends.
—Christine Cragan, Salem, Massachusetts

1 package (8 ounces) cream cheese, softened
1 jar (16 ounces) salsa
1 package (10 ounces) frozen chopped spinach, thawed and squeezed dry
2 cups (8 ounces) shredded Mexican cheese blend, *divided*
Tortilla chips

In a large bowl, combine cream cheese, salsa, spinach and 1 cup Mexican cheese blend. Spread the mixture into an ungreased 9-in. pie plate. Sprinkle with the remaining cheese.

Bake, uncovered, at 350° for 20-25 minutes or until heated through. Serve the dip with tortilla chips. **Yield:** 16 servings (1/4 cup each).

Dreamy S'more Pie

(Pictured above and on page 82)

Prep: 10 min. + chilling **Broil:** 5 min.

I was looking for a way to use chocolate hazelnut spread in a dessert when I dreamed up this treat. With a graham cracker crust and miniature marshmallows, it's sure to remind you of everyone's favorite campfire goodies.
—Karen Bowlden, Boise, Idaho

1 package (8 ounces) cream cheese, softened
1-1/4 cups heavy whipping cream
1 jar (13 ounces) chocolate hazelnut spread
1 graham cracker crust (9 inches)
3 cups miniature marshmallows

In a large bowl, beat the cream cheese and cream until thickened. Add the chocolate hazelnut spread; beat just until combined. Spoon into crust. Cover and refrigerate for at least 3 hours.

Just before serving, top with miniature marshmallows; press gently into the filling. Broil 6 in. from the heat for 1-2 minutes or until marshmallows are golden brown. **Yield:** 8 servings.

Pesto-Olive Chicken

(Pictured at left)

Prep/Total Time: 30 min.

Give weeknights a lift with this dressed-up chicken entree. I keep the ingredients on hand so I can fix it anytime.
—Cristy King, Bridgeport, West Virginia

    4 boneless skinless chicken breast halves
       (6 ounces *each*)
1/2 cup prepared pesto
    2 jars (4-1/2 ounces *each*) sliced mushrooms,
       drained
    1 can (4-1/2 ounces) chopped ripe olives
    1 cup (4 ounces) shredded provolone cheese

Flatten chicken slightly. Place in an ungreased 13-in. x 9-in. baking dish. Spoon pesto over chicken; top with mushrooms and olives.

Bake, uncovered, at 400° for 15 minutes. Sprinkle with provolone cheese. Bake 1-2 minutes longer or until the cheese is melted and chicken juices run clear. **Yield:** 4 servings.

Tender Roasted Potatoes

(Pictured at left)

Prep: 10 min. **Bake:** 35 min.

I prepared this effortless recipe for my uncle, who adores mashed potatoes. I was worried that he wouldn't like this variation, but he couldn't stop raving about it!
—Susan Burk, Saginaw, Michigan

    3 pounds small red potatoes, quartered
    2 tablespoons canola oil
1/3 cup prepared horseradish
1/4 cup stone-ground mustard
    2 tablespoons butter, melted

In a large bowl, toss the potatoes with oil. Place the potatoes on two greased baking sheets. Bake at 400° for 30 minutes.

Meanwhile, in a small bowl, combine the horseradish, mustard and butter. Spoon over the potatoes and toss to coat. Bake 5-7 minutes longer or until tender. **Yield:** 10 servings.

ALL ABOUT MARINADES

• The best way to safely use a marinade as a basting sauce is to set aside a portion of the marinade before adding the remaining marinade to the uncooked meat. Then baste with clean utensils and the reserved marinade when grilling.

• Chicken breasts or cubes of beef require 2 to 4 hours to marinate, and whole chickens or roasts may benefit from 8 hours or longer. Delicate cuts such as fish fillets may need to marinate only 30 minutes.

• Margarita Chicken (recipe above right) flavors chicken in a simple homemade marinade. For an even faster option, try a bottled salad dressing.

Margarita Chicken

(Pictured below)

Prep: 10 min. + marinating **Grill:** 10 min.

Marinated in margarita mix, garlic and lime, this tangy grilled chicken is ready to go whenever the coals are hot. Serve it with roasted corn on the cob and big glasses of cold lemonade for summer eating at its best.
—Kelly Bruneman, Cedar Park, Texas

    1 can (10 ounces) frozen nonalcoholic
       margarita mix, thawed
    3 tablespoons lime juice
    3 garlic cloves, minced
    4 boneless skinless chicken breast halves
       (6 ounces *each*)
1/4 teaspoon salt
1/4 teaspoon pepper

In a small bowl, combine the margarita mix, lime juice and garlic. Pour 1 cup marinade into a large resealable plastic bag. Add the chicken; seal the bag and turn to coat. Refrigerate for 2-4 hours. Cover and refrigerate the remaining marinade.

Using long-handled tongs, moisten a paper towel with cooking oil and lightly coat the grill rack. Drain and discard marinade. Sprinkle chicken with salt and pepper. Grill chicken, covered, over medium heat for 5-7 minutes on each side or until juices run clear, basting frequently with reserved marinade. **Yield:** 4 servings.

Fire-Roasted Salsa

Prep/Total Time: 15 min.

Canned tomatoes never tasted better than they do in this restaurant-worthy salsa you can have ready in 15 minutes flat. Cilantro and lime juice are the key ingredients.
—Missy Kampling, Mountain View, California

- 1 can (14-1/2 ounces) fire-roasted diced tomatoes, drained
- 1/2 cup sliced onion
- 1/3 cup fresh cilantro leaves
- 1 tablespoon lime juice
- 1 teaspoon sugar
- 1/4 teaspoon salt

In a food processor, combine tomatoes, onion, cilantro, lime juice, sugar and salt. Cover and process until desired consistency. **Yield:** 1-1/2 cups.

Foolproof Mushrooms

(Pictured below)

Prep/Total Time: 25 min.

These appetizers really live up to their name because they always turn out well. You can make them up to 4 hours ahead of time and keep them in the fridge before baking. Add some chopped artichoke hearts for extra flair.
—Gail Lucas, Olive Branch, Mississippi

- 1 package (5.2 ounces) garlic-herb cheese spread
- 3 tablespoons grated Parmesan cheese, *divided*
- 30 small fresh mushrooms, stems removed
- Thinly sliced fresh basil, optional

In a small bowl, combine cheese spread and 2 tablespoons Parmesan cheese; spoon into mushroom caps.

Transfer the stuffed caps to a foil-lined baking sheet; sprinkle with remaining Parmesan cheese. Bake at 400° for 10-12 minutes or until lightly browned. Garnish with basil if desired. **Yield:** 2-1/2 dozen.

Smoky Apricot Tarts

(Pictured above)

Prep/Total Time: 25 min.

This recipe is a snap to double, which is a great thing—one batch will disappear quickly! Your party or dinner guests will love the taste of these fall-flavored tarts featuring smoked mozzarella cheese and apricot preserves. —Donna Marie Ryan Topsfield, Massachusetts

- 3/4 cup apricot preserves
- 1/2 teaspoon pumpkin pie spice
- 2 tablespoons brown sugar, *divided*
- 1 package (1.9 ounces) frozen miniature phyllo tart shells
- 1/2 cup shredded smoked part-skim mozzarella cheese

In a small saucepan, combine preserves, pie spice and 1 tablespoon brown sugar. Cook and stir over medium heat until the sugar is dissolved. Spoon into tart shells; arrange on an ungreased baking sheet. Sprinkle with cheese and remaining brown sugar.

Bake at 350° for 5-7 minutes or until cheese is melted. Serve warm. **Yield:** 15 appetizers.

Hazelnut Crescent Rolls
(Pictured above)

Prep/Total Time: 25 min.

With the first bite, these sugar-dusted rolls give way to warm and wonderful chocolate with a hint of hazelnut flavor. What a wonderful way to use refrigerated dough!
—*Phyllis Adkins, South Charleston, West Virginia*

1 tube (8 ounces) refrigerated crescent rolls
1/2 cup chocolate hazelnut spread, warmed
1/3 cup chocolate-covered English toffee bits
Confectioners' sugar

Unroll the crescent roll dough; separate into triangles. Spread each with 1 tablespoon hazelnut spread; sprinkle with toffee bits. Roll up from the wide end and place pointed side down 2 in. apart on greased baking sheets. Curve ends to form crescents.

Bake crescents at 375° for 11-13 minutes or until lightly browned. Dust with confectioners' sugar. **Yield:** 8 servings.

Editor's Note: Look for chocolate hazelnut spread in the peanut butter section.

CRESCENT CRUST

Refrigerated crescent roll dough can make a quick, easy top crust for any potpie. Just roll out the dough to fit the top of the pie, place it over the filling, trim the edges and cut slits in the top before baking.
—*Margaret Baraszu, Lincoln Park, Michigan*

Polenta Parmigiana
(Pictured above)

Prep/Total Time: 30 min.

This oven-baked Italian appetizer can also make a quick, filling lunch. I prefer this veggie version, but my kids like to add pepperoni or sausage to create mini pizzas.
—Carolyn Kumpe, El Dorado, California

    1 tube (1 pound) polenta, cut into 16 slices
  1/4 cup olive oil
    1 cup tomato basil pasta sauce, warmed
  1/2 pound fresh mozzarella cheese, cut into
        16 slices
  1/4 cup grated Parmesan cheese
  1/2 teaspoon salt
  1/8 teaspoon pepper
Fresh basil leaves, optional

Place polenta in a greased 15-in. x 10-in. x 1-in. baking pan; brush with olive oil. Bake at 425° for 15-20 minutes or until edges are golden brown.

Spoon the pasta sauce over polenta slices. Top each with a mozzarella cheese slice; sprinkle with the Parmesan cheese, salt and pepper. Bake 3-5 minutes longer or until the cheese is melted. Garnish with basil if desired. **Yield:** 16 appetizers.

Asian Pear Salad

Prep/Total Time: 15 min.

I came up with this using a handful of leftover ingredients from a party, and I was delighted with the outcome. The combination of pears, nuts, sesame-ginger dressing and cheese gets raves. *—Shirlee Bodfield, Tucson, Arizona*

    1 package (10 ounces) hearts of romaine salad
        mix
    3 medium pears, sliced
    8 ounces fresh mozzarella cheese, sliced
  3/4 cup sesame ginger vinaigrette
    1 package (3-3/4 ounces) oven-roasted sliced
        almonds

Divide the salad mix among six serving plates. Top with the pears and cheese; drizzle with the dressing. Sprinkle with almonds. **Yield: 6 servings.**

Baked Strawberry Salmon
(Pictured below)

Prep: 10 min. + marinating **Bake:** 15 min.

These marinated fillets covered with strawberry preserves are gorgeous…and the taste doesn't disappoint. Whenever I serve them, people think I'm a culinary genius!
—Lisa Speer, Palm Beach, Florida

  3/4 cup soy sauce
    2 tablespoons lemon juice
    1 tablespoon Dijon mustard
  1/4 teaspoon pepper
    4 salmon fillets (6 ounces *each*), skin removed
  2/3 cup strawberry preserves

In a large resealable plastic bag, combine the soy sauce, lemon juice, mustard and pepper. Add salmon; seal bag and turn to coat. Refrigerate for 30 minutes.

Drain and discard marinade. Place salmon in a greased 13-in. x 9-in. baking dish; spoon preserves over fillets. Bake, uncovered, at 375° for 15-20 minutes or until the salmon flakes easily with a fork. **Yield:** 4 servings.

Tomato-Basil Turkey Burgers
(Pictured below)

Prep/Total Time: 30 min.

Choose regular, not lean, ground turkey for these special burgers so they're extra moist and juicy. If you can't use the grill, just cook them under the broiler.
—*Jamie Miller, Maple Grove, Minnesota*

   1 large sweet onion
   1 package (6-1/2 ounces) sun-dried tomato and basil cheese spread, *divided*
1-1/4 pounds ground turkey
   1 large sweet red pepper, quartered
   4 ciabatta rolls, split

Cut sweet onion into three 1/2-in. slices; chop remaining onion and place in a large bowl. Stir in 1/3 cup cheese spread. Crumble turkey over the mixture and mix well. Shape into four patties.

Using long-handled tongs, moisten a paper towel with cooking oil and lightly coat grill rack. Grill burgers, sweet onion slices and sweet red pepper, covered, over medium-high heat for 5-7 minutes on each side or until a meat thermometer reads 165° and juices run clear. Chop grilled onion and red pepper.

Spread rolls with remaining cheese spread; top each with a burger and grilled vegetables. Replace the tops. **Yield:** 4 servings.

Gooey Chocolate-Peanut Bars
(Pictured above)

Prep: 10 min. **Bake:** 20 min. + cooling

Packed with chocolate-covered peanuts, these ooey-gooey goodies are so easy to assemble and take just 10 minutes to get in the oven. They're great to package up for college students craving a sweet treat from home.
—*Elaine Grimme, Sioux Falls, South Dakota*

   1 package (16-1/2 ounces) refrigerated chocolate chip cookie dough
   2 cups chocolate-covered peanuts
   1 cup miniature marshmallows
1/2 cup butterscotch ice cream topping

Press the cookie dough into an ungreased 13-in. x 9-in. baking pan. Bake at 350° for 14-16 minutes or until the edges are lightly browned and the center is set.

Sprinkle with the chocolate-covered peanuts and miniature marshmallows; drizzle with the butterscotch ice cream topping. Bake 6-8 minutes longer or until the marshmallows are puffed. Cool completely and cut into bars. **Yield:** 2 dozen.

BEST TEST

To test Tomato-Basil Turkey Burgers (recipe above right) for doneness, use tongs to hold a burger while inserting an instant-read thermometer horizontally from a side. Make sure the thermometer is far enough in to read the temperature in the center.

Key Lime Mousse Cups

(Pictured above)

Prep/Total Time: 20 min.

Fun, fancy and flavored with a splash of key lime juice, these little phyllo cups are so refreshing as an after-dinner treat. Plus, they take just minutes to prepare.
—Suzanne Pauley, Renton, Washington

    4 ounces cream cheese, softened
  2/3 cup sweetened condensed milk
  1/4 cup key lime juice
  1/2 cup heavy whipping cream, whipped
    2 packages (1.9 ounces *each*) frozen miniature
      phyllo tart shells
Fresh raspberries and lime wedges, optional

In a large bowl, beat the cream cheese, milk and juice until smooth; fold in the whipped cream. Pipe into the tart shells. Garnish with raspberries and lime wedges if desired. Serve immediately. **Yield:** 2-1/2 dozen.

PHYLLO FACTS

Used for the Key Lime Mousse Cups recipe at left, phyllo (also spelled filo) dough is tissue-thin pastry dough used in a variety of sweet and savory dishes. Although phyllo dough can be made by home cooks, it isn't easy to do so. Commercially prepared phyllo dough is a convenient alternative that results in a product that is as good as homemade.

Buttery Cajun Popcorn

Prep/Total Time: 15 min.

This finger-lickin' snack spiced with Cajun seasoning is addictive. Try it for your next movie night at home.
—Beth Stengel, North Hollywood, California

    12 cups air-popped popcorn
   1/4 cup butter, melted
     2 tablespoons lime juice
 4-1/2 teaspoons Cajun seasoning
     4 to 5 tablespoons grated Parmesan cheese

Place the popcorn in a large bowl. Combine the butter and lime juice; drizzle over popcorn and toss to coat.

Combine the Cajun seasoning and grated Parmesan cheese; sprinkle over the popcorn and toss to coat. **Yield:** 3 quarts.

Broccoli Mushroom Salad
(Pictured below)

Prep/Total Time: 20 min.

Fresh broccoli, mushrooms, bacon, cheddar cheese and a tangy dressing—it all adds up to one terrific salad!
—Deb Williams, Peoria, Arizona

     7 cups fresh broccoli florets
     1 cup sliced fresh mushrooms
   1/2 cup shredded cheddar cheese
   1/3 cup prepared honey Dijon salad dressing
     4 bacon strips, cooked and crumbled

In a large saucepan, bring 3 cups water to a boil. Add the broccoli; cover and cook for 3 minutes. Drain and immediately place the broccoli in ice water. Drain and pat dry.

Transfer broccoli to a large bowl; toss with remaining ingredients. **Yield:** 8 servings.

Peach Crisp Delight
(Pictured above)

Prep/Total Time: 25 min.

I love crisps, especially when they come warm and bubbly from the oven. You'll need less than half an hour to whip up the yummy dessert here. Rice Chex makes it different, while peaches and brown sugar provide classic appeal.
—Tracy Golder, Bloomsburg, Pennsylvania

     2 cans (15 ounces *each*) sliced peaches,
       drained
     2 cups Rice Chex, crushed
   1/3 cup packed brown sugar
   1/4 cup all-purpose flour
     3 tablespoons cold butter
 Whipped topping *or* ice cream, optional

Place the peaches in a greased 8-in. square baking dish. In a small bowl, combine the cereal, brown sugar and flour; cut in the butter until the mixture resembles coarse crumbs. Sprinkle over peaches.

Bake, uncovered, at 375° for 15-20 minutes or until topping is golden brown. Serve warm with whipped topping or ice cream if desired. **Yield:** 6 servings.

CHAPTER 6

10 Minutes to the Table

Sauteed Orange Shrimp with Rice...Tomato Salad-Stuffed Avocados...Raspberry-Walnut Brie...Pronto Chicken Fajitas... can recipes this good take only 10 minutes to make from start to finish? The answer is, yes!

Each scrumptious dish in this super-fast chapter will be ready to enjoy in just 10 minutes—or less! From fancy appetizers to family-pleasing main courses, these specialties are quick to fix yet taste like you spent lots of time in the kitchen.

So on your busiest days when you have mere minutes to spare, don't resort to getting food from the drive-thru. Turn to these recipes and serve home cooking in a hurry. ■

TASTE TIMES TEN. Festive Dip (p. 107).

Tomato Salad-Stuffed Avocados
(Pictured below)

Prep/Total Time: 10 min.

My husband requests these dressed-up avocados every year as part of his birthday dinner. They're so pretty and special that your guests will think you fussed. Only you will know how quickly the recipe comes together.
—Charmie Fisher, Fontana, California

    2 small tomatoes, chopped
  2/3 cup crumbled feta cheese
  1/3 cup chopped red onion
    2 tablespoons minced fresh parsley
    2 tablespoons olive oil
    1 tablespoon red wine vinegar
    1 teaspoon minced fresh oregano *or*
      1/4 teaspoon dried oregano
  1/8 teaspoon salt
  1/8 teaspoon pepper
    2 medium ripe avocados, halved, pitted and
      peeled

In a small bowl, combine the first nine ingredients. Spoon into the avocado halves. Serve immediately. **Yield:** 4 servings.

Sauteed Orange Shrimp with Rice
(Pictured above)

Prep/Total Time: 10 min.

Accented with basil and garlic, this restaurant-quality seafood entree takes minutes to prepare but tastes like it took all day. It's just as good served over noodles instead of rice. —Radelle Knappenberger, Oviedo, Florida

    1 package (8.8 ounces) ready-to-serve whole
      grain brown rice
    1 pound uncooked medium shrimp, peeled
      and deveined
    2 garlic cloves, minced
    1 tablespoon olive oil
    1 tablespoon butter
  1/4 teaspoon cornstarch
  1/2 cup orange juice
    2 tablespoons minced fresh basil
  1/4 teaspoon salt

Cook rice according to package directions. Meanwhile, in a large skillet, saute shrimp and garlic in oil and butter for 3-4 minutes or until shrimp turn pink.

Combine cornstarch and orange juice until smooth; stir in the basil and salt. Gradually stir into the skillet. Bring to a boil; cook and stir for 1-2 minutes or until slightly thickened. Serve with rice. **Yield:** 3 servings.

Pronto Chicken Fajitas
(Pictured above)

Prep/Total Time: 10 min.

Mexican food is popular in our family, and this is a really quick way to enjoy it. The fajitas don't require a lot of prep and use only one pan, so you have plenty of time to relax after a busy day. They're also great for turning last night's leftover veggies or chicken into a brand-new meal.

—Robin Poust, Stevensville, Maryland

1 package (14 ounces) frozen pepper strips, thawed
1 medium onion, halved and sliced
1 tablespoon canola oil
2 packages (6 ounces *each*) ready-to-use Southwestern chicken strips
1 tablespoon minced fresh cilantro
1/2 teaspoon salt
1/2 teaspoon garlic powder
1/4 teaspoon pepper
5 flour tortillas (8 inches), warmed
Optional toppings: shredded cheddar cheese, sour cream, guacamole and salsa

In a large skillet, saute pepper strips and onion in oil until tender. Add the chicken strips, cilantro, salt, garlic powder and pepper; heat through.

Spoon onto tortillas; fold in sides. Serve with toppings of your choice. **Yield:** 5 servings.

STORING CILANTRO

Pronto Chicken Fajitas (recipe at left) get zip from cilantro. Like all other fresh herbs, it should be used as soon as possible. For short-term storage, immerse the freshly cut stems in water about 2 inches deep. Cover leaves loosely with a plastic bag and refrigerate it for several days. Wash it just before using.

Sesame Shrimp & Rice
(Pictured above)

Prep/Total Time: 10 min.

With a handful of convenience items and a flash in the skillet, our Test Kitchen home economists were able to prepare a delightfully flavorful, high-quality entree in minutes. Thanks to this recipe, you can, too!

- 1 package (8.8 ounces) ready-to-serve long grain rice
- 1 cup fresh *or* frozen snow peas, thawed
- 2 green onions, sliced
- 1 teaspoon canola oil
- 1 pound cooked medium shrimp, peeled and deveined
- 1 can (20 ounces) pineapple tidbits, drained
- 1 can (11 ounces) mandarin oranges, drained
- 1/4 cup sesame ginger salad dressing
- 2 tablespoons slivered almonds, toasted

Microwave rice according to the package directions. Meanwhile, in a large skillet or wok, stir-fry snow peas and onions in oil for 1 minute. Add the shrimp, pineapple, oranges and salad dressing; cook until heated through and vegetables are crisp-tender.

Sprinkle with the almonds. Serve with the rice. **Yield:** 4 servings.

Irish Cream Coffee

Prep/Total Time: 10 min.

A steaming cup of this jazzed-up coffee makes the perfect pick-me-up any time of day. Try experimenting with other liqueurs or creamers to give each cup a new taste twist.
—*Carol Fate, Waverly, Illinois*

  8 teaspoons sugar
  4 ounces Irish cream liqueur *or* refrigerated
    Irish creme nondairy creamer
  4 cups hot brewed coffee
Whipped cream

Divide sugar and liqueur between four mugs; stir in coffee. Garnish with whipped cream. Serve immediately. **Yield:** 4 servings.

Zippy Peach Spread
(Pictured below)

Prep/Total Time: 10 min.

Don't think twice about the unusual combination of ingredients—this creamy spread is absolutely addictive! If you like, use reduced-fat cream cheese to lighten it up.
—*Laurie Hicks, Troy, Montana*

    1 package (8 ounces) cream cheese, softened
  2/3 cup peach preserves
1-1/2 teaspoons prepared horseradish
1-1/2 teaspoons ground mustard
  1/4 teaspoon white pepper
Assorted crackers

Place cream cheese on a serving plate. In a small bowl, combine peach preserves, horseradish, mustard and pepper; pour over cream cheese. Serve with crackers. **Yield:** 10 servings.

Raspberry-Walnut Brie
(Pictured above)

Prep/Total Time: 10 min.

What could be easier than this creamy, elegant appetizer? Just jam, cheese, crackers, nuts and butter give you an hors d'oeuvre sure to gets oohs and aahs from guests.
—*Janet Edwards, Beaverton, Oregon*

  1/4 cup seedless raspberry jam
    2 rounds (8 ounces *each*) Brie cheese
    1 package (11-1/2 ounces) stone ground
      wheat crackers, *divided*
  1/2 cup finely chopped walnuts
    1 tablespoon butter, melted

In a small microwave-safe bowl, microwave raspberry jam on high for 15-20 seconds or until melted; brush over the Brie.

Crush nine wheat crackers. In a small bowl, combine the cracker crumbs, walnuts and butter; press into the raspberry jam. Serve with the remaining crackers. **Yield:** 16 servings.

Cranberry Cream Cheese Spread
(Pictured above)

Prep/Total Time: 10 min.

With tangy cranberries and a short prep time, this cheery appetizer is perfect for parties during the holiday season. Thanks to the spread's hint of sweetness, both kids and adults will gobble it up. Reduced-fat cream cheese makes it a little lighter. —Frankie Robinson, Lockhart, Texas

    1 package (8 ounces) reduced-fat cream
      cheese
1/2 cup dried cranberries, chopped
1/2 cup chopped dried apricots
    1 teaspoon grated orange peel
Assorted crackers

In a large bowl, beat cream cheese, cranberries, apricots and orange peel until blended. Chill until serving. Serve with crackers. **Yield:** 1-1/2 cups.

CREATIVE CRANBERRIES

Have dried cranberries left over from Cranberry Cream Cheese Spread (recipe above)? They can often be substituted for raisins in recipes or added to salads, breads, stuffings or trail mixes. Commercially dried cranberries contain added sugar, so they can even make a sweet snack alone by the handful.

Strawberry Lime Smoothies

Prep/Total Time: 5 min.

Try this yummy beverage using peak-of-freshness berries, and it's sure to become one of your family's summer staples. —Elizabeth Johnson, Greenville, South Carolina

1/2 cup 2% milk
    2 to 4 tablespoons lime juice
    2 cups fresh strawberries, hulled and halved
    1 cup (8 ounces) strawberry yogurt
    2 tablespoons honey
1/2 teaspoon ground cinnamon

In a blender, combine all ingredients; cover and process until smooth. Pour into chilled glasses. Serve immediately. **Yield:** 3 servings.

Peanut Butter & Banana Smoothie
(Pictured below)

Prep/Total Time: 10 min.

What kid wouldn't love waking up to this cool smoothie flavored with banana, peanut butter and honey? For a fun variation, replace the honey with chocolate syrup.
—Traci Wynne, Denver, Pennsylvania

1/2 cup plain yogurt
    1 medium ripe banana
    2 tablespoons nonfat dry milk powder
    1 tablespoon honey
    1 tablespoon creamy peanut butter
    2 ice cubes

In a blender, combine all ingredients; cover and process for 30-40 seconds or until smooth. Stir if necessary. Pour smoothie into a chilled glass; serve immediately. **Yield:** 1 serving.

Festive Dip

(Pictured above and on page 100)

Prep/Total Time: 10 min.

This colorful snack is great for just about any party or get-together. Convenient bottled Italian salad dressing gives zest to the combination of peppers, onion and black-eyed peas. —Donna Kollar, Austintown, Ohio

1 can (15-1/2 ounces) black-eyed peas, rinsed and drained

1 medium sweet red pepper, finely chopped
1 medium green pepper, finely chopped
1/3 cup finely chopped onion
1 jalapeno pepper, seeded and chopped
1/2 cup Italian salad dressing
Corn chips

In a large bowl, combine the first five ingredients. Drizzle with salad dressing; toss to coat. Serve with corn chips. **Yield:** 4 cups.

Editor's Note: When cutting hot peppers, disposable gloves are recommended. Avoid touching your face.

Creamy Herb Spread
(Pictured at top left)

Prep/Total Time: 5 min.

Whipped up by the expert cooks in our Test Kitchen, this fresh-flavored spread is ideal for chicken, turkey or veggie sandwiches. Plus, the recipe takes just five minutes to prepare. What an easy way to jazz up lunch!

 1 package (3 ounces) cream cheese, softened
1/4 cup loosely packed basil leaves
1/4 cup mayonnaise
 1 tablespoon minced fresh parsley
1/2 teaspoon cider vinegar
1/8 teaspoon pepper
Dash salt

Place all ingredients in a small food processor; cover and process until blended. Store spread in the refrigerator. **Yield:** 1/2 cup.

Lemon-Garlic Spread
(Pictured at center left)

Prep/Total Time: 10 min.

With its tongue-tingling tastes of lemon and garlic, this lively blend from our home economists will complement most any meat or seafood handheld.

1/3 cup mayonnaise
 2 tablespoons olive oil
 1 tablespoon red wine vinegar
 1 garlic clove, minced
 1 teaspoon grated lemon peel
1/4 teaspoon lemon-pepper seasoning

In a small bowl, whisk all ingredients until blended. Store spread in the refrigerator. **Yield:** 1/2 cup.

Roasted Red Pepper Spread
(Pictured at bottom left)

Prep/Total Time: 10 min.

Our Test Kitchen staff took advantage of convenient roasted sweet red pepper strips from a jar to make this colorful condiment. Try tossing the mixture with salad greens before adding it to your sandwich.

 1 cup roasted sweet red pepper strips, drained
 2 teaspoons olive oil
 1 teaspoon balsamic vinegar
1/2 teaspoon sugar
1/2 teaspoon onion powder
1/8 teaspoon salt
1/8 teaspoon pepper

Place all ingredients in a small food processor; cover and process until pureed. Store spread in the refrigerator. **Yield:** 3/4 cup.

 Editor's Note: This recipe was tested with Vlasic roasted red pepper strips.

Berry Blast Smoothies

Prep/Total Time: 5 min.

You'll need just four basic ingredients for these quick morning pick-me-ups. They're also great as a sweet afternoon snack. —Chris Michalowski, Dallas, Texas

- 1/2 cup pomegranate-blueberry V8 juice blend
- 1-1/4 cups frozen unsweetened mixed berries
- 1 medium banana, sliced
- 1/3 cup fat-free plain yogurt

In a blender, combine all ingredients; cover and process until smooth. Pour into chilled glasses; serve immediately. **Yield:** 2 servings.

Watermelon Cooler
(Pictured below)

Prep/Total Time: 10 min.

Summertime means cooling off with a slice of watermelon and a glass of cold lemonade. This recipe gives you two favorites in one. It's so refreshing on a hot day.
—Darlene Brenden, Salem, Oregon

- 2 cups lemonade
- 3 cups seedless watermelon, coarsely chopped
- 1 cup crushed ice

In a blender, combine all ingredients; cover and process until smooth. Pour into chilled glasses; serve immediately. **Yield:** 4 servings.

Chicken Roll-Em Ups
(Pictured above)

Prep/Total Time: 10 min.

Here's a tasty wrap that has it all. It's perfect to grab when you're on the go, and the filling will really satisfy your afternoon appetite. —Deb Perry, Bluffton, Indiana

- 1/2 cup spreadable chive and onion cream cheese
- 1 teaspoon Dijon mustard
- 4 whole wheat tortillas (8 inches)
- 1/2 pound sliced cooked chicken
- 2 cups shredded lettuce
- 1/2 cup crumbled cooked bacon
- 1-1/4 cups (5 ounces) shredded Swiss cheese
- 1 medium tomato, chopped

In a small bowl, combine the cream cheese and Dijon mustard. Spread over tortillas. Top with chicken, lettuce, bacon, Swiss cheese and tomato. Roll up tightly. **Yield:** 4 servings.

BACON BASICS

Chicken Roll-Em Ups (recipe above) get a boost from bacon. Always check the date stamp on packages of vacuum-sealed bacon to make sure it's fresh. The date reflects the last date of sale. Once the package is opened, bacon should be used within a week. For long-term storage, freeze bacon for up to 1 month.

Peach Citrus Smoothies
(Pictured below)

Prep/Total Time: 10 min.

Lemon yogurt and orange juice add a citrusy kick to these peachy keen smoothies. They're slightly icy at first, but they get nice and creamy after a minute or so.
—Joni Rodriguez, Silverton, Oregon

>   3/4 cup orange juice
>   2 cups crushed ice
>   2 cups sliced peeled fresh *or* frozen peaches
>   1/2 cup lemon yogurt
>   1/3 cup honey
>   1 tablespoon lime juice

In a blender, combine all ingredients; cover and process until smooth. Pour into chilled glasses; serve immediately. **Yield:** 4 servings.

Deli Beef Sandwiches with Horseradish Mayonnaise
(Pictured above)

Prep/Total Time: 10 min.

Sweet cherry preserves balance the bold horseradish in this hearty sandwich. What a great noontime treat!
—Greg Fontenot, The Woodlands, Texas

>   1/2 cup mayonnaise
>   2 tablespoons cherry preserves
>   4 teaspoons prepared horseradish
>   8 slices whole wheat bread
>   3/4 pound sliced deli roast beef
>   4 lettuce leaves
>   1 large tomato, thinly sliced
> Dash *each* salt and pepper

In a small bowl, combine mayonnaise, cherry preserves and horseradish. Spread 1 tablespoon over each of four bread slices. Layer with roast beef, lettuce and tomato; sprinkle with salt and pepper. Spread the remaining mayonnaise mixture over remaining bread; place over top. **Yield:** 4 servings.

LIVELY LETTUCE

To keep lettuce crisp and fresh, wash it in cold water and drain it very well. Use a "salad spinner" or pat it dry with paper towels. Store it in a resealable plastic bag or airtight container with a dry paper towel in the bottom to absorb any leftover moisture. Be certain to replace the towel if it gets wet.

Jazzed-Up Clam Chowder
(Pictured above)
Prep/Total Time: 10 min.

No one ever guesses that this dressed-up clam chowder started with a can! It really tastes like homemade.
—Josephine Piro, Easton, Pennsylvania

- 1 can (19 ounces) chunky New England clam chowder
- 1 can (8-3/4 ounces) cream-style corn
- 2/3 cup 2% milk
- 2 tablespoons shredded cheddar cheese
- 2 tablespoons bacon bits
- 2 tablespoons minced chives
- Assorted crackers, optional

In a 1-1/2-qt. microwave-safe dish, combine chowder, corn and milk. Cover and microwave on high for 4-6 minutes or until heated through, stirring every 2 minutes. Sprinkle servings with cheese, bacon and chives. Serve with crackers if desired. **Yield:** 4 servings.

Editor's Note: This recipe was tested in a 1,100-watt microwave.

CHAPTER 7

Shop Once...Eat All Week

Weekdays are your busiest days of all...so wouldn't it be great if you could have dinner for each of those nights all planned out? Thanks to this helpful chapter, you can!

Our Test Kitchen pros have organized some of their own recipe creations into six weeks of Monday-through-Friday suppers. Every evening features a new family-pleasing entree, from Portobello-Chicken Lo Mein to Saucy Italian Orzo.

Many of the recipes make use of leftovers from earlier in the week. Plus, each weekly plan comes with a complete grocery list to make shopping easy.

So stop worrying about what's for dinner. Thanks to this meal plan, you don't have to! ■

WEEKDAY WINNER. Unwrapped Bacon Scallops (p. 127).

Week 1

■ SHOPPING LIST ■

Check for these staples:

- beef broth
- cayenne pepper
- chicken broth
- chili sauce
- cornstarch
- cumin
- dill pickle slices
- flour
- garlic cloves
- ground ginger
- honey
- Italian seasoning
- mayonnaise
- olive oil
- onions
- paprika
- pepper
- prepared mustard
- rice
- rice vinegar
- sage
- salt
- sesame oil
- thyme

Shop for these items:

1 can (15 ounces) black beans
2 cans (14-1/2 ounces each) diced tomatoes with basil, oregano and garlic
1 can (10 ounces) green enchilada sauce
1 package (16 ounces) linguine
1 package (16 ounces) orzo pasta
1 can (6 ounces) tomato paste
1 loaf (1 pound) French bread
4 slices Swiss cheese
1 package (6 ounces) baby spinach
1 package (16 ounces) fresh carrots
1 bunch fresh cilantro
2-1/2 pounds red potatoes
2 packages (8 ounces each) sliced baby portobello mushrooms
1 package (8 ounces) cream cheese
1 pound boneless skinless chicken breasts
4 boneless skinless chicken breast halves (6 ounces each)
1 boneless pork shoulder roast (3 to 4 pounds)
1 pound ground beef

■ TIME-SAVING TIPS ■

- Hearty, earthy portobellos are our first choice in the recipes for Monday and Thursday, but white button mushrooms will work, too.
- Serve Saucy Italian Orzo with crusty Italian bread (or the other half of Friday's French loaf) brushed with garlic butter.
- If you save half of the cooked pork from dinner on Wednesday, you'll have plenty to use for the panini sandwiches on Friday.
- Don't have linguine for the Portobello-Chicken Lo Mein? Try spaghetti or fettuccine.

■ MONDAY ■

Chicken Portobello With Mashed Red Potatoes

(Pictured above)

Prep/Total Time: 30 min.

This family-friendly dish is not only simple enough to enjoy any night of the week, but also nice enough for special occasions. The creamy mushroom sauce pairs perfectly with both the chicken and mashed potatoes.

1-1/2 pounds red potatoes, cubed
1/4 cup all-purpose flour
1-1/4 teaspoons salt, *divided*
1-1/4 teaspoons rubbed sage, *divided*
1/2 teaspoon dried thyme
1/2 teaspoon pepper
4 boneless skinless chicken breast halves (6 ounces *each*)
2 tablespoons olive oil
3/4 pound sliced baby portobello mushrooms
1 package (8 ounces) cream cheese, softened, *divided*
1-1/4 cups chicken broth, *divided*

Place potatoes in a large saucepan and cover with water. Bring to a boil. Reduce heat; cover and cook for 10-15 minutes or until tender.

Meanwhile, in a large resealable plastic bag, combine the flour, 1 teaspoon salt, 1 teaspoon sage, thyme and pepper. Add chicken, one piece at a time, and shake to coat. In a large skillet, cook chicken in oil over medium heat for 5-8 minutes on each side or until a meat thermometer reaches 170°. Remove and keep warm.

In the same skillet, saute mushrooms until tender. Reduce heat; add 6 ounces cream cheese, 1 cup broth and remaining salt and sage. Cook and stir until cheese is melted. Drain potatoes; mash with remaining cream cheese and broth. Serve with chicken and sauce mixture. **Yield:** 4 servings.

TUESDAY

Saucy Italian Orzo
(Pictured below)

Prep/Total Time: 30 min.

Orzo pasta is an interesting twist in this beefy Italian meal-in-one. Spinach adds garden-fresh flavor and gives this dinner a nutritional boost.

    1 pound ground beef
    1 large onion, chopped
    3 garlic cloves, minced
    2 cans (14-1/2 ounces *each*) diced tomatoes
        with basil, oregano and garlic
    1 can (14-1/2 ounces) beef broth
    1 can (6 ounces) tomato paste
  3/4 cup uncooked orzo pasta
    1 teaspoon Italian seasoning
    2 cups fresh baby spinach

In a Dutch oven, cook the beef, onion and garlic over medium heat until meat is no longer pink; drain.

Stir in the tomatoes, beef broth, tomato paste, orzo and Italian seasoning. Bring to a boil. Reduce heat; cover and simmer for 15-20 minutes or until orzo is tender. Add the spinach; cook and stir until spinach is wilted. **Yield:** 6 servings.

WEDNESDAY

Slow-Cooked Pork Verde
(Pictured above)

Prep: 15 min. **Cook:** 4-1/2 hours

Comforting and hearty, this midweek entree is perfect for chilly evenings. Serve it with French bread and a tossed green salad for a well-rounded supper.

    3 medium carrots, sliced
    1 boneless pork shoulder butt roast (3 to
        4 pounds)
    1 can (15 ounces) black beans, rinsed and
        drained
    1 can (10 ounces) green enchilada sauce
  1/4 cup minced fresh cilantro
    1 tablespoon cornstarch
  1/4 cup cold water
Hot cooked rice

Place carrots in a 5-qt. slow cooker. Cut roast in half; place in slow cooker. Add the beans, enchilada sauce and cilantro. Cover and cook on low for 4-1/2 to 5 hours or until a meat thermometer reads 160°.

Remove one half of roast to a serving platter; keep warm. Set aside remaining half to cool.

Skim fat from cooking juices. Transfer the remaining cooking liquid, carrots and beans to a small saucepan. Bring to a boil. Combine the cornstarch and water until smooth. Gradually stir into the pan. Bring to a boil; cook and stir for 2 minutes or until thickened. Serve with the meat and rice.

Cover and refrigerate reserved meat for Pork Panini & Spiced Fries (recipe on page 116) or save for another use. **Yield:** 4 servings.

Pork Panini & Spiced Fries
(Pictured below)

Prep: 25 min. **Bake:** 30 min.

The spread on this delicious panini sandwich combines mayonnaise, chili sauce, mustard and cumin into a unique blend that goes perfectly with pork. Plus, spiced-up french fries are terrific on the side.

    1 tablespoon olive oil
1/2 teaspoon salt
1/2 teaspoon ground cumin
1/2 teaspoon paprika
1/4 teaspoon pepper
1/4 teaspoon cayenne pepper
    1 pound medium red potatoes
PANINI:
    1 loaf (1 pound) French bread
1/3 cup mayonnaise
    4 teaspoons chili sauce
    1 teaspoon prepared mustard
1/8 teaspoon ground cumin
1-1/2 pounds cooked pork, sliced
    8 dill pickle slices
    4 slices Swiss cheese

In a large resealable plastic bag, combine the first six ingredients. Cut the potatoes into 1/4-in. sticks. Add to bag, a few pieces at a time, and shake to coat. Transfer to a greased 15-in. x 10-in. x 1-in. baking pan. Bake at 425° for 30-35 minutes or until crisp and golden brown, stirring once.

Meanwhile, cut the bread in half widthwise (save one half for another use). Cut bread in half horizontally; cut into fourths widthwise. In a small bowl, combine the mayonnaise, chili sauce, mustard and cumin; spread over bread. Layer each with pork, pickles and cheese. Replace tops.

Cook on a panini maker or indoor grill for 2-3 minutes or until the cheese is melted. Serve with the fries. **Yield:** 4 servings.

Portobello-Chicken Lo Mein
(Pictured above)

Prep/Total Time: 30 min.

This Asian-inspired dinner of chicken, vegetables and pasta is highlighted with the flavors of honey and ginger. The slightly sweet sauce brings everything together and makes a meal the whole family will love.

    4 ounces uncooked linguine
    1 tablespoon cornstarch
    1 cup chicken broth
    1 tablespoon rice vinegar
    1 tablespoon honey
3/4 teaspoon salt
1/2 teaspoon ground ginger
    1 pound boneless skinless chicken breasts,
        cut into strips
    2 tablespoons sesame oil, *divided*
    2 medium carrots, sliced
    1 medium onion, chopped
1-3/4 cups sliced baby portobello mushrooms
    2 cups fresh baby spinach

Cook the linguine according to the package directions. Meanwhile, in a small bowl, combine the cornstarch, chicken broth, rice vinegar, honey, salt and ginger until smooth; set aside.

In a large skillet or wok, stir-fry chicken in 1 tablespoon oil for 4-6 minutes or until no longer pink. Remove with a slotted spoon; keep warm.

Stir-fry the carrots and onion in the remaining oil for 2 minutes. Add mushrooms; stir-fry for 2 minutes. Add spinach; stir-fry 1-2 minutes longer or until vegetables are crisp-tender and spinach is wilted.

Stir cornstarch mixture and add to the pan. Bring to a boil; cook and stir for 1-2 minutes or until thickened. Drain linguine. Add chicken and linguine to the pan; heat through. **Yield:** 4 servings.

Week 2

■ SHOPPING LIST ■

Check for these staples:

- butter
- cider vinegar
- eggs
- garlic cloves
- Greek seasoning
- ground cumin
- ground ginger
- honey
- hot pepper sauce
- instant brown rice
- lemon juice
- olive oil
- onions
- pepper
- salt
- sesame seeds
- soy sauce
- thyme

Shop for these items:

1	package (16 ounces) penne pasta
2	cans (2-1/4 ounces each) sliced ripe olives
1	can (15 ounces) tomato sauce
1/4	cup chopped walnuts
2	packages (6 ounces each) fresh baby spinach
1	package (16 ounces) fresh carrots
1	small green pepper
6	medium tomatoes
3	medium yellow summer squash
1	package (12-1/2 ounces) whole pita breads
1	jar (3.5 ounces) prepared pesto
1	package (4 ounces) crumbled garlic and herb feta cheese
1	carton (8 ounces) heavy whipping cream
1	beef top sirloin steak (1 pound)
2-1/2	pounds boneless skinless chicken breasts
4	cod fillets (6 ounces each)
1	package (16 ounces) frozen shelled edamame

■ TIME-SAVING TIPS ■

- Used in Chicken & Pita Salad, edamame is becoming more and more popular in the U.S. These young soybeans pack lots of nutrition and fresh flavor in every bite. You'll find them with the frozen veggies in your grocery store.
- For Tuesday's Mediterranean Steak & Egg Pitas, microwave all four pitas for 15-20 seconds to soften and warm them. For crispier pitas, place each one in a skillet over medium heat until warmed, then turn and heat the other side.
- Cod is a white fish with a tender texture and delicate flavor. Sole, haddock and flounder are similar types of fish that make good substitutes in Thursday's Southwest-Style Cod recipe.
- Garden Vegetable & Chicken Skillet is a fantastic catchall for any leftovers in the fridge.

Chicken & Pita Salad

(Pictured below)

Prep/Total Time: 30 min.

Pita bread makes fantastic croutons for this simple yet tasty main-dish salad. It features a wonderful homemade dressing that's a snap to whip up.

- 1 pita bread (6 inches), chopped
- 1 cup frozen shelled edamame, thawed
- 1 pound boneless skinless chicken breasts, cut into 1/2-inch strips
- 2 teaspoons olive oil
- 1 package (6 ounces) fresh baby spinach
- 1 cup shredded carrots
- 2 medium tomatoes, chopped
- 1/4 cup crumbled garlic and herb feta cheese

DRESSING:
- 2 tablespoons cider vinegar
- 2 tablespoons olive oil
- 2 tablespoons soy sauce
- 2 teaspoons sesame seeds
- 1 garlic clove, minced
- 1 teaspoon honey
- 1/4 teaspoon ground ginger

Dash pepper

Place pita bread on a baking sheet. Bake at 350° for 8-10 minutes or until lightly toasted.

Meanwhile, cook edamame according to the package directions. In a large skillet over medium heat, cook the chicken in oil until chicken juices run clear.

In a large bowl, combine spinach, carrots, tomatoes, cheese, edamame and pita bread. In a small bowl, whisk the dressing ingredients; drizzle over salad and toss to coat. Divide among four serving plates; top with chicken. Serve immediately. **Yield:** 4 servings.

Mediterranean Steak & Egg Pitas
(Pictured below)

Prep/Total Time: 25 min.

Traditional steak and eggs get a Mediterranean makeover in this oh-so-easy entree. Hearty and fun, the pitas are loaded with flavor and make a great dinner.

- 1 beef top sirloin steak (1 pound), cut into 1/2-inch cubes
- 1/2 teaspoon Greek seasoning
- 1/4 teaspoon salt
- 1/4 teaspoon pepper
- 2 teaspoons olive oil
- 4 eggs
- 4 whole pita breads, warmed
- 2 medium tomatoes, chopped
- 1 can (2-1/4 ounces) sliced ripe olives, drained
- 2/3 cup crumbled garlic and herb feta cheese

Sprinkle the beef with the Greek seasoning, salt and pepper. In a large skillet, saute the beef in oil for 4-6 minutes or until no longer pink. Remove from the heat and keep warm.

In a large nonstick skillet coated with cooking spray, fry the eggs as desired. Spoon the steak over the pita breads; top with tomatoes, ripe olives, cheese and eggs. **Yield:** 4 servings.

Creamy Pesto Penne With Vegetable Ribbons
(Pictured above)

Prep/Total Time: 30 min.

This beautiful dish is guaranteed to impress both your family and guests. Colorful veggies make it eye-catching, and the taste doesn't disappoint.

- 2 cups uncooked penne pasta
- 1 cup frozen shelled edamame, thawed
- 4 medium carrots
- 2 yellow summer squash
- 1 medium onion, halved and thinly sliced
- 2 tablespoons butter, *divided*
- 1 garlic clove, minced
- 3/4 cup heavy whipping cream
- 2 tablespoons prepared pesto
- 1/4 teaspoon salt
- 1/4 cup chopped walnuts, toasted

In a large saucepan, cook the pasta according to the package directions, adding the edamame during the last 5 minutes of cooking. Meanwhile, using a vegetable peeler or metal cheese slicer, cut carrots and squash into very thin lengthwise strips.

In a large skillet, saute onion in 1 tablespoon butter until tender. Add the vegetable strips and garlic; saute 2-3 minutes longer or until crisp-tender. Stir in cream, pesto, salt and remaining butter. Bring to a gentle boil; cook for 2-4 minutes or until sauce is slightly thickened and vegetables are tender.

Drain the pasta and edamame; toss with vegetable mixture. Sprinkle with walnuts. **Yield:** 4 servings.

Southwest-Style Cod
(Pictured below)

Prep/Total Time: 30 min.

Make tonight fish night with this festive recipe, and your evening will be anything but boring! Cumin, garlic and hot sauce give the cod fillets their zip.

    1 small onion, chopped
    1 small green pepper, chopped
    2 teaspoons olive oil
    2 garlic cloves, minced
    1 can (15 ounces) tomato sauce
    2 medium tomatoes, chopped
    1 can (2-1/4 ounces) sliced ripe olives, drained
1/2 teaspoon ground cumin
1/4 teaspoon hot pepper sauce
1/8 teaspoon pepper
    4 cod fillets (6 ounces *each*)

In a large skillet, saute the onion and green pepper in oil until tender. Add the garlic; saute 1 minute longer. Stir in the tomato sauce, tomatoes, olives, cumin, pepper sauce and pepper. Bring to a boil. Reduce heat; simmer, uncovered, for 5 minutes.

Add the fillets. Cover and cook over medium heat for 10-14 minutes or until the fish flakes easily with a fork, turning once. **Yield:** 4 servings.

Garden Vegetable & Chicken Skillet
(Pictured above)

Prep: 20 min. **Cook:** 20 min.

Here's a fantastic way to add fresh vegetables to your diet. Featuring squash, onion, carrots and baby spinach, this chicken-and-rice recipe is a complete meal.

1-1/2 pounds boneless skinless chicken breasts, cut
       into 1/2-inch cubes
    1 medium yellow summer squash, chopped
    1 medium onion, chopped
    1 medium carrot, chopped
    2 tablespoons butter
    3 cups fresh baby spinach
    1 garlic clove, minced
1/2 teaspoon salt
1/2 teaspoon dried thyme
1/4 teaspoon pepper
    1 cup uncooked instant brown rice
1-1/4 cups water
    1 tablespoon lemon juice

In a large skillet, saute chicken, squash, onion and carrot in butter for 5-6 minutes or until chicken is no longer pink; drain. Add the spinach, garlic, salt, thyme and pepper; cook 2 minutes longer.

Stir in rice and water. Bring to a boil. Reduce heat; cover and simmer for 10-15 minutes or until rice is tender. Stir in lemon juice. **Yield:** 4 servings.

SQUASH SAVVY

When shopping for this week's meals, choose a firm summer squash with brightly colored skin that's free from spots and bruises. Summer squash may be refrigerated in a plastic bag for up to 5 days. Before using summer squash, wash it and trim both ends.

Week 3

Check for these staples:

- barbecue seasoning
- beef broth
- butter
- chili powder
- chunky peanut butter
- cider vinegar
- crushed red pepper flakes
- Dijon mustard
- dried rosemary
- dried thyme
- eggs
- garlic cloves
- garlic powder
- grated Parmesan cheese
- ground ginger
- Italian seasoning
- olive oil
- onion powder
- onions
- pepper
- rice
- salt
- sugar
- steak seasoning
- soy sauce

Shop for these items:

- 4 hamburger buns
- 1 can (15 ounces) black beans
- 1 tube (1 pound) polenta
- 1 can (14 ounces) bean sprouts
- 1 large bunch romaine
- 1 pint cherry tomatoes
- 2 medium sweet red peppers
- 1 bunch green onions
- 2 small zucchini
- 1 small eggplant
- 1-1/2 pounds small fresh mushrooms
- 1 beef top sirloin steak (1-1/2 pounds)
- 1 pork tenderloin (1 pound)
- 1-1/4 pounds ground turkey
- 1 bunch fresh cilantro

■ TIME-SAVING TIPS ■

- Monday's dinner is a great way to try polenta. Made from cornmeal, it's mild, and in this recipe, slightly crispy. Not feeling adventurous? The ratatouille is great over noodles, too.
- Dress up Tuesday's burgers with a spread of 1/3 cup mayo, 1/4 teaspoon garlic powder, 1/2 teaspoon chives and 1/2 teaspoon horseradish combined.
- Top sirloin is a relatively lean cut of beef that's ideal for broiling or grilling. If you're having trouble finding it, choose your favorite cut of beef or try a 1/2-inch-thick boneless pork chop.
- One of the best things about fried rice is that it's easy to enhance. Turkey Fried Rice features peanut butter and cilantro, flavors that pair perfectly with an added red bell pepper or broccoli.

■ MONDAY ■

Ratatouille with Polenta
(Pictured above)

Prep: 20 min. **Cook:** 15 min.

If you only know Ratatouille as a children's movie, you're in for a treat. Created in the Provence region of France, the seasoned and sauteed vegetable dish is a traditional favorite. Polenta gives this version heartiness.

- 1/2 pound small fresh mushrooms, halved
- 1 medium sweet red pepper, chopped
- 1 small onion, chopped
- 4 teaspoons olive oil, *divided*
- 4 cups cubed peeled eggplant
- 1 small zucchini, chopped
- 1 cup cherry tomatoes
- 2 garlic cloves, minced
- 1-1/2 teaspoons Italian seasoning
- 1/2 teaspoon salt
- 1 tube (1 pound) polenta, cut into 1/2-inch slices

Grated Parmesan cheese, optional

In a large skillet, saute mushrooms, pepper and onion in 2 teaspoons oil until almost tender. Add eggplant, zucchini, tomatoes, garlic, Italian seasoning and salt. Saute for 8-10 minutes or until vegetables are tender.

In another skillet, cook polenta slices in remaining oil over medium-high heat for 3-4 minutes on each side or until lightly browned. Serve with ratatouille; sprinkle with cheese if desired. **Yield:** 4 servings.

Turkey Bean Burgers
(Pictured below)

Prep/Total Time: 30 min.

You won't miss ground beef when you taste these nicely spiced patties made with turkey, black beans and shredded zucchini. They're moist and delicious.

- 3/4 cup canned black beans, rinsed and drained
- 1 egg white
- 1/2 cup shredded zucchini
- 1/2 cup finely chopped sweet red pepper
- 1 teaspoon chili powder
- 1/2 teaspoon onion powder
- 1/2 teaspoon pepper
- 1/4 teaspoon salt
- 3/4 pound ground turkey
- 1 tablespoon olive oil
- 4 hamburger buns, split
- 1 small onion, sliced
- 4 romaine leaves

In a small bowl, coarsely mash the beans. Add the egg white, zucchini, red pepper, chili powder, onion powder, pepper and salt. Crumble turkey over mixture and mix well. Shape into four patties.

In a large skillet, cook burgers in oil over medium heat for 4-5 minutes on each side or until a meat thermometer reads 165° and juices run clear. Serve on buns with onion and lettuce. **Yield:** 4 servings.

Grilled Steaks With Mushroom Sauce
(Pictured above)

Prep/Total Time: 20 min.

With a savory mushroom sauce, this grilled steak entree is sure to make an ordinary midweek day special.

- 1 beef top sirloin steak (1-1/2 pounds)
- 1/2 teaspoon steak seasoning
- 1 pound small fresh mushrooms
- 1/4 cup butter, cubed
- 1/2 cup beef broth
- 1 tablespoon Dijon mustard
- 1/2 teaspoon dried rosemary, crushed
- 1/2 teaspoon dried thyme

Cut the steak into four pieces; sprinkle with the steak seasoning. Grill steaks, covered, over medium heat or broil 4 in. from heat for 5-7 minutes on each side or until the meat reaches desired doneness (for medium-rare, a meat thermometer should read 145°; medium, 160°; well-done, 170°).

Meanwhile, in a large skillet, saute the mushrooms in butter until tender. Stir in remaining ingredients. Bring to a boil; cook until the liquid is reduced by about half. Serve with steaks. **Yield:** 4 servings.

Turkey Fried Rice
(Pictured below)

Prep/Total Time: 30 min.

Generally, fried rice is prepared using leftover rice from the day before, which makes this dish a terrific base for a catchall meal. Just try it and see!

    1 tablespoon olive oil
    2 eggs, beaten
1/2 pound ground turkey
    2 green onions, sliced
    3 cups cold cooked rice
    1 cup canned bean sprouts
1/4 cup minced fresh cilantro
1/4 cup soy sauce
    2 tablespoons chunky peanut butter
    1 teaspoon sugar
1/2 teaspoon garlic powder
1/4 teaspoon crushed red pepper flakes
1/4 teaspoon ground ginger

In a large skillet, heat the oil over medium-high heat. Pour the eggs into the skillet. As the eggs set, lift the edges, letting the uncooked portion flow underneath. When eggs are completely cooked, remove to a plate; set aside.

In the same skillet, cook the turkey and onions over medium heat until the meat is no longer pink. Stir in the rice, bean sprouts and cilantro. In a small bowl, whisk the remaining ingredients until blended; stir into the skillet. Chop the egg into small pieces; stir into skillet and heat through. **Yield:** 4 servings.

Barbecue-Pork Salad
(Pictured above)

Prep/Total Time: 30 min.

All it takes is 2 teaspoons of barbecue seasoning—one for the pork and one for the dressing—to give this simple main-course salad a tasty, unexpected twist.

    1 pork tenderloin (1 pound), cut into 1-inch
       cubes
    1 teaspoon barbecue seasoning
1/8 teaspoon salt
    2 teaspoons olive oil
    1 bunch romaine, torn
    1 cup cherry tomatoes, quartered
3/4 cup canned black beans
VINAIGRETTE:
1/2 cup cider vinegar
1/4 cup olive oil
    2 green onions, sliced
    1 teaspoon barbecue seasoning
1/8 teaspoon salt
1/8 teaspoon pepper

Toss the pork with the barbecue seasoning and salt. In a large skillet, saute the pork in oil until no longer pink; set aside.

In a large bowl, combine romaine, cherry tomatoes, black beans and pork. In a small bowl, combine the vinaigrette ingredients; drizzle over salad and toss to coat. **Yield:** 4 servings.

Week 4

■ SHOPPING LIST ■

Check for these staples:

- butter
- chili powder
- crushed red pepper flakes
- dry bread crumbs
- eggs
- garlic cloves
- garlic powder
- grated Parmesan cheese
- ground cumin
- Italian seasoning
- mayonnaise
- olive oil
- onions
- paprika
- pepper
- salt
- sour cream

Shop for these items:

- 1 package (4 ounces) chopped walnuts
- 1 package flour tortillas (8 inches)
- 1 package (16 ounces) spaghetti
- 1 jar (16 ounces) salsa
- 1 package (16 ounces) shredded Monterey Jack cheese
- 1 bunch fresh cilantro
- 2 medium mangoes
- 1 bunch seedless red grapes
- 2 packages (6 ounces each) fresh baby spinach
- 1 small yellow summer squash
- 5 medium zucchini
- Fresh tarragon
- Fresh thyme
- 3/4 pound boneless skinless chicken breasts
- 1 pound ground beef
- 3/4 pound thick sliced deli ham
- 4 tilapia fillets (6 ounces each)
- 1 package (12 ounces) frozen peas

■ TIME-SAVING TIPS ■

- It's easy to get a nice breading on Monday's tilapia. Cook it in hot oil and leave the fish alone until it's time to flip it.
- Make the filling for Grilled Chicken Salad Wraps a day ahead and chill it. Then, stir it before filling the tortillas and roll them up. If you're taking them on a picnic or another outing, wrap them in plastic wrap and keep them cold.
- Rather than throw away the leftover zucchini pulp from Wednesday's Southwest Zucchini Boats, freeze and save it for zucchini bread. Or, add it to vegetable soups or stews.
- While peas are the traditional green vegetable in carbonara, feel free to prepare Friday's recipe with frozen snap peas or broccoli instead.

MONDAY

Tilapia with Sauteed Spinach
(Pictured above)

Prep: 20 min. **Cook:** 15 min.

Start things off right this week with a restaurant-quality meal fit for guests. Since everything is cooked in the same skillet, cleanup won't be a chore at all.

- 1 egg, beaten
- 1/2 cup dry bread crumbs
- 1 teaspoon Italian seasoning
- 3/4 teaspoon salt, *divided*
- 1/4 teaspoon garlic powder
- 1/4 teaspoon paprika
- 4 tilapia fillets (6 ounces *each*)
- 4 tablespoons olive oil, *divided*
- 1 small onion, chopped
- 1 garlic clove, minced
- 5 cups fresh baby spinach
- 1/8 teaspoon crushed red pepper flakes
- 1/8 teaspoon pepper
- 1/4 cup chopped walnuts, toasted

Place egg in a shallow bowl. In another shallow bowl, combine bread crumbs, Italian seasoning, 1/2 teaspoon salt, garlic powder and paprika. Dip fillets in the egg, then bread crumb mixture.

In a large skillet, cook fillets in 3 tablespoons oil over medium heat for 4-5 minutes on each side or until golden brown and fish flakes easily with a fork. Remove and keep warm.

In the same skillet, saute onion in remaining oil until tender. Add the garlic; cook 1 minute longer. Stir in the spinach, pepper flakes, pepper and remaining salt. Cook and stir for 3-4 minutes or until spinach is wilted. Serve with fillets; sprinkle with walnuts. **Yield:** 4 servings.

Grilled Chicken Salad Wraps

(Pictured below)

Prep/Total Time: 25 min.

Looking for something to perk up your picnic or summer luncheon? Look no further! These tropical delights will dazzle guests and have them coming back for more.

- 3/4 pound boneless skinless chicken breasts
- 1/2 teaspoon salt
- 1/2 teaspoon pepper
- 1 small onion, sliced
- 1 teaspoon olive oil
- 1 cup seedless red grapes, halved
- 2/3 cup chopped peeled mango
- 1/2 cup chopped walnuts, toasted
- 1/2 cup mayonnaise
- 2 teaspoons minced fresh tarragon *or*
  1/2 teaspoon dried tarragon
- 4 flour tortillas (8 inches)
- 1 cup fresh baby spinach

Sprinkle the chicken with the salt and pepper. Place the onion in a grill wok or basket; brush with oil. Grill chicken and onion, covered, over medium heat for 5-7 minutes on each side or until chicken juices run clear and onion is tender. When cool enough to handle, chop the chicken and onion.

In a large bowl, combine the grapes, mango, walnuts, mayonnaise, tarragon, chicken and onion. Place 1 cup filling down the center of each tortilla; top with spinach. Roll up tightly. Serve immediately. **Yield:** 4 servings.

Editor's Note: If you do not have a grill wok or basket, use a disposable foil pan. Poke holes in the bottom of the pan with a meat fork to allow liquid to drain.

Southwest Zucchini Boats

(Pictured above)

Prep/Total Time: 25 min.

These change-of-pace "boats" are packed with a terrific taco-meat filling that's both hearty and family-friendly.

- 4 medium zucchini
- 1 pound ground beef
- 3/4 cup salsa
- 1/4 cup dry bread crumbs
- 1/4 cup minced fresh cilantro
- 1 teaspoon chili powder
- 1/2 teaspoon ground cumin
- 1/4 teaspoon salt
- 1/8 teaspoon pepper
- 1 cup (4 ounces) shredded Monterey
  Jack cheese, *divided*

Sour cream, optional

Cut zucchini in half lengthwise; cut a thin slice from the bottom of each with a sharp knife to allow zucchini to sit flat. Scoop out pulp, leaving 1/4-in. shells.

Place shells in an ungreased 3-qt. microwave-safe dish. Cover and microwave on high for 3 minutes or until crisp-tender; drain and set aside.

Meanwhile, in a large skillet, cook beef over medium heat until no longer pink; drain. Remove from the heat; stir in the salsa, bread crumbs, cilantro, chili powder, cumin, salt, pepper and 1/2 cup cheese. Spoon into the zucchini shells.

Microwave, uncovered, on high for 4 minutes. Sprinkle with remaining cheese. Microwave 3-4 minutes longer or until cheese is melted and zucchini are tender. Serve with sour cream if desired. **Yield:** 4 servings.

Editor's Note: This recipe was tested in a 1,100-watt microwave.

Ham & Mango Quesadillas
(Pictured below)

Prep/Total Time: 25 min.

If you like the ease of quesadillas, especially on busy days, you'll really enjoy this fun and fresh variation featuring jarred salsa enhanced with mangoes.

- 1 tablespoon butter
- 4 flour tortillas (8 inches)
- 2 cups (8 ounces) shredded Monterey Jack cheese
- 1 medium mango, peeled and cubed, *divided*
- 1/4 pound thick sliced deli ham, cut into 1/2-inch strips
- 6 teaspoons minced fresh cilantro, *divided*
- 3/4 cup salsa
- Sour cream, optional

Spread butter over one side of each tortilla. Place the tortillas, butter side down, on a griddle. Sprinkle each with 1/2 cup cheese, 3 tablespoons mango, 1/4 cup ham and 1 teaspoon cilantro. Fold over and cook over low heat for 1-2 minutes on each side or until cheese is melted. Cut into wedges.

Combine the salsa and remaining mango and cilantro; serve with the quesadillas. Garnish with sour cream if desired. **Yield:** 4 servings.

Ham Carbonara
(Pictured above)

Prep/Total Time: 30 min.

The colorful vegetables in this all-in-one pasta dish are sure to brighten up any weeknight meal. The sauce is light but feels rich and comforting, too.

- 8 ounces uncooked spaghetti
- 1 medium zucchini, chopped
- 1 small yellow summer squash, chopped
- 1/4 cup chopped onion
- 2 garlic cloves, minced
- 2 tablespoons olive oil
- 1/2 pound thick sliced deli ham, cubed
- 1 cup frozen peas, thawed
- 2 eggs
- 1/2 cup grated Parmesan cheese, *divided*
- 1 teaspoon minced fresh thyme *or* 1/4 teaspoon dried thyme
- 1/4 teaspoon salt
- 1/8 teaspoon pepper

Cook the spaghetti according to the package directions. Meanwhile, in a large skillet, saute the zucchini, summer squash, onion and garlic in oil until tender. Add ham and peas; heat through. Remove and keep warm.

Reduce heat to low; add eggs to the skillet. Cook and stir until the egg mixture coats the back of a spoon and reaches 160° (mixture will look like a soft frothy egg). Drain spaghetti and place in a bowl. Add eggs; toss to coat. Add the vegetable mixture, 1/4 cup cheese, thyme, salt and pepper; toss gently to coat. Sprinkle with the remaining cheese. **Yield:** 4 servings.

■ SHOPPING LIST ■

Check for these staples:

- chicken broth
- Dijon mustard
- dried thyme
- egg
- garlic cloves
- grated Parmesan cheese
- instant rice
- olive oil
- onion
- pepper
- salt
- seafood seasoning
- seasoned bread crumbs
- seasoned salt

Shop for these items:

- 4 brat buns
- 1 package (20 ounces) refrigerated diced potatoes with onion
- 1 jar (7 ounces) roasted sweet red pepper
- 1 package (8 ounces) shredded Colby-Monterey Jack cheese
- 1 package (5.2 ounces) garlic-herb cheese spread
- 2 pints cherry tomatoes
- 2 packages (6 ounces each) fresh baby spinach
- 1 bunch green onions
- 5 medium ears sweet corn
- 1 medium green pepper
- 1 medium zucchini
- 1 pound thick-sliced bacon strips
- 4 boneless skinless chicken breast halves (5 ounces each)
- 8 uncooked bratwurst links
- 1 pound sea scallops
- 1 package (16 ounces) spaghetti
- 1 bottle (16 ounces) balsamic vinaigrette

■ TIME-SAVING TIPS ■

- Other vinaigrettes, such as sun-dried tomato and Greek, are nice substitutes for balsamic vinaigrette in Bacon & Tomato Spaghetti. As an extra bonus, this main course holds up well, so save any leftovers for a great cold lunch the next day.
- If you can't find sea scallops, feel free to prepare Tuesday's main course with smaller, slightly sweeter bay scallops instead.
- Grill all five ears of corn on Wednesday and save 1 cup of kernels for Bratwurst Hash on Thursday.
- You'll be surprised at how easy it is to fix Friday's elegant stuffed chicken pockets. Simply use a chef's knife and make a lengthwise slit in the thickest part of each breast. Then cut from the edge to the other side, but not through the chicken breast.

■ MONDAY ■

Bacon & Tomato Spaghetti
(Pictured above)

Prep/Total Time: 25 min.

This refreshing, summery pasta dish features baby spinach and a tangy balsamic vinaigrette. They taste terrific with the bacon and cherry tomatoes.

- 8 ounces uncooked spaghetti
- 1/2 pound thick-sliced bacon strips, chopped
- 2 cups cherry tomatoes, halved
- 3 cups fresh baby spinach
- 1/4 cup balsamic vinaigrette
- 1/2 teaspoon salt
- 1/4 teaspoon pepper
- Grated Parmesan cheese

Cook spaghetti according to the package directions.

Meanwhile, in a large skillet, cook the bacon over medium heat until crisp. Remove to paper towels with a slotted spoon; drain, reserving 2 tablespoons drippings. Saute the tomatoes in drippings until tender. Drain the spaghetti; stir into the skillet. Add the spinach, bacon, vinaigrette, salt and pepper; heat through. Sprinkle with cheese. **Yield:** 4 servings.

Unwrapped Bacon Scallops
(Pictured below and on page 112)

Prep/Total Time: 30 min.

With a can't-miss combo of sea scallops and bacon, this 30-minute entree transforms special-occasion food into everyday fare the whole family will love.

- 1-1/2 cups uncooked instant rice
- 1-1/2 cups chicken broth
- 1/2 pound thick-sliced bacon strips, chopped
- 1 medium onion, chopped
- 1 medium zucchini, chopped
- 1 garlic clove, minced
- 1 pound sea scallops
- 1 cup cherry tomatoes, halved
- 1/2 teaspoon seafood seasoning
- 1/2 teaspoon dried thyme
- 2 green onions, chopped

In an ungreased 1-1/2-qt. microwave-safe dish, combine the rice and chicken broth. Cover and microwave on high for 7-8 minutes or until liquid is absorbed and rice is tender. Let stand for 5 minutes.

Meanwhile, in a large skillet, cook bacon over medium heat until crisp; remove to paper towels. Drain, reserving 1 tablespoon drippings.

Saute the onion, zucchini and garlic in drippings until tender. Add scallops; saute for 3 minutes. Add tomatoes, seafood seasoning and thyme; saute 1-2 minutes longer or until scallops are firm and opaque. Fluff rice with a fork; serve with the scallop mixture. Sprinkle with green onions and bacon. **Yield:** 4 servings.

Bratwurst with Grilled Corn Relish
(Pictured above)

Prep/Total Time: 25 min.

Sweet corn is the star of this amazing relish. It really kicks basic brats and hot dogs up a notch. After trying this recipe, you may not want them any other way!

- 3 tablespoons Dijon mustard
- 3 tablespoons balsamic vinaigrette, *divided*
- 4 uncooked bratwurst links
- 2 medium ears sweet corn, husks removed
- 1/4 cup chopped roasted sweet red peppers
- 1 green onion, thinly sliced
- 4 brat buns

Combine Dijon mustard and 2 tablespoons vinaigrette. Grill the bratwurst and corn, covered, over medium heat for 15-20 minutes or until the meat is no longer pink and the corn is tender, turning frequently and basting with mustard mixture.

Remove corn from the cobs. In a small bowl, combine the corn, sweet red peppers, green onion and remaining vinaigrette. Serve the brats in buns with the corn relish. **Yield:** 4 servings.

CORNCOB CLUES

To cut the kernels of corn from a corncob, stand one end of the cob on a cutting board. Starting at the top, run a sharp knife down the cob, cutting deeply to remove whole kernels. One medium corncob yields 1/3 to 1/2 cup kernels.

Spinach-Stuffed Chicken Pockets
(Pictured below)

Prep/Total Time: 30 min.

With a creamy filling and delightfully crispy crust, this elegant stuffed chicken is easy enough for weeknights yet fancy enough for special occasions.

- 4 cups fresh baby spinach
- 1 garlic clove, minced
- 2 teaspoons plus 1/4 cup olive oil, *divided*
- 1/2 cup garlic-herb cheese spread
- 2/3 cup plus 1/4 cup seasoned bread crumbs, *divided*
- 1/2 teaspoon salt, *divided*
- 4 boneless skinless chicken breast halves (5 ounces *each*)
- 1 egg, beaten
- 1/4 teaspoon pepper

In a large skillet, saute spinach and garlic in 2 teaspoons oil until spinach is wilted. Remove from the heat. Stir in the cheese spread, 2/3 cup seasoned bread crumbs and 1/4 teaspoon salt. Cut a pocket in the thickest part of each chicken breast; fill with the spinach mixture. Secure with toothpicks.

Place the egg in a shallow bowl. In another shallow bowl, combine the pepper and remaining bread crumbs and salt. Dip the chicken in egg, then coat with bread crumb mixture.

In a large skillet over medium heat, cook the chicken in remaining oil for 6-8 minutes on each side or until a meat thermometer reads 170°. Discard the toothpicks before serving. **Yield:** 4 servings.

Bratwurst Hash
(Pictured above)

Prep/Total Time: 30 min.

Looking for something homey that's stick-to-your-ribs good? This satisfying, delicious recipe with potatoes, corn, peppers and cheese is the one for you.

- 4 uncooked bratwurst links, halved and sliced
- 1 package (20 ounces) refrigerated diced potatoes with onion
- 1 cup fresh *or* frozen corn
- 1 medium green pepper, chopped
- 1/4 cup chopped roasted sweet red peppers
- 3/4 cup shredded Colby-Monterey Jack cheese, *divided*
- 1/2 teaspoon seasoned salt

In a large skillet, cook the bratwurst over medium heat until meat is no longer pink; drain. Stir in the potatoes, corn and green pepper. Cook, covered, over medium heat for 12-15 minutes or until vegetables are tender, stirring occasionally.

Stir in the red peppers, 1/2 cup cheese and seasoned salt; heat through. Sprinkle with the remaining cheese. **Yield:** 4 servings.

Week 6

■ SHOPPING LIST ■

Check for these staples:

- balsamic vinegar
- bread crumbs
- brown sugar
- butter
- canola oil
- chicken broth
- chili powder
- cider vinegar
- cornstarch
- crushed red pepper flakes
- dried oregano
- dried thyme
- eggs
- garlic cloves
- grated Parmesan cheese
- ground cumin
- honey
- instant brown rice
- milk
- olive oil
- onions
- pepper
- salt
- soy sauce
- sugar

Shop for these items:

- 1 package flour tortillas (8 inches)
- 1 can (11-1/2 ounces) spicy hot V8 juice
- 1 can (15 ounces) black beans
- 1 package (2.20 ounces) beefy onion soup mix
- 1 can (10-3/4 ounces) condensed cream of mushroom with roasted garlic soup, undiluted
- 1 can (10 ounces) enchilada sauce
- 1 package (8 ounces) shredded cheddar cheese
- 1-1/2 pounds brussels sprouts
- 1 medium head cabbage
- 1 medium butternut squash
- 1 bunch broccoli
- 1 large sweet potato
- 1 medium green pepper
- 1 pound medium parsnips
- 1 medium spaghetti squash
- 1 pound Yukon Gold potatoes
- 2 pounds ground beef
- 4 salmon fillets (6 ounces each)
- 1 package (16 ounces) cubed fully cooked ham
- 1 pound boneless skinless chicken breasts

■ TIME-SAVING TIPS ■

- Cutting the sweet potato for Monday into 1/2-inch cubes helps ensure even cooking in the microwave.
- Leftover holiday turkey works well in Thursday's main dish. Just substitute it for the ham.
- A 2-pound head of cabbage yields about 6 cups chopped, enough for Inside-Out Stuffed Cabbage.

Sweet Potato Enchilada Stack
(Pictured below)

Prep: 20 min. **Bake:** 20 min.

Mexican flavors abound in this awesome enchilada stack packed with ground beef, black beans, cheese and sweet potato. What a great way to start off the week!

- 1 large sweet potato, peeled and cut into 1/2-inch cubes
- 1 tablespoon water
- 1 pound ground beef
- 1 medium onion, chopped
- 1 can (15 ounces) black beans, rinsed and drained
- 1 can (10 ounces) enchilada sauce
- 2 teaspoons chili powder
- 1/2 teaspoon dried oregano
- 1/2 teaspoon ground cumin
- 3 flour tortillas (8 inches)
- 2 cups (8 ounces) shredded cheddar cheese

In a large microwave-safe bowl, combine sweet potato and water. Cover and microwave on high for 4-5 minutes or until potato is almost tender.

Meanwhile, in a large skillet, cook the beef and onion over medium heat until meat is no longer pink; drain. Stir in the beans, enchilada sauce, chili powder, oregano, cumin and sweet potato; heat through.

Place a flour tortilla in a greased 9-in. deep-dish pie plate; layer with a third of the beef mixture and cheese. Repeat layers twice. Bake at 400° for 20-25 minutes or until bubbly. **Yield:** 6 servings.

Glazed Salmon With Brussels Sprouts

(Pictured below)

Prep/Total Time: 25 min.

It's hard to believe that this meal gets on the table in less than 30 minutes. It proves that weekday dinners can be fancy and fuss-free at the same time!

- 1-1/2 pounds brussels sprouts, halved
- 4 salmon fillets (6 ounces *each*)
- 2 tablespoons olive oil, *divided*
- 2 garlic cloves, minced
- 1/4 cup honey
- 2 teaspoons chili powder
- 1 teaspoon balsamic vinegar
- 1/2 teaspoon salt
- 1/4 teaspoon pepper

Place brussels sprouts in a large saucepan; cover with water. Bring to a boil. Reduce heat; cover and simmer for 7-9 minutes or until crisp-tender.

Meanwhile, in a large skillet, cook the salmon over medium heat in 1 tablespoon oil for 4-5 minutes on each side or until fish flakes easily with a fork. Remove and keep warm.

Saute garlic in remaining oil for 1 minute; add the honey, chili powder, vinegar, salt and pepper. Cook and stir until blended. Set aside 2 tablespoons glaze. Drain brussels sprouts; add to the skillet. Cook and stir for 1-2 minutes or until tender. Serve with salmon; drizzle with reserved glaze. **Yield:** 4 servings.

Broccoli Chicken Stir-Fry

(Pictured above)

Prep/Total Time: 30 min.

Served on a bed of spaghetti squash, this delicious stir-fry offers a restaurant-quality dish at a fraction of the cost. You'll want to make it again and again.

- 1 medium spaghetti squash

SAUCE:
- 1 cup chicken broth
- 3 tablespoons soy sauce
- 2 tablespoons sugar
- 2 tablespoons cornstarch
- 2 tablespoons cider vinegar
- 1/8 teaspoon crushed red pepper flakes

STIR-FRY:
- 1 egg
- 1 tablespoon soy sauce
- 1/2 cup cornstarch
- 1 pound boneless skinless chicken breasts, cut into 1-inch cubes
- 1/4 cup canola oil
- 2 cups fresh broccoli florets
- 1 medium onion, chopped

Cut spaghetti squash in half lengthwise; discard seeds. Place squash cut side down in a microwave-safe dish. Microwave, uncovered, on high for 12-15 minutes or until tender.

Meanwhile, in a small bowl, combine the broth, soy sauce, sugar, cornstarch, vinegar and pepper flakes until smooth; set aside.

In a shallow bowl, whisk egg and soy sauce. Place cornstarch in another shallow bowl. Dip chicken in egg mixture, then coat with cornstarch. In a large skillet or wok, stir-fry the chicken in oil in batches until no longer pink. Remove and keep warm.

Stir-fry broccoli and onion for 2-3 minutes or until crisp-tender. Stir the sauce mixture and add to the pan. Bring to a boil; cook and stir for 1-2 minutes or until thickened. Add chicken; heat through.

When squash is cool enough to handle, use a fork to separate strands. Serve with stir-fry. **Yield:** 4 servings.

■■■■ **THURSDAY** ■■■■

Parsnip & Ham au Gratin
(Pictured below)

Prep: 20 min. **Bake:** 1 hour

Parsnips, thyme and roasted-garlic soup lend this entree a harvesttime feel, but it's wonderful any time of year. The bread crumbs on top make it rustic and special.

    1 pound medium parsnips, peeled and sliced
    1 pound Yukon Gold potatoes, peeled and
        sliced
    2 cups cubed fully cooked ham
    1 can (10-3/4 ounces) condensed cream of
        mushroom with roasted garlic soup,
        undiluted
    2/3 cup 2% milk
    1/2 cup grated Parmesan cheese, *divided*
    1/2 teaspoon dried thyme
    1/4 teaspoon pepper
    1/4 cup dry bread crumbs
    2 tablespoons butter, melted

Arrange parsnips, potatoes and ham in a greased 13-in. x 9-in. baking dish. Combine cream of mushroom soup, milk, 1/4 cup Parmesan cheese, thyme and pepper; pour over the parsnip mixture.

In a small bowl, combine the bread crumbs, butter and remaining Parmesan cheese. Sprinkle over the top. Cover and bake at 375° for 40 minutes. Uncover; bake 20-25 minutes longer or until the potatoes are tender. **Yield:** 6 servings.

■■■■ **FRIDAY** ■■■■

Inside-Out Stuffed Cabbage
(Pictured above)

Prep/Total Time: 30 min.

Preparing stuffed cabbage rolls can be a time-consuming process, but this version gives you the traditional flavors everyone loves in just half an hour.

    1 pound ground beef
    2 cups cubed peeled butternut squash
    1 medium green pepper, chopped
    6 cups chopped cabbage
    1 can (11-1/2 ounces) spicy hot V8 juice
    1 cup water
    1 envelope beefy onion soup mix
    1 tablespoon brown sugar
  1/2 cup uncooked instant brown rice

In a Dutch oven, cook ground beef, squash and green pepper over medium heat until the meat is no longer pink; drain. Stir in the cabbage, juice, water, soup mix and brown sugar. Bring to a boil. Reduce heat; cover and simmer for 8-10 minutes or until cabbage is tender, stirring occasionally.

Stir in rice. Cover and cook for 5 minutes. Remove from the heat; cover and let stand for 5 minutes or until rice is tender. **Yield:** 4 servings.

CHAPTER 8

Speedy Sides & Salads

Whether you're searching for a crowd-pleasing contribution to a church potluck or looking for a fast dish to round out your family's weekday dinner, you'll want to check the sensational selection here.

From Colorful Green Bean Medley and Garden Zucchini & Corn Saute to Mixed Fruit Salad and Zesty Roasted Vegetables, these recipes come together in a snap to bring you a standout menu addition.

You'll even see Sweet Potato Praline Swirl, Cherry Chiffon Gelatin and other time-tested favorites that are perfect for holiday feasts.

So when you need to complete your menu, the only place you have to look is here! ■

IDEAL ACCOMPANIMENT. Baked Bean Side Dish (p. 145).

Drain and immediately place the vegetables in ice water. Drain; pat dry. Set aside 3/4 cup carrots for garnish.

Discard seasoning packet from noodles or save for another use. Break noodles into small pieces. Place in a large serving bowl; add the blanched vegetables, red pepper, beans sprouts, water chestnuts and 1 tablespoon sesame seeds.

In a small bowl, whisk hoisin sauce, vinegar, canola oil, sesame oil, honey, salt, pepper flakes and pepper. Pour over salad; toss to coat. Garnish with the reserved carrots and remaining sesame seeds. Serve immediately. **Yield:** 9 servings.

Mixed Fruit Salad
(Pictured below)

Prep/Total Time: 20 min.

This recipe is a variation on one I sampled at a work potluck. I added some caramel topping to jazz up the whipped topping and to complement the apples. Featuring crunchy nuts, too, this fruit-filled dish is yummy enough to be a dessert.
—*JayCee Synowiecki, Omaha, Nebraska*

  3 cups chopped apples
  1 cup dried cherries
  1 can (11 ounces) mandarin oranges, drained
  1 medium pear, chopped
1/2 cup chopped walnuts
  1 carton (8 ounces) frozen whipped topping, thawed
  2 tablespoons caramel ice cream topping

Sesame Summer Salad
(Pictured above)

Prep/Total Time: 30 min.

Eye-catching and delicious, this unique salad will impress anytime but is ideal for spring and summer celebrations.
—*Stephanie Matthews, Tempe, Arizona*

  3 large carrots
  2 cups cut fresh asparagus (1-inch pieces)
  2 cups fresh snow peas
  1 package (3 ounces) ramen noodles
  1 medium sweet red pepper, cut into thin strips
  1 can (14 ounces) bean sprouts, drained
  1 can (8 ounces) sliced water chestnuts, drained
  1 tablespoon plus 1 teaspoon sesame seeds, *divided*
1/2 cup hoisin sauce
1/4 cup rice vinegar
1/4 cup canola oil
  2 teaspoons sesame oil
  2 teaspoons honey
1/2 teaspoon salt
1/4 teaspoon crushed red pepper flakes
1/4 teaspoon pepper

Using a vegetable peeler or metal cheese slicer, cut the carrots into very thin lengthwise strips. In a large saucepan, bring 4 cups water to a boil. Add the carrots, asparagus and snow peas; cover and boil for 3 minutes.

Place the fruits and walnuts in a large bowl; fold in the whipped topping. Drizzle with the caramel ice cream topping just before serving. Refrigerate the leftovers. **Yield:** 9 servings.

Dilled Potatoes with Feta

Prep/Total Time: 25 min.

After one taste, people have called this "totally amazing." It's perfect for a picnic, gala or dinner on the patio.
—Sherry Johnston, Green Cove Springs, Florida

1 pound small red potatoes, halved
1 cup (4 ounces) crumbled feta cheese
1/4 cup snipped fresh dill
2 tablespoons olive oil
1 tablespoon lemon juice
1/4 teaspoon salt
1/4 teaspoon pepper

Place potatoes in a large saucepan and cover with water. Bring to a boil. Reduce heat; cover and cook for 10-15 minutes or until tender. Drain.

In a serving bowl, combine the cheese, dill, oil, lemon juice, salt and pepper. Add the potatoes and toss gently to coat. **Yield:** 4 servings.

Heirloom Tomato Salad
(Pictured above)

Prep/Total Time: 20 min.

If you love the fresh-picked flavors of summertime, then this medley from our Test Kitchen staff is a must. Top it all off beautifully with the accompanying dressing.

1 package (5 ounces) spring mix salad greens
3 tablespoons olive oil
2 tablespoons balsamic vinegar
1 teaspoon Dijon mustard
1 garlic clove, minced
1/2 teaspoon sugar
1/4 teaspoon dried oregano
3 large heirloom tomatoes, sliced
1/2 cup fresh basil leaves
1/3 cup pine nuts, toasted
3 tablespoons chopped red onion
2 ounces fresh goat cheese, crumbled

Place salad greens in a large bowl. In a small bowl, whisk oil, vinegar, Dijon mustard, garlic, sugar and oregano. Pour over salad greens; toss to coat. Transfer to a large platter. Arrange the tomato slices over greens. Top with the basil, pine nuts, onion and cheese. Serve immediately. **Yield:** 12 servings.

Potato and Mushroom Gratin
(Pictured below)

Prep: 20 min. **Bake:** 55 min.

Rich and indulgent, this creamy side dish has a splash of wine and plenty of Swiss and Parmesan cheese. It makes the perfect take-along contribution for potlucks or church suppers because it looks impressive and tastes great.
—Laurie LaClair, North Richland Hills, Texas

  2 jars (4-1/2 ounces *each*) sliced mushrooms, drained
  3 shallots, finely chopped
  1 tablespoon olive oil
  2 tablespoons marsala wine
  3 large potatoes (about 1-1/2 pounds), peeled and thinly sliced
  1 cup (4 ounces) shredded Swiss cheese
1/2 cup shredded Parmesan cheese
  2 tablespoons minced fresh basil *or*
  2 teaspoons dried basil
1-1/2 cups heavy whipping cream
  1 tablespoon butter, cubed
1/8 teaspoon salt
1/8 teaspoon pepper

In a large skillet, saute the mushrooms and shallots in oil until tender. Add wine; cook and stir for 2 minutes.

Arrange a third of the potatoes in a greased 10-in. round shallow baking dish. Layer with half of mushroom mixture, cheeses, basil and another third of potatoes. Repeat layers. Pour cream over top. Dot with butter; sprinkle with salt and pepper.

Bake, uncovered, at 350° for 55-65 minutes or until potatoes are tender. **Yield:** 8 servings.

Caribbean Crabmeat Salad
(Pictured above)

Prep/Total Time: 25 min.

This sweet-tart combination brings a delightful blend of colors and flavors to any table. Try it—you'll love it!
—Patrisha Thompson, Sterling, Colorado

  3 cups uncooked tricolor spiral pasta
  1 can (20 ounces) pineapple tidbits, drained
3/4 pound imitation crabmeat, chopped
  1 large sweet red pepper, diced
  1 jalapeno pepper, seeded and chopped
  2 tablespoons minced fresh cilantro
  3 tablespoons lime juice
  2 tablespoons olive oil
  1 tablespoon honey
  1 teaspoon grated lime peel
1/2 teaspoon ground cumin
1/4 teaspoon salt
1/4 teaspoon ground ginger

Cook pasta according to package directions. Meanwhile, in a serving bowl, combine the pineapple, crab, red and jalapeno peppers and cilantro.

Drain and rinse pasta in cold water; add to the crab mixture. In a small bowl, whisk the remaining ingredients. Pour over the salad and toss to coat. Chill until serving. **Yield:** 13 servings (3/4 cup each).

Editor's Note: When cutting hot peppers, disposable gloves are recommended. Avoid touching your face.

Rosemary Roasted Potatoes

(Pictured below)

Prep: 15 min. **Bake:** 40 min.

A sprinkling of fresh rosemary is the key to these attractive, delicious spuds. Like carrots? You can substitute those for the sweet potatoes with equally pleasing results.
—Shannon Koene, Blacksburg, Virginia

1-1/2 pounds potatoes, peeled and cut into 1-inch
    cubes
1-1/2 pounds sweet potatoes, peeled and cut into
    1-inch cubes
    1 large onion, cut into wedges
    2 garlic cloves, minced
    3 tablespoons olive oil
4-1/2 teaspoons minced fresh rosemary *or*
    1-1/2 teaspoons dried rosemary, crushed
1-1/2 teaspoons Creole seasoning
    1/4 teaspoon salt
    1/4 teaspoon pepper

In a large bowl, combine the potatoes, onion and garlic; drizzle with oil. Sprinkle with rosemary, Creole seasoning, salt and pepper; toss to coat. Transfer to a greased 15-in. x 10-in. x 1-in. baking pan.

Bake at 425° for 40-50 minutes or until tender, stirring occasionally. **Yield:** 8 servings.

Editor's Note: The following spices may be substituted for 1 teaspoon Creole seasoning: 1/4 teaspoon each salt, garlic powder and paprika; and a pinch each of dried thyme, ground cumin and cayenne pepper.

Au Gratin Potato Pancakes

(Pictured above)

Prep/Total Time: 25 min.

People who sample these often declare the well-seasoned pancakes to be among the best they've ever had. I think these are really good with barbecued ribs and chicken.
—Cathy Hall, Phoenix, Arizona

    2 cups mashed potatoes (without added milk
    and butter)
    1 egg, lightly beaten
    1 tablespoon minced chives
    1 teaspoon minced fresh parsley
    3/4 teaspoon salt
    1/8 teaspoon dried minced garlic
    1/8 teaspoon pepper
Dash dried rosemary, crushed
    1/2 cup shredded sharp cheddar cheese
    4 tablespoons canola oil, *divided*

In a large bowl, combine the first eight ingredients. Stir in cheese.

Heat 2 tablespoons oil in a large nonstick skillet over medium heat. Drop the batter by 1/4 cupfuls into oil; press lightly to flatten. Cook in batches for 2-3 minutes on each side or until golden brown, using the remaining oil as needed. Drain pancakes on paper towels. **Yield:** 8 potato pancakes.

Summertime Melon Salad
(Pictured above)
Prep/Total Time: 25 min.

Fun and refreshing, this easy medley is like a plateful of summer—served up in a melon half and coated with a tangy citrus sauce. —Sally Maloney, Dallas, Georgia

1-1/2 cups cantaloupe balls
1-1/2 cups honeydew balls
   1 can (20 ounces) pineapple chunks, drained
   1 can (11 ounces) mandarin oranges, drained
   1 cup halved fresh strawberries
  3/4 cup thawed lemonade concentrate
  1/2 cup orange marmalade
   4 medium cantaloupe melons, halved and
     seeded
Fresh mint leaves

In a large bowl, combine the first five ingredients. In a small bowl, combine the lemonade concentrate and orange marmalade; pour over the fruit and toss to coat. Spoon into the cantaloupe halves. Garnish with mint.
Yield: 8 servings.

Green Bean Salad
Prep/Total Time: 25 min.

Each year, I can't wait to get fresh green beans from the garden because I use them to fix this wonderful vegetable dish. It's so good, I could eat it all myself!
—Kathy Smith, Pittsburgh, Pennsylvania

   1 pound fresh green beans, trimmed
   1 small red onion, sliced
 12 cherry tomatoes, halved
 12 pitted ripe olives, halved
1/4 cup shredded Parmesan cheese
   2 tablespoons bacon bits
1/3 cup olive oil
   2 tablespoons balsamic vinegar
   1 garlic clove, minced
1/2 teaspoon ground mustard
1/2 teaspoon salt
Dash pepper

Place beans in a steamer basket. Place in a large saucepan over 1 in. of water; bring to a boil. Cover and steam for 7-8 minutes or until crisp-tender.

In a large bowl, combine the beans, onion, tomatoes, ripe olives, Parmesan cheese and bacon. In a jar with a tight-fitting lid, combine the oil, vinegar, garlic, mustard, salt and pepper. Drizzle with the dressing; toss to coat. **Yield:** 8 servings.

Cherry Chiffon Gelatin
(Pictured below)

Prep: 10 min. + chilling

I've made this gelatin mold so many times, I can hardly read the well-worn recipe card any longer. It's a beautiful treat your family will ask for again and again.
—Michelle Smith, Sykesville, Maryland

 2 packages (3 ounces *each*) cherry gelatin, *divided*
1-1/2 cups boiling water, *divided*
 2 cups cold water, *divided*
 1 can (15 ounces) pitted dark sweet cherries, drained
 2 cups whipped topping

In a large bowl, dissolve 1 package of gelatin in 3/4 cup boiling water. Add 1 cup cold water; stir. Refrigerate until partially set, about 1 hour. Stir in cherries. Pour into a 7-cup mold coated with cooking spray. Refrigerate for 1 hour or until firm.

In a small bowl, dissolve the remaining gelatin in the remaining boiling water. Stir in remaining cold water. Refrigerate until partially set, about 1 hour. Fold in the whipped topping. Carefully spread over top. Refrigerate for 4 hours or until firm. Unmold onto a serving platter. **Yield:** 8 servings.

Golden Potato Salad
(Pictured above)

Prep: 25 min. **Cook:** 15 min. + cooling

What's a cookout without potato salad? This one using Yukon Golds, red pepper, onion and carrot is a winner.
—Linda Behrman, North Merrick, New York

2-1/2 pounds Yukon Gold potatoes, peeled and cut into 1/2-inch cubes
 1 medium sweet red pepper, chopped
 1 small red onion, chopped
 1/2 cup shredded carrot
 1 cup mayonnaise
 2 tablespoons olive oil
 2 tablespoons balsamic vinegar
 2 tablespoons spicy brown mustard
 1 tablespoon mustard seed
 3 teaspoons snipped fresh dill, *divided*
1-1/2 teaspoons sugar
 3/4 teaspoon salt
 1/2 teaspoon pepper

Place potatoes in a large saucepan and cover with water. Bring to a boil. Reduce heat; cover and simmer for 10-15 minutes or until tender. Drain; cool for 15 minutes.

In a large bowl, combine the sweet red pepper, red onion, carrot and potatoes. In a small bowl, whisk the mayonnaise, oil, balsamic vinegar, spicy brown mustard, mustard seed, 2 teaspoons dill, sugar, salt and pepper. Pour over potato mixture; gently toss to coat. Sprinkle with the remaining dill. Refrigerate salad until serving. **Yield:** 10 servings.

Summer Garden Couscous Salad
(Pictured below)

Prep/Total Time: 30 min.

This recipe makes the most of summer's bounty. I used to prepare it with a mayonnaise dressing but then lightened it up with a vinaigrette. The new version is even better!
—Priscilla Yee, Concord, California

3 medium ears sweet corn, husks removed
1 cup reduced-sodium chicken broth *or* vegetable broth
1 cup uncooked couscous
1 medium cucumber, halved and sliced
1-1/2 cups cherry tomatoes, halved
1/2 cup crumbled feta cheese
1/4 cup chopped red onion
3 tablespoons minced fresh parsley
3 tablespoons olive oil
3 tablespoons lemon juice
1 teaspoon dried oregano
3/4 teaspoon ground cumin
1/2 teaspoon salt
1/2 teaspoon pepper

Place corn in a Dutch oven; cover with water. Bring to a boil; cover and cook for 6-9 minutes or until tender. Meanwhile, in a small saucepan, bring broth to a boil. Stir in couscous. Remove from the heat; cover and let stand for 5-10 minutes or until water is absorbed. Fluff with a fork and set aside to cool slightly.

In a large bowl, combine the cucumber, tomatoes, feta cheese, red onion and parsley. Drain the corn and immediately place in ice water. Drain and pat dry; cut the kernels from the cobs. Add to the cucumber mixture. Stir in couscous.

In a small bowl, whisk oil, lemon juice and seasonings. Pour dressing over the couscous mixture; toss to coat. Serve immediately or cover and refrigerate until chilled. **Yield:** 9 servings.

Rice Vegetable Salad
(Pictured above)

Prep/Total Time: 25 min.

I first tried this at a party and fell in love with the bright look and taste. Packed with vegetables, the colorful salad offers a touch of Indian flair and is a cinch to double.
—Sandy Heley, Grand Junction, Colorado

1/2 cup uncooked basmati rice
1 can (15 ounces) black beans, rinsed and drained
2 medium carrots, finely chopped
3/4 cup fresh *or* frozen corn, thawed
3/4 cup chopped tomatoes
1/4 cup minced fresh cilantro
1/4 cup minced fresh parsley
2 tablespoons finely chopped red onion
1/4 cup lime juice
1/4 cup olive oil
1 teaspoon ground cumin
1/8 teaspoon salt
1/8 teaspoon pepper

Cook rice according to package directions. Meanwhile, in a large bowl, combine the black beans, carrots, corn, tomatoes, cilantro, parsley and onion.

In a small bowl, whisk the lime juice, oil, cumin, salt and pepper. Stir the rice into the bean mixture. Drizzle with the dressing; toss to coat. **Yield:** 5 servings.

Sweet Potato Praline Swirl
(Pictured below)

Prep: 25 min. **Bake:** 30 min.

Bored with the same old marshmallows on your holiday sweet potatoes? Serve this yummy side instead—it's sure to be a hit.   —Amanda Dalvine, Orange Park, Florida

  2 medium sweet potatoes, peeled and cubed
1/2 cup heavy whipping cream
  2 eggs
1/4 cup packed brown sugar
  3 teaspoons vanilla extract
  1 teaspoon ground cinnamon
1/2 teaspoon ground ginger
1/2 cup chopped pecans
PRALINE SAUCE:
1/3 cup packed brown sugar
1/4 cup sweetened condensed milk
  2 teaspoons butter, melted
1/2 teaspoon vanilla extract

Place sweet potatoes in a large saucepan and cover with water. Bring to a boil. Reduce heat; cover and cook for 10-15 minutes or until tender.

Drain potatoes and place in a large bowl; mash until smooth. Beat in the cream, eggs, brown sugar, vanilla, cinnamon and ginger; fold in pecans.

Transfer the mixture to a greased 8-in. square baking dish. Combine the sauce ingredients; spoon over potato mixture. Cut through with a knife to swirl the sauce.

Bake, uncovered, at 325° for 30-40 minutes or until a thermometer reads 160°. **Yield:** 6 servings.

Greek Country Salad
(Pictured above)

Prep/Total Time: 15 min.

With Mediterranean ingredients, this refreshing medley is a favorite with everyone and virtually a meal in itself.
    —Christine Chinchilla, Hinckley, Illinois

    6 large tomatoes, chopped
    1 large cucumber, seeded and chopped
    1 medium green pepper, chopped
1-1/4 cups chopped sweet onion
  1/3 cup olive oil
    2 tablespoons red wine vinegar
    1 tablespoon Greek seasoning
    2 packages (4 ounces *each*) crumbled feta
       cheese
Sliced French bread

In a large salad bowl, combine the tomatoes, cucumber, pepper and onion. In a small bowl, whisk the oil, vinegar and seasoning. Drizzle over salad and toss to coat. Chill until serving. Just before serving, sprinkle with cheese. Serve with bread. **Yield:** 8 servings.

▮ HOT POTATOES ▮

Why save sweet potatoes for holidays? In summer, I cut peeled, washed spuds into 1/2-inch slices and cook them on the grill. I brush each side with butter several times and turn them often until tender.
    —Keri Hains Riker, Wellesley, Massachusetts

Pina Colada Fruit Salad
(Pictured above)

Prep/Total Time: 15 min.

On warm summer days, give friends the taste of a favorite beverage by serving this refreshing fruit blend. For a little extra punch, you could add a splash of coconut rum.
—Carol Farnsworth, Greenwood, Indiana

1-1/2 cups green grapes
1-1/2 cups seedless red grapes
1-1/2 cups fresh blueberries
1-1/2 cups halved fresh strawberries
   1 can (8 ounces) pineapple chunks, drained
  1/2 cup fresh raspberries
   1 can (10 ounces) frozen nonalcoholic pina colada mix, thawed
  1/2 cup sugar
  1/2 cup pineapple-orange juice
  1/8 teaspoon almond extract
  1/8 teaspoon coconut extract

In a serving bowl, combine the first six ingredients. In a small bowl, whisk the pina colada mix, sugar, juice and extracts until sugar is dissolved. Pour over fruit; toss to coat. Chill until serving. **Yield:** 9 servings.

Colorful Green Bean Medley

Prep/Total Time: 25 min.

With green beans, sweet pepper and water chestnuts, this side is a great partner for all kinds of meat entrees.
—Elke Rose, Waukesha, Wisconsin

   1 pound fresh green beans, cut into 2-inch pieces
   1 medium sweet orange pepper, cut into strips
   1 can (8 ounces) sliced water chestnuts, drained

   2 tablespoons butter
   2 garlic cloves, minced
  1/2 teaspoon salt
  1/4 teaspoon onion powder
  1/4 teaspoon dried basil
  1/4 teaspoon coarsely ground pepper

Place green beans in a steamer basket; place in a large saucepan over 1 in. of water. Bring to a boil; cover and steam for 8-10 minutes or until crisp-tender.

Meanwhile, in a large skillet, saute the sweet orange pepper and water chestnuts in the butter until tender. Add the garlic, salt, onion powder, basil and pepper; cook 1 minute longer. Add green beans; toss to coat. **Yield:** 6 servings.

Zesty Roasted Vegetables
(Pictured below)

Prep: 15 min. **Cook:** 30 min.

I've found that even picky eaters will devour these tangy vegetables. They require only 15 minutes of prep, leaving you with plenty of time to make the rest of your menu.
—Aims62, Taste of Home Online Community

   1 pound medium fresh mushrooms
   3 cups fresh baby carrots, cut in half lengthwise
   2 medium green peppers, cut into 1-inch strips
   2 medium onions, cut into wedges
  2/3 cup Italian salad dressing
  1/2 cup plus 2 tablespoons grated Parmesan cheese, *divided*
  1/4 teaspoon salt
  1/4 teaspoon pepper

In a large bowl, combine the mushrooms, carrots, green peppers, onions, Italian salad dressing, 1/2 cup cheese, salt and pepper. Transfer to an ungreased 15-in. x 10-in. x 1-in. baking pan.

Bake, uncovered, at 425° for 30-40 minutes or until tender, stirring once. Sprinkle with remaining cheese. **Yield:** 9 servings.

Shrimp Salad
(Pictured above)

Prep: 15 min. + chilling

I have vivid memories of my mom fixing this for get-togethers when I was a child. And now, it just wouldn't be the Fourth of July without Grandma's Shrimp Salad. A big bowl is a must-have alongside all of the other traditional picnic fixings.
—Delores Hill, Helena, Montana

2-1/3 cups uncooked small pasta shells
  1/3 pound cooked salad shrimp
    3 celery ribs, chopped
    1 small onion, chopped
    4 radishes, halved and sliced
    4 hard-cooked eggs, chopped
    1 cup mayonnaise
    1 tablespoon prepared mustard
1-1/2 teaspoons salt
  1/8 teaspoon pepper

Cook pasta according to package directions. Meanwhile, in a large bowl, combine shrimp, celery, onion, radishes and eggs. In a small bowl, combine the mayonnaise, mustard, salt and pepper.

Drain the pasta and rinse in cold water; add to the shrimp mixture. Add the dressing mixture; toss to coat. Cover and refrigerate the salad for at least 2 hours. **Yield:** 9 servings.

Asparagus Tomato Salad
(Pictured below)

Prep/Total Time: 15 min.

This colorful, light vegetable salad proved popular at our church's cooking club. The asparagus, tomatoes, zucchini and green onions go well with just about any main course. Plus, the simple homemade dressing is a tongue-tingling accent. It all comes together in only 15 minutes.
— Dorothy Buhr, Ogden, Illinois

- 1 pound fresh asparagus, trimmed and cut into 1-inch pieces
- 1 small zucchini, halved and cut into 1/4-inch slices
- 1 cup grape *or* cherry tomatoes
- 1/4 cup sliced green onions
- 1/4 cup minced fresh parsley
- 3 tablespoons olive oil
- 2 tablespoons red wine vinegar
- 1 garlic clove, minced
- 1/4 teaspoon seasoned salt
- 1/4 teaspoon Dijon mustard
- 1/4 cup shredded Parmesan cheese, optional
- 2 tablespoons sunflower kernels, toasted, optional

Place the asparagus and zucchini in a steamer basket; place in a saucepan over 1 in. of water. Bring to a boil; cover and steam for 2 minutes. Rinse in cold water.

In a large bowl, combine the asparagus, zucchini, cherry tomatoes, green onions and parsley.

In a small bowl, whisk the next five ingredients. Pour over the asparagus mixture; toss to coat. Sprinkle with Parmesan cheese and sunflower kernels if desired. **Yield:** 6 servings.

Apple-Pecan Salad With Honey Vinaigrette
(Pictured above)

Prep/Total Time: 15 min.

Sweet-tart apple varieties, such as Braeburn and Empire, pair well with the Parmesan cheese in this fresh-tasting combination. It's a fantastic way to enjoy just-picked fall fruit. If you like, you could prepare this using a Bosc or Bartlett pear and crumbled blue cheese instead.
— Anna Russell, Peterborough, Ontario

- 7 cups torn Bibb *or* Boston lettuce
- 1 medium apple, sliced
- 1/3 cup pecan halves, toasted
- 1/4 cup cider vinegar
- 3 tablespoons honey
- 2 tablespoons olive oil
- 1/2 teaspoon honey mustard
- 1/8 teaspoon salt
- 1/8 teaspoon pepper
- 1 cup shredded Parmesan cheese

In a serving bowl, combine the lettuce, apple and pecan halves. In a small bowl, whisk the cider vinegar, honey, oil, mustard, salt and pepper.

Pour dressing over salad; toss to coat. Sprinkle with cheese. **Yield:** 10 servings.

Asparagus Mozzarella Salad
(Pictured below)

Prep/Total Time: 25 min.

This refreshing favorite is ideal for picnics, barbecues and other warm-weather gatherings. Toss any leftovers with some pasta. —Lisa Gibbs, Muskegon, Michigan

  2 pounds fresh asparagus, trimmed and cut into 1-inch pieces
  1 pound fresh mozzarella cheese, cubed
  2 cups grape tomatoes
  1 medium red onion, halved and sliced
1/4 cup minced fresh basil
DRESSING:
1/4 cup olive oil
  2 tablespoons balsamic vinegar
  1 garlic clove, minced
1/2 teaspoon salt
1/2 teaspoon Dijon mustard
1/4 teaspoon pepper
  2 tablespoons lemon juice

In a large saucepan, bring 1/2 in. of water to a boil. Add the asparagus; cover and boil for 3 minutes. Drain and immediately place asparagus in ice water. Drain and pat dry. Transfer to a large bowl. Add the cheese, tomatoes, onion and basil.

In a small bowl, whisk the oil, balsamic vinegar, garlic, salt, mustard and pepper. Pour over the salad; toss to coat. Drizzle with lemon juice. Chill until serving. **Yield:** 15 servings (2/3 cup each).

Baked Bean Side Dish
(Pictured above and on page 132)

Prep: 10 min. **Bake:** 45 min.

Everyone who samples these beans is pleasantly surprised by the unique flavor. It's my daughter's recipe.
—Lilas Umphrey, Davenport, Florida

  1 can (28 ounces) baked beans, drained
  1 medium tart apple, peeled and chopped
  1 large onion, chopped
  1 cup barbecue sauce
1/3 cup packed brown sugar
1/4 cup raisins
  1 jalapeno pepper, seeded and chopped
  3 bacon strips, diced

In a large bowl, combine the first seven ingredients. Transfer to a greased 11-in. x 7-in. baking dish. Sprinkle with the bacon. Cover and bake at 350° for 20 minutes. Uncover; bake 25-30 minutes longer or until bubbly and beans reach desired thickness. **Yield:** 7 servings.

Editor's Note: When cutting hot peppers, disposable gloves are recommended. Avoid touching your face.

POTLUCK PRESENT

Turn your Asparagus Mozzarella Salad (recipe above left) or other potluck contribution into a gift for the hostess by serving the food in a new bowl for her to keep. She'll get a pretty addition to her kitchen, and you won't have to tote a bowl home afterward.

Grilled Chicken Salad with Blueberry Vinaigrette
(Pictured above)

Prep: 20 min. + marinating **Grill:** 10 min.

Here's a delightfully different mix of colors, textures and flavors. Enjoy it with some crusty bread and a frosty glass of lemonade. —Susan Gauthier, Falmouth, Maine

3 tablespoons olive oil
1 garlic clove, minced
1 teaspoon salt
1 teaspoon pepper
2 boneless skinless chicken breast halves (6 ounces *each*)

VINAIGRETTE:
1/4 cup olive oil
1/4 cup blueberry preserves
2 tablespoons maple syrup
2 tablespoons balsamic vinegar
1/4 teaspoon ground mustard
1/8 teaspoon salt
Dash pepper
SALAD:
1 package (10 ounces) ready-to-serve salad greens
1 cup fresh blueberries
1 snack-size cup (4 ounces) mandarin oranges, drained
1 cup crumbled goat cheese

In a large resealable plastic bag, combine the oil, garlic, salt and pepper; add the chicken. Seal the bag and turn to coat; refrigerate for 30 minutes. Place the vinaigrette ingredients in a jar with a tight-fitting lid; shake well. Cover and refrigerate until ready to use.

Drain and discard marinade. Grill chicken, covered, over medium heat for 5-7 minutes on each side or until juices run clear. When cool enough to handle, cut the chicken into slices.

Divide salad greens among four serving plates. Top each with chicken, blueberries and oranges. Shake the vinaigrette and drizzle over salads; sprinkle with cheese. **Yield:** 4 servings.

Summer Chicken Salad with Raspberry Vinaigrette

(Pictured below)

Prep/Total Time: 20 min.

This best-of-the-season dish is always popular. It's piled high with fresh fruits, veggies, chicken and greens, then drizzled with a homemade raspberry vinaigrette.
—*Heidi Farnworth, Riverton, Utah*

　1 package (10 ounces) ready-to-serve salad greens
3-1/2 cups cubed cooked chicken
　1 cup fresh sugar snap peas
　1 cup fresh blueberries
　1 cup fresh raspberries
　1 celery rib, thinly sliced

1/4 cup olive oil
　3 tablespoons balsamic vinegar
　1 tablespoon seedless red raspberry preserves
1/2 teaspoon salt
1/2 teaspoon onion powder
1/2 teaspoon pepper
1/4 cup slivered almonds, toasted

Place the salad greens, chicken, peas, berries and celery in a large bowl. In a small bowl, whisk the oil, balsamic vinegar, raspberry preserves, salt, onion powder and pepper. Drizzle over salad; toss gently to coat. Top with almonds. **Yield:** 4 servings.

Crunchy Tuna Salad

(Pictured above)

Prep/Total Time: 15 min.

My husband and son don't really care for salads—except for this one! I can't seem to fix enough of it. Try it as a fast, tasty lunch. —*Pat Ashworth, Elk Grove, California*

1/3 cup mayonnaise
1/3 cup sour cream
3/4 teaspoon garlic powder
1/2 teaspoon salt
1/8 teaspoon pepper
　1 head iceberg lettuce, torn
　1 can (12 ounces) tuna, drained and flaked
　1 cup frozen peas, thawed
　1 can (5 ounces) chow mein noodles

In a small bowl, combine the mayonnaise, sour cream, garlic powder, salt and pepper. In a large bowl, combine lettuce, tuna and peas. Add mayonnaise mixture; toss to coat. Stir in the chow mein noodles. Serve immediately. **Yield:** 6 servings.

Orzo Cheesecake Fruit Salad
(Pictured below)

Prep: 30 min. + chilling

With cheesecake pudding mix, this medley of my favorite fruits and orzo pasta is luscious enough to be a dessert.
—Priscilla Gilbert, Indian Harbour Beach, Florida

- 1 cup uncooked orzo pasta
- 1 package (3.4 ounces) instant cheesecake *or* vanilla pudding mix
- 1/3 cup sour cream
- 1 can (20 ounces) crushed pineapple, undrained
- 1 large banana, sliced
- 2 teaspoons lemon juice
- 2 cans (11 ounces *each*) mandarin oranges, drained
- 2 cups miniature marshmallows
- 1 cup chopped pecans, toasted
- 1 cup canned sliced peaches, drained and chopped
- 1/2 cup maraschino cherries, drained and quartered
- 1 carton (8 ounces) frozen whipped topping, thawed
- 1/2 cup flaked coconut, toasted

Cook orzo according to package directions. Drain and rinse in cold water; set aside.

In a large bowl, combine pudding mix, sour cream and pineapple. Toss banana with lemon juice; stir into pudding mixture. Stir in oranges, marshmallows, pecans, peaches, cherries and orzo. Fold in whipped topping. Sprinkle with coconut. Cover and refrigerate 2 hours or until chilled. **Yield:** 16 servings.

Fruity Sangria Salad
(Pictured above)

Prep: 30 min. + chilling

Here's a lovely and refreshing salad for any warm summer day. Add a dollop of whipped topping for a special treat.
—Corvilia Thykkuttathil, Renton, Washington

- 1-1/4 cups water
- 1/2 cup sugar
- 1/4 cup white wine *or* white grape juice
- 1 medium lime, peeled and quartered
- 3 tablespoons honey
- 2 peeled fresh gingerroot slices (1/2 inch *each*)
- 1 teaspoon grated lime peel
- 3 medium Granny Smith apples, cubed
- 2 medium nectarines, cubed
- 1 tablespoon lime juice
- 2-1/2 cups green grapes
- 2 cups cubed honeydew
- 2 cups cubed cantaloupe
- Whipped topping

In a small saucepan, combine the water, sugar, wine, lime, honey, ginger and lime peel. Cook and stir over medium heat for 10 minutes. Remove and discard lime and gingerroot. Cool syrup completely.

In a large bowl, combine the apples and nectarines. Add lime juice; toss gently to coat. Stir in the grapes, honeydew and cantaloupe. Drizzle with syrup and toss to coat. Cover and refrigerate for at least 1 hour. Serve with a slotted spoon. Garnish with whipped topping. **Yield:** 16 servings (3/4 cup each).

Garden Zucchini & Corn Saute

Prep/Total Time: 25 min.

My vegetable saute pairs well with nearly any barbecued entree, and it also makes a great filling for an omelet. It's even good cold! —Trisha Kruse, Eagle, Idaho

2 medium zucchini, thinly sliced
1/3 cup sliced onion
1-1/2 teaspoons olive oil
3/4 cup fresh whole kernel corn
2 garlic cloves, minced
1/2 teaspoon sugar
1/4 teaspoon salt
1/4 teaspoon lemon-pepper seasoning

In a large skillet, saute the zucchini and onion in oil until crisp-tender. Add corn and garlic; saute 2 minutes longer or until vegetables are tender. Sprinkle with sugar, salt and lemon-pepper. **Yield:** 4 servings.

Tropical Spinach & Ham Salad
(Pictured below)

Prep/Total Time: 20 min.

Capture the flavor of paradise with this easy recipe from our Test Kitchen home economists. It features cucumber, mango, spinach and a homemade vinaigrette.

4 cups fresh baby spinach
3/4 pound thick sliced deli ham, cut into
    1-1/2-inch strips
1 medium mango, peeled and cubed
1 medium cucumber, halved and sliced
1 cup slivered almonds, toasted
1 small red onion, halved and thinly sliced
VINAIGRETTE:
1/4 cup olive oil
2 tablespoons balsamic vinegar
2 teaspoons Dijon mustard
1 teaspoon molasses
1/4 teaspoon salt
1/8 teaspoon pepper

In a large bowl, combine the spinach, ham, mango, cucumber, almonds and onion.
    In a small bowl, whisk vinaigrette ingredients. Drizzle over salad; toss to coat. **Yield:** 8 servings.

Layered Ranch Salad
(Pictured above)

Prep/Total Time: 20 min.

This wonderful dish is a breeze to put together. Spinach and greens provide the ideal backdrop for the crisp bacon, hard-cooked eggs and yummy ranch dressing.
—*Suzanne Zick, Maiden, North Carolina*

5 cups torn mixed salad greens
5 cups fresh baby spinach
1/2 pound sliced fresh mushrooms
6 hard-cooked eggs, chopped
1 bunch green onions, sliced
1/2 cup bacon bits
3/4 cup mayonnaise
1/3 cup sour cream
3-1/2 teaspoons ranch salad dressing mix
1 tablespoon minced fresh parsley

In a 3-qt. glass serving bowl, layer the first six ingredients in order listed. In a small bowl, combine the mayonnaise, sour cream and ranch dressing mix. Spread over salad. Sprinkle with parsley. Cover and refrigerate until serving. **Yield:** 10 servings.

Bacon & Gorgonzola Potato Salad
(Pictured below)

Prep: 25 min. **Cook:** 15 min. + chilling

Dressed in a creamy sauce featuring Gorgonzola cheese, chives and bacon, this potato medley is a sure hit. I like to make it in advance so the flavors have time to blend.
—Barbara Spitzer, Lodi, California

    1-3/4 pounds potatoes, peeled and cubed
      3/4 cup mayonnaise
      3/4 cup sour cream
        4 green onions, thinly sliced
        1 celery rib, finely chopped
        2 tablespoons minced chives, *divided*
      1/2 teaspoon salt
      1/2 teaspoon coarsely ground pepper
      1/4 teaspoon sugar
        1 cup (4 ounces) crumbled Gorgonzola cheese
        1 cup bacon bits, *divided*
        2 plum tomatoes, peeled, seeded and chopped

Place potatoes in a large saucepan and cover with water. Bring to a boil. Reduce heat; cover and cook for 10-15 minutes or until tender. Drain and cool.

Meanwhile, in a large bowl, combine the mayonnaise, sour cream, green onions, celery, 1 tablespoon chives, salt, pepper and sugar. Stir in cheese and 1/2 cup bacon bits. Fold in tomatoes and potatoes. Cover and refrigerate for at least 1 hour. Just before serving, sprinkle with the remaining chives and bacon. **Yield:** 6 servings.

Tossed Pepperoni Pizza Salad

Prep/Total Time: 20 min.

Love pizza? Here's a salad for you! Purchased sun-dried tomato dressing is the perfect complement to the peppers, mozzarella, Parmesan and pepperoni in this rave-winning recipe. Plus, it's ready to serve in just 20 minutes.
—Lisa Demarsh, Mt. Solon, Virginia

      1/4 cup sun-dried tomatoes (not packed in oil)
        1 cup boiling water
        3 cups torn leaf lettuce
      3/4 cup cubed part-skim mozzarella cheese
        2 ounces sliced pepperoni, quartered (about 1/2 cup)
        6 slices red onion, separated into rings
      1/2 cup chopped green pepper
      1/2 cup chopped sweet red pepper
      1/2 cup grape tomatoes, halved
      1/4 cup grated Parmesan cheese
      1/4 cup sun-dried tomato salad dressing
        1 teaspoon Italian seasoning
      1/2 teaspoon garlic powder

In a small bowl, combine sun-dried tomatoes and water. Let stand for 5 minutes; drain.

In a large bowl, combine lettuce, mozzarella cheese, pepperoni, onion, peppers, grape tomatoes, Parmesan cheese and sun-dried tomatoes. In a small bowl, whisk the salad dressing, Italian seasoning and garlic powder; drizzle over salad and toss to coat. Serve immediately. **Yield:** 5 servings.

Coconut Twice-Baked Sweet Potatoes

Prep: 30 min. **Bake:** 20 min.

Even if you can't travel to a tropical paradise, you can get a taste of it with these breezy sweet potatoes. They're a special menu addition during the holidays or anytime.
—Nancy Sobel, Bay Shore, New York

        4 medium sweet potatoes
      1/2 cup coconut milk
        1 tablespoon maple syrup
        1 teaspoon minced fresh gingerroot
        1 teaspoon adobo sauce
      1/2 teaspoon salt
      1/4 cup chopped pecans
      1/4 cup flaked coconut

Scrub and pierce potatoes; place on a microwave-safe plate. Microwave, uncovered, on high for 10-12 minutes or until tender, turning once.

When cool enough to handle, cut each potato in half lengthwise. Scoop out the pulp, leaving thin shells. In a large bowl, mash the pulp with the coconut milk. Stir in maple syrup, ginger, adobo sauce and salt. Spoon into potato shells.

Place on a baking sheet. Sprinkle with pecans and coconut. Bake at 350° for 20-25 minutes or until heated through. **Yield:** 8 servings.

Italian Orzo Salad
(Pictured above)

Prep/Total Time: 30 min.

This pasta toss is an ideal summer side dish for a potluck or picnic. It can even make a light weeknight dinner.
—*Cindy Springsteen, Denver, Colorado*

  6 cups chicken broth
  1 package (16 ounces) orzo pasta
1/3 cup olive oil
1/4 cup red wine vinegar
  2 tablespoons lemon juice
  1 tablespoon honey
1/2 teaspoon salt
1/2 teaspoon pepper
  2 cups chopped plum tomatoes
  1 cup chopped seeded peeled cucumber
  1 cup fresh basil leaves, thinly sliced
  4 green onions, chopped
1/2 cup fresh baby spinach, chopped
1-3/4 cups (7 ounces) crumbled feta cheese
1/2 cup pine nuts, toasted

In a large saucepan, bring the chicken broth to a boil; add the pasta. Return to a boil. Cook, uncovered, for 10-12 minutes or until pasta is tender. Meanwhile, in a small bowl, whisk the oil, vinegar, lemon juice, honey, salt and pepper.

In a large bowl, combine plum tomatoes, cucumber, basil, green onions and spinach. Drain the pasta; add to the tomato mixture. Drizzle with dressing; toss to coat. Chill until serving.

Just before serving, stir in the cheese and pine nuts. **Yield:** 12 servings.

CHAPTER 9

Plan an Instant Party

Wish you had enough time to entertain family and friends? You do! Simply use the festive but fast dishes in this chapter to host a great bash in a flash.

We've featured four popular party themes for you to choose from. Is the big game on TV? Invite the gang over to watch and munch on Smoked Sausage Appetizers. Like the idea of a Mexican fiesta? Spice it up with Effortless Guacamole.

Plus, you'll find "fake-out takeout"—tasty knockoffs of restaurant foods—and special beverages to enjoy after work on a Friday night or anytime.

With these crowd-pleasing recipes, planning a get-together will seem virtually fuss-free. ■

FUN-FILLED FAVORITE. Beef & Bean Enchiladas (p. 159).

When the big game is on TV and the whole gang is coming over to watch, make the food you're serving just as memorable as the on-screen competition. Simply toss together the delicious, done-in-a-snap snacks featured here.

Your fellow sports fans are sure to like high-scoring munchies such as Party Cheese Bread, Fig & Ham Pinwheels, Five-Spice Pecans and Smoked Sausage Appetizers. What a winning combination! ■

Fig & Ham Pinwheels
(Pictured below)

Prep: 25 min. **Bake:** 15 min.

The blend of ingredients in these baked snacks may seem unusual, but give them a try—you'll be glad you did! The figs, ham and marmalade go really well together.
—Bonnie Buckley, Kansas City, Missouri

- 1 cup finely chopped dried figs
- 1/3 cup orange marmalade
- 2 tablespoons stone-ground mustard
- 1 tablespoon brown sugar
- 1 tube (8 ounces) refrigerated crescent rolls
- 4 slices deli ham

In a small bowl, combine the figs, marmalade, mustard and brown sugar. Separate the crescent dough into four rectangles; seal perforations. Top each with ham and spread 1/4 cup filling to within 1/4 in. of the edges. Roll up each jelly-roll style, starting with a short side; pinch seams to seal. Cut each into six slices.

Place slices cut side down on greased baking sheets. Bake at 375° for 12-14 minutes or until golden brown. Serve warm. **Yield:** 24 appetizers.

Smoked Sausage Appetizers
(Pictured above)

Prep/Total Time: 25 min.

A sweet-savory sauce with a touch of currant jelly glazes these yummy little sausages. They're ready in less than 30 minutes, and guests of all ages snatch them up.
—Kathryn Bainbridge, PA Furnace, Pennsylvania

- 3/4 cup red currant jelly
- 3/4 cup barbecue sauce
- 3 tablespoons prepared mustard
- 2 packages (1 pound *each*) miniature smoked sausages, drained

In a large saucepan, combine the jelly, barbecue sauce and mustard. Cook, uncovered, over medium heat, for 15-20 minutes or until the jelly is melted and mixture is smooth, stirring occasionally.

Add sausages; stir to coat. Cover; cook 5-6 minutes longer or until heated through, stirring occasionally. Serve with toothpicks. **Yield:** 8 dozen.

Party Cheese Bread
(Pictured below)
Prep: 25 min. **Bake:** 25 min.

People just flock to this! Cheesy, buttery and finger-licking good, the no-fuss loaf also makes a tasty side for pasta.
—Karen Gran, Tulare, California

    1/2 cup butter, melted
      2 tablespoons lemon juice
      2 tablespoons Dijon mustard
1-1/2 teaspoons garlic powder
    1/2 teaspoon onion powder
    1/2 teaspoon celery salt
      1 round loaf sourdough bread (1 pound)
      1 pound Monterey Jack cheese, thinly sliced

In a small bowl, combine the first six ingredients; set aside. Cut the bread diagonally into 1-in. slices to within 1/2 in. of the bottom of loaf. Repeat cuts in the opposite direction. Arrange the cheese slices in the cuts. Drizzle the butter mixture over the bread.

Wrap the loaf in foil; place on a baking sheet. Bake at 350° for 15 minutes. Uncover; bake 10 minutes longer or until cheese is melted. **Yield:** 8 servings.

Five-Spice Pecans
Prep: 10 min. **Cook:** 10 min. + cooling

After the first handful, it's hard to stop reaching for this sugar-and-spice treat. It's great sprinkled on salads, too.
—Anne Leslie, Chandler, Indiana

      2 cups pecan halves
      2 tablespoons brown sugar
      2 tablespoons maple syrup
      1 teaspoon Chinese five-spice powder

In a large nonstick skillet, cook the pecans over medium heat until toasted, about 4 minutes. Add brown sugar, maple syrup and five-spice powder. Cook and stir for 2-4 minutes or until sugar is melted. Spread on foil to cool. Store in an airtight container. **Yield:** 2 cups.

Getting together with friends for a special dinner doesn't have to mean driving to an out-of-the-way eatery and paying high prices. Instead, treat your group to restaurant-quality flavor in the comfort of your home. It's easy with these authentic-tasting versions of popular takeout dishes.

Create your own out-on-the-town atmosphere for this at-home party using plenty of candlelight and music. Who knows...your house might just become your friends' favorite place to eat! ■

Three-Cheese Quesadillas
(Pictured below)

Prep/Total Time: 20 min.

When people take a bite, they can't believe these cheesy slices didn't come from a Mexican restaurant. If you like, lighten up the quesadillas using reduced-fat products.
—Sandy Smith, Saugerties, New York

- 1 tablespoon butter
- 4 flour tortillas (8 inches)
- 2 ounces cream cheese, softened
- 1/4 cup shredded sharp cheddar cheese
- 1/4 cup shredded Monterey Jack cheese
- 2 tablespoons thinly sliced green onion
- 1 tablespoon minced fresh cilantro
- 2 teaspoons chopped ripe olives
- 1/4 cup salsa
- Sour cream, optional

Spread the butter over one side of each tortilla. Spread the cream cheese over the unbuttered side on half of the tortillas. Sprinkle with the cheeses, onion, cilantro and olives. Top with remaining tortillas, buttered side up.

Cook on a griddle over medium heat for 1-2 minutes on each side or until the cheese is melted. Cut quesadillas into wedges. Serve with salsa and sour cream if desired. **Yield:** 2 servings.

Kickin' Hawaiian Pizza
(Pictured above)

Prep: 30 min. **Bake:** 15 min.

Why wait for great pizza to be delivered? Thanks to this recipe, you don't have to! It tingles taste buds with lots of pineapple, pepperoni and a homemade sauce.
—John Weakland, Springfield, Oregon

- 4 plum tomatoes, coarsely chopped
- 1 can (6 ounces) tomato paste
- 1/4 cup water
- 1/4 cup roasted sweet red peppers
- 1 tablespoon dried oregano
- 1 tablespoon honey
- 2 teaspoons dried minced garlic
- 2 teaspoons paprika
- 1 teaspoon salt
- 1/4 teaspoon crushed red pepper flakes
- 2 tubes (13.8 ounces *each*) refrigerated pizza crust
- 2 cups (8 ounces) shredded part-skim mozzarella cheese, *divided*
- 1 cup (4 ounces) shredded Romano cheese, *divided*
- 1 package (3-1/2 ounces) sliced pepperoni
- 1 cup pineapple tidbits, drained

For the sauce, place the first 10 ingredients in a food processor; cover and process until blended. Transfer to a small saucepan; heat through.

Meanwhile, press pizza crust dough into a greased 15-in. x 10-in. x 1-in. baking pan; build up edges slightly and seal the seam. Bake at 425° for 6-8 minutes or until lightly browned.

Spread 1-3/4 cups sauce over the crust (refrigerate remaining sauce for another use). Sprinkle with 1 cup mozzarella and 1/2 cup Romano; top with pepperoni, pineapple and remaining cheeses.

Bake for 14-18 minutes or until cheese is melted and crust is golden brown. **Yield:** 12 pieces.

Gyro-Style Turkey Pitas
(Pictured below)

Prep/Total Time: 30 min.

These are so good—they'll remind you of specialties from a Greek deli. Everyone who samples these hearty stuffed pitas loves them. —Wanda Allende, Orlando, Florida

- 1 **pound ground turkey**
- 1 **small onion, chopped**
- 1/2 **cup sauerkraut, rinsed and well drained**
- 2 **tablespoons brown sugar**
- 1/2 **teaspoon salt**
- 2/3 **cup sour cream**
- 3 **tablespoons mayonnaise**
- 2 **tablespoons prepared ranch salad dressing**
- 1 **small tomato, chopped**
- 1/3 **cup chopped cucumber**
- 4 **pita breads (6 inches), halved and warmed**

Shredded lettuce

In a large skillet, cook ground turkey, onion, sauerkraut, brown sugar and salt over medium heat until the meat is no longer pink; drain.

In a small bowl, combine the sour cream, mayonnaise and ranch salad dressing. Stir in tomato and cucumber. Fill pita halves with turkey mixture, lettuce and sauce. **Yield:** 4 servings.

Thai Chicken Stir-Fry
(Pictured above)

Prep/Total Time: 25 min.

Instead of getting Thai food by going out, why not whip up this sensational stir-fry in your own kitchen? It takes less than half an hour. —Sally Bailey, Wooster, Ohio

- 1 **pound boneless skinless chicken breasts, cut into 1-inch strips**
- 1 **tablespoon olive oil**
- 1 **package (16 ounces) frozen stir-fry vegetable blend, thawed**
- 1/4 **cup unsweetened apple juice**
- 1/4 **cup soy sauce**
- 1/4 **cup creamy peanut butter**
- 2 **tablespoons brown sugar**
- 2 **teaspoons garlic powder**
- 1/4 **teaspoon ground ginger**
- 1/4 **teaspoon cayenne pepper**

Hot cooked rice

In a large skillet or wok, stir-fry the chicken in the oil for 3-4 minutes or until no longer pink. Stir in the vegetable blend; cook, uncovered, for 4-6 minutes or until the vegetables are tender.

Meanwhile, in a small bowl, combine the apple juice, soy sauce, peanut butter, brown sugar, garlic powder, ginger and cayenne. Stir into the chicken mixture; heat through. Serve with rice. **Yield:** 4 servings.

Everyone will say "Olé!" to the festive idea here—a south-of-the-border bash that features special foods guests are sure to love.

Your party spread will have lots of appeal thanks to colorful Shrimp & Avocado Salads, hearty Beef & Bean Enchiladas, Effortless Guacamole and Mexican Chicken and Rice. Don't forget to add a big basket of tortilla chips and plenty of salsa! ■

Mexican Chicken and Rice
(Pictured below)

Prep/Total Time: 30 min.

Fans of Southwest-style fare just can't get enough of this delicious dish. I've served it at many casual get-togethers, passing the toppings around for a fun presentation.
—Trisha Kruse, Eagle, Indiana

- 1 pound boneless skinless chicken breasts, cut into 1/2-inch strips
- 2 tablespoons butter
- 1-3/4 cups salsa
- 1 envelope (5.4 ounces) Mexican-style rice and pasta mix
- 1 can (2-1/4 ounces) sliced ripe olives, drained
- 2 tablespoons lime juice
- 1/2 cup shredded cheddar cheese
- 1 cup (8 ounces) sour cream
- 1 medium ripe avocado, peeled and cubed
- 1 medium tomato, chopped

In a large skillet, brown the chicken in butter. Stir in the salsa, rice mix, ripe olives and lime juice. Bring to a boil. Reduce heat; cover and simmer for 8-10 minutes or until rice is tender.

Sprinkle with cheese. Serve with sour cream, avocado and tomato. **Yield:** 4 servings.

Shrimp & Avocado Salads
(Pictured above)

Prep/Total Time: 25 min.

This gorgeous, refreshing salad has such authentic flavor, you'll feel like you're relaxing at a beachside cantina in Acapulco! The homemade vinaigrette is a breeze to whip up and perfectly accents the shrimp and veggies.
—Heidi Hall, North St. Paul, Minnesota

- 1 pound uncooked large shrimp, peeled and deveined
- 1 small garlic clove, minced
- 1/2 teaspoon chili powder
- 1/4 teaspoon salt
- 1/4 teaspoon ground cumin
- 2 teaspoons olive oil
- 5 cups hearts of romaine salad mix
- 1 cup fresh or frozen corn, thawed
- 1 cup frozen peas, thawed
- 1/2 cup chopped sweet red pepper
- 1 medium ripe avocado, peeled and thinly sliced

CILANTRO VINAIGRETTE:
- 7 tablespoons olive oil
- 1/4 cup minced fresh cilantro
- 1/4 cup lime juice
- 1-1/2 teaspoons sugar
- 1 small garlic clove, minced
- 1/2 teaspoon salt
- 1/4 teaspoon pepper

In a large skillet, cook the shrimp, garlic, chili powder, salt and cumin in oil over medium heat for 3-4 minutes or until shrimp turn pink; set aside.

In a large bowl, combine romaine salad mix, corn, peas and red pepper; divide among four serving plates. Top each with shrimp and avocado. In a small bowl, whisk the vinaigrette ingredients and drizzle over salads. **Yield:** 4 servings.

Effortless Guacamole

Prep/Total Time: 15 min.

Here's a super-easy classic you'll find yourself turning to time and again when entertaining. I've been counting on this 15-minute recipe ever since I started cooking.
—Deann Lokvam, Tijeras, New Mexico

    2 medium ripe avocados, peeled
    2 green onions, chopped
    1 tablespoon salsa
    1 tablespoon mayonnaise
    2 to 3 teaspoons lime juice, optional
    1/2 teaspoon ground cumin
    1/2 teaspoon chili powder
    1/4 teaspoon garlic salt
Tortilla chips

In a small bowl, mash avocados. Stir in the green onions, salsa, mayonnaise, lime juice if desired, cumin, chili powder and garlic salt. Serve the guacamole with tortilla chips. **Yield:** 1 cup.

Beef & Bean Enchiladas
(Pictured above and on page 152)

Prep/Total Time: 30 min.

These tried-and-true enchiladas are great not only when you're having a fiesta, but also on rushed weeknights.
—Myra Innes, Auburn, Kansas

        1 pound ground beef
        2 cans (16 ounces *each*) refried beans
    1-1/2 teaspoons dried minced onion
        1 to 2 teaspoons chili powder
      1/2 teaspoon salt
       10 flour tortillas (8 inches), warmed
      1/4 cup chopped onion
    1-1/2 cups (6 ounces) shredded cheddar cheese,
            divided
        1 can (10 ounces) enchilada sauce, warmed
        1 can (2-1/2 ounces) sliced ripe olives,
            drained

In a large saucepan, cook beef over medium heat until no longer pink; drain. Stir in the beans, dried onion, chili powder and salt; heat through.

Place about 1/3 cupful down center of each tortilla. Sprinkle each with onion and cheese. Fold bottom and sides over filling. Pour sauce over the top; garnish with olives. **Yield:** 10 enchiladas.

Stay cool on any hot day by inviting friends over for some sensational sippers. Whether it's after work on a weeknight or a weekend evening, everyone will feel refreshed with these extra-special beverages.

Quench their thirst by blending up gorgeous Blue Lagoon Margaritas, Lemon-Pineapple Punch, Mojito Slush and Cran-Grape Cooler. Keep these colorful favorites in mind for holidays, too! ■

Blue Lagoon Margaritas
(Pictured below)

Prep/Total Time: 15 min.

This super drink will have your friends asking, "What's that?" They'll definitely be requesting the recipe.
—*Willie DeWaard, Coralville, Iowa*

- 4 lime slices
- 3 tablespoons coarse sugar
- 1/2 cup lemon-lime soda, chilled
- 1/2 cup tequila
- 1/3 cup frozen limeade concentrate, partially thawed
- 1/2 cup blue curacao
- 2 cups ice cubes

Using lime slices, moisten the rims of four margarita or cocktail glasses. Set aside lime slices for garnish. Sprinkle the coarse sugar on a plate; hold each glass upside down and dip rim into sugar. Set aside. Discard the remaining sugar on plate.

In a blender, combine the remaining ingredients; cover and process until blended. Pour into the prepared glasses. Garnish with the reserved lime slices. Serve immediately. **Yield:** 4 servings.

Lemon-Pineapple Punch
(Pictured at left in photo at right)

Prep/Total Time: 20 min.

Our Test Kitchen staff stirred pineapple juice and sherbet into this fresh-tasting punch. It's a hit with children and adults alike, especially on scorching-hot days.

- 1 can (46 ounces) unsweetened pineapple juice
- 2 cans (12 ounces *each*) frozen lemonade concentrate, thawed
- 1/4 cup sugar
- 1/4 cup lemon juice
- 2 liters lemon-lime soda, chilled
- 2 pints pineapple sherbet, softened
- 5 drops yellow food coloring, optional
- Pineapple chunks and maraschino cherries, optional

In a large punch bowl, combine the pineapple juice, lemonade concentrate, sugar and lemon juice. Add the lemon-lime soda, sherbet and food coloring if desired; stir until blended.

Serve immediately, garnishing servings with pineapple and maraschino cherries if desired. **Yield:** 21 servings (about 5 quarts).

Cran-Grape Cooler
(Pictured at far right in photo at right)

Prep/Total Time: 10 min.

You're just a few simple ingredients and 10 minutes away from sipping this tangy cooler. The cranberry flavor and ruby-red color make it festive for Christmastime, too.
—*Didi Desjardins, Dartmouth, Massachusetts*

- 6 cups cranberry-grape juice, chilled
- 3 cups lemon-lime soda, chilled
- 2 tablespoons lime juice
- Ice cubes
- Lime slices and maraschino cherries, optional

In a large pitcher, combine the cranberry-grape juice, lemon-lime soda and lime juice. Serve over ice; garnish servings with lime slices and cherries if desired. **Yield:** 9 servings (2-1/4 quarts).

Mojito Slush

(Pictured at center in photo above)

Prep: 30 min. + freezing

Whether you're splashing poolside or enjoying relaxation time indoors, this slushy drink has just the right balance of minty crispness and limey tartness to tingle taste buds.
—*Jessica Ring, Chicago, Illinois*

1 package (3 ounces) lime gelatin
2 tablespoons sugar
1 cup boiling water
1 cup fresh mint leaves
2 cans (12 ounces *each*) frozen limeade
   concentrate, thawed
2 cups cold water
1 cup grapefruit soda
1 cup rum *or* additional grapefruit soda
EACH SERVING:
2/3 cup grapefruit soda
GARNISH:
Lime wedge *and/or* fresh mint leaves

In a small bowl, dissolve the lime gelatin and sugar in the boiling water; add the mint leaves. Cover and steep for 20 minutes.

Press through a sieve; discard the mint leaves. Stir in the limeade concentrate, cold water, grapefruit soda and rum. Pour into a 2-1/2-qt. freezer container. Freeze overnight or until set.

For each serving, scoop 2/3 cup slush into a glass. Pour grapefruit soda into the glass; garnish as desired.
Yield: 13 servings (about 2 quarts slush mix).

CHAPTER 10

Slow-Cooked Sensations

Want to make dinner prep as fast as can be? Just take things slow—in the slow cooker!

When you rely on this handy kitchen appliance, you can get your meal started well before suppertime arrives. Then, after returning from a busy day of work or running errands, you'll have hot home cooking ready and waiting for you.

Just page through this chapter to see the wide variety of tasty specialties—24 in all—you and your family can enjoy.

From Fiesta Beef Bowls and Potato Pizza Casserole to Zesty Chicken Marinara and Super Short Ribs, these slow-cooked creations will have you taking it easy in no time. ■

SLOW BUT SURE. Tangy Beef Brisket (p. 170).

Veggie Potato Soup
(Pictured above)

Prep: 20 min. **Cook:** 5-1/2 hours

Chock-full of potatoes, this vegetarian soup is as filling as it is flavorful. Serve it with crusty bread on a cold night... and take any leftovers in a thermos to work the next day. With this in store, you'll really look forward to lunch!
— *Hannah Thompson, Scotts Valley, California*

    6 medium potatoes, cubed
    3 cans (14-1/2 ounces *each*) vegetable broth
    1 medium carrot, thinly sliced
    1 large leek (white portion only), chopped
  1/4 cup butter, cubed
    1 garlic clove, minced
    1 teaspoon dried thyme
  3/4 teaspoon salt
  1/4 teaspoon dried marjoram
  1/4 teaspoon pepper
  1/4 cup all-purpose flour
1-1/2 cups half-and-half cream
    1 cup frozen peas, thawed

In a 5-qt. slow cooker, combine the first 10 ingredients. Cover and cook on low for 5-6 hours or until vegetables are tender.

In a small bowl, combine the flour and cream until smooth; add to the slow cooker. Stir in peas. Cover and cook on high for 30 minutes or until slightly thickened. **Yield:** 11 servings (2-3/4 quarts).

▐ LIVELY LEEKS ▐

Refrigerate leeks in a plastic bag for up to 5 days. Before using them, cut off the roots and trim the tough leaf ends. Slit the leek from end to end and wash it thoroughly under cold water to remove dirt trapped between the leaf layers.

Melt-in-Your-Mouth Chuck Roast
(Pictured below)

Prep: 20 min. **Cook:** 5 hours

My husband and I are always interested in well-seasoned recipes, and this one is fantastic. After 5 hours of slow cooking, the roast comes out nice and tender, too.
— *Bette McCumber, Schenectady, New York*

    1 large onion, sliced
    1 medium green pepper, sliced
    1 celery rib, chopped
    1 boneless beef chuck roast (2 to 3 pounds)
    1 can (14-1/2 ounces) Italian stewed tomatoes
  1/2 cup beef broth
  1/2 cup ketchup
    3 tablespoons brown sugar
    2 tablespoons Worcestershire sauce
4-1/2 teaspoons prepared mustard
    3 garlic cloves, minced
    1 tablespoon soy sauce
    2 teaspoons pepper
  1/4 teaspoon crushed red pepper flakes
    3 tablespoons cornstarch
  1/4 cup cold water

Place the onion, green pepper and celery in a 5-qt. slow cooker; add the roast. In a large bowl, combine tomatoes, beef broth, ketchup, brown sugar, Worcestershire sauce, mustard, garlic, soy sauce, pepper and pepper flakes; pour over meat. Cover and cook on low for 5-6 hours or until meat is tender.

Remove meat and vegetables; keep warm. Skim fat from the cooking juices if necessary; transfer to a small saucepan. Combine the cornstarch and cold water until smooth; stir into the cooking juices. Bring to a boil; cook and stir for 2 minutes or until thickened. Serve with the roast. **Yield:** 6 servings.

Pork Chops & Potatoes
In Mushroom Sauce
(Pictured above)
Prep: 25 min. **Cook:** 3-1/2 hours

For anyone who craves home-style, meat-and-potatoes comfort food, this recipe is a keeper! Plus, it couldn't be much easier to prepare. You don't need to precook any of the ingredients before popping them in the slow cooker.
—*Linda Foreman, Locust Grove, Oklahoma*

  1 can (10-3/4 ounces) condensed cream of
     mushroom soup, undiluted
1/4 cup chicken broth
1/4 cup country-style Dijon mustard
  1 garlic clove, minced
1/2 teaspoon dried thyme
1/4 teaspoon salt
1/4 teaspoon pepper
  6 medium red potatoes, sliced
  1 medium onion, halved and thinly sliced
  6 boneless pork loin chops (5 ounces *each*)

In a 5-qt. slow cooker, combine the first seven ingredients. Stir in potatoes and onion. Top with pork chops. Cover and cook on low for 3-1/2 to 4-1/2 hours or until meat is tender. **Yield:** 6 servings.

Mexican Chicken Chili
Prep: 30 min. **Cook:** 5 hours

Corn, black beans and green chilies give this chicken chili some south-of-the-border flair. Reduce or eliminate the cayenne pepper if your gang prefers a little less zip.
—*Stephanie Rabbitt-Schappacher, West Chester, Ohio*

  1 pound boneless skinless chicken breasts,
     cubed
  1 tablespoon canola oil
  2 cans (14-1/2 ounces *each*) diced tomatoes,
     undrained
  2 cups frozen corn
  1 can (15 ounces) black beans, rinsed and
     drained
  1 can (14-1/2 ounces) reduced-sodium chicken
     broth
  1 can (4 ounces) chopped green chilies
  2 tablespoons chili powder
  1 tablespoon ground cumin
1/2 teaspoon salt
1/4 teaspoon cayenne pepper

In a small skillet, brown chicken in oil. Transfer to a 5-qt. slow cooker. Stir in the remaining ingredients. Cover and cook on low for 5-6 hours or until the chicken is no longer pink. **Yield:** 6 servings.

Super Short Ribs
(Pictured below)

Prep: 20 min. **Cook:** 8 hours

These lip-smacking ribs came from an old oven recipe of my mom's. They make a great meal on a bed of pasta.
—Coleen Carter, Malone, New York

    3 medium onions, cut into wedges
    3 to 3-1/2 pounds bone-in beef short ribs
    1 bay leaf
    1 bottle (12 ounces) light beer *or* nonalcoholic
      beer
    2 tablespoons brown sugar
    2 tablespoons Dijon mustard
    2 tablespoons tomato paste
    2 teaspoons dried thyme
    2 teaspoons beef bouillon granules
    1 teaspoon salt
  1/4 teaspoon pepper
    3 tablespoons all-purpose flour
  1/2 cup cold water
Hot cooked noodles

Place the onions in a 5-qt. slow cooker; add the ribs and bay leaf. Combine the beer, brown sugar, Dijon mustard, tomato paste, thyme, bouillon, salt and pepper. Pour over the meat. Cover and cook on low for 8-10 hours or until meat is tender.

Remove the meat and vegetables to a serving platter; keep warm. Discard the bay leaf. Skim fat from cooking juices; transfer the juices to a small saucepan. Bring the liquid to a boil. Combine flour and water until smooth. Gradually stir into the pan. Bring to a boil; cook and stir for 2 minutes or until thickened. Serve with meat and noodles. **Yield:** 6 servings.

Zesty Chicken Marinara
(Pictured above)

Prep: 15 min. **Cook:** 4 hours

A friend served this saucy Italian dinner before a church social, and I fell in love! Now I make this dish often.
—Linda Baumann, Richfield, Wisconsin

    4 bone-in chicken breast halves (12 to
      14 ounces *each*), skin removed
    2 cups marinara sauce
    1 medium tomato, chopped
  1/2 cup Italian salad dressing
1-1/2 teaspoons Italian seasoning
    1 garlic clove, minced
  1/2 pound uncooked angel hair pasta
  1/2 cup shredded part-skim mozzarella cheese

Place the chicken in a 4-qt. slow cooker. In a small bowl, combine marinara sauce, tomato, Italian dressing, Italian seasoning and garlic; pour over the chicken. Cover and cook on low for 4-5 hours or until chicken is tender.

Meanwhile, cook the pasta according to the package directions; drain. Serve chicken and sauce with pasta; sprinkle with cheese. **Yield:** 4 servings.

PASTA POINTER

To cook 8 ounces of pasta, bring 3 quarts of water to a full rolling boil. Add 1 tablespoon salt for flavor if desired. Stir in the pasta all at once. Return to a boil; boil, uncovered, stirring occasionally. Pasta should be cooked until "al dente," or firm yet tender.

Fiesta Beef Bowls
(Pictured below)

Prep: 25 min. **Cook:** 8-1/2 hours

In the mood for Mexican? South-of-the-border ingredients turn this round steak into a terrific all-in-one supper.
—*Deborah Linn, Valdez, Arkansas*

1-1/2 pounds boneless beef top round steak
   1 can (10 ounces) diced tomatoes and green chilies
   1 medium onion, chopped
   2 garlic cloves, minced
   1 teaspoon dried oregano
   1 teaspoon chili powder
   1 teaspoon ground cumin
1/4 teaspoon salt
1/4 teaspoon pepper
   2 cans (15 ounces *each*) pinto beans, rinsed and drained
   3 cups hot cooked rice
1/2 cup shredded cheddar cheese
   6 tablespoons sliced ripe olives
   6 tablespoons thinly sliced green onions
   6 tablespoons guacamole

Place round steak in a 3-qt. slow cooker. In a small bowl, combine the tomatoes, onion, garlic and seasonings; pour over steak. Cover and cook on low for 8-9 hours or until meat is tender.

Remove meat from slow cooker. Add beans to tomato mixture. Cover and cook on high for 30 minutes or until beans are heated through. When cool enough to handle, slice meat. In individual bowls, layer the rice, meat and bean mixture. Top with cheddar cheese, olives, onions and guacamole. **Yield:** 6 servings.

Creamy Crab Dip
(Pictured above)

Prep: 20 min. **Cook:** 2 hours

This is wonderful for entertaining because it frees up your oven for other foods. Crab lovers will adore it! Enjoy any leftovers on a baked potato for lunch the next day.
—*Susan D'Amore, West Chester, Pennsylvania*

   1 package (8 ounces) cream cheese, softened
   2 green onions, chopped
1/4 cup chopped sweet red pepper
   2 tablespoons minced fresh parsley
   2 tablespoons mayonnaise
   1 tablespoon Dijon mustard
   1 teaspoon Worcestershire sauce
1/4 teaspoon salt
1/4 teaspoon pepper
   2 cans (6 ounces *each*) crabmeat, drained, flaked and cartilage removed
   2 tablespoons capers, drained
Dash hot pepper sauce
Assorted crackers

In a 1-1/2-qt. slow cooker, combine the first nine ingredients; stir in crab. Cover and cook on low for 1-1/2 hours. Stir in capers and pepper sauce; cook 30 minutes longer or until heated through. Serve with crackers. **Yield:** 2-1/3 cups.

Rosemary Mushroom Chicken
(Pictured below)

Prep: 30 min. **Cook:** 7 hours

A delicate hint of rosemary lightly seasons this rich and creamy dish. Cooking the chicken and mushroom gravy together cuts so much time from your dinner prep. For a complete and filling meal, add egg noodles or rice.
—Genny Monchamp, Redding, California

    6 chicken leg quarters, skin removed
    2 cups sliced fresh mushrooms
    2 cans (10-3/4 ounces *each*) condensed cream
      of mushroom soup, undiluted
1/2 cup white wine *or* chicken broth
    1 teaspoon garlic salt
    1 teaspoon dried rosemary, crushed
1/2 teaspoon paprika
1/8 teaspoon pepper
Hot cooked egg noodles

Place chicken in a 5- or 6-qt. slow cooker coated with cooking spray; top with the mushrooms. Combine the cream of mushroom soup, wine, garlic salt, rosemary, paprika and pepper; pour over top. Cover and cook on low for 7-9 hours or until chicken is tender. Serve with the noodles. **Yield:** 6 servings.

Potato Pizza Casserole
(Pictured above)

Prep: 25 min. **Cook:** 4 hours

If your kids love pizza, forget about delivery and get this cheesy casserole going early in the day. Later, you'll have a ready-to-eat, homemade supper that's sure to please.
—Tyler Sherman, Williamsburg, Virginia

    1 pound ground beef
1/2 pound sliced fresh mushrooms
    1 medium green pepper, chopped
    1 small onion, chopped
    2 jars (14 ounces *each*) pizza sauce
    1 can (10-3/4 ounces) condensed cheddar
      cheese soup, undiluted
1/2 cup 2% milk
    1 teaspoon Italian seasoning
1/2 teaspoon garlic salt
1/4 teaspoon crushed red pepper flakes
    1 package (32 ounces) frozen cubed hash
      brown potatoes, thawed
   15 slices pepperoni, chopped
    2 cups (8 ounces) shredded Italian cheese
      blend

In a large skillet, cook ground beef, mushrooms, green pepper and onion until the meat is no longer pink; drain. Meanwhile, in a large bowl, combine the pizza sauce, cheese soup, milk, Italian seasoning, garlic salt and pepper flakes. Stir in the potatoes, pepperoni and beef mixture.

Transfer half of the meat mixture to a 5-qt. slow cooker. Sprinkle with half of the cheese; repeat layers. Cover and cook on low for 4-5 hours or until potatoes are tender. **Yield:** 8 servings.

Crispy Snack Mix
(Pictured above)

Prep: 10 min. **Cook:** 2-1/2 hours

You can make just about anything in the slow cooker—this recipe proves it's true! With lots of cereal, chow mein noodles and more, the snack mix is delightfully crispy.
—Jane Sims, De Leon, Texas

4-1/2 cups chow mein noodles
    4 cups Rice Chex
    1 can (9-3/4 ounces) salted cashews
    1 cup flaked coconut, toasted
1/2 cup butter, melted
    2 tablespoons soy sauce
2-1/4 teaspoons curry powder
    3/4 teaspoon ground ginger

In a 5-qt. slow cooker, combine the chow mein noodles, cereal, cashews and coconut.

In a small bowl, whisk the butter, soy sauce, curry powder and ginger; drizzle over cereal mixture and mix well. Cover and cook on low for 2-1/2 hours, stirring every 30 minutes. Serve warm or at room temperature. **Yield:** about 2-1/2 quarts.

COCONUT CLUE

To toast coconut for Crispy Snack Mix (recipe above), spread the coconut in a 15-in. x 10-in. x 1-in. baking pan. Bake it at 350° for 5-10 minutes or until the coconut is lightly browned, stirring occasionally.

Or, use the stovetop. Spread the coconut in a dry nonstick skillet and heat it over low heat until the coconut is lightly browned, stirring occasionally.

Zesty Sausage & Beans
(Pictured below)

Prep: 30 min. **Cook:** 5 hours

If the guys in your life crave classic "man" food, consider this. Jam-packed with sausage, beans and bacon, it's guaranteed to satisfy the biggest appetites at the table.
—Melissa Just, Minneapolis, Minnesota

    2 pounds smoked kielbasa *or* Polish sausage, halved and sliced
    2 cans (15 ounces *each*) black beans, rinsed and drained
    1 can (15 ounces) great northern beans, rinsed and drained
    1 can (15 ounces) thick and zesty tomato sauce
    1 medium green pepper, chopped
    1 medium onion, chopped
    5 bacon strips, cooked and crumbled
    3 tablespoons brown sugar
    2 tablespoons cider vinegar
    3 garlic cloves, minced
1/4 teaspoon dried thyme
1/4 teaspoon dried marjoram
1/4 teaspoon cayenne pepper
Hot cooked rice

In a large skillet, brown the sausage. Transfer to a 4-qt. slow cooker; add beans, tomato sauce, green pepper, onion, bacon, brown sugar, cider vinegar, garlic, thyme, marjoram and cayenne.

Cover and cook on low for 5-6 hours or until the vegetables are tender. Serve with hot cooked rice. **Yield:** 10 servings.

Tangy Beef Brisket

(Pictured above and on page 162)

Prep: 10 min. **Cook:** 6 hours

This fork-tender brisket will keep your oven off and your kitchen cool on a hot day. Plus, the recipe uses just six ingredients. —Stephanie Strong, Mt. Juliet, Tennessee

- **1 fresh beef brisket (3 pounds)**
- **1 cup chili sauce**
- **1 cup cola**
- **1 envelope onion soup mix**
- **1 tablespoon cornstarch**
- **1 tablespoon cold water**

Cut the brisket in half and place in a 5-qt. slow cooker. Combine the chili sauce, cola and soup mix; pour over brisket. Cover and cook on low for 6-7 hours or until the meat is tender.

Remove the meat to a serving platter and keep warm. Skim fat from cooking juices; transfer to a small saucepan. Bring the liquid to a boil. Combine cornstarch and water until smooth. Gradually stir into the pan. Bring to a boil; cook and stir for 2 minutes or until thickened. Thinly slice the meat across the grain; serve with gravy. **Yield:** 7 servings (2 cups gravy).

Editor's Note: This is a fresh beef brisket, not corned beef.

GREAT GRAVY

The recipe for Tangy Beef Brisket (at left) includes an easy gravy that's made on the stovetop after the brisket comes out of the slow cooker. For a delicious side dish to round out your meal, serve the gravy over instant mashed potatoes or noodles.

Chili Coney Dogs

Prep: 15 min. **Cook:** 4 hours

Everyone in our family, from the smallest children to the oldest adults, loves these special dogs. They're smothered with a beefy chili sauce, cheese, onion and relish.
—Michele Harris, Vicksburg, Michigan

    1 pound lean ground beef (90% lean)
    1 can (15 ounces) tomato sauce
1/2 cup water
    2 tablespoons Worcestershire sauce
    1 tablespoon dried minced onion
1/2 teaspoon garlic powder
1/2 teaspoon ground mustard
1/2 teaspoon chili powder
1/2 teaspoon pepper
Dash cayenne pepper
    8 hot dogs
    8 hot dog buns, split
Shredded cheddar cheese, relish and chopped
    onion, optional

In a large skillet, cook beef over medium heat until meat is no longer pink; drain. Stir in the tomato sauce, water, Worcestershire sauce, onion and spices.

Place hot dogs in a 3-qt. slow cooker; top with beef mixture. Cover and cook on low for 4-5 hours or until heated through. Serve on buns with cheese, relish and onion if desired. **Yield:** 8 servings.

Pineapple Chicken
(Pictured below)

Prep: 15 min. **Cook:** 4 hours

The taste of this quick-to-fix main dish may remind you of traditional sweet-and-sour chicken. It's delicious!
—Francisca Mesiano, Newport News, Virginia

    4 bone-in chicken breast halves (12 to
    14 ounces *each*), skin removed

    1 tablespoon canola oil
    1 can (20 ounces) sliced pineapple
1/3 cup packed brown sugar
1/4 cup cornstarch
    2 tablespoons lemon juice
3/4 teaspoon salt
1/4 teaspoon ground ginger
Hot cooked rice

In a large skillet, brown the chicken in oil. Transfer to a greased 4-qt. slow cooker. Drain pineapple; reserving juice. Place pineapple over chicken. Whisk the brown sugar, cornstarch, lemon juice, salt, ginger and reserved juice until smooth; pour over top.

Cover and cook on low for 4-5 hours or until chicken is tender. Serve with rice. **Yield:** 4 servings.

Country-Style Ribs
(Pictured above)

Prep: 15 min. **Cook:** 5-1/2 hours

This was a favorite in our house when I was a kid, and now I enjoy making it myself. To save time the next day, I often whip up the tangy sauce the night before.
—Bethany Mott, Provo, Utah

1-1/2 pounds boneless country-style pork ribs
    1 medium onion, sliced
    2 cups tomato juice
1/2 cup packed brown sugar
1/4 cup cider vinegar
1/4 cup ketchup
    2 tablespoons Worcestershire sauce
    1 teaspoon ground mustard
1/4 teaspoon chili powder

Place ribs and onion in a 3-qt. slow cooker. In a small bowl, combine the remaining ingredients. Pour over the ribs. Cover and cook on low for 5-1/2 to 6 hours or until a meat thermometer reads 160°. **Yield:** 4 servings.

French Dip au Jus

(Pictured below)

Prep: 30 min. **Cook:** 8 hours

I came up with this homemade sandwich because other French Dips I've tried tasted bland. This recipe is a snap to fix, and I like it better than restaurant versions.
— *Lindsay Ebert, Orem, Utah*

1-1/2 teaspoons beef base
  1 teaspoon dried thyme
  1 beef rump roast *or* bottom round roast
    (3 pounds)
  1 medium onion, quartered
1/2 cup soy sauce
  2 garlic cloves, minced
  1 bay leaf
1/2 teaspoon pepper
  8 cups water
  2 tablespoons Dijon mustard
  2 loaves French bread (1 pound *each*), split
    and toasted
 12 slices part-skim mozzarella cheese
  1 jar (4-1/2 ounces) sliced mushrooms,
    drained

Combine the beef base and thyme; rub over roast and place in a 5-qt. slow cooker. Combine the onion, soy sauce, garlic, bay leaf and pepper; pour over the roast. Add the water.

Cover and cook on low for 8-9 hours or until meat is tender. Discard the bay leaf. Remove meat to a cutting board. Let stand for 10 minutes. Thinly slice the meat across the grain.

To assemble sandwiches, spread mustard over bread. Layer with beef, cheese, mushrooms and onion. Replace tops. Cut each loaf into four slices; serve with cooking juices. **Yield:** 8 servings.

Editor's Note: Look for beef base near the broth and bouillon.

Slow-Cooked Spaghetti Sauce

(Pictured above)

Prep: 15 min. **Cook:** 8 hours

The flavor of this easy sauce has store-bought ones beat. Just boil spaghetti and indulge in an Italian classic.
— *Kim Stewart, North Little Rock, Arkansas*

  2 pounds lean ground beef (90% lean)
  1 large green pepper, chopped
  1 large onion, chopped
1-1/2 cups water
  1 can (14-1/2 ounces) diced tomatoes,
    undrained
  1 can (8 ounces) tomato sauce
  1 can (6 ounces) tomato paste
  2 garlic cloves, minced
  4 bay leaves
  2 tablespoons Italian seasoning
  1 teaspoon salt
  1 teaspoon sugar
  1 teaspoon dried parsley flakes
1/2 teaspoon pepper
1/4 teaspoon dried rosemary, crushed
Hot cooked spaghetti

In a large skillet over medium heat, cook beef until no longer pink; drain. Transfer to a 5-qt. slow cooker. Stir in the green pepper, onion, water, tomatoes, tomato sauce, paste, garlic and seasonings. Cover and cook on low for 8 hours or until bubbly. Discard bay leaves; serve over spaghetti. **Yield:** 2 quarts.

SAUCY SOLUTION

I like to cut a loaf of French bread lengthwise and spread leftover spaghetti sauce on each half. Then I sprinkle on cheddar and Parmesan cheeses. Toasted under the broiler, the slices make a quick snack.
— *Jean Monigold, Spirit Lake, Idaho*

Vegetable Chicken Soup

(Pictured below)

Prep: 25 min. **Cook:** 5 hours

This satisfying veggie soup really hits the spot for lunch or dinner on a chilly day. Add a side salad and slices of whole grain bread for a filling and nutritious meal.
—Amy Cheatham, Sandusky, Ohio

  1 large sweet onion, chopped
  1 cup sliced baby portobello mushrooms
1/2 cup chopped green pepper
1/2 cup chopped sweet red pepper
  5 garlic cloves, minced
  1 tablespoon butter
  1 tablespoon olive oil
3/4 pound boneless skinless chicken breasts,
     cut into 1/2-inch cubes
  1 can (49-1/2 ounces) chicken broth
  1 can (28 ounces) crushed tomatoes,
     undrained
  2 medium carrots, cut into 1/4-inch slices
1/2 cup medium pearl barley
1-3/4 teaspoons Italian seasoning
1-1/2 teaspoons pepper
1/2 teaspoon salt

In a large skillet, saute the onion, portobello mushrooms, green and red peppers and garlic in butter and oil until tender. Transfer to a 5-qt. slow cooker. Add the remaining ingredients. Cover and cook on low for 5-6 hours or until the chicken and barley are tender. **Yield:** 7 servings (2-3/4 quarts).

Italian Sausage Dinner

(Pictured above)

Prep: 20 min. **Cook:** 6 hours

Everyone in my family loves this delicious combination of sausage, onion, potatoes, zucchini and peppers. It goes together in a flash before I leave in the morning, and it makes the house smell so good at the end of the day. —Kathy Kasprowicz
Arlington Heights, Illinois

  1 pound small red potatoes
  2 large zucchini, cut into 1-inch slices
  2 large green peppers, cut into 1-1/2-inch
     pieces
  1 large onion, cut into wedges
1/4 teaspoon salt
1/4 teaspoon pepper
  1 pound Italian sausage links, cut into
     1-1/2-inch pieces
  1 tablespoon olive oil
1/2 cup white wine *or* chicken broth
  1 tablespoon Italian seasoning

Place the first six ingredients in a 6-qt. slow cooker. In a large skillet, brown the sausages in oil. Reduce heat. Add wine and Italian seasoning, stirring to loosen browned bits from the pan. Transfer to slow cooker. Cover and cook on low for 6-8 hours or until potatoes are tender. **Yield:** 5 servings.

Parmesan Pork Roast
(Pictured above)

Prep: 15 min. **Cook:** 5-1/2 hours

Honey, soy sauce and other pantry staples give this easy pork roast sweet-and-savory flavor. You'll love it!
—Karen Warner, Louisville, Ohio

- 1 boneless whole pork loin roast (4 pounds)
- 2/3 cup grated Parmesan cheese
- 1/2 cup honey
- 3 tablespoons soy sauce
- 2 tablespoons dried basil
- 2 tablespoons minced garlic
- 2 tablespoons olive oil
- 1/2 teaspoon salt
- 2 tablespoons cornstarch
- 1/4 cup cold water

Cut roast in half. Transfer to a 3-qt. slow cooker. In a small bowl, combine the cheese, honey, soy sauce, basil, garlic, oil and salt; pour over pork. Cover and cook on low for 5-1/2 to 6 hours or until a meat thermometer reads 160° and meat is tender.

Remove meat to a serving platter; keep warm. Skim fat from the cooking juices; transfer to a small saucepan. Bring liquid to a boil. Combine the cornstarch and water until smooth. Gradually stir into the pan. Bring to a boil; cook and stir for 2 minutes or until thickened. Slice roast; serve with gravy. **Yield:** 10 servings.

TOMATO TIDBITS

A bit of tomato paste can enhance many dishes. To store leftover tomato paste, line a baking sheet with waxed paper. Mound the tomato paste in 1-tablespoon portions on the waxed paper. Freeze until firm, then transfer to a resealable freezer bag.

Beef with Red Wine Gravy
(Pictured below)

Prep: 10 min. **Cook:** 6-1/4 hours

Slow cooker convenience means you can prep this in the morning and come home to a restaurant-worthy entree.
—Maybrie, Taste of Home Online Community

- 3 pounds beef stew meat, cut into 1-inch cubes
- 1 pound medium fresh mushrooms, halved
- 1 medium onion, sliced
- 1 can (10-1/2 ounces) condensed beef broth, undiluted
- 1 cup dry red wine
- 1 envelope brown gravy mix
- 2 tablespoons tomato paste
- 1/4 teaspoon salt
- 1 bay leaf
- 1/4 cup cornstarch
- 1/4 cup cold water
- Hot cooked egg noodles

Place beef, mushrooms and onion in a 5-qt. slow cooker. In a small bowl, combine beef broth, wine, gravy mix, tomato paste, salt and bay leaf. Pour over top.

Cover and cook on low for 6-7 hours or until beef is tender. Discard bay leaf. Combine cornstarch and water until smooth; stir into meat mixture. Cover and cook on high for 15 minutes or until thickened. Serve with egg noodles. **Yield:** 6 servings.

Barbecue Meatballs
(Pictured above)

Prep: 20 min. **Cook:** 7 hours

I whipped up these saucy little morsels for my son's first birthday so I could serve something hearty before the cake and ice cream. —Tara Reeder, Mason, Michigan

   1 egg, beaten
1/2 cup shredded Colby-Monterey Jack cheese
1/4 cup seasoned bread crumbs
1/4 cup finely chopped onion
   2 pounds ground beef
SAUCE:
   2 cups ketchup
   2 tablespoons prepared mustard
   1 tablespoon brown sugar
   1 tablespoon cider vinegar
   1 tablespoon lemon juice
   1 tablespoon soy sauce

In a large bowl, combine egg, cheese, seasoned bread crumbs and onion. Crumble the beef over the mixture and mix well. Shape into 1-1/2-in. balls. Transfer to a 3-qt. slow cooker.

In a small bowl, combine the sauce ingredients; pour over meatballs. Cover and cook on low for 7-8 hours or until meat is no longer pink. **Yield:** 6 servings.

Country Rib Sandwiches

Prep: 30 min. **Cook:** 6-1/4 hours

Whether you're looking for an effortless weeknight dinner or a cozy weekend meal, this recipe is terrific. It gives you delicious, fall-off-the-bone tender meat for sandwiches. —Margaret Luchsinger, Jupiter, Florida

   1 large onion, chopped
   2 pounds boneless country-style pork ribs
1/2 cup ketchup
1/4 cup plum sauce
1/4 cup chili sauce
   2 tablespoons brown sugar
   1 teaspoon celery seed
   1 teaspoon garlic powder
   1 teaspoon Liquid Smoke, optional
1/2 teaspoon ground allspice
   8 kaiser rolls, split

Place the onion in a 3-qt. slow cooker; top with the ribs. Combine the ketchup, plum sauce, chili sauce, brown sugar, celery seed, garlic powder, Liquid Smoke if desired and allspice; pour over ribs.

Cover and cook on low for 6-7 hours or until meat is tender. Shred meat with two forks and return to the slow cooker. Cover and cook 15 minutes longer or until heated through. Serve on rolls. **Yield:** 8 servings.

CHAPTER 11

Breakfast & Brunch Favorites

Whatever the weather, your day will have a sunny start when you put these bright delights on the morning menu. They're not only scrumptious, but also a snap to prepare.

Need to get the kids off to school pronto? They'll love the grab-and-go ease of Breakfast Burritos. Looking for something special but speedy for a holiday brunch? You can't miss with Spinach & Sausage Egg Bake.

In this chapter, you'll also find a convenient homemade muffin mix you can whip up in advance, then keep handy for baking a fresh batch anytime.

So rise and shine with some delicious sunrise specialties. It's easier than ever! ■

A.M. FAVORITE. Peach & Sausage Breakfast Squares (p. 181).

Nutty Maple Muffins
(Pictured above)

Prep: 15 min. **Bake:** 20 min.

Sweet and moist, these morsels are full of maple flavor. They freeze well and are just as good with walnuts instead of pecans. —Betty Rupert, Chatham, Ontario

   1 egg
   1 cup (8 ounces) sour cream
   1 cup maple syrup
 1/3 cup canola oil
2-1/2 cups Oatmeal Crisp Almond cereal
1-1/3 cups all-purpose flour
 1/4 cup packed brown sugar
   1 teaspoon baking soda
 2/3 cup chopped pecans

In a large bowl, whisk the egg, sour cream, syrup and oil; stir in cereal. Let stand for 5 minutes. In another large bowl, combine the flour, brown sugar and baking soda. Stir in sour cream mixture just until moistened. Fold in pecans.

Fill greased or paper-lined muffin cups two-thirds full. Bake at 375° for 18-22 minutes or until a toothpick comes out clean. Cool for 5 minutes before removing from the pans to wire racks. Serve muffins warm. **Yield:** 1-1/2 dozen.

▮ FRUITFUL FACT ▮

With lemon zest in the dough and lemon juice in the icing, scrumptious Lemon-Nut Twists (recipe above right) boast a citrusy flavor that's doubly delightful. One medium lemon yields 2-3 teaspoons zest and about 3 tablespoons juice.

Lemon-Nut Twists
(Pictured below)

Prep: 20 min. **Bake:** 15 min. + rising

With a pretty drizzle of icing, these golden-brown twists from the Taste of Home Test Kitchen look so yummy... and don't disappoint when you take a bite.

 1/2 cup sliced almonds, toasted
 1/3 cup packed brown sugar
   1 tablespoon grated lemon peel
   1 loaf (16 ounces) frozen white bread dough, thawed
   2 tablespoons butter, melted, *divided*
   1 cup confectioners' sugar
   4 to 5 teaspoons lemon juice

Combine almonds, brown sugar and lemon peel. Roll dough to a 21-in. x 8-in. rectangle. Brush middle third of dough with 1 tablespoon melted butter. Sprinkle buttered area with half of almond-brown sugar mixture. Fold one of the remaining dough thirds over filling. Brush folded dough with remaining melted butter. Sprinkle with remaining filling. Fold remaining dough third over filling; pinch edges to seal. Cut into eight (1-in.-wide) strips. Hold each strip at both ends, twist in opposite directions three times.

Place on a greased baking sheet. Cover; let rise in a warm place until doubled in size, about 30-40 minutes. Bake at 375° for 15 minutes or until golden brown. Remove from baking sheet to wire rack to cool. Combine confectioners' sugar and lemon juice. Beat until smooth. Drizzle over twists. **Yield:** 8 servings.

Breakfast Burritos
(Pictured above)

Prep/Total Time: 30 min.

Get everyone in your family up and ready for a busy day by serving these hearty handhelds. The flour tortillas are packed with sausage, eggs, cheese and favorite taco toppings. With these Southwestern wraps, breakfast is like a fiesta!
—Jenny White, Glen, Mississippi

    1/4 pound bulk pork sausage
      5 eggs
    1/3 cup chopped tomato
    1/4 cup chopped onion
      2 tablespoons canned chopped green chilies
    1/4 teaspoon pepper
      5 slices process American cheese
      5 flour tortillas (10 inches), warmed
    1/2 cup chunky salsa
    1/2 cup sour cream

In a large skillet, cook sausage over medium heat until no longer pink; drain. In a large bowl, whisk the eggs, tomato, onion, chilies and pepper. Add to the skillet; cook and stir until set.

Place a cheese slice on each tortilla. Spoon filling off center on each tortilla. Top with salsa and sour cream. Fold the sides and ends over the filling and roll up. **Yield:** 5 servings.

Sweet Potato Waffles With Nut Topping
(Pictured at right)

Prep: 20 min. **Cook:** 5 min./batch

Ready in minutes, these tender homemade waffles have a crunchy topping made with brown sugar and two kinds of nuts. They make a wonderful treat for the holidays or anytime. —Christine Keating, Norwalk, California

      2 cups biscuit/baking mix
      2 tablespoons brown sugar
    1/2 teaspoon ground cinnamon
    1/4 teaspoon ground ginger
    1/4 teaspoon ground nutmeg
      1 egg
  1-1/3 cups 2% milk
      1 cup canned sweet potatoes, mashed
      2 tablespoons canola oil
      1 teaspoon vanilla extract
TOPPING:
      1 tablespoon butter
    1/2 cup chopped pecans
    1/2 cup chopped walnuts
      2 tablespoons brown sugar
      1 tablespoon water
    1/8 teaspoon ground cinnamon
Dash salt
Dash ground nutmeg
Maple syrup

In a large bowl, combine the biscuit mix, brown sugar and spices. In another bowl, whisk the egg, milk, sweet potatoes, oil and vanilla. Stir into dry ingredients just until combined.

Bake in a preheated waffle iron according to the manufacturer's directions until golden brown.

Meanwhile, in a small skillet, melt the butter over medium heat. Add pecans and walnuts. Cook and stir for 2 minutes. Add brown sugar, water, cinnamon, salt and nutmeg. Cook and stir until sugar is dissolved. Serve waffles with topping and syrup. **Yield:** 12 waffles.

All-Star Muffin Mix

(Pictured below)

Prep/Total Time: 30 min.

You can keep this handy starter in your pantry or freezer. I love the fact that one mix can create so many different varieties of muffins, from carrot-raisin to cappuccino.
—Nancy Mackey, Madison, Ohio

    8 cups all-purpose flour
    3 cups sugar
    3 tablespoons baking powder
    2 teaspoons salt
    2 teaspoons ground cinnamon
    2 teaspoons ground nutmeg
ADDITIONAL INGREDIENTS:
    1 egg
    1 cup 2% milk
    1/2 cup butter, melted
FOR BANANA MUFFINS:
    1 cup mashed ripe bananas (about 2 medium)
FOR BLUEBERRY MUFFINS:
    1 cup fresh *or* frozen blueberries
FOR CRANBERRY-PECAN MUFFINS:
    1 cup chopped fresh *or* frozen cranberries
    1/2 cup chopped pecans
    3 tablespoons sugar
FOR APRICOT-CHERRY MUFFINS:
    1/2 cup chopped dried apricots
    1/2 cup dried cherries
FOR CAPPUCCINO MUFFINS:
    1 cup miniature semisweet chocolate chips
    2 teaspoons instant coffee granules
FOR CARROT-RAISIN MUFFINS:
    3/4 cup shredded carrots
    1/3 cup golden raisins
FOR APPLE-CHEESE MUFFINS:
    1/2 cup shredded peeled apple
    1/2 cup shredded Colby-Monterey Jack cheese
FOR RHUBARB-ORANGE MUFFINS:
    3/4 cup diced fresh *or* frozen rhubarb
    1/3 cup orange marmalade

In a large bowl, combine the first six ingredients. Store in airtight containers in a cool dry place or in the freezer for up to 6 months. **Yield:** 4 batches (11 cups).

To prepare plain muffins: Place 2-3/4 cups muffin mix in a large bowl. Whisk the egg, milk and butter; stir into dry ingredients just until moistened. Fill paper-lined muffin cups three-fourths full. Bake at 400° for 18-21 minutes or until a toothpick comes out clean. Cool for 5 minutes before removing to a wire rack. Serve warm.

To prepare Banana Muffins: Place 2-3/4 cups muffin mix in a large bowl. Whisk the egg, milk, butter and bananas; stir into dry ingredients just until moistened. Fill muffin cups and bake as directed for plain muffins.

To prepare Blueberry Muffins: Place 2-3/4 cups muffin mix in a large bowl. Whisk the egg, milk and butter; stir into dry ingredients just until moistened. Fold in blueberries. Fill muffin cups and bake as directed for plain muffins.

To prepare Cranberry-Pecan Muffins: In a large bowl, combine 2-3/4 cups muffin mix, cranberries, pecans and sugar. Whisk the egg, milk and butter; stir into dry ingredients just until moistened. Fill muffin cups and bake as directed for plain muffins.

To prepare Apricot-Cherry Muffins: In a large bowl, combine 2-3/4 cups muffin mix, apricots and cherries. Whisk the egg, milk and butter; stir into dry ingredients just until moistened. Fill muffin cups and bake as directed for plain muffins.

To prepare Cappuccino Muffins: In a large bowl, combine 2-3/4 cups muffin mix, chocolate chips and coffee granules. Whisk the egg, milk and butter; stir into dry ingredients just until moistened. Fill muffin cups and bake as directed for plain muffins.

To prepare Carrot-Raisin Muffins: In a large bowl, combine 2-3/4 cups muffin mix, carrots and raisins. Whisk the egg, milk and butter; stir into dry ingredients just until moistened. Fill muffin cups and bake as directed for plain muffins.

To prepare Apple-Cheese Muffins: In a large bowl, combine 2-3/4 cups muffin mix, apple and cheese. Whisk the egg, milk and butter; stir into dry ingredients just until moistened. Fill muffin cups and bake as directed for plain muffins.

To prepare Rhubarb-Orange Muffins: In a large bowl, combine 2-3/4 cups muffin mix, rhubarb and orange marmalade. Whisk the egg, milk and butter; stir into dry ingredients just until moistened. Fill muffin cups and bake as directed for plain muffins. **Yield:** 1 dozen per batch.

FRESH ADVICE

Have extra muffins after baking a batch of them using All-Star Muffin Mix (recipe above)? To keep those or other muffins fresh and flavorful for several days, it's important to store them properly.

Muffins are often quite moist. To prevent them from spoiling, let them cool completely after coming out of the oven, then wrap them tightly in foil or plastic wrap and let them stand overnight. Refrigerate any leftover muffins the next day.

Peach & Sausage Breakfast Squares
(Pictured above and on page 176)
Prep: 15 min. **Bake:** 30 min.

The combination of ingredients may sound unusual, but this breakfast bake is delicious! Sausage, peaches and pancake mix come together for a complete meal in one.
—*Judith Bowden, Sanford, North Carolina*

    1 can (15-1/4 ounces) sliced peaches
1/4 cup sugar
    1 tablespoon cornstarch
3/4 cup maple syrup
    1 tablespoon butter
    2 cups pancake mix
    1 egg, beaten
    2 tablespoons canola oil
    1 package (7 ounces) brown-and-serve
       sausage links, halved lengthwise

Drain peaches, reserving the juice; set aside. In a small saucepan, combine sugar and cornstarch; stir in 1/2 cup reserved peach juice until smooth. Bring to a boil. Cook and stir for 1-2 minutes or until thickened. Stir in syrup and butter; set aside and keep warm.

Combine the remaining juice and enough water to measure 1 cup. In a small bowl, combine pancake mix, egg, oil and juice mixture. Pour into a greased 13-in. x 9-in. baking dish. Arrange the sausages and peaches over the top.

Bake, uncovered, at 350° for 30-40 minutes or until a toothpick inserted near the center comes out clean. Cut into squares; serve warm with peach syrup. **Yield:** 6 servings.

Hearty Sausage 'n' Hash Browns
Prep/Total Time: 30 min.

Rich and meaty, this scrumptious skillet dish has a smoky flavor and cheesy topping. The recipe is quick to fix and just as good for a late-night supper as it is for breakfast.
—*Violet Beard, Marshall, Illinois*

    4 cups frozen cubed hash brown potatoes
1/4 cup chopped green pepper
1/3 cup canola oil
1/4 pound smoked sausage, halved lengthwise
       and cut into 1/4-inch slices
    3 slices process American cheese

In a large skillet, cook potatoes and pepper in oil over medium heat until potatoes are golden brown. Stir in sausage; heat through. Remove from heat; top with cheese. Cover and let stand for 5 minutes or until cheese is melted. **Yield:** 3 servings.

Pat dough into a 9-in. x 7-in. rectangle. Cut in half horizontally. Cut each half into four rectangles; separate and place on a greased baking sheet. Brush with the remaining cream. Bake at 400° for 20-25 minutes or until golden brown. Cool on a wire rack for 5 minutes.

For glaze, in a small bowl, combine the confectioners' sugar, lemon juice, butter and milk; drizzle over warm scones. **Yield:** 8 scones.

Corned Beef Hash
(Pictured below)

Prep/Total Time: 20 min.

Chock-full of eggs, potatoes and corned beef, this hearty scramble is great any time of day. Serve it with a side of Texas toast and just wait for the compliments!
—Susanna Bellamy, Cremona, Alberta

　　3 tablespoons butter, *divided*
　　4 cups refrigerated diced potatoes with onion
1-1/2 cups leftover cooked corned beef, diced
　　1 medium green pepper, diced
　　1 cup sliced fresh mushrooms
　　1 teaspoon salt
　　6 eggs
　1/2 teaspoon pepper

In a large skillet, melt 2 tablespoons butter; stir in the potatoes, corned beef, green pepper, mushrooms and salt. Cook, covered, over medium heat for 10-12 minutes or until vegetables are tender, stirring occasionally.

Meanwhile, in a small bowl, whisk eggs and pepper. In another skillet, heat remaining butter over medium heat. Add the egg mixture; cook and stir until the eggs are completely set. Stir into the potato mixture. **Yield:** 6 servings.

Strawberry Scones
With Lemon Glaze
(Pictured above)

Prep: 25 min.　**Bake:** 20 min.

You won't believe how tender these rich, buttery scones are. Plus, the lemony glaze adds a burst of sweet-tart flavor and a pretty finishing touch. Whip up a batch for your next Sunday brunch, at holiday time or whenever you want a treat.
　　—Kathy Harding, Richmond, Missouri

　　2 cups all-purpose flour
　　2 tablespoons sugar
　　1 tablespoon baking powder
　1/2 teaspoon salt
　　5 tablespoons cold butter
1-1/4 cups plus 2 tablespoons heavy whipping
　　　　cream, *divided*
　　1 cup frozen unsweetened strawberries,
　　　　chopped
GLAZE:
　　2 cups confectioners' sugar
　　3 tablespoons lemon juice
　　1 tablespoon butter, melted
　　1 tablespoon 2% milk

In a large bowl, combine the flour, sugar, baking powder and salt. Cut in butter until mixture resembles coarse crumbs. Stir in 1-1/4 cups cream just until moistened. Fold in strawberries. Turn onto a floured surface; knead 10 times.

Italian Mini-Frittatas

(Pictured above)

Prep: 20 min. **Bake:** 15 min.

These adorable miniature frittatas from the Taste of Home Test Kitchen bake in under 15 minutes, so they're nice for special events or breakfasts on the run.

    1 cup coarsely shredded yellow summer
      squash
    1 cup coarsely shredded zucchini
    1 cup chopped fresh mushrooms
    2 tablespoons butter
  1/2 teaspoon salt
  1/4 teaspoon pepper
  1/2 cup all-purpose flour
    4 eggs, beaten
    5 tablespoons chopped ripe olives, *divided*
    2 tablespoons grated Parmesan cheese
    1 teaspoon dried basil
  1/2 teaspoon garlic salt
    1 small onion, thinly sliced
  1/2 cup diced grape tomatoes
  1/2 cup shredded Monterey Jack cheese
English muffins, split and toasted, optional

In a large nonstick skillet, saute squash and mushrooms in the butter until tender. Season with salt and pepper; set aside.

In a bowl, whisk flour and eggs until smooth. Stir in reserved vegetables and 1/4 cup olives. Coat 12 muffin cups with cooking spray; fill half full with egg mixture. Bake at 450° for 6-8 minutes or until set.

Combine the Parmesan cheese, basil and garlic salt; sprinkle over egg mixture. Combine the onion, tomatoes and remaining olives; spoon over the top. Sprinkle with Monterey Jack cheese. Bake for 5 minutes or until the cheese is melted. Serve on English muffins if desired. **Yield:** 6 servings.

Sweet Potato Muffins

(Pictured below)

Prep/Total Time: 25 min.

I came up with this muffin recipe and prepare it often, especially for guests. My grandchildren gobble these up.
—Christine Johnson, Ricetown, Kentucky

    2 cups self-rising flour
    2 cups sugar
    2 teaspoons ground cinnamon
    1 egg
    2 cups cold mashed sweet potatoes (without
      added butter or milk)
    1 cup canola oil
GLAZE:
    1 cup confectioners' sugar
    2 tablespoons plus 1-1/2 teaspoons 2% milk
1-1/2 teaspoons butter, melted
    1 teaspoon vanilla extract
  1/2 teaspoon ground cinnamon

In a small bowl, combine the flour, sugar and cinnamon. In another bowl, whisk the egg, sweet potatoes and oil. Stir into dry ingredients just until moistened.

Fill greased muffin cups two-thirds full. Bake at 375° for 15-18 minutes or until a toothpick comes out clean. Cool for 5 minutes before removing from pans to wire racks. In a small bowl, combine glaze ingredients; drizzle over warm muffins. **Yield:** 2 dozen.

Editor's Note: As a substitute for each cup of self-rising flour, place 1-1/2 teaspoons baking powder and 1/2 teaspoon salt in a measuring cup. Add all-purpose flour to measure 1 cup.

Brunch Pizza
(Pictured below)

Prep: 35 min. **Bake:** 15 min.

This breakfast-style pizza is one of our favorite morning dishes. Filling and satisfying with lots of veggies, it brings raves whenever I serve it to guests for brunch.
—Marty Schwartz, Sarasota, Florida

- 1 tube (8 ounces) refrigerated crescent rolls
- 1/2 pound sliced bacon, chopped
- 1/2 pound bulk pork sausage
- 1/2 pound sliced fresh mushrooms
- 1 small onion, finely chopped
- 1 small green pepper, finely chopped
- 1 tablespoon butter
- 8 eggs, lightly beaten
- 1 package (3 ounces) cream cheese, softened
- 1/3 cup sour cream
- 1 garlic clove, minced
- 1/4 teaspoon Italian seasoning
- 2 plum tomatoes, chopped
- 1-1/2 cups (6 ounces) shredded part-skim mozzarella cheese
- Picante sauce and additional sour cream, optional

Unroll the crescent dough into a greased 13-in. x 9-in. baking dish; seal seams and perforations. Bake at 375° for 6-8 minutes or until golden brown.

Meanwhile, in a small skillet, cook bacon and sausage over medium heat until bacon is crisp and sausage is no longer pink. Using a slotted spoon, remove meat to paper towels; drain, reserving 2 tablespoons drippings. In the drippings, saute the mushrooms, onion and green pepper. Remove and set aside.

Heat butter in a large skillet over medium heat. Add eggs; cook and stir until almost set.

In a small bowl, beat the cream cheese, sour cream, garlic and Italian seasoning; spread over crust. Layer

with eggs, sausage and bacon, sauteed vegetables, tomatoes and mozzarella.

Bake at 375° for 15-18 minutes or until cheese is melted. Serve with picante sauce and additional sour cream if desired. **Yield:** 12 pieces.

Spinach & Sausage Egg Bake
(Pictured above)

Prep: 20 min. **Bake:** 30 min.

I've made this zippy egg bake for my coworkers, and it always disappears in no time. You'll want to keep the leftovers, too! Simply pop a serving in the microwave for a few seconds, and it's just as good as fresh.
—Paula Crockett, West Columbia, South Carolina

- 1 pound bulk pork sausage
- 1 package (10 ounces) frozen chopped spinach, thawed and squeezed dry
- 6 bacon strips, cooked and crumbled
- 1/4 cup finely chopped onion
- 1/4 cup finely chopped sweet red pepper
- 1 cup (4 ounces) shredded Monterey Jack cheese
- 1 cup (4 ounces) shredded cheddar cheese
- 10 eggs
- 3/4 cup 2% milk
- 2 teaspoons snipped fresh dill *or* 1/2 teaspoon dill weed
- 1-1/2 teaspoons chili powder
- 1 teaspoon garlic powder
- 1 teaspoon pepper
- 1/4 teaspoon salt

In a large skillet, cook sausage over medium heat until no longer pink; drain. Spoon into a greased 13-in. x 9-in. baking dish. Layer with spinach, bacon, onion, red pepper and cheeses.

In a large bowl, beat the eggs, milk and seasonings; pour over top. Bake at 375° for 30-35 minutes or until a knife inserted near the center comes out clean. Let stand for 5 minutes before cutting. **Yield:** 12 servings.

Lemon-Blueberry Muffins
(Pictured below)

Prep: 30 min. **Bake:** 25 min.

Bursting with berries and drizzled with a light, lemony glaze, these muffins are moist, tender and truly something special. They're a great treat for family and friends.
—Kathy Harding, Richmond, Missouri

      1/2 cup butter, softened
        1 cup sugar
        2 eggs
      1/2 cup 2% milk
        2 tablespoons lemon juice
        2 teaspoons grated lemon peel
        2 cups all-purpose flour
        2 teaspoons baking powder
Dash salt
        2 cups fresh *or* frozen blueberries
GLAZE:
  1-1/2 cups confectioners' sugar
        2 tablespoons lemon juice
        1 teaspoon butter, melted
      1/4 teaspoon vanilla extract

In a large bowl, cream butter and sugar until light and fluffy. Add eggs, one at a time, beating well after each addition. Beat in milk, lemon juice and peel. Combine the flour, baking powder and salt; add to creamed mixture just until moistened. Fold in blueberries.

Fill paper-lined muffin cups three-fourths full. Bake at 400° for 25-30 minutes or until a toothpick inserted in muffin comes out clean. Cool for 5 minutes before removing from pan to a wire rack.

In a small bowl, combine the confectioners' sugar, lemon juice, butter and vanilla; drizzle over warm muffins. **Yield:** 11 muffins.

Editor's Note: If using frozen blueberries, use without thawing to avoid discoloring the batter.

Chocolate Chip Zucchini Bread
(Pictured above)

Prep: 20 min. **Bake:** 1 hour + cooling

Every summer, my mom and I try to bake as many loaves of this yummy zucchini bread as possible. It's hard—my five children eat them as soon as they're cool enough!
—Beth Sine, Faulkner, Maryland

        3 cups all-purpose flour
        2 cups sugar
        3 teaspoons ground cinnamon
        1 teaspoon baking soda
        1 teaspoon salt
      1/2 teaspoon baking powder
        3 eggs
        1 cup canola oil
        3 teaspoons vanilla extract
        2 cups shredded zucchini
  1-1/2 cups semisweet chocolate chips
        1 can (8 ounces) unsweetened crushed
          pineapple, drained

In a large bowl, combine the flour, sugar, cinnamon, baking soda, salt and baking powder. In a small bowl, whisk the eggs, oil and vanilla. Stir into dry ingredients just until moistened. Fold in the remaining ingredients.

Transfer to two greased 8-in. x 4-in. loaf pans. Bake at 350° for 60-65 minutes or until a toothpick inserted near the center comes out clean. Cool for 10 minutes before removing from pans to wire racks. **Yield:** 2 loaves (12 slices each).

PICK OF THE CROP

To pick the freshest zucchini for your recipes, look for a firm, heavy squash that has a moist stem end and a shiny skin. Smaller squash are generally sweeter and more tender than larger ones.

Apple Pancakes with Cider Syrup
(Pictured above)

Prep/Total Time: 30 min.

What a delightful way to start the day! Sweet apple flavor fills every delectable bite of these flapjacks. For an extra treat, top them with sour cream before adding the syrup.
—Janet Vardaman, Zephyrhills, Florida

2 cups complete pancake mix
1-1/2 cups water
3/4 cup grated apple
1/2 teaspoon ground cinnamon
CIDER SYRUP:
1/2 cup sugar
1 tablespoon cornstarch
1/8 teaspoon ground cinnamon
1/8 teaspoon ground nutmeg
1 cup apple cider *or* juice
2 tablespoons butter, cubed
1 tablespoon lemon juice

In a small bowl, stir the pancake mix, water, apple and cinnamon just until moistened.

Pour batter by 1/4 cupfuls onto a greased hot griddle; turn when bubbles form on top. Cook until second side is golden brown.

Meanwhile, for syrup, in a small saucepan, combine the sugar, cornstarch, cinnamon and nutmeg. Stir in cider until smooth. Cook and stir over medium-high heat until thickened and bubbly, about 5 minutes. Reduce heat to low; cook and stir 2 minutes longer. Stir in butter and lemon juice. Serve with pancakes. **Yield:** 12 pancakes (1-1/4 cups syrup).

Enchilada Hash Brown Casserole
(Pictured below)

Prep: 15 min. **Bake:** 40 min. + standing

Here's a wonderfully different combination of Mexican flavors that's guaranteed to spice up any family brunch, breakfast or supper. You'll want to try this delicious casserole soon—it just may become a new favorite!
—Geraldine Saucier, Albuquerque, New Mexico

1-1/2 cups enchilada sauce
1 garlic clove, minced
1 teaspoon onion powder
1/2 teaspoon pepper
1/4 teaspoon ground coriander
1/8 teaspoon ground cumin
3 cups frozen cubed hash brown potatoes, thawed
1-1/4 cups (5 ounces) shredded Mexican cheese blend, *divided*
1 cup cubed fully cooked ham
1 cup canned black beans, rinsed and drained
1 can (4 ounces) chopped green chilies
6 eggs
2 tablespoons butter

In a large bowl, combine the first six ingredients; stir in potatoes, 1 cup cheese, ham, beans and green chilies. Transfer to a greased 8-in. square baking dish; sprinkle with remaining cheese.

Cover and bake at 350° for 30 minutes. Uncover; bake 10-15 minutes longer or until heated through and cheese is melted. Let stand for 10 minutes.

Meanwhile, in a large skillet, fry eggs in butter as desired. Serve with casserole. **Yield:** 6 servings.

Spinach & Bacon Hash Brown Quiche
(Pictured below)

Prep: 25 min. **Bake:** 25 min. + standing

With a crust of crispy hash browns and a rich, creamy filling featuring spinach and bacon, this cheesy quiche is comfort food at its most satisfying. Don't save this for mornings—it's terrific for a luncheon or dinner, too.
—*Sonya Labbe, Santa Monica, California*

    3 cups frozen shredded hash brown potatoes,
        thawed
    1/4 cup butter, melted
      6 bacon strips, diced
      1 small onion, chopped
      3 eggs
      1 cup half-and-half cream
    1/4 teaspoon salt
    1/8 teaspoon pepper
      2 cups chopped fresh spinach
    2/3 cup shredded part-skim mozzarella cheese
    1/3 cup shredded Swiss cheese

Press hash browns between paper towels to remove excess moisture; toss with butter. Press onto the bottom and up the sides of a 9-in. pie plate. Bake at 425° for 20-25 minutes or until edges are browned.

Meanwhile, in a large skillet, cook bacon and onion over medium heat until bacon is crisp. Remove to paper towels to drain. In a large bowl, combine the eggs, cream, salt and pepper. Stir in the spinach, cheeses and bacon mixture; pour into crust.

Bake at 350° for 25-30 minutes or until a knife inserted near the center comes out clean. Let quiche stand for 10 minutes before cutting. **Yield:** 6 servings.

Spicy Egg Bake
(Pictured above)

Prep/Total Time: 30 min.

This baked egg dish makes a great brunch offering served with muffins and fresh fruit. It's also a simple way to use up extra taco meat from dinner the night before. Adjust the heat by choosing a hotter or milder salsa.
—*Michelle Jibben, Springfield, Minnesota*

      1 tube (8 ounces) refrigerated crescent rolls
    10 eggs
    1/3 cup water
      3 tablespoons butter
    1-1/2 cups prepared taco meat
      1 cup (4 ounces) shredded cheddar cheese
      1 cup (4 ounces) shredded Monterey Jack
        cheese
      1 cup salsa

Unroll crescent roll dough into a greased 13-in. x 9-in. baking dish. Seal seams and perforations; set aside.

In a small bowl, whisk eggs and water. In a large skillet, heat butter until hot. Add egg mixture; cook and stir over medium heat until eggs are almost set. Remove from the heat.

Sprinkle the taco meat over the dough. Layer with eggs, cheeses and salsa. Bake, uncovered, at 375° for 14-16 minutes or until bubbly and cheese is melted. **Yield:** 8 servings.

CHAPTER 12

Quick Soups & Sandwiches

Warm up a wintry day with a steaming bowl of Spicy Fajita Chili...savor a fast but filling lunch of Egg Salad Pockets... whenever you're craving the comfort of a soup or sandwich, this is the chapter for you!

You'll enjoy family favorites as well as new twists on classics. From Caesar Chicken Burgers and Fruited Tuna Salad Pitas to Potato-Lentil Stew and Ham & Corn Chowder, these irresistible creations are guaranteed to please everyone at the table.

Plus, most of the recipes are ready to serve in just 30 minutes or less! So you won't need to spend hours in the kitchen before you can sit down to a home-cooked meal. ■

DOUBLY DELECTABLE. Creamy Tomato Soup and Grilled Tomato-Cheese Sandwiches (both recipes on p. 193).

Spicy Fajita Chili

(Pictured below)

Prep: 15 min. **Cook:** 30 min.

You'll want to serve this with fresh-baked rolls or corn bread to soak up every delicious drop. Prefer more heat? Just choose spicier versions of V8 juice and chili beans.
—Cathy Bell, Joplin, Missouri

1-1/2 pounds ground pork
  1 medium onion, chopped
  1 medium green pepper, chopped
  1 medium sweet red pepper, chopped
  1 garlic clove, minced
  2 cans (11-1/2 ounces *each*) V8 juice
  1 can (16 ounces) chili beans, undrained
  1 can (10 ounces) diced tomatoes and
     green chilies
  2 tablespoons chili powder
  1 teaspoon seasoned salt
1/2 teaspoon seasoned pepper
Shredded cheddar cheese

In a Dutch oven, cook the ground pork, onion, peppers and garlic over medium heat until the meat is no longer pink; drain.

Stir in the V8 juice, beans, tomatoes, chili powder, seasoned salt and seasoned pepper. Bring to a boil. Reduce heat; simmer, uncovered, for 20 minutes or until slightly thickened. Serve with cheese. **Yield:** 8 servings (2 quarts).

Chipotle Roast Beef Sandwiches

(Pictured above)

Prep/Total Time: 25 min.

Rustic ciabatta bread is the perfect choice for this simple yet tasty sandwich featuring tender roast beef, bold blue cheese and chipotle. You'll love it! —Andre Houseknecht South Williamsport, Pennsylvania

  1 loaf (14 ounces) ciabatta bread, halved
     lengthwise
2/3 cup mayonnaise
  1 tablespoon chipotle pepper in adobo sauce,
     chopped
  1 small garlic clove, minced
  1 teaspoon lime juice
1/4 teaspoon pepper
1/8 teaspoon salt
1/2 cup crumbled blue cheese
3/4 pound sliced deli roast beef
  1 small onion, thinly sliced
  1 medium tomato, sliced
  4 lettuce leaves

Place the halves of ciabatta bread, cut side up, on a baking sheet. Broil 3-4 in. from the heat for 2-3 minutes or until toasted.

Meanwhile, in a small bowl, combine the mayonnaise, chipotle pepper, garlic, lime juice, pepper and salt; spread over the cut sides of bread. Sprinkle the bottom half of bread with blue cheese. Layer with the roast beef, onion, tomato and lettuce; replace top. Cut into four sandwiches. **Yield:** 4 servings.

Asian Chicken Noodle Soup
(Pictured below)
Prep: 15 min. **Cook:** 40 min.

One night I didn't have any noodles to put in my chicken soup, so I gave it an Asian twist with strips of wonton wrappers instead. It was great! You won't want to skip the celery leaves; they bring extra flavor to every bowlful.
—Noelle Myers, Grand Forks, North Dakota

1-1/2 pounds boneless skinless chicken breasts, cut
    into 1-inch cubes
   1 tablespoon sesame oil
   3 medium carrots, sliced
   2 celery ribs, chopped
   1 medium onion, chopped
   6 cups chicken broth
 1/3 cup teriyaki sauce
 1/4 cup chili garlic sauce
   1 package (12 ounces) wonton wrappers,
    cut into 1/4-inch strips
   2 cups sliced fresh shiitake mushrooms
 1/3 cup chopped celery leaves
 1/4 cup minced fresh basil
   2 tablespoons minced fresh cilantro
   2 green onions, sliced

In a Dutch oven, cook the chicken in sesame oil over medium heat until no longer pink. Remove and keep warm. In the same pan, saute the carrots, celery and onion until tender.

Stir in chicken broth, teriyaki sauce, garlic sauce and chicken. Bring to a boil. Reduce heat; simmer, uncovered, for 20 minutes.

Add the wonton strips, mushrooms, celery leaves, basil and cilantro. Cook and stir for 4-5 minutes or until wonton strips and mushrooms are tender. Sprinkle with green onions. **Yield:** 10 servings (2-1/2 quarts).

Fruited Tuna Salad Pitas
(Pictured above)
Prep/Total Time: 15 min.

Bite into one of these pitas, and you'll feel like you're at a restaurant. The bistro-worthy rounds are a breeze to put together, yet they're special enough for lunch guests.
—Shelly Fisher, Hermiston, Oregon

 1/2 cup mayonnaise
   1 tablespoon honey
   1 can (12 ounces) white water-packed tuna,
    drained
   1 can (11 ounces) mandarin oranges, drained
   1 medium apple, chopped
 1/3 cup chopped pecans
   1 celery rib, thinly sliced
 1/4 cup dried cranberries
 1/8 teaspoon salt
   4 whole wheat pita breads (6 inches)
2-3/4 cups alfalfa sprouts

In a large bowl, combine mayonnaise and honey. Stir in tuna, oranges, apple, pecans, celery, berries and salt. Serve on pita breads with sprouts. **Yield:** 4 servings.

▌ BEYOND BREAD ▐

Tired of the usual sliced bread for sandwiches? Pita breads are a great way to jazz things up and bring a little variety to your lunchtime routine. You could also try hard rolls, biscuits, buns, bagels, tortillas, English muffins or even pastry shells.

Egg Salad Pockets
(Pictured above)

Prep/Total Time: 20 min.

Here's a delectable sandwich that's perfect for spring and summer outings. The pita-bread pockets keep the filling neatly contained. —*Karen Ann Bland, Gove, Kansas*

    1 package (3 ounces) cream cheese, softened
1/4 cup Miracle Whip
    1 celery rib, finely chopped
    2 tablespoons finely chopped onion
    1 tablespoon sweet pickle relish
3/4 teaspoon dill weed
1/2 teaspoon salt
1/2 teaspoon ground mustard
    6 hard-cooked eggs, chopped
    3 pita breads (6 inches), halved
    6 lettuce leaves

In a small bowl, combine cream cheese and Miracle Whip. Add the celery, onion, relish, dill weed, salt and mustard. Gently stir in eggs. Line pita halves with lettuce; fill each with 1/2 cup egg salad. **Yield:** 3 servings.

POTATO POINTERS

Select sweet potatoes that are firm with no cracks or bruises. If stored in a cool, dark, well-ventilated place, sweet potatoes will remain fresh for about 2 weeks. If the temperature is above 60°, they'll sprout sooner or become woody.

Caribbean Potato Soup
(Pictured below)

Prep/Total Time: 30 min.

The blend of vegetables in this tasty, colorful meatless soup includes okra, black-eyed peas, sweet potatoes and kale. If you don't have kale, just use spinach.
—*Crystal Bruns, Iliff, Colorado*

    2 medium onions, chopped
    2 teaspoons canola oil
    3 garlic cloves, minced
    2 teaspoons minced fresh gingerroot
    2 teaspoons ground coriander
    1 teaspoon ground turmeric
1/2 teaspoon dried thyme
1/4 teaspoon ground allspice
    5 cups vegetable broth
    2 cups cubed peeled sweet potato
    3 cups chopped fresh kale
    1 cup frozen sliced okra
    1 cup coconut milk
    1 cup canned diced tomatoes, drained
    1 cup canned black-eyed peas, rinsed and
       drained
    2 tablespoons lime juice

In a Dutch oven, saute onions in oil until tender. Add the garlic, ginger and spices; cook 1 minute longer.

Stir in broth and potato. Bring to a boil. Reduce heat; cover and simmer for 5 minutes. Stir in kale and okra. Return to a boil; cover and simmer 10 minutes longer or until potato is tender. Add the milk, tomatoes, peas and lime juice; heat through. **Yield:** 6 servings.

Creamy Tomato Soup
(Pictured above and on page 188)

Prep/Total Time: 15 min.

I first tried this at a restaurant, and the waiter revealed the ingredients. I changed the recipe a bit, and now people say it's the best tomato soup they've ever tasted.
—Beth Ann Slough, Mountville, Pennsylvania

    1 can (29 ounces) tomato sauce
    1 cup heavy whipping cream
1-1/2 teaspoons brown sugar
    1 teaspoon Italian seasoning
  1/4 teaspoon salt
  1/8 teaspoon white pepper
Dash hot pepper sauce
Salad croutons, shredded cheddar cheese, quartered grape tomatoes *and/or* thinly sliced green onions

In a large saucepan, combine the first seven ingredients. Cook and stir over medium heat until heated through (do not boil). Garnish with croutons, cheese, tomatoes and/or onions. **Yield:** 4 servings.

Grilled Tomato-Cheese Sandwiches
(Pictured above and on page 188)

Prep/Total Time: 20 min.

Give a classic sandwich an awesome twist! Turn plain ol' grilled cheese into something extra-special by using four kinds of cheese, grape tomatoes and green onion.
—Elaine Haskins, Troutville, Pennsylvania

3/4 cup grape tomatoes, chopped
  1 green onion, sliced
  8 slices Italian bread
  4 slices cheddar cheese
  4 slices Swiss cheese
  4 slices provolone cheese
  4 slices Colby-Monterey Jack cheese
  8 teaspoons butter, softened

Sprinkle the tomatoes and onion over four bread slices. Layer with cheese slices; top with the remaining bread. Butter outsides of sandwiches.

Toast on a heated griddle for 2-3 minutes on each side or until bread is golden brown and cheese is melted. **Yield:** 4 servings.

Creamy Butternut Soup

(Pictured above top)

Prep/Total Time: 30 min.

Thick and filling, this lovely soup topped with chives and a drizzle of sour cream looks as special as it tastes.
—Amanda Smith, Cincinnati, Ohio

- 1 **butternut squash, peeled, seeded and cubed (about 6 cups)**
- 5 **cups water**
- 3 **medium potatoes, peeled and cubed**
- 1 **large onion, diced**
- 2 **chicken bouillon cubes**
- 2 **garlic cloves, minced**

Sour cream and chives, optional

In a Dutch oven, combine the squash, water, potatoes, onion, bouillon and garlic. Bring to a boil. Reduce heat; cover and simmer for 15-20 minutes or until vegetables are tender.

Remove from the heat; cool slightly. In a blender, puree the mixture in batches. Return to the pan; heat through. Serve with sour cream and chives if desired. **Yield:** 10 servings (2-1/2 quarts).

Spinach Tortellini Soup
(Pictured at left)

Prep: 20 min. **Cook:** 30 min.

I'm always searching for easy recipes that fit my busy schedule, and this one is great. Try it with crusty bread.
—Jacqueline Dintino, Westminster, Maryland

- 3 small red potatoes, peeled and cubed
- 2 medium carrots, sliced
- 1 celery rib, chopped
- 1 small onion, chopped
- 2 tablespoons plus 1-1/2 teaspoons chicken bouillon granules
- 2 quarts water
- 3 cups cubed cooked chicken
- 1 package (10 ounces) frozen chopped spinach, thawed and squeezed dry
- 1 teaspoon dried parsley flakes
- 1/2 teaspoon garlic powder
- 1/2 teaspoon dried oregano
- 1/2 teaspoon pepper
- 1/4 teaspoon salt
- 2 packages (9 ounces *each*) refrigerated cheese tortellini

In a Dutch oven, combine the potatoes, carrots, celery, onion, bouillon and water. Bring to a boil. Reduce heat; cover and simmer for 10 minutes.

Stir in the chicken, spinach, parsley, garlic powder, oregano, pepper and salt; return to a boil. Add tortellini; cook, uncovered, for 7-9 minutes or until tortellini is tender. **Yield:** 10 servings (3-3/4 quarts).

Three-Cheese French Onion Soup
(Pictured far left)

Prep/Total Time: 30 min.

This satisfying blend is fantastic for chilly fall or winter days. The combination of Swiss, Parmesan and mozzarella gives it a richness onion-soup fans will eat up.
—Gina Berry, Chanhassen, Minnesota

- 2 large red onions, thinly sliced
- 1/4 cup butter, cubed
- 2 cans (14-1/2 ounces *each*) chicken broth
- 3 cups water
- 1 envelope onion soup mix
- 1 teaspoon pepper
- 1 teaspoon Worcestershire sauce
- 1/2 teaspoon garlic powder
- 7 slices French bread (3/4 inch thick)
- 1/2 cup shredded Swiss cheese
- 1/2 cup shredded part-skim mozzarella cheese
- 1/4 cup grated Parmesan cheese

In a Dutch oven, saute onions in butter until tender. Add chicken broth, water, soup mix, pepper, Worcestershire sauce and garlic powder. Bring to a boil. Reduce heat; cover and simmer for 5 minutes.

Meanwhile, place the bread slices on an ungreased baking sheet. Sprinkle with the Swiss and mozzarella cheeses. Broil 4 in. from the heat for 1-2 minutes or until cheese is melted. Ladle soup into serving bowls; top each with a toast slice. Sprinkle with Parmesan cheese. **Yield:** 7 servings.

Turkey & Swiss With Herbed Greens
(Pictured below)

Prep/Total Time: 30 min.

Here, a simple homemade dressing lends a burst of flavor to turkey, cheese and other classic sandwich ingredients.
—Pam Norby, Amery, Wisconsin

- 2 tablespoons balsamic vinegar
- 1 tablespoon olive oil
- 1/2 teaspoon dried oregano
- 1/4 teaspoon garlic powder
- 1/4 teaspoon dried basil
- 4 cups torn mixed salad greens
- 2 tablespoons finely chopped onion
- 16 slices multigrain bread
- 3/4 pound thinly sliced deli turkey
- 8 slices Swiss cheese
- 2 large tomatoes, sliced

In a large bowl, whisk the balsamic vinegar, oil, oregano, garlic powder and basil. Add salad greens and onion; toss to coat.

On eight slices of bread, layer turkey, Swiss cheese, tomatoes and salad greens. Top with remaining bread. **Yield:** 8 servings.

Ham & Corn Chowder
(Pictured below)

Prep/Total Time: 25 min.

Generous amounts of corn and more make this a filling favorite. It's a great way to use up leftover ham from the holidays. —*Marion St. Jean, Homosassa, Florida*

>   1 can (10 3/4 ounces) reduced-fat
>   reduced-sodium condensed cream of celery
>   soup, undiluted
> 1-1/2 cups fat-free milk
>   1 can (15-1/4 ounces) whole kernel corn,
>   drained
>   1 can (14-3/4 ounces) cream-style corn
>   1/2 cup cubed fully cooked ham
>   2 tablespoons dried minced onion
>   2 tablespoons minced fresh parsley
>   1 can (14-1/2 ounces) diced potatoes, drained
> Sour cream, shredded cheddar cheese *and/or*
>   paprika, optional

In a large saucepan, combine the soup and milk. Heat through, stirring frequently. Stir in the corn, ham, onion and parsley. Bring to a boil. Reduce heat; cover and simmer for 5 minutes. Stir in the potatoes; heat through. Garnish with sour cream, cheddar cheese and/or paprika if desired. **Yield:** 6 servings.

Summer Veggie Sandwiches
(Pictured above)

Prep/Total Time: 15 min.

These standouts are perfect for lunch or dinner. Look for pepperoncinis in the pickle/olive section of your grocery store. —*Mary Lou Timpson, Colorado City, Arizona*

>   4 ounces cream cheese, softened
>   8 slices whole wheat bread
>   1 small cucumber, sliced
>   1/2 cup alfalfa sprouts
>   2 teaspoons olive oil
>   2 teaspoons red wine vinegar
>   1 large tomato, sliced
>   4 lettuce leaves
>   3/4 cup sliced pepperoncinis
>   1 medium ripe avocado, peeled and mashed

Spread cream cheese over four slices of bread; layer with cucumber and alfalfa sprouts. Combine oil and vinegar; drizzle over the sprouts. Layer with tomato, lettuce and pepperoncinis. Spread avocado over remaining bread; place over top. **Yield:** 4 servings.

CHOWDER CHOICES

• When I have leftover au gratin potatoes, I combine them in a saucepan with sauteed chopped onions, carrots and celery. I add milk and stir for a nice rich chowder. —*Margo Seegrist, Shelton, Washington*

• A tasty potato chowder recipe can be very versatile. I like to use mine as a hearty base when making clam or corn chowder. —*Mary Jo Elam, Cedar Rapids, Iowa*

Pasta and Bean Soup

(Pictured below)

Prep: 10 min. **Cook:** 30 min.

Packed with pasta shells, ham and vegetables, this recipe transforms canned soup from ordinary to amazing.
—Julia Cox, Chesapeake, Virginia

- 1 cup cubed fully cooked ham
- 1 small onion, chopped
- 1 celery rib, chopped
- 1 garlic clove, minced
- 1 tablespoon canola oil
- 1 can (18.8 ounces) ready-to-serve chunky savory vegetable soup
- 1 can (16 ounces) kidney beans, rinsed and drained
- 1-3/4 cups water
- 2 teaspoons minced fresh thyme *or* 1/2 teaspoon dried thyme
- 1 bay leaf
- 1/8 teaspoon pepper
- 1/2 cup uncooked medium pasta shells

In a large saucepan, saute ham, onion, celery and garlic in oil for 3-4 minutes or until vegetables are tender.

Stir in the vegetable soup, kidney beans, water, thyme, bay leaf and pepper. Bring to a boil. Stir in the pasta shells. Reduce heat; simmer, uncovered, for 20-25 minutes or until pasta is tender. Discard bay leaf. **Yield:** 5 servings.

Potato-Lentil Stew

(Pictured above)

Prep: 20 min. **Cook:** 40 min.

Chock-full of nutritious veggies, this chunky main-dish soup makes a stick-to-your-ribs meatless meal the whole family will love. Pair it with a crusty loaf of bread, and dinner's done!   —Krista Goodwin, Ypsilanti, Michigan

- 1 large onion, chopped
- 2 medium carrots, chopped
- 2 teaspoons olive oil
- 4 teaspoons chili powder
- 3 garlic cloves, minced
- 3 teaspoons ground cumin
- 1 teaspoon dried oregano
- 1 carton (32 ounces) vegetable broth
- 3/4 cup dried lentils, rinsed
- 2 cans (10 ounces *each*) diced tomatoes and green chilies
- 3-1/2 cups frozen cubed hash brown potatoes, thawed
- 1 can (16 ounces) kidney beans, rinsed and drained
- 1/2 teaspoon salt
- 1/4 teaspoon pepper

In a Dutch oven, saute the onion and carrots in oil until tender. Add the chili powder, garlic, cumin and oregano; cook 1 minute longer.

Stir in broth and lentils. Bring to a boil. Reduce heat; cover and simmer for 18-22 minutes or until lentils are tender. Stir in the tomatoes, potatoes, beans, salt and pepper. Return to a boil. Reduce heat; cover and simmer 10-15 minutes longer or until potatoes are tender. **Yield:** 6 servings (2-1/2 quarts).

Caesar Chicken Burgers

(Pictured above)

Prep/Total Time: 20 min.

My family loves this casual mainstay recipe. And since it's so easy to fix, we enjoy it often. I use the indoor grill or oven to make these zippy chicken sandwiches during winter, and they're great on the barbecue in summer.
—Andrea VanDinter, Prince George, British Columbia

    4 boneless skinless chicken breast halves
        (4 ounces *each*)
1/4 teaspoon salt
1/4 teaspoon pepper
    4 slices red onion
    2 tablespoons butter, softened
    4 hamburger buns, split
    2 cups torn romaine
    1 tablespoon grated Parmesan cheese
1/2 cup creamy Caesar salad dressing, *divided*

Sprinkle chicken with salt and pepper. Grill on an indoor grill coated with cooking spray for 4-5 minutes or until juices run clear. Grill the onion slices for 4-5 minutes or until tender.

Meanwhile, spread butter over the cut sides of the hamburger buns. Place buttered side up on an ungreased baking sheet. Broil 3-4 in. from the heat for 1 minute or until golden brown.

Toss the romaine with Parmesan cheese and 1/4 cup dressing; spoon onto bun bottoms. Top with onions, chicken and remaining dressing. Replace bun tops.
Yield: 4 servings.

Vegetable Dumpling Soup

(Pictured below)

Prep: 25 min. **Cook:** 20 min.

As a busy working mother, I often rely on this soup. I can combine common pantry items to put a wholesome and hearty main dish on the table for my family to enjoy. A fruit salad is a refreshing way to round out dinner.
Graciela Sandvigen, Rochester, New York

    1 medium onion, chopped
    1 tablespoon canola oil
4-1/2 cups chicken broth
    1 package (16 ounces) frozen sugar snap
        stir-fry vegetable blend, thawed
    1 can (15-1/2 ounces) great northern beans,
        rinsed and drained
    1 teaspoon ground mustard
    1 cup biscuit/baking mix
2/3 cup cornmeal
1/4 teaspoon dried oregano
1/4 teaspoon dried basil
2/3 cup 2% milk
1/2 cup uncooked orzo pasta

In a Dutch oven, saute the onion in oil until tender. Stir in the broth, vegetable blend, beans and mustard. Bring to a boil. Reduce heat; simmer for 6-8 minutes or until heated through.

For dumplings, in a bowl, combine the baking mix, cornmeal, oregano and basil. Stir in the milk just until moistened; set aside.

Stir the orzo into soup. Drop the dumpling batter by tablespoonfuls onto simmering soup. Cover and simmer for 20 minutes or until a toothpick inserted in a dumpling comes out clean (do not lift the cover while simmering).
Yield: 6 servings (2 quarts).

Peanut Chicken Pockets
(Pictured above)

Prep/Total Time: 30 min.

A friend gave me this recipe, and it's a hit every time I serve it. The ingredients are as pleasing to the eye as they are to the palate. —Esther Davis, Chelan, Washington

- 2 cups cubed cooked chicken
- 2 celery ribs, chopped
- 1/4 cup chopped cucumber
- 1/4 cup bean sprouts
- 1/4 cup chopped peanuts
- 1/4 cup mayonnaise
- 2 green onions, chopped
- 1 tablespoon minced fresh parsley
- 1 tablespoon lemon juice
- 1/4 teaspoon salt
- 1/4 teaspoon pepper
- 4 pita breads (6 inches), halved
- 8 lettuce leaves
- 8 tomato slices

In a large bowl, combine the first 11 ingredients. Line pita halves with lettuce leaves and tomato slices. Spoon chicken mixture into pitas. **Yield:** 4 servings.

Chicken Bruschetta Sandwiches

Prep/Total Time: 25 min.

Regular bruschetta is wonderful as an hors d'oeuvre but rarely makes a meal. Inspired by that popular Italian appetizer, this satisfying sandwich adds grilled chicken to the mix of fresh plum tomatoes, basil and onion.
—Bette Giles, Dedham, Massachusetts

- 2 cups chopped plum tomatoes
- 1/2 cup minced fresh basil
- 1/3 cup finely chopped red onion
- 3/4 cup Italian salad dressing, divided
- 4 boneless skinless chicken breast halves (4 ounces *each*)
- 4 slices Italian bread (1 inch thick), toasted
- 4 slices part-skim mozzarella cheese

In a small bowl, combine the tomatoes, basil, onion and 1/2 cup salad dressing; set aside. Flatten the chicken to 1/4-in. thickness.

Grill the chicken, covered, over medium heat for 3-5 minutes on each side or until juices run clear, basting occasionally with remaining dressing.

Layer each slice of toast with a chicken breast, cheese slice and tomato mixture. **Yield:** 4 servings.

CHAPTER 13

Express Entrees

On hectic weeknights and busy weekends, you simply don't have the time to spend hours cooking up a complicated main dish. That's where this chapter comes in handy!

Each and every recipe can be prepared from start to finish in just 30 minutes—or less. In all, you get over 30 mouthwatering entrees that are on the table in only half an hour.

Southwest Beef Burritos... Seafood Pasta Alfredo...Sweet & Sour Sausage...Bacon-Chicken Club Pizza...with variety like this, you'll have a great selection to choose from, too.

And because these favorites came from time-crunched cooks just like you, you can be sure each one is a family-pleaser. ■

MAIN ATTRACTION. Hearty Red Beans & Rice (p. 212).

Orange-Glazed Pork Chops

(Pictured above)

Prep/Total Time: 30 min.

I first made these citrusy chops for my husband after we were married, and they're still one of his favorite ways to eat pork. —Amy Theis, Huron, South Dakota

  4 boneless pork loin chops (6 ounces *each*)
  1 tablespoon butter
  3 tablespoons honey
  2 tablespoons lemon juice
  2 tablespoons orange juice
  1 tablespoon soy sauce
1/8 teaspoon pepper
  2 tablespoons cold butter
  4 orange slices

In a large skillet, brown the pork chops in 1 tablespoon butter over medium heat. Combine the honey, lemon juice, orange juice, soy sauce and pepper; pour over the pork chops.

Cover and cook for 10-12 minutes or until a meat thermometer reads 160°, turning once. Remove pork chops to a serving plate; keep warm. Whisk cold butter into cooking juices until melted. Serve with pork. Garnish with orange slices. **Yield:** 4 servings.

Tomato Tart with Three Cheeses

Prep/Total Time: 30 min.

This quick and easy recipe from our Test Kitchen staff will please any pizza lovers in your home. Preparation is so simple using convenient frozen puff pastry.

  1 sheet frozen puff pastry, thawed
3/4 cup shredded part-skim mozzarella cheese
3/4 cup shredded provolone cheese
1/4 cup minced fresh basil
  4 plum tomatoes, thinly sliced
Salt and pepper to taste
1/4 cup shredded Parmesan cheese
Additional minced fresh basil

Unfold the pastry sheet on a lightly floured surface. Roll into a 12-in. square; transfer to a parchment paper-lined baking sheet. Prick with a fork.

Combine the mozzarella, provolone and basil; sprinkle over the pastry to within 1 in. of edges. Arrange tomato slices over cheese. Season with salt and pepper; sprinkle with Parmesan cheese.

Bake at 400° for 15-20 minutes or until the pastry is golden brown. Remove the tart from baking sheet to a wire rack to cool for 5 minutes. Sprinkle with additional basil. Cut into slices. Serve hot or at room temperature. **Yield:** 4 servings.

Chicken Tortellini Alfredo

(Pictured below)

Prep/Total Time: 25 min.

I frequently get home too late to spend lots of time fixing supper, so I'm always on the lookout for cooking shortcuts. Here's a great-tasting dish we enjoy often.
—Christie Wethington, Lexington, Kentucky

  1 package (9 ounces) refrigerated spinach *or* cheese tortellini
  2 cups fresh broccoli florets
  1 cup fresh baby carrots
  3 tablespoons olive oil, *divided*
  2 cups sliced fresh mushrooms
  1 large onion, cut into wedges
1-1/2 teaspoons minced garlic

3/4 pound boneless skinless chicken breasts,
   cut into strips
1 jar (15 ounces) Alfredo sauce
1/4 teaspoon Italian seasoning
1/4 teaspoon dried basil
1/4 teaspoon dried oregano

Cook the tortellini according to the package directions. Meanwhile, in a large skillet, saute broccoli and carrots in 2 tablespoons oil for 5-6 minutes or until crisp-tender. Stir in mushrooms, onion and garlic; saute the vegetables 3-4 minutes longer or until the vegetables are tender. Remove vegetables and keep warm.

In the same skillet, cook chicken in remaining oil over medium heat for 4-6 minutes or until no longer pink. Return vegetables to the skillet. Stir in Alfredo sauce and seasonings; heat through. Drain tortellini; add to chicken mixture. Toss to coat. **Yield:** 6 servings.

Mixed Paella
(Pictured above)

Prep/Total Time: 30 min.

Packed with chicken, shrimp, rice and veggies, this filling main dish will make a complete meal served alongside a tossed green salad...or even all by itself. I bring leftovers to work for lunch.   —Libby Walp, Chicago, Illinois

1-1/4 pounds boneless skinless chicken breasts,
   thinly sliced
2 tablespoons olive oil
1 medium onion, chopped
2 garlic cloves, minced
2-1/4 cups chicken broth
1 cup uncooked long grain rice
1 teaspoon dried oregano
1/2 teaspoon ground turmeric
1/2 teaspoon paprika
1/4 teaspoon salt
1/4 to 1/2 teaspoon pepper
1 pound cooked medium shrimp, peeled and
   deveined
1 can (14-1/2 ounces) diced tomatoes,
   undrained
3/4 cup frozen peas, thawed
1/2 cup sliced pimiento-stuffed olives

In a large skillet, saute the chicken in oil until no longer pink. Remove and keep warm. In the same skillet, saute onion until tender. Add garlic; cook 1 minute longer. Stir in the broth, rice and seasonings. Bring to a boil. Reduce heat; cover and simmer for 15-18 minutes or until the rice is tender.

Stir in the shrimp, tomatoes, peas, olives and chicken; cover and cook for 3-4 minutes or until heated through. **Yield:** 6 servings.

Peanut Chicken Stir-Fry
(Pictured below)

Prep/Total Time: 30 min.

This Asian pasta dish gets a touch of heat from crushed red pepper. The recipe calls for broccoli and carrots, but you could add some frozen stir-fry veggies, too.
—Lisa Erickson, Ripon, Wisconsin

    8 ounces uncooked thick rice noodles
  1/3 cup water
  1/4 cup reduced-sodium soy sauce
  1/4 cup peanut butter
4-1/2 teaspoons brown sugar
    1 tablespoon lemon juice
    2 garlic cloves, minced
  1/2 teaspoon crushed red pepper flakes
    1 pound boneless skinless chicken breasts,
      cut into 1/2-inch strips
    2 tablespoons canola oil, *divided*
    1 bunch broccoli, cut into florets
  1/2 cup shredded carrot

Cook the noodles according to the package directions. Meanwhile, in a small bowl, combine water, soy sauce, peanut butter, brown sugar, lemon juice, garlic and red pepper flakes; set aside.

In a large skillet or wok, stir-fry chicken in 1 tablespoon oil until no longer pink. Remove and keep warm. Stir-fry broccoli and carrot in remaining oil for 4-6 minutes or until vegetables are crisp-tender. Stir the sauce mixture; add the sauce and chicken to skillet. Return the chicken to skillet. Drain the noodles; toss with chicken mixture. **Yield:** 6 servings.

Smothered Home-Style Chicken
(Pictured above)

Prep/Total Time: 30 min.

Here is comfort food at its best! My favorite way to serve this is over basmati rice that's sauteed in butter for about a minute, then cooked in chicken stock and water.
—Billy Hensley, Temperance, Michigan

  1/3 cup all-purpose flour
    1 teaspoon salt
    1 teaspoon garlic powder
    1 teaspoon Cajun seasoning
    1 teaspoon pepper
    5 boneless skinless chicken thighs (about
      1-1/2 pounds)
    3 tablespoons olive oil, *divided*
    2 medium carrots, chopped
    1 small onion, chopped
  1/2 cup chopped green pepper
    2 garlic cloves, minced
  1/2 cup white wine *or* chicken broth
    1 can (10-3/4 ounces) condensed cream of
      chicken soup, undiluted
  1/2 cup chicken broth
Hot cooked rice

In a large resealable plastic bag, combine the flour, salt, garlic powder, Cajun seasoning and pepper. Add chicken thighs, one at a time, and shake to coat. In a large skillet, brown chicken in 2 tablespoons oil in batches. Remove and keep warm.

In the same skillet, saute the carrots, onion and green pepper in remaining oil until tender. Add garlic; cook 1 minute longer. Add wine, stirring to loosen browned bits from pan. Stir in soup and broth.

Return chicken to skillet. Bring to a boil. Reduce heat; cover and simmer for 10-15 minutes or until the chicken juices run clear. Serve with rice. **Yield:** 5 servings.

Bacon & Rosemary Chicken
(Pictured below)
Prep/Total Time: 30 min.

Simple ingredients—chicken, bacon and seasonings—combine for simply fantastic flavor in this recipe. It comes together in a mere 30 minutes on the stovetop. You'll need just one pan, so you won't have to spend a lot of time on cleanup, either.
—*Yvonne Starlin, Hermitage, Tennessee*

    4 boneless skinless chicken breast halves
      (5 ounces *each*)
1/2 teaspoon salt
1/4 teaspoon pepper
1/4 cup all-purpose flour
    5 bacon strips, chopped
    1 tablespoon butter
    4 garlic cloves, thinly sliced
    1 tablespoon minced fresh rosemary *or*
      1 teaspoon dried rosemary, crushed
1/8 teaspoon crushed red pepper flakes
    1 cup reduced-sodium chicken broth
    2 tablespoons lemon juice

Flatten the chicken breasts to an even thickness; sprinkle with salt and pepper. Place the flour in a large resealable plastic bag. Add the chicken breasts, one at a time, and shake to coat.

In a large skillet, cook bacon over medium heat until crisp. Remove to paper towels with a slotted spoon; drain, reserving 2 tablespoons bacon drippings. Cook the chicken in the butter and reserved drippings for 4-6 minutes on each side or until a meat thermometer reads 170°. Remove and keep warm.

Add the garlic, rosemary and red pepper flakes to the skillet; cook for 1 minute. Add the chicken broth and lemon juice; bring to a boil. Cook until liquid is reduced by half. Return the chicken and bacon to the skillet; heat through. **Yield:** 4 servings.

Cranberry-Maple Pork Chops
(Pictured above)
Prep/Total Time: 30 min.

Featuring a sweet sauce with a hint of maple syrup, these juicy pork chops are company-special but easy enough for weeknights. Try a side of roasted potato wedges or rice.
—*Heather Bates, Athens, Maine*

    6 boneless pork loin chops (5 ounces *each*)
1/2 teaspoon salt
1/2 teaspoon pepper
    2 tablespoons butter
    1 can (14 ounces) whole-berry cranberry
      sauce
1/3 cup grape jelly
    2 tablespoons ketchup
    1 tablespoon soy sauce
1/3 cup maple syrup

Sprinkle the pork chops with salt and pepper. In a large skillet, brown the pork chops in the butter. Remove and keep warm.

In the same skillet, combine cranberry sauce, grape jelly, ketchup and soy sauce; cook and stir until blended. Return chops to the pan; drizzle with syrup. Bring to a boil. Reduce heat; cover and simmer for 15-20 minutes or until meat is tender. **Yield:** 6 servings.

Hearty Sausage Stew
(Pictured above)

Prep/Total Time: 30 min.

My daughters shared this recipe with me, and I've since passed it on to many others. The two-sausage stew with pasta and veggies is economical, quick and delicious.
—Nellie Lamb, Muskogee, Oklahoma

- 1/2 pound fresh kielbasa *or* Polish sausage links, cut into 1/2-inch slices
- 1/2 pound Italian sausage links, cut into 1/2-inch slices
- 1 medium onion, chopped
- 1 medium green pepper, chopped
- 3-1/2 cups beef broth
- 1 can (14-1/2 ounces) diced tomatoes, undrained
- 1 cup apple juice
- 1 tablespoon minced fresh parsley
- 1 garlic clove, minced
- 1/4 teaspoon dried basil
- 1/4 teaspoon dried oregano
- 4 ounces uncooked spiral pasta

In a large saucepan, cook the sausages over medium heat until no longer pink. Remove with a slotted spoon; drain, reserving 2 tablespoons drippings.

In the drippings, saute the onion and pepper until crisp-tender. Stir in broth, tomatoes, apple juice, parsley, garlic, basil, oregano and sausages. Bring to a boil; add pasta. Reduce heat; cover and simmer for 10-15 minutes or until pasta is tender. **Yield:** 4 servings.

Greek Pizzas

Prep/Total Time: 20 min.

This is fast, fresh and packed with Mediterranean flavor from the artichokes, feta cheese, Greek olives, herbs and flatbread crust. —Cathi Schuett, Omaha, Nebraska

- 2 Italian herb flatbread wraps
- 1 tablespoon Greek vinaigrette
- 1/2 cup crumbled feta cheese
- 1/4 cup grated Parmesan cheese
- 1/2 cup pitted Greek olives, sliced
- 1/2 cup water-packed artichoke hearts, rinsed, drained and chopped

1/2 cup ready-to-use grilled chicken breast
   strips, chopped
1/8 teaspoon dried oregano
1/8 teaspoon dried basil
Dash pepper
   1 cup (4 ounces) shredded part-skim
      mozzarella cheese

Place the flatbread on an ungreased baking sheet; brush with vinaigrette. Layer with the remaining ingredients.
   Bake at 400° for 8-10 minutes or until the cheese is melted. **Yield:** 4 servings.

Crab Sandwiches
With Horseradish Sauce
(Pictured below)

Prep/Total Time: 30 min.

Do you love crab cakes—but not spending lots of time in the kitchen? Here's a great solution! The easy sandwiches get a zesty kick from a homemade horseradish sauce.
   —Margaret Lowenberg, Kingman, Arizona

 10 saltines, crushed
   2 egg whites, lightly beaten
   2 tablespoons Dijon-mayonnaise blend
   1 green onion, chopped
   4 drops hot pepper sauce
   4 pouches (3.53 ounces *each*) premium
      crabmeat, drained
1/3 cup sour cream
   1 tablespoon prepared horseradish
   1 teaspoon lemon juice
   4 sandwich buns, split
   4 lettuce leaves
   4 slices tomato

In a small bowl, combine the first five ingredients. Fold in crabmeat; let stand for 5 minutes. Shape mixture by 1/2 cupfuls into 1/2-in.-thick patties. Place on a greased baking sheet. Bake at 425° for 4-5 minutes on each side or until golden brown.
   Meanwhile, in a small bowl, combine the sour cream, horseradish and lemon juice. Serve patties on buns with lettuce, tomato and sauce. **Yield:** 4 servings.

Stroganoff-Style
Spaghetti 'n' Meatballs
(Pictured above)

Prep/Total Time: 30 min.

This is perfect for those chilly nights when you're craving something hot and comforting. The rich, creamy noodles and meatballs taste like they simmered for hours.
   —Sharon Ylkanen, Marenisco, Michigan

1/2 pound uncooked spaghetti
   1 package (12 ounces) frozen fully cooked
      Italian meatballs, thawed
   2 tablespoons finely chopped onion
   1 garlic clove, minced
   1 tablespoon olive oil
   1 can (10-3/4 ounces) condensed cream of
      mushroom soup, undiluted
1/4 cup 2% milk
   1 tablespoon concentrated au jus sauce
1/8 teaspoon Cajun seasoning
   1 cup (8 ounces) sour cream

Cook the spaghetti according to the package directions. Meanwhile, in a large skillet, saute the meatballs, onion and garlic in oil for 4-5 minutes or until meatballs are browned. Stir in soup, milk, au jus sauce and seasoning. Bring to a boil. Reduce heat; simmer, uncovered, for 10-12 minutes or until heated through.
   Gradually stir in sour cream; heat through (do not boil). Drain spaghetti; stir into skillet. Serve immediately. **Yield:** 4 servings.

Chicken Fettuccine Alfredo
(Pictured below)

Prep/Total Time: 30 min.

This is a favorite in our house, and one of the best things about it is that you need only two pans. My son does the dishes, so the less for him to clean, the happier he is!
—Sandy Schmitzer, Swartz Creek, Michigan

    1 package (12 ounces) fettuccine
    8 bacon strips, cut into 1-inch pieces
    1 pound boneless skinless chicken breasts, cubed
    2 cups sliced fresh mushrooms
    6 green onions, thinly sliced
    1 garlic clove, minced
1-1/2 cups half-and-half cream
  1/2 cup shredded Parmesan cheese
    1 teaspoon paprika
  1/2 teaspoon coarsely ground pepper
Additional shredded Parmesan cheese

Cook the fettuccine according to the package directions. Meanwhile, in a large skillet, cook the bacon until crisp. Remove bacon to paper towels to drain, reserving 1-2 tablespoons drippings.

Saute chicken in drippings until no longer pink. Add mushrooms and green onions; cook until mushrooms are tender. Add garlic; cook 1 minute longer. Stir in the cream, Parmesan cheese, paprika and pepper. Reduce heat; simmer, uncovered, for 5-10 minutes. Stir in the reserved bacon.

Drain fettuccine; place in a serving bowl. Add chicken mixture; toss to coat. Garnish with additional cheese. **Yield:** 6 servings.

Spicy Sausage Linguine
(Pictured above)

Prep/Total Time: 30 min.

Crushed red pepper brings a bit of a kick to the sausage, veggies and linguine in this satisfying stovetop meal.
—Susie Van Etten, Chapmansboro, Tennessee

    9 ounces uncooked linguine
    1 pound Italian sausage links, cut into 1/2-inch slices
    1 medium onion, chopped
  1/2 medium sweet red pepper, cut into thin strips
  1/2 medium green pepper, cut into thin strips
    1 garlic clove, minced
    1 teaspoon fennel seed
  1/4 teaspoon salt
  1/4 teaspoon crushed red pepper flakes
  1/4 teaspoon pepper
    3 plum tomatoes, chopped
    3 tablespoons heavy whipping cream

Cook the linguine according to the package directions.

Meanwhile, in a large skillet, cook the sausage, onion, red pepper and green pepper over medium heat until the meat is no longer pink and the vegetables are tender; drain. Add the garlic, fennel, salt, red pepper flakes and pepper; cook 1 minute longer. Stir in the tomatoes and cream; heat through.

Drain the linguine; serve with the sausage mixture. **Yield:** 4 servings.

Ham and Penne Milano
(Pictured below)

Prep/Total Time: 30 min.

I came up with this recipe one night when I had to stretch leftover ham to feed our family of five. I tossed in pasta, broccoli, peppers and more. Everyone loved it!
—Kathleen Mancuso, Niskayuna, New York

- 1 package (16 ounces) penne pasta
- 2-2/3 cups frozen broccoli florets
- 2 garlic cloves, minced
- 2 tablespoons butter
- 3 tablespoons all-purpose flour
- 1 can (14-1/2 ounces) reduced-sodium chicken broth
- 1/4 cup 2% milk
- 1-1/2 pounds boneless fully cooked ham, julienned
- 1 jar (7-1/2 ounces) roasted sweet red peppers, drained and julienned
- 2/3 cup grated Parmesan cheese
- 1/2 cup chopped walnuts
- 1 teaspoon pepper

In a Dutch oven, cook pasta according to the package directions, adding the broccoli during the last 5 minutes of cooking.

Meanwhile, in a large skillet, saute the garlic in butter for 1 minute. Stir in flour until blended; gradually add chicken broth and milk. Bring to a boil; cook and stir for 1-2 minutes or until thickened. Stir in ham, red peppers, cheese, walnuts and pepper.

Drain pasta and broccoli. Add ham mixture; toss to coat. **Yield:** 8 servings.

Antipasto Pizza
(Pictured above)

Prep/Total Time: 25 min.

A prebaked crust and ready-made pizza sauce really cut the prep work for this deliciously different, versatile pie. You can serve it as either an entree or a hot appetizer.
—Mindee Curtis, Omaha, Nebraska

- 1 prebaked 12-inch pizza crust
- 3/4 cup pizza sauce
- 2 cups (8 ounces) shredded part-skim mozzarella cheese, *divided*
- 1/2 cup roasted sweet red peppers, drained and cut into strips
- 1/2 cup marinated quartered artichoke hearts, drained
- 1/4 pound thinly sliced hard salami, julienned
- 1/4 pound sliced deli ham, julienned
- 1/4 cup minced fresh basil

Place the crust on an ungreased pizza pan. Spread sauce over the crust; sprinkle with 1 cup cheese. Top with red peppers, artichokes, salami and ham; sprinkle with the remaining cheese.

Bake at 450° for 10-12 minutes or until the cheese is melted. Sprinkle with basil. **Yield:** 8 slices.

▌ COLOR SCHEME ▐

I use a different color plastic cutting board for each ingredient I'm using (white for raw meats, pink for veggies, etc.). It saves having to repeatedly clean one board and helps prevent food contamination.
—Adele Shreckengost, Cottonwood, Arizona

Lemon Chicken Primavera

(Pictured below)

Prep/Total Time: 30 min.

With a refreshing hint of citrus from grated lemon peel, this entree is a great change of pace for my husband and me when our three sons stay with their grandparents.
— *Mary Linda King, Florence, South Carolina*

    1 cup uncooked spiral pasta
    1 pound boneless skinless chicken breasts,
      cut into 2-inch strips
  1/2 cup chopped sweet red pepper
    2 garlic cloves, minced
    2 tablespoons canola oil
    2 tablespoons all-purpose flour
1-1/2 cups 2% milk
    2 cups frozen peas, thawed
    1 teaspoon salt
    1 teaspoon grated lemon peel
  1/2 teaspoon dill weed
  1/4 teaspoon pepper
  1/4 cup grated Parmesan cheese
    2 tablespoons minced fresh parsley

Cook spiral pasta according to the package directions. Meanwhile, in a large skillet, saute chicken, red pepper and garlic in oil until chicken juices run clear. Combine flour and milk until smooth; gradually stir into chicken mixture. Bring to a boil. Cook and stir for 2 minutes or until thickened.

Drain pasta. Add the pasta, peas, salt, lemon peel, dill and pepper to pan. Cook and stir until heated through. Sprinkle with cheese and parsley. **Yield:** 4 servings.

Sausage & Penne Marinara

Prep/Total Time: 30 min.

Love Italian food? It's hard to beat the classic flavors of this favorite featuring sausage, pasta and a homemade marinara sauce. For milder fare, omit the pepper flakes.
— *Tammy Rowe, Bellevue, Ohio*

2-1/2 cups uncooked penne pasta
    1 pound Italian sausage links, cut into 1-inch
      pieces
    1 large onion, halved and sliced
    1 medium green pepper, sliced
    1 tablespoon canola oil
    1 can (14-1/2 ounces) stewed tomatoes,
      cut up
    1 can (8 ounces) tomato sauce
    1 teaspoon garlic powder
    1 teaspoon dried basil
    1 teaspoon dried oregano
  1/2 teaspoon salt
  1/2 teaspoon pepper
  1/4 teaspoon crushed red pepper flakes
Grated Parmesan cheese, optional

Cook penne pasta according to the package directions. Meanwhile, in a large skillet, cook the Italian sausage, onion and green pepper in oil over medium heat until the sausage is no longer pink and the vegetables are tender. Add the tomatoes, tomato sauce and seasonings; heat through.

Drain pasta; toss with tomato mixture. Sprinkle with cheese if desired. **Yield:** 6 servings.

Grilled Veggie Pita Pizzas

Prep/Total Time: 30 min.

Grilling these personal-size pizzas is a nice alternative to using the oven. When you can't grill, just pop them in a 350° oven for 4-5 minutes or until the cheese is melted.
— *Bonnie Hawkins, Elkhorn, Wisconsin*

    1 large onion, thinly sliced
    1 tablespoon plus 1 teaspoon olive oil, *divided*
    2 garlic cloves, minced
    2 cups fresh arugula *or* baby spinach
    4 pita breads (6 inches)
    8 ounces fresh mozzarella cheese, thinly sliced
    2 plum tomatoes, cut into 1/4-inch slices
  1/4 cup sliced ripe olives
    2 tablespoons capers, drained

In a small skillet, saute the onion in 1 tablespoon oil until tender. Add garlic; saute 1 minute longer. Remove and keep warm. In same pan, cook arugula just until wilted; remove and keep warm.

Brush one side of each pita with remaining oil. Layer with the cheese, plum tomatoes, arugula, onion mixture, olives and capers.

Grill the pizzas, covered, over medium heat for 2-4 minutes or until the cheese is melted. Serve immediately. **Yield:** 4 servings.

Springtime Salmon Salad
(Pictured above)

Prep/Total Time: 20 min.

This filling main-dish salad gets my family to eat a mix of nutritious foods. It's so tasty, they don't even realize they're eating healthy! —Trisha Kruse, Eagle, Idaho

1 can (11 ounces) mandarin oranges, undrained
3 cups cut fresh asparagus (1-inch pieces)
1 package (5 ounces) spring mix salad greens
1/2 cup slivered almonds, toasted
1/2 cup frozen peas, thawed
3/4 pound smoked salmon fillet, flaked

DRESSING:
1/4 cup olive oil
2 tablespoons lemon juice
1 teaspoon Dijon mustard
1/2 teaspoon salt
1/4 teaspoon pepper

Drain mandarin oranges, reserving 1/4 cup juice. Set oranges aside. In a small saucepan, bring 2 cups water to a boil. Add asparagus; cover and boil for 3 minutes. Drain and immediately place asparagus in ice water. Drain and pat dry.

In a large bowl, toss salad greens, asparagus, oranges, almonds and peas. Divide among four serving plates. Top with the salmon. In a small bowl, whisk the dressing ingredients and reserved juice; drizzle over salads. Serve immediately. **Yield:** 4 servings.

Place the buns cut side up on an ungreased baking sheet. Broil 3-4 in. from the heat for 1-2 minutes or until golden brown. Spread the cut side of each bottom half with 2 tablespoons cream cheese mixture. Layer with the chicken, onion and lettuce; replace the bun tops. **Yield:** 4 servings.

Hearty Red Beans & Rice
(Pictured below and on page 200)

Prep/Total Time: 30 min.

My husband loves this filling supper loaded with sausage. And I love the fact that it's so simple to prepare!
—Sherri Miller, Greencastle, Indiana

1-1/2 cups uncooked instant rice
   1 pound bulk Italian sausage
   1 medium green pepper, chopped
   1 small onion, chopped
   1 garlic clove, minced
   1 can (16 ounces) kidney beans, rinsed and drained
   1 can (15 ounces) pinto beans, rinsed and drained
   1 can (10-3/4 ounces) condensed tomato soup, undiluted
   1 cup salsa
   1 teaspoon Italian seasoning

Prepare rice according to package directions. Meanwhile, in a Dutch oven, cook the sausage, green pepper, onion and garlic over medium heat until the meat is no longer pink; drain.

Add the beans, soup, salsa and Italian seasoning; heat through. Serve with rice. **Yield:** 6 servings.

Broiled Chicken Sandwiches
(Pictured above)

Prep/Total Time: 30 min.

I'm always searching for new ways to serve chicken, and these tangy sandwiches spread with a quick cream cheese blend have become a favorite in our household.
—Jessica Dieters, Laramie, Wyoming

   1 package (3 ounces) cream cheese, softened
   2 tablespoons butter, softened
 1/2 teaspoon lemon-pepper seasoning, *divided*
 1/4 teaspoon dried basil
 1/8 teaspoon garlic salt
   1 tablespoon canola oil
   1 tablespoon lemon juice
1-1/2 pounds chicken tenderloins, cut into 1/2-inch strips
   4 Italian sandwich buns, split
   1 small red onion, sliced
   4 lettuce leaves

In a small bowl, beat cream cheese, butter, 1/4 teaspoon lemon-pepper seasoning, basil and garlic salt until smooth; set aside. In another small bowl, combine the oil, lemon juice and remaining lemon-pepper seasoning; set aside.

Place chicken on a greased broiler pan. Spoon half of the lemon juice mixture over top. Broil 3-4 in. from the heat for 4-5 minutes. Turn chicken; top with remaining lemon juice mixture. Broil 4-5 minutes longer or until the chicken juices run clear.

Grilled Halibut With Blueberry Salsa
(Pictured above)

Prep/Total Time: 30 min.

Give halibut fillets a summery spin with this easy recipe. The salsa may seem sophisticated, but it's really a cinch to make. —Donna Goutermont, Juneau, Alaska

    2 cups fresh blueberries, *divided*
    1 small red onion, chopped
  1/4 cup minced fresh cilantro
    1 jalapeno pepper, seeded and chopped
    2 tablespoons orange juice
    1 tablespoon balsamic vinegar
    1 teaspoon plus 2 tablespoons olive oil, *divided*
  1/8 teaspoon plus 1 teaspoon salt, *divided*
  1/8 teaspoon pepper
    6 halibut fillets (5 ounces *each*)

In a small bowl, coarsely mash 1 cup blueberries. Stir in onion, cilantro, jalapeno pepper, orange juice, vinegar, 1 teaspoon oil, 1/8 teaspoon salt, pepper and remaining blueberries. Cover and chill until serving.

Meanwhile, brush fillets with remaining oil; sprinkle with remaining salt. Grill halibut, covered, over medium heat for 4-5 minutes on each side or until the fish flakes easily with a fork. Serve with salsa. **Yield:** 6 servings.

Editor's Note: When cutting hot peppers, disposable gloves are recommended. Avoid touching your face.

PARSLEY POINTER

Parsley adds fresh flavor to Shrimp Penne with Garlic Sauce (recipe above right). To keep fresh parsley in the refrigerator for several weeks, wash the entire bunch in warm water, shake off all excess moisture, wrap it in a paper towel and seal it in a plastic bag.

Shrimp Penne with Garlic Sauce
(Pictured below)

Prep/Total Time: 25 min.

Can you get a restaurant-quality main course from your own kitchen in under half an hour? Yes, you can—this recipe proves it! —Christy Martell, Round Hill, Virginia

    2 cups uncooked penne pasta
    2 garlic cloves, minced
  1/4 cup butter, cubed
  1/4 cup all-purpose flour
    1 can (14-1/2 ounces) chicken broth
    1 can (5 ounces) evaporated milk
    1 pound cooked medium shrimp, peeled and deveined
  2/3 cup shredded Parmesan cheese
    2 tablespoons minced fresh parsley
1-1/2 teaspoons seafood seasoning

Cook the penne pasta according to package directions. Meanwhile, in a large saucepan, saute garlic in butter. Stir in flour until blended; gradually add the broth and milk. Bring to a boil; cook and stir for 2 minutes or until thickened. Stir in shrimp, cheese, parsley and seafood seasoning; heat through.

Drain the penne pasta; place in a large bowl. Add the shrimp mixture; toss to coat. Serve immediately. **Yield:** 4 servings.

Southwest Beef Burritos
(Pictured above)

Prep/Total Time: 20 min.

Mealtime is all wrapped up when you take advantage of this super-easy recipe. Loaded with beef, vegetables and cheese, the burritos are ready to eat in just 20 minutes.
—Patricia Harmon, Baden, Pennsylvania

   1 package (17 ounces) refrigerated beef tips with gravy
   1 medium onion, chopped
   1 tablespoon canola oil
   2 cups frozen mixed vegetables, thawed
   1 can (4 ounces) chopped green chilies, drained
3/4 teaspoon ground cumin
   4 flour tortillas (10 inches), warmed
3/4 cup shredded Mexican cheese blend

Cut the beef tips into 1/2-inch pieces. In a large skillet, saute the onion in the oil until tender. Add the beef tips with gravy, mixed vegetables, green chilies and cumin; heat through.

   Spoon 3/4 cup filling off center on each flour tortilla. Sprinkle with cheese. Fold sides and ends over filling and roll up. **Yield:** 4 servings.

Pronto Paella

Prep/Total Time: 30 min.

I saw a chef making paella on a TV show and decided to create a quick version I could fix after work. Everyone is amazed it comes together so fast! I often prepare the pilaf with reduced-sodium chicken broth instead of water.
—Peter Halferty, Corpus Christi, Texas

   1 package (6.09 ounces) rice pilaf
1-1/2 cups ready-to-use grilled chicken breast strips
   1 medium sweet onion, cut into wedges
   2 garlic cloves, minced
1-1/2 teaspoons Cajun seasoning
   3 tablespoons butter
   1 can (11 ounces) Mexicorn, drained
   1 package (9 ounces) frozen baby peas, thawed
1/2 pound cooked medium shrimp, peeled and deveined

Microwave rice pilaf according to package directions. Meanwhile, in a large skillet, saute the chicken, onion, garlic and Cajun seasoning in butter until the onion is tender. Stir in the corn, peas, shrimp and prepared pilaf; heat through. **Yield:** 4 servings.

Seafood Pasta Alfredo

(Pictured below)

Prep/Total Time: 30 min.

My husband loves seafood, and I put together this entree one night using a little of this and a little of that. Luckily, I wrote down what I did because he asks for it often!
—Rebekah Beyer, Sabetha, Kansas

    8 ounces uncooked linguine
    1 small zucchini, quartered and sliced
    1 cup julienned carrots
    1 small onion, chopped
    1 tablespoon olive oil
    1 garlic clove, minced
Dash crushed red pepper flakes
    1 cup heavy whipping cream
  1/2 cup grated Parmesan cheese
    2 tablespoons butter
  1/2 teaspoon salt
  1/8 teaspoon pepper
    1 pound cooked medium shrimp, peeled and
      deveined
    2 plum tomatoes, chopped
    1 can (6 ounces) crabmeat, drained, flaked
      and cartilage removed
    4 ounces imitation crabmeat, chopped
    3 green onions, sliced

Cook the linguine according to the package directions. Meanwhile, in a large skillet, saute the zucchini, carrots and onion in oil until crisp-tender. Add garlic and pepper

flakes; cook 1 minute longer. Stir in the cream, cheese, butter, salt and pepper.

Bring to a gentle boil; cook for 1-2 minutes or until slightly thickened. Add the shrimp, tomatoes, crabmeat and green onions. Drain linguine; toss with the shrimp mixture. **Yield:** 6 servings.

Sweet & Sour Sausage

(Pictured above)

Prep/Total Time: 20 min.

This fuss-free main dish gives sweet-and-sour flavor to smoked Polish sausage. We always keep that ingredient handy in the freezer so we can enjoy this anytime.
—Carol Matthews, Lima, New York

    1 can (20 ounces) pineapple chunks
  1/2 cup apricot preserves
    2 teaspoons cornstarch
    1 tablespoon cider vinegar
    1 tablespoon soy sauce
  1/2 teaspoon ground ginger
    1 pound smoked Polish sausage, cut into
      1/2-inch slices
    1 large onion, cut into 1-inch pieces
    1 medium green pepper, cut into 1-inch pieces
    1 tablespoon canola oil
Hot cooked rice

Drain pineapple, reserving 1/4 cup juice; set pineapple aside. In a small bowl, combine the preserves, cornstarch, vinegar, soy sauce, ginger and reserved juice.

In a large skillet, saute the sausage, onion and pepper in oil until vegetables are tender. Add sauce mixture and pineapple. Bring to a boil; cook and stir for 2 minutes or until thickened. Serve with rice. **Yield:** 4 servings.

Meat Lover's Pizza

(Pictured below)

Prep/Total Time: 30 min.

This hefty meal-on-a-crust is stacked with three different meats and lots of mozzarella. It's sure to score with your sports-watching gang and anyone with a big appetite.
—Edgar Peavy, Oxnard, California

    2 packages (6-1/2 ounces *each*) pizza crust mix
    1 tablespoon olive oil
1-1/2 teaspoons garlic powder, *divided*
  1/4 pound ground beef
  1/2 teaspoon onion powder
  2/3 cup spaghetti sauce
    1 package (3-1/2 ounces) sliced pepperoni
    6 ounces Canadian bacon, quartered
  1/4 cup sliced fresh mushrooms
    2 tablespoons sliced ripe olives
    2 cups (8 ounces) shredded part-skim
      mozzarella cheese

Prepare pizza dough according to the package directions. With floured hands, press dough onto a greased 14-in. pizza pan. Bake at 425° for 7-9 minutes or until lightly browned. Combine oil and 1 teaspoon garlic powder; brush over crust edges.

In a large skillet over medium heat, cook beef with onion powder and remaining garlic powder until no longer pink; drain.

Spread spaghetti sauce over crust to within 1 in. of the edges. Top with beef mixture, pepperoni, Canadian bacon, mushrooms, olives and cheese.

Bake at 425° for 10-15 minutes or until the cheese is melted and the crust is golden brown. **Yield:** 8 slices.

Southwest Beef & Rice Skillet

(Pictured above)

Prep/Total Time: 25 min.

My family loves this because it's so tasty, and I love the one-dish prep! Sometimes I add a can of drained corn.
—Jane Porras, Plano, Texas

1-1/2 cups uncooked instant rice
    1 pound ground beef
    1 medium onion, chopped
    1 garlic clove, minced
    1 can (15 ounces) Ranch Style beans (pinto
      beans in seasoned tomato sauce)
    1 cup beef broth
    1 cup tomato sauce
    2 teaspoons chili powder
  1/2 teaspoon salt
  1/2 teaspoon ground cumin
  1/4 teaspoon pepper
  1/2 cup shredded pepper Jack cheese

Cook rice according to package directions. Meanwhile, in a large skillet, cook the beef, onion and garlic over medium heat until meat is no longer pink; drain. Stir in the rice, beans, broth, tomato sauce, chili powder, salt, cumin and pepper; heat through. Sprinkle with cheese. Cover and cook for 1-2 minutes or until cheese is melted. **Yield:** 5 servings.

CRUST WITH A KICK

I usually don't have time to make pizza crust from scratch, but I can usually find a few moments to dress up a mix. To make a delicious herbed crust, I simply add 1 teaspoon basil and 1 teaspoon oregano to a boxed pizza crust mix. It's so easy to do, and it's a great way to give your pie some added zip.
—Michelle Durfee, Gregory, Michigan

Santa Fe Skillet

(Pictured below)

Prep/Total Time: 30 min.

As a mother who works full-time, I'm always looking for quick meals to prepare. I started fixing this Southwestern skillet many years ago, and it's still a favorite.
—Lorie VanHorn, Waddell, Arizona

  1 pound lean ground beef (90% lean)
  1 small onion, chopped
  1 package (6 ounces) four-cheese corkscrew
    pasta mix
  2 cups salsa
  1 cup hot water
  1 tablespoon chili powder
  1/2 teaspoon salt
Dash cayenne pepper
  1 can (14-1/2 ounces) diced tomatoes,
    undrained
  1 can (2-1/4 ounces) sliced ripe olives, drained
  1 cup (4 ounces) shredded cheddar cheese
Sour cream, optional

In a large skillet, cook beef and onion over medium heat until meat is no longer pink; drain. Stir pasta, contents of seasoning packet, salsa, water, chili powder, salt and cayenne into the skillet.

  Bring to a boil. Reduce heat; cover and simmer for 15 minutes or until pasta is tender, adding more water if necessary. Stir in the tomatoes; sprinkle with the ripe olives and cheese. Cover and simmer for 3-4 minutes or until heated through. Serve with sour cream if desired.
Yield: 6 servings.

  Editor's Note: This recipe was tested with Pasta Roni mix.

Bacon-Chicken Club Pizza

(Pictured above)

Prep/Total Time: 25 min.

Pizza topped with lettuce, tomato and ranch dressing? It may sound unusual, but you're in for a real treat!
—Debbie Reid, Clearwater, Florida

  1 prebaked 12-inch pizza crust
  4 ounces cream cheese, softened
  1 shallot, minced
  2 cups shredded rotisserie chicken
1-1/2 cups (6 ounces) shredded Monterey Jack
    cheese
  1 cup (4 ounces) shredded sharp cheddar
    cheese
  8 slices ready-to-serve fully cooked bacon,
    cut into 1-inch pieces
1/4 cup sour cream
  3 tablespoons 2% milk
  2 teaspoons ranch salad dressing mix
  1 cup shredded lettuce
  1 plum tomato, seeded and chopped

Place crust on an ungreased pizza pan. Combine cream cheese and shallot; spread over crust. Top with chicken, cheeses and bacon.

  Bake at 425° for 12-15 minutes or until the edges are lightly browned and the cheese is melted.

  Meanwhile, in a small bowl, combine the sour cream, milk and dressing mix. Sprinkle lettuce and tomato over pizza; drizzle with dressing. **Yield:** 8 slices.

CHAPTER 14

Delectable Desserts

Think you simply don't have time to make a dessert to top off your meal? Think again!

Whether it's a hectic weekday or a holiday, you can rely on this chapter for blissfully sweet treats that'll get you out of the kitchen in a jiffy.

To surprise your family on even the busiest weeknights, try recipes such as Crescent Apple Dumplings, Crunchy Lime & Berry Parfaits and Caramelized Angel Food Cake Sundaes.

On special occasions, you'll impress everyone with speedy sensations such as Cranberry Ice Cream Pie, Chocolate Pecan Cheesecake and Over-the-Top Blueberry Bread Pudding.

No matter which you serve, you're sure to see smiles! ■

DECADENT DELIGHTS. Lemon Burst Tartlets (p. 227).

Butterscotch Torte

(Pictured below)

Prep: 15 min. + chilling

I wanted a butterscotch-flavored pudding dessert. After searching many cookbooks, I came up with this yummy layered delight. —Judith Kuehl, Merrill, Wisconsin

- 1 package (16 ounces) cream-filled vanilla sandwich cookies, crushed
- 1/2 cup butter, melted
- 1 package (8 ounces) cream cheese, softened
- 1 cup confectioners' sugar
- 1 carton (12 ounces) frozen whipped topping, thawed, *divided*
- 2-1/2 cups cold 2% milk
- 2 packages (3.4 ounces *each*) instant butterscotch pudding mix

Set aside 1 cup cookie crumbs. Combine the remaining cookie crumbs and butter; press into a greased 13-in. x 9-in. dish. In a large bowl, beat the cream cheese and confectioners' sugar until smooth. Fold in 1-1/2 cups whipped topping. Spread over crust.

In a small bowl, whisk the milk and pudding mix for 2 minutes; let stand for 2 minutes or until soft-set. Spoon over cream cheese layer. Top with remaining whipped topping. Sprinkle with the reserved crumbs. Cover and refrigerate for at least 2 hours. **Yield:** 15 servings.

Editor's Note: To make the garnish shown below, melt butterscotch chips in the microwave and stir until smooth. Drizzle onto waxed paper and refrigerate until set. Then peel or lift off with a spatula.

Orange-Lemon Cake

(Pictured above)

Prep: 15 min. **Bake:** 35 min. + cooling

You'll taste refreshing citrus flavor in both this cake and its sweet icing. A big slice always makes eyes light up. —Ann Robinson, Bloomington, Indiana

- 1 package (18-1/4 ounces) lemon cake mix
- 1 package (3 ounces) orange gelatin
- 2/3 cup water
- 2/3 cup canola oil
- 4 eggs

ICING:
- 1 cup confectioners' sugar
- 3 to 4 teaspoons orange juice

In a large bowl, combine the first five ingredients; beat on low speed for 30 seconds. Beat on medium speed for 2 minutes. Pour into a greased and floured 10-in. fluted tube pan.

Bake at 350° for 35-40 minutes or until a toothpick inserted near the center comes out clean. Cool for 10 minutes before removing from pan to a wire rack to cool completely. Combine the confectioners' sugar and enough orange juice to achieve desired consistency. Drizzle over cake. **Yield:** 12 servings.

BETTER BOXED MIX

To dress up a box of super-moist cake mix, I prepare the batter as directed, then stir in a small package of instant vanilla pudding mix. This gives the cake such great flavor, you'd think it was homemade.
—Cindy Shehee, Butte, Montana

Refrigerator Lime Cheesecake

(Pictured below)

Prep: 25 min. **Cook:** 5 min. + chilling

I served this at a party for Father's Day, and the creamy cheesecake was a hit. It's so pretty covered with ladyfingers and fruit. —Cher Anjema, Kleinburg, Ontario

- 38 ladyfingers, split
- 1 envelope unflavored gelatin
- 1/4 cup lime juice, chilled
- 2 packages (8 ounces *each*) cream cheese, softened
- 1 cup sugar
- 6 ounces white baking chocolate, melted and cooled
- 2 teaspoons grated lime peel
- 1 cup heavy whipping cream, whipped

Fresh strawberry and lime slices, optional

Arrange 22 split ladyfingers around edges and 16 split ladyfingers on bottom of an ungreased 8-in. springform pan; set aside. In a small saucepan, sprinkle unflavored gelatin over the cold lime juice; let stand for 1 minute. Heat over low heat, stirring until the gelatin is completely dissolved; cool.

   Meanwhile, in a large bowl, beat cream cheese and sugar until smooth. Gradually beat in melted chocolate, lime peel and gelatin mixture. Fold in whipped cream. Pour into the prepared pan. Cover and refrigerate for 3 hours or until set. Garnish with strawberry and lime slices if desired. **Yield:** 12 servings.

Crescent Apple Dumplings

(Pictured above)

Prep: 10 min. **Bake:** 25 min.

Kids can help assemble these scrumptious treats…and everyone will enjoy polishing off the entire pan! The recipe goes together in a snap thanks to refrigerated crescent roll dough. In a mere 10 minutes, you'll have a batch of dumplings in the oven. —Vera Grovier, Rantoul, Illinois

- 1 tube (8 ounces) refrigerated crescent rolls
- 1 medium Granny Smith apple, peeled
- 16 red-hot candies
- 1/2 cup sugar
- 1/4 cup butter, melted
- 1 teaspoon vanilla extract
- 6 tablespoons grapefruit *or* citrus soda
- 1 to 2 teaspoons pumpkin pie spice

Vanilla ice cream, optional

Unroll the crescent rolls and separate into eight triangles. Cut apple into eight wedges. Place an apple wedge and two red-hots on each crescent triangle. Bring up corners of dough to the center; pinch edges to seal. Place in a greased 8-in. square baking dish.

   In a small bowl, combine the sugar, butter and vanilla; spoon over the rolls. Slowly pour the soda around the rolls (do not stir). Sprinkle with pumpkin pie spice. Bake, uncovered, at 350° for 25-30 minutes or until golden brown. Serve dumplings warm with vanilla ice cream if desired. **Yield:** 8 dumplings.

Chocolate Almond Dessert
(Pictured above)

Prep: 20 min. **Cook:** 10 min. + chilling

Who wouldn't love this decadent chocolate finale? It's made with convenience items but tastes from-scratch.
—Heidi Hall, North St. Paul, Minnesota

   1 prepared angel food cake (8 to 10 ounces), cut into 1-inch cubes
   4 cups cold 2% milk
   2 packages (3.4 ounces *each*) cook-and-serve chocolate pudding mix
   1 milk chocolate candy bar (1.55 ounces), chopped
3/4 cup sliced almonds, toasted, *divided*
   1 cup heavy whipping cream, whipped

Arrange half of the cake cubes in an ungreased 13-in. x 9-in. dish; set aside. In a large saucepan, whisk the milk and pudding mixes. Add candy bar. Cook and stir over medium heat until mixture comes to a boil. Cook and stir 1-2 minutes longer or until thickened.

Pour half of the pudding over the cake cubes. Sprinkle with half of the almonds; cover and refrigerate. Transfer remaining pudding to a small bowl; cover and refrigerate until chilled.

Arrange the remaining cake cubes over dessert. Whisk the chilled pudding; fold in the whipped cream. Spread over the top and sprinkle with the remaining almonds. Cover and refrigerate for at least 1 hour. Cut into squares. **Yield:** 15 servings.

Buttermilk Bread Pudding with Caramel Creme Fraiche
(Pictured below)

Prep: 20 min. + standing **Bake:** 55 min.

This special-sounding recipe really lives up to its name. The oven-baked pudding is wonderful with coffee after dinner, but you could also enjoy it in the morning for brunch. Either way, there's no better use for day-old French bread! —Janice Elder Charlotte, North Carolina

   8 cups cubed day-old French bread, crusts removed
   5 eggs
   3 cups buttermilk
   1 can (15 ounces) cream of coconut
   1 cup flaked coconut
   1 cup pineapple preserves
1/2 cup sugar
   1 teaspoon ground cinnamon
3/4 cup heavy whipping cream
1/2 cup sour cream
1/2 cup caramel ice cream topping
   1 tablespoon rum *or* 1 teaspoon rum extract
Toasted flaked coconut, optional

Place the bread in a greased 13-in. x 9-in. baking dish. In a large bowl, combine the eggs, buttermilk, cream of coconut, coconut, preserves, sugar and cinnamon. Pour the mixture over bread cubes. Let stand for 15 minutes or until bread is softened. Bake, uncovered, at 350° for 55-65 minutes or until a knife inserted near the center comes out clean.

In a large bowl, beat the cream, sour cream, caramel topping and rum until soft peaks form. Serve with warm or cooled bread pudding. Sprinkle with toasted coconut if desired. **Yield:** 15 servings (2 cups cream).

Kitchen Sink Cookies
(Pictured above)

Prep: 25 min. **Bake:** 10 min./batch

Crisp outside and soft inside, these fun goodies are packed with everything but the kitchen sink—candies, coconut, oats and more.   —Brittney Musgrove, Dallas, Georgia

      1 cup butter, softened
1-1/4 cups packed brown sugar
      2 eggs
      3 teaspoons vanilla extract
      2 teaspoons 2% milk
      2 cups quick-cooking oats
1-3/4 cups all-purpose flour
      1 teaspoon baking soda
   1/2 teaspoon salt
   1/4 teaspoon ground nutmeg
      1 cup (6 ounces) semisweet chocolate chips
   1/3 cup Reese's pieces
   1/3 cup flaked coconut
   1/3 cup chopped walnuts
   1/3 cup milk chocolate M&M's

In a large bowl, cream the butter and brown sugar until light and fluffy. Beat in eggs, vanilla and milk. Combine the oats, flour, baking soda, salt and nutmeg; gradually add to the creamed mixture and mix well. Stir in the remaining ingredients.

Drop dough by rounded tablespoonfuls 3 in. apart onto ungreased baking sheets. Flatten slightly with the bottom of a glass coated with cooking spray.

Bake at 375° for 8-10 minutes or until golden brown. Cool for 1 minute before removing from pans to wire racks. **Yield:** 5 dozen.

Peanut Butter Crispy Bars
(Pictured above)

Prep: 15 min. **Bake:** 15 min. + cooling

When I needed something quick for a gathering, I whipped up these bars. Everyone likes the pairing of chocolate and peanut butter.   —Gail Anderson, Jefferson, Wisconsin

      1 tube (16-1/2 ounces) refrigerated peanut
        butter cookie dough
      4 cups miniature marshmallows
      2 cups (12 ounces) semisweet chocolate chips
   1/2 cup creamy peanut butter
   1/4 cup butter, cubed
      2 cups crisp rice cereal
   1/2 cup salted peanuts

Press the cookie dough into an ungreased 13-in. x 9-in. baking pan. Bake at 350° for 10-14 minutes or until the center is set.

Sprinkle with marshmallows; bake 4-5 minutes longer or until marshmallows are puffed. Cool for 5 minutes.

In a small saucepan, combine chocolate chips, peanut butter and butter. Cook and stir until smooth. Remove from the heat; stir in cereal and nuts. Drop by spoonfuls over top; gently spread over marshmallows. Cool and cut into bars. **Yield:** 3 dozen.

Chocolate Pecan Cheesecake
(Pictured below)

Prep: 25 min. + chilling

Present this pie to guests, and mouths will water at the sight alone! It's dressed up with a drizzle of hot fudge and a sprinkle of nuts. —Christy Bowles, Garfield, Arizona

- 25 caramels
- 1/4 cup evaporated milk
- 3/4 cup chopped pecans, *divided*
- 1 chocolate crumb crust (9 inches)
- 2 packages (3 ounces *each*) cream cheese, softened
- 1/2 cup sour cream
- 1-1/4 cups cold 2% milk
- 1 package (3.9 ounces) instant chocolate pudding mix
- 1/2 cup hot fudge ice cream topping, warmed

In a small saucepan, combine caramels and evaporated milk. Cook and stir over medium-low heat until smooth; stir in 1/2 cup pecans. Pour into crumb crust. Refrigerate for 15 minutes.

Meanwhile, in a large bowl, beat cream cheese and sour cream until smooth. In a small bowl, whisk the milk and pudding mix for 2 minutes; beat into cream cheese mixture until blended. Spread over the caramel mixture. Refrigerate for at least 30 minutes. Before serving, drizzle with hot fudge topping and sprinkle with the remaining pecans. **Yield:** 8 servings.

Upside-Down Berry Cake
(Pictured above)

Prep: 20 min. **Bake:** 30 min. + cooling

This moist cake is wonderful warm or cold...and is even better topped with whipped topping or ice cream. Keep it in mind when you have just-picked berries in summer. —Candy Scholl, West Sunbury, Pennsylvania

- 1/2 cup chopped walnuts
- 1 cup fresh *or* frozen blueberries
- 1 cup fresh *or* frozen raspberries, halved
- 1 cup sliced fresh strawberries
- 3/4 cup sugar
- 1 package (3 ounces) raspberry gelatin
- 1-1/2 cups miniature marshmallows
- 1 package (18-1/4 ounces) yellow cake mix
- 2 eggs
- 1-1/4 cups water
- 2 tablespoons canola oil

In a greased 13-in. x 9-in. baking dish, layer the walnuts and berries; sprinkle with sugar, raspberry gelatin and marshmallows. In a large bowl, combine the cake mix, eggs, water and oil; beat on low speed for 30 seconds. Beat on medium for 2 minutes. Pour over top.

Bake at 350° for 30-35 minutes or until a toothpick inserted near the center of the cake comes out clean. Cool for 5 minutes before inverting cake onto a serving platter. Refrigerate leftovers. **Yield:** 15 servings.

Blueberry Banana Cream Pie

Prep: 15 min. + chilling

I came across this easy recipe in a book years ago. People always comment on the combination of tangy blueberries and mellow bananas. —Loraine Meyer, Bend, Oregon

2 packages (3 ounces *each*) cream cheese, softened
1 can (14 ounces) sweetened condensed milk
3/4 cup cold water
1 package (3.4 ounces) instant vanilla pudding mix
1 cup heavy whipping cream, whipped
2 medium bananas, cut into 1/4-inch slices
2 teaspoons lemon juice
35 vanilla wafers
1 cup fresh blueberries

In a large bowl, beat cream cheese until smooth. Beat in the milk, water and vanilla pudding mix. Fold in the whipped cream.

In a resealable plastic bag, add bananas and lemon juice; toss until bananas are coated. Drain and discard lemon juice.

Line an ungreased deep-dish 9-in. pie plate with the vanilla wafers. Spread with half of the cream cheese mixture. Top with bananas and blueberries. Spread with remaining cream cheese mixture. Refrigerate for 3 hours or until set. **Yield:** 8 servings.

Caramelized Angel Food Cake Sundaes
(Pictured below)

Prep/Total Time: 20 min.

A prepared angel food cake gets a sinfully good makeover in these heavenly sundaes. If you have fresh strawberries on hand, slice them and add them to each serving.
—Jessica Ring, Chicago, Illinois

1 package (3 ounces) cream cheese, softened
1/4 cup sour cream
2 tablespoons confectioners' sugar
1/4 cup butter, softened

1/4 cup packed brown sugar
1/8 teaspoon ground cinnamon
6 slices angel food cake
6 scoops fudge ripple ice cream

In a small bowl, beat the cream cheese, sour cream and confectioner's sugar until smooth. In another bowl, cream the butter, brown sugar and cinnamon until light and fluffy.

Spread butter mixture over the top and sides of each cake slice. Place on an ungreased baking sheet. Broil 4-6 in. from the heat for 1-2 minutes or until bubbly. Cool slightly. Serve with ice cream and sour cream mixture. **Yield:** 6 servings.

White Chocolate Mousse Tarts
(Pictured above)

Prep/Total Time: 30 min.

These yummy individual tarts come together with just a handful of basic ingredients, including purchased graham cracker shells. Colorful fruit makes the perfect garnish.
—Angela Lively, Cookeville, Tennessee

6 ounces white baking chocolate, chopped
1 can (14 ounces) sweetened condensed milk
1/4 teaspoon vanilla extract
2 cups heavy whipping cream, whipped
2 packages (6 count *each*) individual graham cracker tart shells
Assorted fresh fruit, optional

In a microwave, melt the chocolate; stir until smooth. Transfer to a large bowl; whisk in milk and vanilla. Fold in whipped cream. Spoon into tart shells. Garnish with fruit if desired. Chill until serving. **Yield:** 12 servings.

Cranberry Ice Cream Pie
(Pictured above)

Prep: 25 min. + freezing

My mother served this often during the year—always at Thanksgiving and Christmas. We love the tongue-tingling combination of sweet ice cream and tart cranberries.
—Geordyth Sullivan, Miami, Florida

Pastry for single-crust pie (9 inches)
   3/4 cup cold 2% milk
   1 package (3.4 ounces) instant vanilla pudding
      mix
   3 cups vanilla ice cream, softened
   1 can (14 ounces) jellied cranberry sauce,
      cut into slices
   2 cups whipped topping
Red food coloring, optional

Line a 9-in. pie plate with pie pastry; trim and flute the edges. Line unpricked pastry with a double thickness of heavy-duty foil. Bake at 450° for 8 minutes. Remove foil; bake 5-7 minutes longer or until golden brown. Cool on a wire rack.

In a large bowl, whisk the milk and pudding mix for 2 minutes. Let stand for 2 minutes or until soft-set. Fold in the ice cream. Arrange half of the cranberry slices in the crust. Spread with half of the ice cream mixture; repeat layers.

Cover and freeze for at least 2 hours or until firm. In a small bowl, tint the whipped topping with red food coloring if desired. Just before serving, spread over pie. **Yield:** 8 servings.

Lemon-Berry Shortcake
(Pictured below)

Prep: 30 min. **Bake:** 20 min. + cooling

Here's a quick-and-easy take on a summer classic. The shortcake base is tender and not too sweet. For the Fourth of July, add blueberries for a red-white-and-blue look.
—Meryl Herr, Overland Park, Kansas

1-1/3 cups all-purpose flour
   1/2 cup sugar
   2 teaspoons baking powder
   1/4 teaspoon salt
   1 egg
   2/3 cup buttermilk
   1/4 cup butter, melted
   1 tablespoon lemon juice
   1 teaspoon grated lemon peel
   1 teaspoon vanilla extract
   1 cup sliced fresh strawberries
TOPPING:
 1-1/2 cups sliced fresh strawberries
   1 tablespoon lemon juice
   1 teaspoon sugar
   2 cups reduced-fat whipped topping

In a large bowl, combine the flour, sugar, baking powder and salt. In another bowl, combine the egg, buttermilk, butter, lemon juice, lemon peel and vanilla. Stir into the dry ingredients just until moistened. Fold in strawberries. Pour the batter into a greased and floured 9-in. round baking pan.

Bake at 350° for 20-25 minutes or until a toothpick inserted near the center of cake comes out clean. Cool for 10 minutes before removing from pan to a wire rack to cool completely.

For topping, in a large bowl, combine berries, lemon juice and sugar. Cover and refrigerate until serving. Spread whipped topping over the cake. Drain berries; arrange over top. **Yield:** 8 servings.

Crunchy Lime & Berry Parfaits

(Pictured above)

Prep/Total Time: 25 min.

When we want something lighter, I prepare these yummy parfaits using reduced-fat whipped topping. The crunchy pretzels are a nice contrast to the smooth, creamy layers.
—Elizabeth Hayes, Brazil, Indiana

   1 cup coarsely crushed pretzels
1/4 cup sugar
1/4 cup butter, melted
   1 carton (8 ounces) frozen whipped topping, thawed
1/2 cup confectioners' sugar
   2 tablespoons lime juice
1-1/2 teaspoons grated lime peel
1-1/3 cups sliced fresh strawberries
1-1/3 cups fresh raspberries
1-1/3 cups fresh blueberries

In a small bowl, combine the pretzels, sugar and butter; press mixture into a greased 9-in. square baking pan. Bake, uncovered, at 350° for 8-10 minutes or until lightly browned. Set aside.

In a large bowl, combine the whipped topping, confectioners' sugar, lime juice and peel. In another bowl, combine the berries. Break pretzel mixture into small pieces.

Spoon 2 tablespoons lime mixture into each of eight parfait glasses. Layer each with 1 tablespoon pretzel pieces and 1/2 cup berries. Top each with the remaining lime mixture and pretzel pieces. Serve immediately. **Yield:** 8 servings.

Lemon Burst Tartlets

(Pictured below and on page 218)

Prep/Total Time: 30 min.

These fancy-looking bites are wonderful for a wedding shower, ladies' luncheon… any get-together at all. The tartlets may appear complicated and fussy, but the recipe calls for a time-saving ingredient— ready-made phyllo shells. —Pam Javor North Huntingdon, Pennsylvania

   2 packages (1.9 ounces *each*) frozen miniature phyllo tart shells
   1 jar (10 ounces) lemon curd
   1 carton (8 ounces) frozen whipped topping, thawed
   5 to 6 drops yellow food coloring, optional
2/3 cup raspberry cake and pastry filling
30 fresh raspberries

Bake phyllo shells according to package directions; cool completely on wire rack.

In a large bowl, combine the lemon curd, whipped topping and food coloring if desired until smooth.

Spoon 1 teaspoon raspberry filling into each phyllo shell. Pipe or spoon lemon mixture over filling. Garnish each tartlet with a raspberry. Refrigerate leftovers. **Yield:** 30 servings.

Editor's Note: This recipe was tested with Solo brand cake and pastry filling. Look for it in the baking aisle.

Lemon Panna Cotta with Berries

(Pictured above)

Prep: 25 min. + chilling

Cool, creamy and pretty as a picture, this luscious Italian specialty is elegant enough for the fanciest dinner party. Instead of molding this dessert in ramekins, try serving it in cocktail glasses and add the berry mixture on top.
—*Mariela Petroski, Helena, Montana*

    1 envelope unflavored gelatin
1-1/3 cups half-and-half cream
    2 cups heavy whipping cream
  1/3 cup honey
    1 teaspoon grated lemon peel
Dash salt
  2/3 cup *each* fresh blackberries, blueberries
        and raspberries
    2 tablespoons sugar
    2 tablespoons lemon juice
    1 tablespoon Amaretto, optional

In a small saucepan, sprinkle gelatin over half-and-half; let stand for 1 minute. Heat over low heat, stirring until gelatin is completely dissolved. Stir in whipping cream, honey, lemon peel and salt. Cook and stir until blended. Pour into seven 6-ounce ramekins or custard cups.

Cover and refrigerate for at least 5 hours or until set. In a small bowl, combine berries, sugar, lemon juice and Amaretto if desired. Cover and refrigerate for at least 30 minutes. Unmold panna cotta onto dessert plates; serve with berry mixture. **Yield:** 7 servings.

Plum-Topped Chocolate Kuchen

(Pictured at right)

Prep: 25 min. + standing **Bake:** 35 min. + cooling

Rich and chocolaty, this cake is a comforting, traditional treat for holidays. Four to five medium plums will yield 2 cups sliced. —*Patricia Harmon, Baden, Pennsylvania*

    2 cups sliced fresh plums
  1/4 cup port wine
    1 tablespoon honey
  1/2 cup butter, *divided*
    5 tablespoons finely chopped hazelnuts,
        divided
    2 ounces unsweetened chocolate, coarsely
        chopped
    2 eggs
  2/3 cup plus 3 tablespoons sugar, *divided*
    2 tablespoons 2% milk
1-1/2 cups all-purpose flour
    2 teaspoons baking powder
  1/2 teaspoon salt
  1/2 teaspoon baking soda
  1/2 teaspoon ground cinnamon
Whipped cream and confectioners' sugar, optional

In a small bowl, combine plums, port wine and honey; let stand for 30 minutes.

Meanwhile, grease bottom and 1 in. up the sides of a 9-in. springform pan with 1 tablespoon butter. Sprinkle with 3 tablespoons hazelnuts. Place the pan on a baking sheet; set aside.

In a microwave, melt chocolate and remaining butter; stir until smooth. Cool to room temperature. In a large bowl, combine the eggs, 2/3 cup sugar and milk. Add chocolate mixture. Combine flour, baking powder, salt and baking soda; add to chocolate mixture and beat just until combined. Transfer to prepared pan.

Drain plums, reserving 2 tablespoons liquid. Arrange plums over the batter; drizzle with the reserved liquid. Combine cinnamon and remaining sugar and hazelnuts; sprinkle over top.

Bake at 375° for 35-40 minutes or until a toothpick inserted near the center comes out clean. Cool on a wire rack for 10 minutes. Carefully run a knife around the edge of pan to loosen. Serve warm or cold. Garnish with whipped cream and confectioners' sugar if desired. **Yield:** 12 servings.

Over-the-Top
Blueberry Bread Pudding
(Pictured above)

Prep: 15 min. + standing **Bake:** 50 min.

This delectable Southern pudding boasts out-of-this-world flavor and eye appeal. Dotted with blueberries and draped with a cream sauce, it's a favorite for summer gatherings. You'll want to skip the main course and go straight to dessert!
—Marilyn Haynes, Sylacauga, Alabama

3 eggs
4 cups heavy whipping cream
2 cups sugar
3 teaspoons vanilla extract
2 cups fresh *or* frozen blueberries
1 package (10 to 12 ounces) white baking chips
1 loaf (1 pound) French bread, cut into 1-inch cubes

SAUCE:
1 package (10 to 12 ounces) white baking chips
1 cup heavy whipping cream

In a large bowl, combine eggs, heavy whipping cream, sugar and vanilla. Stir in blueberries and white baking chips. Stir in bread cubes; let stand for 15 minutes or until the bread is softened.

Transfer to a greased 13-in. x 9-in. baking dish. Bake, uncovered, at 350° for 50-55 minutes or until a knife inserted near the center comes out clean. Let stand for 5 minutes before serving.

For the sauce, place the white baking chips in a small bowl. In a small saucepan, bring the heavy whipping cream just to a boil. Pour over the baking chips; whisk until smooth. Serve the sauce with the bread pudding.
Yield: 12 servings.

Sweet Potato Cheesecake Bars
(Pictured above)

Prep: 20 min. **Bake:** 25 min. + chilling

Your house will be filled with the aroma of pumpkin spice after baking these rich squares. They look complicated but are so easy, you can whip up a batch anytime.
—Nancy Whitford, Edwards, New York

  1 package (18-1/4 ounces) yellow cake mix
1/2 cup butter, softened
  1 egg
FILLING:
  1 can (15 ounces) sweet potatoes, drained
  1 package (8 ounces) cream cheese, cubed
1/2 cup plus 1/4 cup sugar, *divided*
  1 egg
1-1/2 teaspoons pumpkin pie spice
  1 cup (8 ounces) sour cream
1/4 teaspoon vanilla extract
TOPPING:
1-1/4 cups granola without raisins
1/2 cup white baking chips
1/4 teaspoon pumpkin pie spice

In a large bowl, beat the yellow cake mix, butter and egg until crumbly. Press onto the bottom of a greased 13-in. x 9-in. baking dish.

Place sweet potatoes, cream cheese, 1/2 cup sugar, egg and pie spice in a food processor; cover and process until blended. Spread over crust.

Bake at 350° for 20-25 minutes or until the center is almost set. Meanwhile, in a small bowl, combine the sour cream, vanilla and remaining sugar. Spread over the filling. Combine the topping ingredients; sprinkle over the top. Bake 5-8 minutes longer or just until set. Cool on a wire rack.

Refrigerate for at least 2 hours and cut into bars. Refrigerate leftovers. **Yield:** 2 dozen.

Blueberry-Blackberry Rustic Tart

Prep: 20 min. + chilling **Bake:** 55 min.

When you want something extra-special for a summer get-together, it's hard to beat this impressive tart. Fresh berries pack the golden-brown cornmeal crust. If it doesn't disappear after dinner, it will as a late-night snack!
—Priscilla Gilbert, Indian Harbour Beach, Florida

  2 cups all-purpose flour
1/3 cup sugar
1/4 cup yellow cornmeal
2/3 cup cold butter
1/2 cup buttermilk
FILLING:
  4 cups fresh blueberries
  2 cups fresh blackberries
2/3 cup sugar
1/3 cup all-purpose flour
  2 tablespoons lemon juice
  1 egg, beaten
  2 tablespoons turbinado (washed raw) sugar
    or coarse sugar
Whipped cream, optional

In a large bowl, combine the flour, sugar and cornmeal; cut in the butter until crumbly. Gradually add buttermilk, tossing with a fork until dough forms a ball. Cover and refrigerate for at least 30 minutes.

On a lightly floured surface, roll chilled dough into a 14-in. circle. Transfer dough to a parchment paper-lined baking sheet.

In a large bowl, combine the berries, sugar, flour and lemon juice; spoon over the pastry to within 2 in. of the edges. Fold up the edges of the pastry over the filling, leaving the center uncovered. Brush folded pastry with egg; sprinkle with sugar.

Bake at 375° for 55-60 minutes or until crust is golden brown and filling is bubbly. Using the parchment paper, slide tart onto a wire rack to cool. Serve with whipped cream if desired. **Yield:** 8 servings.

Carrot-Spice Cake With Caramel Frosting
(Pictured above right)

Prep: 45 min. **Bake:** 25 min. + cooling

This cake begins with a convenient boxed mix, but it's loaded with extras to give it that from-scratch flavor.
—Nora Fitzgerald, Sevierville, Tennessee

  1 package (18-1/4 ounces) spice cake mix
  1 package (3.4 ounces) instant vanilla
    pudding mix
  4 eggs
3/4 cup water
1/2 cup sour cream
1/4 cup canola oil
  1 cup shredded carrots
  1 can (8 ounces) unsweetened crushed
    pineapple, drained
1/2 cup flaked coconut

1/2 cup chopped pecans
1/4 cup raisins
FROSTING:
   1 cup butter, softened
   1 package (8 ounces) cream cheese, softened
   6 cups confectioners' sugar
1/2 cup caramel ice cream topping
   1 to 2 tablespoons 2% milk

In a large bowl, combine the cake mix, pudding mix, eggs, water, sour cream and oil; beat on low speed for 30 seconds. Beat on medium for 2 minutes. Fold in the carrots, pineapple, coconut, pecans and raisins just until blended. Pour into two greased and floured 9-in. round baking pans.

Bake at 350° for 25-30 minutes or until a toothpick inserted near the center of cake comes out clean. Cool for 10 minutes before removing from pans to wire racks to cool completely.

For the frosting, in a large bowl, beat the butter and cream cheese until fluffy. Add the confectioners' sugar, caramel ice cream topping and enough milk to achieve the desired consistency. Spread the frosting between the layers and over the top and sides of cake. Store in the refrigerator. **Yield:** 12 servings.

GRATE GLOVE

My husband loves carrot cake, but I always seemed to scrape my fingers when grating the carrots. Now I wear a new, unused garden glove while grating. It's just the thing to grasp the carrot and save my hands.
—*Debbie Douglass, Jacksonville, Florida*

Banana-Berry Pie
(Pictured below)

Prep: 30 min. + chilling

Here's a gorgeous pie that makes guests think you fussed. It features a ginger-spiced graham cracker crust, lovely strawberry layer and yummy banana cream topping.
—*Julie Guntzel, Bemidji, Minnesota*

1-1/4 cups graham cracker crumbs
   5 tablespoons butter, melted
   2 tablespoons sugar
   1 teaspoon ground ginger
FILLING:
3/4 cup sugar
   2 tablespoons plus 3/4 teaspoon cornstarch
   1 tablespoon strawberry gelatin
3/4 cup cold water
   2 cups sliced fresh strawberries, *divided*
   1 can (14 ounces) sweetened condensed milk
   1 package (8 ounces) reduced-fat cream cheese
1/4 cup cold 2% milk
   1 package (3.4 ounces) instant banana cream pudding mix

Combine the graham cracker crumbs, butter, sugar and ginger. Press onto the bottom and up the sides of an ungreased 9-in. pie plate. Bake at 350° for 8-10 minutes or until lightly browned. Cool on a wire rack.

For filling, in a small saucepan, combine the sugar, cornstarch and gelatin. Stir in water until smooth. Bring to a boil; cook and stir for 2 minutes or until thickened. Cool slightly. Arrange 1 cup strawberries over the crust. Pour the gelatin mixture over strawberries. Refrigerate for 2 hours or until set.

In a large bowl, beat the sweetened condensed milk, cream cheese, milk and banana cream pudding mix for 1 minute. Spread over top of pie. Refrigerate for 2 hours or until set. Garnish with the remaining strawberries. Refrigerate leftovers. **Yield:** 8 servings.

Raisin Cake Cookies

(Pictured above)

Prep: 15 min. **Bake:** 15 min./batch

A little cinnamon and lots of raisins and nuts make these a nice change from the usual chocolate chip cookies.
—Jacqueline Deibert, Klingerstown, Pennsylvania

    2 cups raisins
    1 cup water
    1 cup butter, softened
1-1/2 cups sugar
    2 eggs
    1 teaspoon vanilla extract
    4 cups all-purpose flour
    3/4 teaspoon baking soda
    3/4 teaspoon baking powder
    1/2 teaspoon salt
    1/2 teaspoon ground cinnamon
    1/2 cup chopped pecans

In a small saucepan, combine raisins and water. Bring to a boil. Reduce heat; simmer, uncovered, for 3 minutes. Set aside to cool. In a large bowl, cream the butter and sugar. Add the eggs, one at a time, beating well after each addition. Beat in vanilla. Combine the flour, baking soda, baking powder, salt and cinnamon; gradually add to the creamed mixture. Stir in the pecans and raisins with liquid.

Drop the cookie dough by rounded tablespoonfuls 2 in. apart onto greased baking sheets. Bake at 350° for 12-15 minutes or until lightly browned. Remove to wire racks to cool. **Yield:** 5 dozen.

Chocolate Cake Mix Cookies

(Pictured above)

Prep: 15 min. **Bake:** 10 min./batch

These gooey, peanut-buttery treats taste like two desserts—cookies and cake—in one. The recipe is perfect when you need something fuss-free but yummy to whip up for a school party or bake sale. You'll save time using a convenient boxed mix.
—Kathy Lazor, Vienna, Ohio

    1 package (8 ounces) cream cheese, softened
1/2 cup butter, softened
    1 egg
    1 teaspoon vanilla extract
    1 package (18-1/4 ounces) chocolate cake mix

1 cup semisweet chocolate chips
1 cup peanut butter chips

In a large bowl, beat the cream cheese and butter until smooth. Beat in the egg and vanilla. Add the cake mix; beat on low speed until blended. Stir in chocolate and peanut butter chips.

Drop by rounded tablespoonfuls 2 in. apart onto greased baking sheets. Bake at 375° for 10-12 minutes or until set. Cool for 3 minutes before removing to wire racks. Store in an airtight container. **Yield:** 4 dozen.

Toffee Ice Cream Pie
(Pictured below)

Prep: 25 min. + freezing

This is my sister's recipe, which I modified a bit to save me time in the kitchen. Everyone who tastes it wants a second slice. —Janell Greisen, San Dimas, California

1 quart vanilla ice cream, softened
1 Heath candy bar (1.4 ounces), crushed
1 chocolate crumb crust (8 inches)
CHOCOLATE SAUCE:
1 cup (6 ounces) semisweet chocolate chips
1/4 cup butter, cubed
1 cup confectioners' sugar
1 can (5 ounces) evaporated milk
1 teaspoon vanilla extract

In a large bowl, combine ice cream and crushed candy; spread into crust. Cover and freeze until firm.

In a small saucepan, melt chocolate chips and butter over medium-low heat. Add confectioners' sugar and evaporated milk; cook and stir for 4-5 minutes or until thickened. Remove from the heat; stir in vanilla. Cut pie into slices and drizzle with sauce. **Yield:** 8 servings.

Berries with Vanilla Custard
(Pictured above)

Prep: 20 min. + chilling

What a simple, delectable way to savor fresh raspberries! For variety, try the custard with strawberries or peaches. —Sarah Vasques, Milford, New Hampshire

1 cup half-and-half cream
2 egg yolks
2 tablespoons sugar
2 teaspoons vanilla extract
2 cups fresh raspberries

In a small saucepan, combine the cream, egg yolks and sugar. Cook and stir over medium heat until mixture reaches 160° and is thick enough to coat the back of a spoon. Remove from the heat; stir in vanilla. Cover and chill until serving. Serve with berries. **Yield:** 4 servings.

CREAM CLUE

Want to make Berries with Vanilla Custard (recipe above) but don't usually keep half-and-half cream on hand? For half-and-half cream in dishes that are cooked or baked, you may substitute 4-1/2 teaspoons melted butter plus enough whole milk to equal 1 cup. One cup of evaporated milk may also be substituted for each cup of half-and-half cream.

CHAPTER 15

Make-Ahead Marvels

Get a head start on your busy weekdays, hectic holidays or any occasion by preparing these convenient recipes in advance. You and your family will be glad you did!

Make mouthwatering dishes such as Chicken Pasta Casserole, Grilled Asian Flank Steak and yummy Toffee Apple Cheese Pie the night before to ensure meal prep is a breeze the next day.

Or, for even more of a jump on things, pop favorites such as Quick Pizza Rolls, Southwestern Pork & Pasta and Banana Split Brownie Cake in the freezer well ahead of time.

Later on, when you have only moments to spare, you can turn to your own home cooking—all ready and waiting for you! ■

FIX FOR THE FUTURE. Grilled Teriyaki Pork Tenderloin (p. 241).

Quick Pizza Rolls
(Pictured above)

Prep: 35 min. **Bake:** 10 min.

These are great for a casual party or movie night at home. You can freeze a bunch, then thaw and bake as many as you need. —Debbie Gray, Gilbert, Iowa

     1 pound ground beef
 1/2 cup chopped green pepper
 1/4 cup chopped onion
     1 can (8 ounces) tomato sauce
     1 can (6 ounces) tomato paste
 1/4 cup water
     1 garlic clove, minced
     1 teaspoon sugar
     1 teaspoon Italian seasoning
 1/2 teaspoon salt
     6 French rolls
 3/4 cup shredded cheddar cheese
 3/4 cup shredded part-skim mozzarella cheese

In a large skillet, cook ground beef, green pepper and onion over medium heat until the meat is no longer pink; drain. Add the tomato sauce, tomato paste, water, garlic, sugar, Italian seasoning and salt. Bring to a boil. Reduce heat; simmer, uncovered, for 10 minutes or until heated through.

Cut 1/4 in. off the top of each roll; set aside. Carefully hollow out bottom of roll, leaving a 1/4-in. shell (discard the removed bread or save for another use). Fill each roll with 1/2 cup meat mixture. Sprinkle with cheeses. Replace bread tops.

Place the needed number of sandwiches on a baking sheet. Bake at 350° for 10-15 minutes or until heated through. Individually wrap the remaining unbaked sandwiches tightly in foil; freeze for up to 3 months.

To use frozen sandwiches: Thaw in the refrigerator overnight. Remove from the refrigerator 30 minutes before baking. Place foil-wrapped sandwiches on baking sheet. Bake at 350° for 30-35 minutes or until heated through. **Yield:** 6 servings.

Chicken Pasta Casserole
(Pictured below)

Prep: 25 min. + chilling **Bake:** 55 min.

Take a little time to put together this family favorite on Sunday, and your Monday dinner will be fuss-free. —Marianna Pickering, Neenah, Wisconsin

     5 cups uncooked egg noodles
 1/2 cup grated Parmesan cheese
     1 egg, lightly beaten
     1 tablespoon garlic powder
 1-1/4 teaspoons pepper, *divided*
     1 pound chicken tenderloins
     1 medium onion, sliced
     2 celery ribs, chopped
     3 tablespoons butter
 1-3/4 cups half-and-half cream, *divided*
     2 cups (8 ounces) shredded part-skim mozzarella cheese
     1 can (10-3/4 ounces) condensed cream of celery soup, undiluted
 1/2 cup white wine *or* chicken broth
     1 tablespoon dried parsley flakes

Cook the noodles according to the package directions. Meanwhile, in a large bowl, combine the Parmesan cheese, egg, garlic powder and 1 teaspoon pepper; set aside. Drain noodles and rinse in cold water; add to egg mixture. Set aside.

In a large skillet, cook the chicken, onion, celery and remaining pepper in butter over medium heat for 12-15 minutes or until chicken is no longer pink. Stir in 1/2 cup cream; heat through.

In a greased 13-in. x 9-in. baking dish, layer half of noodle mixture, chicken mixture and mozzarella cheese. Repeat layers. Combine the celery soup, wine, parsley and remaining cream; pour over the top. Cover and refrigerate overnight.

Remove from refrigerator 30 minutes before baking. Cover and bake at 350° for 40 minutes. Bake, uncovered, for 15-20 minutes longer or until bubbly and cheese is melted. **Yield:** 6 servings.

Ham and Egg Breakfast Casseroles
(Pictured above)

Prep: 25 min. **Bake:** 30 min. + standing

I created this one day while trying to use up leftovers in the refrigerator. Even my picky children loved it!
—Lisa Pogue, Keithville, Louisiana

- 1 pound large fresh mushrooms, coarsely chopped
- 1/3 cup butter, cubed
- 1/2 teaspoon Italian seasoning
- 1/8 teaspoon pepper
- 4 cups (16 ounces) shredded sharp cheddar cheese
- 1-3/4 cups cubed fully cooked ham
- 1/2 cup shredded Parmesan cheese
- 2 tablespoons all-purpose flour
- 24 eggs
- 2 cups heavy whipping cream
- 1 tablespoon Dijon mustard
- 1/8 teaspoon white pepper

In a Dutch oven, saute mushrooms in butter until tender. Add the Italian seasoning and pepper; saute 1 minute longer. Spread the mushroom mixture evenly into two greased 13-in. x 9-in. baking dishes. In a large bowl, combine cheddar cheese, ham, Parmesan cheese and flour. Sprinkle over mushroom mixture.

In a large bowl, whisk the eggs, cream, mustard and white pepper. Pour over cheese mixture. Cover and freeze one casserole for up to 3 months. Bake remaining casserole, uncovered, at 350° for 30-35 minutes or until a knife inserted near the center comes out clean. Let stand 10 minutes before cutting.

To use frozen casserole: Remove casserole from the freezer 30 minutes before baking (do not thaw). Cover and bake at 350° for 55 minutes. Uncover; bake 15-20 minutes longer or until a knife inserted near the center comes out clean. Let stand for 10 minutes before cutting.
Yield: 2 casseroles (12 servings each).

Chicken 'n' Berry Salad
(Pictured below)

Prep: 15 min. + marinating **Grill:** 10 min.

We like this hearty main-dish salad any time of year, but especially in summer when blueberries and strawberries are in season. —Sheri Abernathy, Lemont, Illinois

- 1/2 cup sugar
- 1/2 cup red wine vinegar
- 1/2 cup olive oil
- 1 garlic clove, minced
- 1/2 teaspoon salt
- 1/4 teaspoon pepper
- 2 pounds boneless skinless chicken breasts
- 6 cups torn romaine
- 6 cups torn red leaf lettuce
- 1 pint fresh blueberries
- 1 pint fresh strawberries, sliced
- 2 cups (8 ounces) shredded part-skim mozzarella cheese
- 1 cup chopped walnuts

In a large bowl, whisk the first six ingredients. Pour 3/4 cup marinade into a large resealable plastic bag; add the chicken. Seal bag and turn to coat; refrigerate overnight. Cover and refrigerate remaining marinade.

Drain and discard marinade. Grill chicken, covered, over medium heat for 5-8 minutes on each side or until juices run clear. Cut into strips.

In a large bowl, combine the lettuces, blueberries, strawberries, mozzarella cheese and walnuts. Add the reserved marinade; toss to coat. Top with sliced chicken.
Yield: 9 servings.

Southwestern Pork & Pasta
(Pictured above)

Prep: 25 min. **Cook:** 20 min.

This filling stovetop supper features green chilies, beans, salsa and spices for south-of-the-border taste. Also try it with boneless, skinless chicken breast instead of pork.
—Nicole Filizetti, Grand Marais, Michigan

1 package (16 ounces) penne pasta
2 pork tenderloins (1 pound *each*), cut into
   1-inch cubes
2 tablespoons olive oil
8 green onions, chopped
4 garlic cloves, minced
3 cans (14-1/2 ounces *each*) diced tomatoes
   with mild green chilies, undrained
2 cans (15 ounces *each*) black beans, rinsed
   and drained
1 package (16 ounces) frozen corn, thawed
1 jar (16 ounces) salsa
1 tablespoon chili powder
1 teaspoon salt
1 teaspoon ground cumin
1 teaspoon paprika *or* smoked paprika
1/2 teaspoon pepper
1/4 teaspoon cayenne pepper
1 tablespoon cornstarch
2 tablespoons cold water
Sour cream

Cook the pasta according to the package directions. Meanwhile, in a Dutch oven, cook pork in oil in batches over medium heat for 6-7 minutes or until juices run clear; return all to the pan. Add onions and garlic; cook 1 minute longer. Stir in tomatoes, beans, corn, salsa and spices. Bring to a boil. Reduce heat; simmer, uncovered, for 5 minutes.

Combine the cornstarch and cold water until smooth. Gradually stir into pan. Bring to a boil; cook and stir for 2 minutes or until slightly thickened. Drain pasta; add to pork mixture and toss to coat.

Serve desired amount of pasta with sour cream. Cool remaining pasta; transfer to freezer containers. Cover and freeze for up to 3 months.

To use frozen pasta: Thaw pasta in the refrigerator. Place in an ungreased shallow microwave-safe dish. Cover and microwave on high until heated through. **Yield:** 10 servings.

Pesto-Chicken Penne Casseroles
(Pictured below)

Prep: 20 min. **Bake:** 40 min.

With this make-ahead recipe, you get two family-pleasing meals—one for now, one to pop in the freezer for later.
—Laura Kayser, Ankeny, Iowa

- 1 package (16 ounces) penne pasta
- 6 cups cubed cooked chicken
- 4 cups (16 ounces) shredded Italian cheese blend
- 3 cups fresh baby spinach
- 1 can (15 ounces) crushed tomatoes
- 1 jar (15 ounces) Alfredo sauce
- 1 jar (10 ounces) prepared pesto
- 1-1/2 cups 2% milk
- 1/2 cup seasoned bread crumbs
- 1/2 cup grated Parmesan cheese
- 1 tablespoon olive oil

Cook pasta according to package directions. Meanwhile, in a large bowl, combine the chicken, cheese blend, spinach, tomatoes, Alfredo sauce, pesto and milk. Drain pasta and add to chicken mixture; toss to coat.

Transfer to two greased 8-in. square baking dishes. In a small bowl, combine the bread crumbs, Parmesan cheese and oil; sprinkle over casseroles.

Cover and freeze one casserole for up to 3 months. Cover and bake remaining casserole at 350° for 40-45 minutes or until bubbly.

To use frozen casserole: Thaw in the refrigerator overnight. Remove from the refrigerator 30 minutes before baking. Cover and bake at 350° for 50-60 minutes or until bubbly. **Yield:** 2 casseroles (6 servings each).

Grilled Caesar Chicken Breasts
(Pictured above)

Prep: 10 min. + marinating **Grill:** 15 min.

Marinated overnight in creamy Caesar salad dressing and a few other ingredients, this chicken grills up juicy, tender and flavorful. It's great with garden-fresh veggies.
—Marcia Wallenfeldt, Kent, Ohio

- 1/2 cup creamy Caesar salad dressing
- 3 tablespoons olive oil
- 3 tablespoons Dijon mustard
- 6 garlic cloves, minced
- 4 boneless skinless chicken breast halves (5 ounces *each*)

In a large resealable plastic bag, combine the dressing, oil, mustard and garlic. Add the chicken; seal bag and turn to coat. Refrigerate for 8 hours or overnight.

Drain and discard the marinade. Grill the chicken, covered, over medium heat or broil 4 in. from the heat for 6-8 minutes on each side or until a meat thermometer reads 170°. **Yield:** 4 servings.

COOKED CONVENIENCE

I buy several packages of chicken pieces at once and bake it all, skin side up, on foil-lined pans. When it's cool, I remove the skin and bones, cube the meat and freeze it in measured portions for casseroles and other dishes. —*Marilyn Wolfe, Des Moines, Iowa*

into a freezer container. Waffles and syrup may be frozen for up to 2 months.

To use frozen waffles and syrup: Reheat waffles in a toaster. Microwave syrup until heated through and serve with waffles. **Yield:** 14 waffles (1 cup syrup).

Frozen Strawberry Delight
(Pictured below)

Prep: 20 min. + freezing

Pretty and refreshing, this frosty dessert is sure to become a favorite. Mix fresh blueberries in with the strawberries to create a patriotic look for the Fourth of July.
—*Barbara Christensen, Jacksonville, Florida*

    1 can (14 ounces) sweetened condensed milk
1/4 cup lemon juice
    4 cups sliced fresh strawberries, *divided*
    1 carton (8 ounces) frozen whipped topping,
      thawed and *divided*
    8 cream-filled chocolate sandwich cookies,
      crushed

Line an 8-in. x 4-in. loaf pan with foil, letting edges hang over sides; set aside.

In a large bowl, combine milk and lemon juice; fold in 2 cups strawberries and 2 cups whipped topping. Transfer half of the mixture to prepared pan. Sprinkle with cookie crumbs; top with remaining strawberry mixture. Cover and freeze for 6 hours or overnight.

To serve, using the foil, lift the dessert out of the pan. Invert onto a serving plate; discard the foil. Spread the remaining whipped topping over the top and sides of dessert; garnish with remaining strawberries. Cut into slices. **Yield:** 10 servings.

Easy Morning Waffles
(Pictured above)

Prep: 20 min. **Cook:** 5 min./batch

Making your own fluffy waffles from scratch takes no time at all, as this recipe from our Test Kitchen staff proves. With a hint of cinnamon and homemade syrup, it has the frozen store-bought versions beat.

    2 cups all-purpose flour
    1 tablespoon brown sugar
    2 teaspoons baking powder
1/2 teaspoon salt
1/2 teaspoon ground cinnamon
    3 eggs, *separated*
    2 cups 2% milk
1/4 cup canola oil
3/4 teaspoon vanilla extract
SYRUP:
1/2 cup butter, cubed
1/2 cup honey
    1 teaspoon ground cinnamon

In a large bowl, combine the flour, brown sugar, baking powder, salt and cinnamon. In a small bowl, whisk the egg yolks, milk, oil and vanilla; stir into dry ingredients just until moistened. In a small bowl, beat egg whites until stiff peaks form; fold into batter.

Bake in a preheated waffle iron according to the manufacturer's directions until golden brown.

In a microwave, melt the butter, honey and cinnamon; stir until smooth.

Serve the desired amount of waffles with the syrup. Arrange the remaining waffles in a single layer on sheet pans. Freeze overnight or until frozen. Transfer to a resealable plastic freezer bag. Pour the remaining syrup

Grilled Teriyaki Pork Tenderloin

(Pictured below and on page 234)

Prep: 10 min. + marinating **Grill:** 25 min.

In this five-ingredient recipe, pork tenderloin is treated to a mustard-and-teriyaki sauce marinade and dressed up with a sprinkling of sliced green onion. The result is an elegant from-the-grill entree that's ready in a flash.
—Tahnia Fox, Trenton, Michigan

  3/4 cup honey mustard
  3/4 cup teriyaki marinade
    1 pork tenderloin (1 pound)
    2 garlic cloves, minced
    1 green onion, chopped

In a small bowl, combine the honey mustard and teriyaki marinade; pour 1 cup into a large resealable plastic bag. Add the pork and garlic; seal the bag and turn to coat. Refrigerate for 6 hours or overnight. Cover and refrigerate remaining marinade.

Using long-handled tongs, dip a paper towel in cooking oil and lightly coat grill rack. Prepare grill for indirect heat. Drain and discard the marinade from pork. Grill, covered, over indirect medium-hot heat for 25-30 minutes or until a meat thermometer reads 160°, basting with the reserved marinade and turning occasionally.

Let stand for 5 minutes before slicing. Sprinkle with onion. **Yield:** 4 servings.

Frozen Banana Treats

(Pictured above)

Prep: 15 min. + freezing

I love making these with my young son. He's in charge of cutting the bananas with a butter knife, pushing in the sticks and rolling the treats in the granola. The next day, we both enjoy eating the fruits of our labor!
—Aimee Lawrence, Wimberley, Texas

1-1/2 cups granola without raisins, crushed
    1 cup (6 ounces) semisweet chocolate chips
  1/3 cup creamy peanut butter
    8 Popsicle sticks
    4 large firm bananas, halved widthwise

Sprinkle the granola onto a large piece of waxed paper; set aside. In a microwave, melt the semisweet chocolate chips; stir until smooth. Stir in the creamy peanut butter until blended.

Insert a Popsicle stick into each banana half. Spread with chocolate mixture; roll in granola. Wrap in foil and freeze for 24 hours. **Yield:** 8 servings.

▮ MELTING METHOD ▮

To melt the semisweet chocolate for yummy Frozen Banana Treats (recipe above), place the chocolate in a microwave-safe bowl. Melt it on high (100% power) for 1 minute, then stir. Microwave at additional 10- to 20-second intervals, stirring until smooth.

Chicken & Sausage Manicotti
(Pictured below)

Prep: 25 min. **Bake:** 55 min. + standing

This hearty meal-in-one is sure to please meat-lovers and anyone with a big appetite. For a change of pace, try it with ground turkey or beef instead of sausage.
—*Fran Scott, Birmingham, Michigan*

- 1 pound sliced fresh mushrooms
- 2 medium green peppers, chopped
- 2 medium onions, chopped
- 1 tablespoon olive oil
- 4 garlic cloves, minced
- 3 jars (26 ounces *each*) spaghetti sauce
- 1-1/4 cups water
- 1-1/2 pounds chicken tenderloins, halved lengthwise
- 4 teaspoons dried basil
- 2 teaspoons chicken seasoning
- 2 packages (8 ounces *each*) uncooked manicotti shells
- 1 pound fully cooked andouille *or* Italian sausage links, halved lengthwise and sliced
- 2 cups (8 ounces) shredded part-skim mozzarella cheese
- 2 cups (8 ounces) shredded cheddar cheese

In a Dutch oven, saute mushrooms, peppers and onions in oil until tender; add garlic, cook 1 minute longer. Stir in spaghetti sauce and water.

Sprinkle the chicken with basil and chicken seasoning. Stuff chicken into uncooked manicotti shells. Spread 1 cup sauce mixture in each of two greased 13-in. x 9-in. baking dishes. Arrange the manicotti over sauce; sprinkle with sausage. Pour remaining sauce over top; sprinkle with cheeses.

Cover and freeze one casserole for up to 3 months. Cover and bake remaining casserole at 375° for 55-65 minutes or until bubbly and pasta is tender. Let stand for 10 minutes before serving.

To use frozen manicotti: Thaw in the refrigerator overnight. Remove from refrigerator 30 minutes before baking. Cover and bake at 375° for 55-65 minutes or until bubbly and pasta is tender. Let stand for 10 minutes before serving. **Yield:** 2 casseroles (7 servings each).

Editor's Note: This recipe was tested with McCormick's Montreal Chicken Seasoning. Look for it in the spice aisle.

Carolina Marinated Pork Tenderloin

Prep: 10 min. + marinating **Grill:** 25 min.

You'll need just molasses, mustard and vinegar to make this melt-in-your-mouth marinade for pork tenderloin.
—*Sharisse Dunn, Rocky Point, North Carolina*

- 1/4 cup molasses
- 2 tablespoons spicy brown mustard
- 1 tablespoon cider vinegar
- 1 pork tenderloin (1 pound)

In a large resealable plastic bag, combine the molasses, mustard and vinegar; add the pork. Seal bag and turn to coat; refrigerate for 8 hours or overnight.

Prepare the grill for indirect heat, using a drip pan. Drain and discard marinade. Using long-handled tongs, moisten a paper towel with cooking oil and lightly coat the grill rack. Place the pork over the drip pan and grill, covered, over indirect medium-hot heat for 25-30 minutes or until a meat thermometer reads 160°, turning occasionally. Let pork stand for 5 minutes before slicing. **Yield:** 4 servings.

Grilled Asian Flank Steak

Prep: 10 min. + marinating **Grill:** 15 min.

Friends and family keep asking me to fix this tasty entree that combines three of my favorites: Asian food, ginger and steak.
—*Warren Paulson, Mesa, Arizona*

- 1/4 cup thinly sliced green onions
- 1/4 cup unsweetened pineapple juice
- 1/4 cup soy sauce
- 1/4 cup ketchup
- 1/4 cup plum sauce
- 2 tablespoons minced fresh cilantro
- 3 garlic cloves, minced
- 1 tablespoon minced fresh gingerroot
- 1 beef flank steak (1-1/4 pounds)

In a small bowl, combine the first eight ingredients. Pour 3/4 cup marinade into a large resealable plastic bag; add the beef flank steak. Seal the bag and turn to coat; refrigerate for 4 hours or overnight. Cover and refrigerate remaining marinade.

Drain and discard the marinade. Grill steak, covered, over medium heat 6-8 minutes on each side or until the meat reaches desired doneness (for medium-rare, the meat thermometer should read 145°; medium, 160°;

well-done, 170°), basting occasionally with reserved marinade. To serve, thinly slice steak across the grain. **Yield:** 4 servings.

Chicken Potpies
(Pictured above)

Prep: 20 min. **Bake:** 35 min. + standing

My aunt came up with this recipe, and I tweaked it to fit my family's tastes. I think they like it so much because of the sage. —Lysa Davis, Pine Bluff, Arkansas

- 2 cans (9-3/4 ounces *each*) chunk white chicken, drained
- 1 can (15-1/4 ounces) lima beans, drained
- 1 can (15 ounces) sliced carrots, drained
- 1 jar (4-1/2 ounces) sliced mushrooms, drained
- 1 can (14-1/2 ounces) sliced potatoes, drained
- 1 can (10-3/4 ounces) condensed cream of chicken soup, undiluted
- 1 can (10-3/4 ounces) condensed cream of mushroom soup, undiluted
- 1-1/2 teaspoons rubbed sage
- 1/4 teaspoon salt
- 1/4 teaspoon pepper
- 2 packages (15 ounces *each*) refrigerated pie pastry
- 1 tablespoon butter, melted

In a large bowl, combine the first 10 ingredients. Line two 9-in. pie plates with bottom crusts. Add the filling. Roll out the remaining pastry to fit the tops of pies; place over the filling. Trim, seal and flute the edges. Cut slits in pastry; brush with butter.

Cover and freeze one potpie for up to 3 months. Bake remaining pie at 375° for 35-40 minutes or until golden brown. Let stand for 10 minutes before cutting.

To use frozen potpie: Remove the potpie from the freezer 30 minutes before baking. Cover edges of crust loosely with foil; place on a baking sheet.

Bake at 425° for 30 minutes. Reduce heat to 375°; remove foil. Bake 55-60 minutes longer or until golden brown. Let stand for 10 minutes before cutting. **Yield:** 2 pies (6 servings each).

Creamy Ham Noodle Casserole
(Pictured below)

Prep: 20 min. **Bake:** 25 min.

Top this bake with crushed butter-flavored crackers for a little crunch, and you've got a dish everyone will love. —Marion Little, Humboldt, Tennessee

- 10 cups uncooked tricolor spiral pasta
- 4 celery ribs, chopped
- 1 medium green pepper, chopped
- 1/2 cup chopped onion
- 1/4 cup butter, cubed
- 3 cans (10-3/4 ounces *each*) condensed cheddar cheese soup, undiluted
- 3 cups 2% milk
- 1 teaspoon salt
- 4 cups cubed fully cooked ham
- 2 cans (8 ounces *each*) mushroom stems and pieces, drained
- 1 cup crushed butter-flavored crackers

Cook the pasta according to the package directions. Meanwhile, in a Dutch oven, saute the celery, pepper and onion in butter until tender. Stir in the soup, milk and salt. In a very large bowl, combine the soup mixture, ham and mushrooms. Drain pasta; add to soup mixture and toss to coat.

Transfer to two greased 13-in. x 9-in. baking dishes. Top with cracker crumbs. Cover and freeze one casserole for up to 3 months. Bake remaining casserole, uncovered, at 350° for 20-25 minutes or until golden brown.

To use frozen casserole: Thaw the casserole in the refrigerator overnight. Remove from the refrigerator 30 minutes before baking. Bake, uncovered, at 350° for 50-55 minutes or until the casserole is heated through. **Yield:** 2 casseroles (9 servings each).

Butterfinger Ice Cream
(Pictured above)

Prep: 10 min. **Process:** 20 min./batch + freezing

Crushed Butterfinger candy bars are mixed right into this homemade ice cream. It's a sweet treat everyone loves.
—*Tammy Drost, Cheyenne, Wyoming*

- 1/2 gallon whole milk
- 1 can (14 ounces) sweetened condensed milk
- 1 carton (16 ounces) frozen whipped topping, thawed
- 6 Butterfinger candy bars (2.1 ounces *each*), crushed

In a large bowl, whisk milk and condensed milk. Whisk in the whipped topping until combined; stir in crushed candy bars.

Fill cylinder of ice cream freezer two-thirds full; freeze according to the manufacturer's directions. Refrigerate remaining mixture until ready to freeze.

When the ice cream is frozen, transfer to a freezer container; freeze ice cream for 2-4 hours before serving. **Yield:** 4 quarts.

Toffee Apple Cheese Pie

Prep: 15 min. **Bake:** 40 min. + chilling

With a vanilla wafer crust, this cheesecake-like dessert is decadent from top to bottom. Try it for Thanksgiving or other fall feasts. —*Marie Rizzio, Interlochen, Michigan*

- 1 cup crushed vanilla wafers (about 30 wafers)
- 1/4 cup butter, melted
- 2 tablespoons sugar

FILLING:
- 2 packages (8 ounces *each*) cream cheese, softened
- 1/2 cup sugar
- 1/2 cup reduced-fat sour cream
- 1/2 teaspoon almond extract
- 2 eggs, beaten
- 1-1/2 cups apple pie filling
- 1/3 cup chopped walnuts
- 1/3 cup toffee bits

TOPPING:
- 1/3 cup chopped walnuts
- 1/3 cup toffee bits

Combine the vanilla wafer crumbs, butter and sugar; press onto the bottom and up the sides of an ungreased 9-in. pie plate.

In a large bowl, beat the cream cheese, sugar, sour cream and extract until smooth. Add eggs; beat on low speed just until combined. Coarsely chop the pie filling; cover and refrigerate 3/4 cup for the topping. Stir the walnuts, toffee bits and remaining pie filling into cream cheese mixture. Pour into crust.

Bake at 325° for 40-45 minutes or until the center is almost set. Cool on a wire rack for 1 hour. Refrigerate for 4 hours or overnight. Just before serving, top the pie with reserved pie filling, walnuts and toffee bits. **Yield:** 8 servings.

Banana Split Brownie Cake
(Pictured below)

Prep: 20 min. + freezing

"Yum" is the word when it comes to this creative freezer cake from our Test Kitchen home economists. They put brownies on the bottom and topped them with two kinds of ice cream, bananas, hot fudge and nuts.

- 2 packages (13 ounces *each*) fudge brownies
- 1 quart strawberry ice cream, softened

3 large firm bananas, halved lengthwise
1 cup hot fudge ice cream topping, warmed
1 quart vanilla ice cream, softened
3/4 cup chopped pecans

Arrange the brownies in a greased 9-in. springform pan, cutting them to fit and filling in small holes. Spread with the strawberry ice cream. Cover and freeze for 3 hours or until firm.

Arrange bananas over the ice cream, cutting them to fit as needed. Spread with fudge topping and vanilla ice cream. Sprinkle with pecans. Cover tightly and freeze overnight. May be frozen for up to 2 months.

Remove from the freezer 10 minutes before serving. Carefully run a knife around the edge of pan to loosen; remove sides of pan. **Yield:** 14 servings.

Editor's Note: This recipe was prepared with Little Debbie fudge brownies.

SOFT SOLUTION

Soften ice cream by transferring it from the freezer to the refrigerator 20-30 minutes before using it. Or, let it stand at room temperature for 10-15 minutes. Hard ice cream can also be softened in the microwave at 30% power for about 30 seconds.

Marinated Pork Medallions
(Pictured above)

Prep: 15 min. + marinating   **Grill:** 10 min.

Serve this simple main course with a tossed green salad, corn and a dinner roll for a summery, standout supper.
—*Melanie Miller, Bascom, Ohio*

1/2 cup packed brown sugar
1/2 cup Italian salad dressing
1/4 cup unsweetened pineapple juice
3 tablespoons soy sauce
2 pork tenderloins (1 pound *each*), cut into 3/4-inch slices

In a small bowl, combine brown sugar, salad dressing, pineapple juice and soy sauce. Pour 1/2 cup marinade into a large resealable plastic bag. Add the pork; seal bag and turn to coat. Refrigerate overnight. Cover and refrigerate remaining marinade.

Drain and discard the marinade. Using long-handled tongs, moisten a paper towel with cooking oil and lightly coat the grill rack.

Grill pork, covered, over medium heat or broil 4 in. from the heat for 5-7 minutes on each side or until a meat thermometer reads 160°, basting occasionally with reserved marinade. **Yield:** 5 servings.

CHAPTER 16

Casseroles & Oven Suppers

Pull an ooey-gooey casserole or other piping-hot entree from the oven, and family members come running! In this chapter, you'll find dozens of delicious choices that go together quickly before baking.

For casual dinners anytime, enjoy favorites such as Hearty Shepherd's Pie, Creamy Onion Lasagna, Stuffed-Crust Chicken Pizza and Vegetarian Tacos.

We've featured lots of main courses for special occasions, too. Try Three-Cheese Turkey Manicotti, Savory Stuffed Pork Chops, Meat Loaf Wellington and Reuben Quiche.

All of these from-the-oven options can be assembled in mere minutes. After that, just bake—and dinner's done! ∎

HEAT IT UP. Spinach Chicken Casserole (p. 250).

Three-Cheese Turkey Manicotti

(Pictured above)

Prep: 25 min. **Bake:** 35 min.

My husband always requests this dinner. With a hearty meat sauce and three kinds of cheese, it's his favorite.
—LuAnne Wallace Bennett, Powder Springs, Georgia

     12 uncooked manicotti shells
      1 pound ground turkey
      1 large sweet onion, chopped
      1 jar (26 ounces) three-cheese spaghetti sauce
      2 teaspoons sugar
      2 teaspoons Italian seasoning
      1 teaspoon onion powder
      1 teaspoon garlic powder
      2 cups (8 ounces) shredded cheddar-Monterey Jack cheese
      1 carton (15 ounces) ricotta cheese
   1/2 cup grated Parmesan cheese, *divided*
      1 egg

Cook manicotti shells according to package directions. Meanwhile, in a large skillet, cook turkey and onion over medium heat until meat is no longer pink; drain. Stir in the spaghetti sauce, sugar, Italian seasoning, onion powder and garlic powder. Place 1 cup meat sauce into a greased 13-in. x 9-in. baking dish.

Drain manicotti shells. In a large bowl, combine the cheddar-Monterey Jack cheese, ricotta cheese, 1/4 cup Parmesan cheese and egg. Stuff into shells. Place shells over meat sauce. Top with remaining sauce. Sprinkle with remaining Parmesan. Cover and bake at 350° for 35-40 minutes or until bubbly. **Yield:** 6 servings.

Creole Beef Casserole

Prep: 25 min. **Bake:** 40 min.

Savor the flavor of Cajun country with this distinctively seasoned dish. Ground beef and hash browns make it filling. —Nicki Austin, Lawrenceville, Illinois

      2 cans (10-3/4 ounces *each*) condensed cream of chicken soup, undiluted
      2 cups (16 ounces) sour cream
      1 small onion, chopped
   1/4 teaspoon pepper
      1 package (30 ounces) frozen shredded hash brown potatoes, thawed
      2 cups (8 ounces) shredded cheddar cheese
   1-1/2 pounds ground beef
      1 cup ketchup
   1/4 cup packed brown sugar
      3 teaspoons Creole seasoning
      1 teaspoon garlic salt
      1 teaspoon dried oregano
   1/4 teaspoon cayenne pepper
   3/4 cup crushed cornflakes
   1/4 cup butter, melted

In a large bowl, combine the soup, sour cream, onion and pepper. Stir in potatoes and cheese; transfer to a greased 3-qt. baking dish.

In a large skillet, cook the ground beef over medium heat until no longer pink; drain. Stir in ketchup, brown sugar and seasonings; spread over potatoes. Combine the cornflakes and butter; sprinkle over the top. Bake, uncovered, at 350° for 40-45 minutes or until bubbly. **Yield:** 8 servings.

Editor's Note: The following spices may be substituted for 1 teaspoon Creole seasoning: 1/4 teaspoon each salt, garlic powder and paprika; and a pinch each of dried thyme, ground cumin and cayenne pepper.

Savory Stuffed Pork Chops

Prep: 10 min. **Bake:** 40 min.

Who'd ever guess stuffed chops could be so simple? Baby spinach and stuffing mix are the secrets to this elegant recipe. —Rebecca Nossaman, Hurricane, West Virginia

      8 boneless pork loin chops (1 inch thick and 8 ounces *each*)
      1 small onion, chopped
   1/2 cup butter, cubed
      5 cups fresh baby spinach
      1 package (6 ounces) sage stuffing mix
   1-1/2 cups (12 ounces) sour cream
   1/2 teaspoon rubbed sage
   1/2 teaspoon lemon-pepper seasoning

Using a sharp knife, cut a pocket in each pork chop. In a large skillet, saute onion in butter until tender. Add spinach, cook until wilted. Stir in the stuffing mix, sour cream and sage.

Fill each chop with about 1/3 cup stuffing mixture; secure with toothpicks if necessary. Place chops on a greased 15-in. x 10-in. x 1-in. baking pan. Sprinkle with lemon-pepper seasoning.

Bake, uncovered, at 350° for 35-40 minutes or until a meat thermometer reads 160°. Discard toothpicks. **Yield:** 8 servings.

Mom's Meat Loaf
(Pictured below)

Prep: 10 min. **Bake:** 35 min.

If you're looking for home-style comfort food, this moist and tender loaf will fill the bill! When I was a child, my mother prepared it for supper at least every other week. She always served scalloped potatoes on the side.
—Helen Lipko, Martinsburg, Pennsylvania

    1 egg, lightly beaten
    1 can (5-1/2 ounces) V8 juice
1/2 cup seasoned bread crumbs
    1 envelope onion soup mix
1/4 cup grated Parmesan cheese
1/4 teaspoon garlic powder
1-1/2 pounds ground beef
1/3 cup ketchup

In a large bowl, combine egg, V8 juice, bread crumbs, onion soup mix, cheese and garlic powder. Crumble beef over mixture and mix well. Pat into an ungreased 9-in. x 5-in. loaf pan.

Bake, uncovered, at 350° for 30 minutes. Spread the ketchup over the top; bake 5-10 minutes longer or until no pink remains and a meat thermometer reads 160°. **Yield:** 8 servings.

Tex-Mex Pizza
(Pictured above)

Prep: 25 min. **Bake:** 15 min.

Loaded with toppings that include beans and corn, this knife-and-fork pie is packed with Southwest taste. It's a great change of pace from the usual pepperoni or sausage pizza. Add avocado and sour cream as garnishes.
—Charlene Chambers, Ormond Beach, Florida

1/2 pound lean ground beef (90% lean)
2/3 cup chopped red onion
    2 garlic cloves, minced
    1 cup salsa
    1 can (4 ounces) chopped green chilies, drained
    1 prebaked 12-inch pizza crust
1-1/2 cups (6 ounces) shredded cheddar cheese
    1 cup canned black beans, rinsed and drained
1/2 cup frozen corn, thawed
    1 can (2-1/4 ounces) sliced ripe olives, drained
    1 medium ripe avocado, peeled and cubed
    2 teaspoons lemon juice
1/2 cup sour cream

In a large skillet, cook the beef, onion and garlic over medium heat until meat is no longer pink; drain. Stir in salsa and chilies.

Place crust on an ungreased pizza pan. Top with the beef mixture, cheese, beans, corn and olives.

Bake at 425° for 15-20 minutes or until edges are lightly browned and cheese is melted. Toss the avocado with lemon juice. Serve the pizza with avocado and sour cream. **Yield:** 8 slices.

Spinach Chicken Casserole

(Pictured below and on page 246)

Prep: 20 min. **Bake:** 20 min.

This is my variation on a recipe I found on the label of a spaghetti sauce jar. After making a few substitutions and additions, I was quite pleased with the results.
—Jackie Wood, Jackson, Tennessee

- 2 cups uncooked penne pasta
- 3/4 pound boneless skinless chicken breasts, cubed
- 1 small onion, chopped
- 1/2 cup chopped green pepper
- 1 jar (26 ounces) spaghetti sauce
- 1 package (16 ounces) frozen leaf spinach, thawed and squeezed dry
- 1 jar (6 ounces) sliced mushrooms, drained
- 1 can (2-1/4 ounces) sliced ripe olives, drained
- 2 cups (8 ounces) shredded part-skim mozzarella cheese, *divided*

Cook the pasta according to the package directions. Meanwhile, in a large nonstick saucepan coated with cooking spray, saute the chicken until no longer pink; set aside.

In the same pan, saute the onion and green pepper until crisp-tender. Add the spaghetti sauce, spinach, mushrooms and ripe olives. Bring to a boil. Reduce heat; simmer, uncovered, for 5 minutes. Drain the pasta; add

chicken and pasta to the pan. Sprinkle with 1 cup cheese and toss to coat.

Transfer to a 13-in. x 9-in. baking dish coated with cooking spray; sprinkle with remaining cheese. Cover and bake at 350° for 20-25 minutes or until cheese is melted. **Yield:** 6 servings.

Beef & Tater Bake

(Pictured above)

Prep: 25 min. **Bake:** 25 min.

The whole family will enjoy this meal-in-one. It combines kid-favorite Tater Tots, ground beef, french-fried onions, veggies and cheese. —Mike Tchou, Pepper Pike, Ohio

- 4 cups frozen Tater Tots
- 1 pound ground beef
- 1 package (16 ounces) frozen chopped broccoli, thawed
- 1 can (10-3/4 ounces) condensed cream of broccoli soup, undiluted
- 1 medium tomato, chopped
- 1 can (2.8 ounces) french-fried onions, *divided*
- 1 cup (4 ounces) shredded Colby-Monterey Jack cheese, *divided*
- 1/3 cup 2% milk
- 1/4 teaspoon garlic powder
- 1/8 teaspoon pepper

Place Tater Tots in an ungreased 13-in. x 9-in. baking dish. Bake, uncovered, at 400° for 10 minutes.

Meanwhile, in a large skillet, cook the ground beef over medium heat until no longer pink; drain. Stir in the broccoli, soup, tomato, 3/4 cup french-fried onions,

1/2 cup cheese, milk, garlic powder and pepper; heat through. Pour over Tater Tots.

Cover and bake for 20 minutes. Uncover; sprinkle with remaining onions and cheese. Bake 5-10 minutes longer or until cheese is melted. **Yield:** 12 servings.

Spicy Shrimp Pizza

Prep: 30 min. **Bake:** 10 min.

A sophisticated blend of seasonings, shrimp and a splash of white wine make this distinctive pizza a winner with adults. It's special enough to serve at a casual get-together but quick enough to whip up on weeknights, too.
— *Debra Udden, Colorado Springs, Colorado*

  1 pound uncooked medium shrimp, peeled and deveined
1/2 to 3/4 teaspoon crushed red pepper flakes
  2 tablespoons olive oil
  1 medium onion, chopped
  5 garlic cloves, minced
 12 cherry tomatoes, halved
  1 can (15 ounces) crushed tomatoes, undrained
  1 cup white wine *or* chicken broth
1/2 teaspoon dried oregano
1/8 teaspoon pepper
  3 tablespoons minced fresh parsley
  1 prebaked 12-inch thin pizza crust
  1 cup (4 ounces) shredded Italian cheese blend
  1 cup (4 ounces) shredded Parmesan *or* Parmigiano-Reggiano cheese

In a large skillet over medium heat, cook the shrimp and pepper flakes in oil for 2-3 minutes or until shrimp turn pink. Remove and keep warm.

In the same skillet, saute onion and garlic until tender. Add cherry tomatoes, crushed tomatoes, white wine, oregano and pepper. Bring to a boil; cook until liquid is reduced, stirring occasionally. Add the shrimp and parsley; heat through.

Place pizza crust on an ungreased pizza pan. Spread the shrimp mixture over crust to within 1/2 in. of edges; sprinkle with cheeses. Bake at 450° for 8-10 minutes or until the cheese is melted and edges are lightly browned. **Yield:** 6 slices.

PRIMPING SHRIMP

To peel and devein shrimp, start on the underside by the head area to remove the shell. Pull the legs and first section of the shell to one side. Continue pulling the shell up around the top and to the other side. Pull off the shell by the tail if desired.

Remove the black vein running down the back of shrimp by making a shallow slit with a paring knife along the back from the head area to the tail. Rinse shrimp under cold water to remove the vein.

Chicken Artichoke Casserole
(Pictured below)

Prep: 20 min. **Bake:** 25 min.

With a flavor that's similar to artichoke dip, this creamy and comforting pasta entree is guaranteed to warm you up on chilly evenings. Keep it in mind when you want to use up cooked chicken that's left over from dinner the night before.
— *Amy Nutoni, La Crescent, Minnesota*

  2 cups uncooked bow tie pasta
  2 cups cubed cooked chicken
  1 can (14 ounces) water-packed artichoke hearts, rinsed, drained and chopped
  1 can (10-3/4 ounces) condensed cream of chicken soup, undiluted
  1 cup shredded Parmesan cheese
  1 cup mayonnaise
1/3 cup 2% milk
  1 garlic clove, minced
1/2 teaspoon onion powder
1/2 teaspoon pepper
  1 cup onion and garlic salad croutons, coarsely crushed

Cook pasta according to package directions. Meanwhile, in a large bowl, combine the chicken, artichokes, soup, cheese, mayonnaise, milk, garlic, onion powder and pepper. Drain pasta; add to chicken mixture.

Transfer to a greased 2-qt. baking dish. Sprinkle with croutons. Bake, uncovered, at 350° for 25-30 minutes or until heated through. **Yield:** 6 servings.

Meat Loaf Wellington

(Pictured below)

Prep: 20 min. **Bake:** 50 min.

Mix up a moist and tasty meat loaf, wrap it in a golden crust and add a wonderfully creamy sauce on the side... you'll have one impressive entree to serve guests!
— *KyAna44, Taste of Home Online Community*

    1 egg, lightly beaten
1/2 cup dry bread crumbs
    1 can (10-3/4 ounces) condensed golden
        mushroom soup, undiluted, *divided*
1/3 cup finely chopped onion
1/4 cup ketchup
    1 garlic clove, minced
    1 teaspoon Worcestershire sauce
    2 pounds lean ground beef (90% lean)
    1 tube (8 ounces) refrigerated crescent rolls
1/3 cup reduced-fat sour cream

In a large bowl, combine egg, bread crumbs, 1/2 cup soup, onion, ketchup, garlic and Worcestershire sauce. Crumble the beef over mixture and mix well. Shape into a 9-in. x 5-in. rectangle and place in a greased 15-in. x 10-in. x 1-in. baking pan.

Bake, uncovered, at 375° for 40 minutes. Unroll the crescent dough; seal the seams and perforations. Drape dough over meat loaf to cover the top, sides and ends; seal the ends. Bake 12-15 minutes longer or until a meat thermometer reads 160° and crust is golden brown. Let stand for 5 minutes.

Meanwhile, in a small microwave-safe bowl, combine sour cream and remaining soup. Cover and microwave on high for 30-40 seconds or until heated through. Serve with meat loaf. **Yield:** 10 servings.

Hearty Shepherd's Pie

(Pictured above)

Prep: 35 min. **Bake:** 20 min.

This comforting recipe relies on instant mashed potatoes, canned soup and other convenience products, but fresh rosemary lends a burst of just-picked flavor. The beefy pie makes a very filling meal with a side of corn bread.
— *Melissa Birdsong, Gilbert, South Carolina*

    1 pound lean ground beef (90% lean)
    1 medium onion, chopped
    1 can (10-3/4 ounces) condensed cream of
        celery soup, undiluted
    1 can (8-1/2 ounces) peas and carrots, drained
    1 jar (4-1/2 ounces) sliced mushrooms,
        drained
1/4 cup water
    1 tablespoon minced fresh rosemary *or*
        1 teaspoon dried rosemary, crushed
    1 teaspoon garlic powder, *divided*
1/2 teaspoon salt
1/4 teaspoon pepper
    2 cups prepared instant mashed potatoes
    1 package (3 ounces) cream cheese, softened
        and cubed
1/4 cup sour cream
1/4 cup grated Parmesan cheese

In a large skillet, cook the ground beef and onion over medium heat until the meat is no longer pink; drain. Stir in the cream of celery soup, peas and carrots, mushrooms, water, rosemary, 1/2 teaspoon garlic powder, salt and pepper; heat through. Transfer mixture to a greased 9-in. deep-dish pie plate.

In a large bowl, beat mashed potatoes, cream cheese, sour cream and remaining garlic powder until blended. Spread over the top. Sprinkle with Parmesan cheese.

Bake, uncovered, at 350° for 20-25 minutes or until heated through and the mashed potatoes are lightly browned. **Yield:** 6 servings.

Three-Cheese Veggie Pizza
(Pictured below)

Prep: 30 min. **Bake:** 20 min.

We love pizza so much, we consider ourselves connoisseurs! This version with a breadstick-dough crust is great when time is short. —Sue Ellen Clark, Wyoming, New York

- 2 tubes (8 ounces *each*) refrigerated garlic breadsticks
- 3 plum tomatoes, seeded and finely chopped
- 1 small yellow summer squash, finely chopped
- 1 small zucchini, finely chopped
- 4 tablespoons Italian salad dressing, *divided*
- 1 tablespoon minced fresh parsley
- 2 teaspoons garlic powder, *divided*
- 1 teaspoon dried basil
- 1/2 teaspoon Italian seasoning
- 1/2 cup grated Romano *or* Parmesan cheese
- 2 cups (8 ounces) shredded Monterey Jack cheese, *divided*
- 2/3 cup ricotta cheese

Unroll breadsticks; place in a greased 15-in. x 10-in. x 1-in. baking pan. Press onto the bottom and up the sides of pan to form a crust; pinch seams to seal. Bake at 350° for 6-8 minutes or until lightly browned.

Meanwhile, in a small bowl, combine the tomatoes, yellow squash, zucchini, 2 tablespoons salad dressing, parsley, 1 teaspoon garlic powder, basil and Italian seasoning; set aside.

Spread the remaining dressing over the crust; sprinkle with Romano cheese and 1 cup Monterey Jack cheese. Top with the vegetable mixture; dot ricotta cheese over the vegetables. Sprinkle with remaining Monterey Jack and garlic powder.

Bake for 20-25 minutes or until cheese is melted and crust is golden brown. **Yield:** 12 pieces.

Creamy Chicken-Rice Casserole
(Pictured above)

Prep: 20 min. **Bake:** 50 min.

Gravy, chicken soup and sour cream make this a rich and hearty casserole you'll want to curl up with on a blustery winter day. —Nancy Foust, Stoneboro, Pennsylvania

- 3 cups cubed cooked chicken
- 2-2/3 cups chicken gravy
- 2 cups uncooked instant rice
- 1 can (10-3/4 ounces) condensed cream of chicken soup, undiluted
- 1 cup (8 ounces) sour cream
- 1 can (8 ounces) mushroom stems and pieces, drained
- 1 medium onion, chopped
- 2/3 cup chopped celery
- 2/3 cup water
- 1/4 cup chopped pitted green olives
- 1/4 cup chopped ripe olives
- 2 teaspoons dried parsley flakes
- 1/8 teaspoon pepper

In a large bowl, combine all ingredients. Transfer to a greased 13-in. x 9-in. baking dish.

Cover and bake at 375° for 30 minutes. Uncover and stir; bake 20-25 minutes longer or until bubbly and rice and vegetables are tender. **Yield:** 9 servings.

ON-HAND EXTRAS

When I buy fresh celery, onions and carrots, I chop them up, use what I need and freeze the rest in small amounts. That way, I always have veggies on hand for when I want to make casseroles, soups or stews.
—Joan Fraley, Columbus, Ohio

Chicken Potpie with Cheddar Biscuit Topping
(Pictured above)

Prep: 20 min. **Bake:** 45 min.

With tender chicken, veggies and a golden biscuit topping, this meal rivals made-from-scratch dishes from home.
—*Sala Houtzer, Goldsboro, North Carolina*

  4 cups cubed cooked chicken
  1 package (12 ounces) frozen broccoli and cheese sauce
  1 can (10-3/4 ounces) condensed cream of chicken and mushroom soup, undiluted
  1 can (10-3/4 ounces) condensed cream of chicken soup, undiluted
  2 medium potatoes, cubed
  3/4 cup chicken broth
  2/3 cup sour cream
  1/2 cup frozen peas
  1/4 teaspoon pepper
TOPPING:
1-1/2 cups biscuit/baking mix
  3/4 cup shredded sharp cheddar cheese
  3/4 cup 2% milk
  3 tablespoons butter, melted

In a Dutch oven, combine the first nine ingredients; bring to a boil. Transfer mixture to a greased 13-in. x 9-in. baking dish.

In a small bowl, combine the topping ingredients; spoon over the top. Bake, uncovered, at 350° for 40-45 minutes or until bubbly and the topping is golden brown. Let potpie stand for 10 minutes before serving. **Yield:** 9 servings.

Pastry-Topped Salmon Casserole
(Pictured below)

Prep: 20 min. **Bake:** 30 min.

What a yummy way to eat salmon! You'll be amazed at how much it adds to this potpie-like casserole full of peas, carrots, potatoes and cream cheese. Store-bought phyllo dough creates the flaky top and bottom crust.
—*Tyler Sherman, Williamsburg, Virginia*

  1 large onion, chopped
  1 garlic clove, minced
  5 tablespoons butter, *divided*
1-1/4 cups 2% milk
  1 package (8 ounces) cream cheese, softened, cubed
  2 cups frozen peas and carrots, thawed
  1 can (14-1/2 ounces) diced potatoes, drained
  2 pouches (6 ounces *each*) boneless skinless pink salmon, flaked
  1/2 teaspoon salt
  1/4 teaspoon pepper
  10 sheets phyllo dough (14 inches x 9 inches)

In a large skillet, saute onion and garlic in 2 tablespoons butter for 5 minutes or until crisp-tender. Add milk; heat over medium heat until bubbles form around the side of pan. Add cream cheese; stir until the cheese is melted. Remove from the heat; stir in peas and carrots, potatoes, salmon, salt and pepper.

Melt the remaining butter; brush some of the butter over the bottom and sides of a 2-1/2-qt. round baking dish. Line with five sheets of phyllo dough. Pour in the salmon mixture. Crimp the remaining sheets of dough; place over the filling to cover the top. Brush dough with remaining butter.

Bake at 375° for 30-35 minutes or until crust is lightly browned. **Yield:** 6 servings.

Stuffed-Crust Chicken Pizza
(Pictured above)

Prep: 35 min. **Bake:** 10 min.

This recipe may sound complicated, but it really couldn't be much easier to make. For the stuffed crust, I simply tuck string cheese around the edges of refrigerated pizza dough. The ooey-gooey center you find when you take a bite is worth it!
—Pamela Brooks, South Berwick, Maine

  2 tubes (13.8 ounces *each*) refrigerated pizza crust
 10 pieces string cheese
1/2 pound boneless skinless chicken breasts, cut into 1/2-inch cubes
  1 small onion, chopped
  2 tablespoons olive oil
  3 garlic cloves, minced
1/2 cup oil-packed sun-dried tomatoes, julienned
  1 teaspoon dried rosemary, crushed
1/2 teaspoon salt
1/2 teaspoon pepper
3/4 cup pizza sauce
  2 cups (8 ounces) shredded part-skim mozzarella cheese
1/2 cup pitted ripe olives, chopped

Unroll pizza dough and place in a greased 15-in. x 10-in. x 1-in. baking pan, letting dough drape 1 in. over the edges. Pinch center seam to seal.

Place string cheese around edges of pan. Fold dough over cheese; pinch to seal. Bake at 425° for 5 minutes.

Meanwhile, in a large skillet, saute the chicken and onion in oil until chicken is no longer pink. Add garlic; cook 1 minute longer. Stir in the tomatoes, rosemary, salt and pepper.

Spread sauce over crust. Top with chicken mixture. Sprinkle with the mozzarella cheese and olives. Bake for 10-15 minutes or until cheese is melted and crust is golden brown. **Yield:** 12 pieces.

Creamy Onion Lasagna
(Pictured below)

Prep: 25 min. **Bake:** 55 min. + standing

Give an Italian classic a simple but delicious twist with an unusual ingredient—purchased French onion dip. It brings a creamy richness to this saucy, meaty lasagna.
—Ann Schroeder, Peosta, Iowa

  1 pound ground beef
  1 jar (26 ounces) roasted garlic Parmesan spaghetti sauce
  1 egg
  1 cup (8 ounces) 4% cottage cheese
  1 carton (8 ounces) French onion dip
  1 jar (25.6 ounces) Italian sausage and garlic spaghetti sauce
 12 no-cook lasagna noodles
  3 cups (12 ounces) shredded part-skim mozzarella cheese

In a Dutch oven, cook the beef over medium heat until no longer pink; drain. Stir in the roasted garlic Parmesan spaghetti sauce. Combine the egg, cottage cheese and onion dip.

Spread 1 cup Italian sausage and garlic spaghetti sauce into a greased 13-in. x 9-in. baking dish. Top with four lasagna noodles. Layer with half of cottage cheese mixture, half of beef mixture and 1 cup mozzarella cheese. Repeat layers. Top with the remaining noodles, sauce and mozzarella cheese.

Cover and bake at 375° for 50 minutes. Uncover; bake 5-10 minutes longer or until the cheese is melted. Let lasagna stand for 15 minutes before cutting. **Yield:** 12 servings.

Classic Spinach Pizza
(Pictured above)

Prep: 35 min. **Bake:** 10 min.

Your family and friends will really go for the combination of flavors in this fresh-tasting pizza. The cheesy slices are hard to resist and definitely special enough for guests.
—*Gilda Lester, Millsboro, Delaware*

    2 ounces pancetta *or* sliced bacon, finely
      chopped
    4 garlic cloves, minced
    1 package (6 ounces) fresh baby spinach
    1 cup sliced fresh mushrooms
    1 tablespoon olive oil
  1/4 teaspoon crushed red pepper flakes
  1/8 teaspoon salt
  1/8 teaspoon pepper
  1/3 cup Mascarpone cheese
  1/4 cup chopped ripe olives
    1 prebaked 12-inch pizza crust
    1 cup (4 ounces) shredded provolone cheese
  1/3 cup grated Romano cheese

In a large skillet, cook pancetta over medium heat until crisp. Using a slotted spoon, remove to paper towels to drain. Saute garlic in drippings. Add spinach; cook just until wilted. Drain spinach mixture on paper towels.

In same skillet, saute mushrooms in oil until tender; add the pepper flakes, salt and pepper. Remove from heat; transfer to a small bowl and let stand for 5 minutes. Stir in Mascarpone cheese, olives and pancetta.

Place the crust on an ungreased pizza pan. Spread the mushroom mixture over the crust; layer with spinach mixture, provolone and Romano.

Bake at 450° for 10-12 minutes or until the cheese is melted. **Yield:** 6 slices.

QUICK GARLIC

Minced garlic available in stores, garlic that's been finely chopped by hand and garlic that's been put through a press can all be used interchangeably in recipes, including Classic Spinach Pizza (at left). Choose whichever is the most convenient for you.

Roasted Vegetable Penne Bake

(Pictured below)

Prep: 30 min. **Bake:** 20 min.

For a twist, poke holes in a disposable foil-lined pan and grill these seasoned and coated vegetables, covered, over medium heat for 4-5 minutes on each side or until they're crisp-tender. —Robyn Cavallaro, Easton, Pennsylvania

    2 large zucchini, cut into 1-inch pieces
    1 medium sweet red pepper, cut into 1-inch
      pieces
  1/2 pound medium fresh mushrooms, halved
    1 small onion, cut into 1-inch pieces
    2 tablespoons olive oil
1-1/2 teaspoons Italian seasoning
    2 cups uncooked penne pasta
    1 can (15 ounces) crushed tomatoes,
      undrained
    2 ounces provolone cheese, shredded
  3/4 cup frozen peas, thawed
  1/4 cup shredded part-skim mozzarella cheese
  1/4 cup plus 2 tablespoons grated Parmesan
      cheese, *divided*
  1/2 teaspoon salt
  1/2 teaspoon pepper
    1 tablespoon butter, cubed

In a large bowl, combine the zucchini, sweet red pepper, mushrooms, onion, oil and Italian seasoning; toss to coat. Arrange in a single layer in an ungreased 15-in. x 10-in. x 1-in. baking pan. Bake, uncovered, at 425° for 20-25 minutes or until tender.

Meanwhile, cook the penne pasta according to the package directions; drain. In a large bowl, combine the pasta, roasted vegetables, tomatoes, provolone cheese, peas, mozzarella cheese, 1/4 cup Parmesan cheese, salt and pepper. Transfer mixture to a greased 11-in. x 7-in.

baking dish. Sprinkle with remaining Parmesan cheese; dot with butter.

Cover and bake at 350° for 10 minutes. Uncover; bake 10-15 minutes longer or until casserole is bubbly. **Yield:** 6 servings.

Vegetarian Tacos

(Pictured above)

Prep: 20 min. **Bake:** 20 min.

*I wasn't sure about trying a vegetarian recipe—especially because I have a meat-and-potatoes husband. But this one was so tasty, he couldn't get enough! Even our young children enjoy the bean- and veggie-stuffed tacos.
    —Mischelle Jewell, Clermont, Florida*

    6 plum tomatoes, seeded and cut into wedges
    2 medium green peppers, cut into 1/2-inch
      slices
    2 medium onions, cut into 1/2-inch wedges
    1 envelope taco seasoning
    3 tablespoons olive oil
    1 can (16 ounces) vegetarian refried beans,
      warmed
   12 taco shells, warmed
    1 cup taco sauce

In a large bowl, combine the plum tomatoes, green peppers, onions, taco seasoning and oil. Arrange in a single layer on two 15-in. x 10-in. x 1-in. baking pans. Bake, uncovered, at 475° for 20-25 minutes or until lightly browned.

Spread refried beans over half of each taco shell. Fill with vegetable mixture; drizzle with taco sauce. Serve immediately. **Yield:** 6 servings.

Reuben Quiche
(Pictured below)

Prep: 25 min. **Bake:** 25 min.

Here, deli ingredients bring the taste of the classic Reuben sandwich to a favorite breakfast and brunch dish. The hearty quiche has a cracker crust and plenty of corned beef. Serve a little Thousand Island dressing on the side.
—Barbara Nowakowski, North Tonawanda, New York

   1 cup plus 3 tablespoons finely crushed Rye Triscuits *or* other crackers
   1 tablespoon rye *or* all-purpose flour
   2 tablespoons plus 1-1/2 teaspoons butter, melted
FILLING:
   5 green onions, chopped
   1 tablespoon butter
1-1/2 cups (6 ounces) shredded Swiss cheese, *divided*
   1 package (2-1/2 ounces) deli corned beef, cut into 2-inch strips
1/2 cup sauerkraut, well drained
   4 eggs
   1 cup half-and-half cream
   1 tablespoon all-purpose flour
1/2 teaspoon ground mustard
1/4 teaspoon salt

In a small bowl, combine the cracker crumbs, flour and butter; press onto the bottom and up the sides of an ungreased 9-in. pie plate. Bake at 375° for 8-10 minutes or until edges are lightly browned.

Meanwhile, in a small skillet, saute onions in butter until tender; set aside. Sprinkle 1/2 cup cheese over crust. Top with corned beef, sauerkraut and remaining cheese. Beat the eggs, cream, flour, mustard, salt and reserved onion mixture; pour over cheese.

Bake, uncovered, at 375° for 25-30 minutes or until a knife inserted near the center comes out clean. Let stand for 5 minutes before cutting. **Yield:** 6 servings.

Nacho Pizza
(Pictured above)

Prep: 30 min. **Bake:** 15 min.

I love Mexican food, and I love pizza. This pie featuring ground beef, crushed tortilla chips, salsa and chili powder combines the best of both in one satisfying recipe.
—Laura Stonesifer, Luck, Wisconsin

   1 package (6-1/2 ounces) pizza crust mix
   1 teaspoon cornmeal
3/4 pound ground beef
1/3 cup chopped onion
   1 teaspoon chili powder
1/4 teaspoon salt
1/8 teaspoon pepper
   1 cup salsa
1/2 cup sour cream
   1 medium tomato, chopped
   2 tablespoons chopped ripe olives
   2 cups (8 ounces) shredded cheddar cheese
1/2 cup crushed tortilla chips

Prepare pizza dough according to package directions. Coat a 12-in. pizza pan with cooking spray; sprinkle with cornmeal. With floured hands, press dough onto pan. Bake at 425° for 6-8 minutes or until lightly browned.

Meanwhile, in a small skillet, cook beef and onion over medium heat until meat is no longer pink; drain. Stir in the chili powder, salt and pepper.

Combine salsa and sour cream; spread over crust to within 1 in. of the edges. Top with beef mixture, tomato, olives and cheese. Bake for 10 minutes.

Sprinkle with crushed tortilla chips; bake 5-6 minutes longer or until cheese is melted and crust is golden brown. **Yield:** 8 slices.

Chicken Spaghetti Casserole

(Pictured above)

Prep: 25 min. **Bake:** 25 min.

This creamy, cheesy spaghetti casserole is so heartwarming and homey, second helpings are practically a must!
—Lynne German, Cumming, Georgia

>   8 ounces uncooked spaghetti, broken into 3-inch pieces
>   3 cups cubed cooked chicken
>   1 can (10-3/4 ounces) condensed cream of chicken soup, undiluted
>   1 medium onion, chopped
>   1 cup 2% milk
>   1 cup (4 ounces) shredded sharp cheddar cheese, *divided*
>   1 cup (4 ounces) shredded Swiss cheese, *divided*
>   1 can (4 ounces) mushroom stems and pieces, drained
> 1/2 cup chopped roasted sweet red peppers
>   3 tablespoons mayonnaise
> 1-1/2 teaspoons steak seasoning
> 1/2 teaspoon dried basil

Cook the spaghetti according to the package directions. Meanwhile, in a large bowl, combine the chicken, cream of chicken soup, onion, milk, 1/2 cup cheddar cheese, 1/2 cup Swiss cheese, mushrooms, peppers, mayonnaise, steak seasoning and basil.

Drain the spaghetti. Add to the chicken mixture; toss to coat. Transfer to a greased 13-in. x 9-in. baking dish. Cover and bake at 350° for 20 minutes. Uncover; sprinkle with the remaining cheese. Bake 5-10 minutes longer or until casserole is heated through and cheese is melted. **Yield:** 6 servings.

Editor's Note: This recipe was tested with McCormick's Montreal Steak Seasoning. Look for it in the spice aisle.

Deep-Dish Chicken Pizza

(Pictured below)

Prep: 20 min. + rising **Bake:** 25 min. + standing

I've been putting together this loaded pizza for my family for years. It's the only one we make ourselves and is also good meatless. —*Edward Smulski, Lyons, Illinois*

>   1 package (16 ounces) hot roll mix
>   1 pound boneless skinless chicken breasts, cut into 1/2-inch cubes
>   2 tablespoons olive oil, *divided*
> 1/2 pound sliced fresh mushrooms
>   1 large sweet red pepper, cut into strips
>   1 large green pepper, cut into strips
>   1 medium onion, sliced
> 1/2 teaspoon Italian seasoning
> 1/4 teaspoon dried basil
> 1/4 teaspoon dried oregano
> 1/4 teaspoon pepper
>   1 jar (14 ounces) pizza sauce
>   2 cups (8 ounces) shredded part-skim mozzarella cheese
>   1 cup grated Parmesan cheese

Prepare the roll mix according to the package directions. Meanwhile, in a large skillet over medium heat, cook chicken in 1 tablespoon oil until no longer pink. Remove and keep warm.

In the same skillet, saute mushrooms, peppers, onion and seasonings in the remaining oil until vegetables are tender. Return chicken to the pan.

Roll dough into a 17-in. x 12-in. rectangle. Transfer to a greased 15-in. x 10-in. x 1-in. baking pan; build up the edges slightly. Spread sauce over dough. Top with chicken mixture and cheeses.

Bake at 375° for 25-30 minutes or until the crust and cheeses are lightly browned. Let stand for 10 minutes before serving. **Yield:** 12 pieces.

CHAPTER 17

Lightened-Up Delights

Whether you're watching your waistline, following a special diet or just want to eat healthier, this is the chapter for you! It's packed with tasty favorites that cut calories, sodium and fat but not great flavor.

You'll be amazed when you sample home-cooked specialties such as saucy Italian Beef and Shells, Sour Cream Chicken, Mexican Spoon Bread, Broccoli Mushroom Casserole, Confetti Tilapia Packets and Plum-Good Pork Chops.

What's more, each delicious dish includes nutrition facts at the end of the recipe, so you'll have all of the information you need to make the best choices for you and your family. ■

GUILT-FREE FAVORITE. Special Scallops Salad (p. 265).

Chipotle-Marmalade Chicken
(Pictured below)

Prep: 15 min. **Cook:** 4 hours

This zippy main course takes advantage of a slow cooker. If yours tends to cook food fast, check the chicken earlier to ensure it comes out moist and tender, not overcooked.
—Cittie, Taste of Home Online Community

  4 boneless skinless chicken breast halves
    (6 ounces *each*)
  1/4 teaspoon salt
Dash pepper
  1/2 cup chicken broth
  1/3 cup orange marmalade
    1 tablespoon canola oil
    1 tablespoon balsamic vinegar
    1 tablespoon minced chipotle pepper in
      adobo sauce
    1 tablespoon honey
    1 teaspoon chili powder
  1/4 teaspoon garlic powder
    4 teaspoons cornstarch
    2 tablespoons cold water

Sprinkle chicken with salt and pepper. Transfer to a 4- or 5-qt. slow cooker. In a small bowl, combine the chicken broth, orange marmalade, oil, vinegar, chipotle pepper, honey, chili powder and garlic powder; pour over the chicken. Cover and cook on low for 4-5 hours or until a meat thermometer reads 170°.

Remove the chicken to a serving platter; keep warm. Skim fat from cooking juices; transfer to a small saucepan. Bring liquid to a boil. Combine the cornstarch and water until smooth. Gradually stir into the pan. Bring to a boil; cook and stir for 2 minutes or until thickened. Serve with chicken. **Yield:** 4 servings.

Nutrition Facts: 1 chicken breast half with 1/3 cup sauce equals 315 calories, 8 g fat (1 g saturated fat), 95 mg cholesterol, 400 mg sodium, 26 g carbohydrate, 1 g fiber, 35 g protein. **Diabetic Exchanges:** 5 lean meat, 2 starch, 1/2 fat.

All recipes in this chapter include Nutrition Facts. Most include Diabetic Exchanges.

Italian Beef and Shells
(Pictured above)

Prep/Total Time: 30 min.

A hearty dinner will come easy tonight when you rely on this pasta and vegetable combo. Red wine lends an extra touch of flavor and sophistication to the sauce.
—Mike Tchou, Pepper Pike, Ohio

1-1/2 cups uncooked medium pasta shells
    1 pound lean ground beef (90% lean)
    1 small onion, chopped
    1 garlic clove, minced
    1 jar (23 ounces) marinara sauce
    1 small yellow summer squash, quartered and
      sliced
    1 small zucchini, quartered and sliced
  1/4 cup dry red wine *or* reduced-sodium beef
      broth
  1/2 teaspoon salt
  1/2 teaspoon Italian seasoning
  1/2 teaspoon pepper

Cook the pasta according to the package directions.

Meanwhile, in a Dutch oven, cook the beef, onion and garlic over medium heat until the meat is no longer pink; drain. Stir in the marinara sauce, squash, zucchini, red wine and seasonings. Bring to a boil. Reduce heat; simmer, uncovered, for 10-15 minutes or until thickened. Drain the pasta; stir into beef mixture and heat through. **Yield:** 4 servings.

Nutrition Facts: 1-3/4 cups equals 396 calories, 10 g fat (4 g saturated fat), 71 mg cholesterol, 644 mg sodium, 45 g carbohydrate, 5 g fiber, 29 g protein. **Diabetic Exchanges:** 3 starch, 3 lean meat.

Sour Cream Chicken
(Pictured above)

Prep: 15 min. **Bake:** 45 min.

Here's a great make-ahead entree. Chill the chicken and sour cream mixture together overnight, then coat it with crumbs the next day. —Nancy Stec, Upperco, Maryland

- 1 cup (8 ounces) reduced-fat sour cream
- 2 tablespoons minced chives
- 2 tablespoons lemon juice
- 2 teaspoons celery salt
- 2 teaspoons paprika
- 2 teaspoons Worcestershire sauce
- 1 small garlic clove, minced
- 1-1/4 cups seasoned bread crumbs
- 1 broiler/fryer chicken (2 to 3 pounds), cut up and skin removed
- 2 tablespoons reduced-fat butter, melted

In a shallow bowl, combine the first seven ingredients. Place the seasoned bread crumbs in a separate shallow bowl. Coat chicken with sour cream mixture, then coat with bread crumbs.

Arrange the chicken on a rack in a foil-lined 15-in. x 10-in. x 1-in. baking pan. Bake, uncovered, at 350° for 30 minutes. Drizzle with butter; bake 15-20 minutes longer or until juices run clear. **Yield:** 4 servings.

Nutrition Facts: 1 serving equals 365 calories, 15 g fat (6 g saturated fat), 97 mg cholesterol, 899 mg sodium, 26 g carbohydrate, 1 g fiber, 32 g protein.

Mexican Spoon Bread
(Pictured above)

Prep: 10 min. **Bake:** 50 min.

Mmmm—this warm and comforting dish is fluffy, cheesy and stick-to-your-ribs good! It requires just 10 minutes of prep before going in the oven. Try this side with everyday meals, but it will be a hit at family gatherings, too.
—Sherry Thompson, Seneca, South Carolina

- 3 eggs
- 1 cup (8 ounces) reduced-fat sour cream
- 3/4 cup fat-free milk
- 1 can (11 ounces) Mexicorn, drained
- 1 cup yellow cornmeal
- 3/4 cup shredded sharp cheddar cheese
- 1 small onion, chopped
- 3 tablespoons butter, melted
- 1 teaspoon baking powder
- 1/4 teaspoon salt

In a large bowl, whisk the eggs, sour cream and milk until smooth. Stir in the remaining ingredients. Pour the mixture into a 2-qt. round baking dish coated with cooking spray.

Bake, uncovered, at 400° for 50-60 minutes or until a knife inserted near the center comes out clean. Serve immediately. **Yield:** 6 servings.

Nutrition Facts: 3/4 cup equals 329 calories, 16 g fat (9 g saturated fat), 150 mg cholesterol, 653 mg sodium, 33 g carbohydrate, 3 g fiber, 13 g protein.

Chili Steak & Peppers

(Pictured below)

Prep/Total Time: 30 min.

Our Test Kitchen pros didn't stop with this well-seasoned steak. They made it even more special by adding sauteed peppers and a creamy horseradish sauce.

- 2 tablespoons chili sauce
- 1 tablespoon lime juice
- 1 teaspoon brown sugar
- 1/2 teaspoon crushed red pepper flakes
- 1/2 teaspoon salt, *divided*
- 1 beef top sirloin steak (1-1/4 pounds), cut into four steaks
- 1 medium onion, halved and sliced
- 1 medium green pepper, cut into strips
- 1 medium sweet yellow pepper, cut into strips
- 2 teaspoons olive oil
- 1 small garlic clove, minced
- 1/8 teaspoon pepper
- 1/4 cup reduced-fat sour cream
- 1 teaspoon prepared horseradish

Combine the chili sauce, lime juice, brown sugar, pepper flakes and 1/4 teaspoon salt; brush over the steaks. Broil the steaks 4-6 in. from the heat for 5-7 minutes on each side or until the meat reaches the desired doneness (for medium-rare, a meat thermometer should read 145°; medium, 160°; well-done, 170°).

Meanwhile, in a large skillet, saute onion and green and yellow peppers in oil until tender. Add garlic, pepper and remaining salt; cook 1 minute longer. In a small bowl, combine sour cream and horseradish. Serve steaks with pepper mixture and sauce. **Yield:** 4 servings.

Nutrition Facts: 1 steak with 1/3 cup pepper mixture and 1 tablespoon sauce equals 265 calories, 9 g fat (3 g saturated fat), 62 mg cholesterol, 491 mg sodium, 12 g carbohydrate, 2 g fiber, 32 g protein. **Diabetic Exchanges:** 4 lean meat, 1 vegetable, 1 fat.

Confetti Tilapia Packets

(Pictured above)

Prep/Total Time: 30 min.

This tasty, summery recipe came to mind after I watched a friend grilling fish wrapped in foil. You could also use flounder or cod. —Barbara Schindler, Napoleon, Ohio

- 1 medium green pepper, cut into 3/4-inch pieces
- 4 green onions, sliced
- 3 bacon strips, chopped
- 1 celery rib, chopped
- 1 large tomato, chopped
- 1/2 teaspoon salt
- 1/8 teaspoon pepper
- 4 tilapia fillets (4 ounces *each*)
- 4 teaspoons lemon juice

In a large skillet, saute the green pepper, onions, bacon and celery until vegetables are tender and bacon is crisp; drain. Add the tomato, salt and pepper; heat through.

Place each fillet on a double thickness of heavy-duty foil (about 12 in. square). Drizzle the fillets with lemon juice. Top with the vegetable mixture. Fold foil around the fish and seal tightly. Grill, covered, over medium-hot heat for 15-20 minutes or until the fish flakes easily with a fork. Open the foil carefully to allow steam to escape. **Yield:** 4 servings.

Nutrition Facts: 1 packet equals 141 calories, 3 g fat (1 g saturated fat), 60 mg cholesterol, 459 mg sodium, 5 g carbohydrate, 2 g fiber, 24 g protein. **Diabetic Exchanges:** 3 lean meat, 1 vegetable.

Special Scallops Salads

(Pictured below and on page 260)

Prep/Total Time: 20 min.

You'll be amazed at how easy it is to prepare this elegant dish. It's ready to put on the table in just 20 minutes. The vinegar, tarragon and honey blend beautifully.
—Mary Relyea, Canastota, New York

1-1/2 pounds sea scallops
  1/4 teaspoon salt
  1/8 teaspoon pepper
    3 tablespoons olive oil, *divided*
    1 tablespoon fresh minced chives
    1 tablespoon balsamic vinegar
    2 garlic cloves, minced
    2 teaspoons minced fresh tarragon
    2 teaspoons honey
    1 teaspoon Dijon mustard
    1 package (5 ounces) spring mix salad greens
    1 cup shredded carrots
  1/2 cup chopped tomato

Sprinkle scallops with salt and pepper. In a large skillet, saute scallops in 2 tablespoons oil until firm and opaque. Remove and keep warm.

In the same skillet, combine chives, balsamic vinegar, garlic, tarragon, honey, Dijon mustard and remaining oil. Bring to a boil; cook and stir for 30 seconds or until slightly thickened.

Divide the salad greens among four plates; top with the carrots, tomato and scallops. Drizzle with dressing. **Yield:** 4 servings.

Nutrition Facts: 1 serving equals 278 calories, 12 g fat (2 g saturated fat), 56 mg cholesterol, 482 mg sodium, 13 g carbohydrate, 2 g fiber, 30 g protein. **Diabetic Exchanges:** 4 lean meat, 2 fat, 1 vegetable, 1/2 starch.

Lightened-Up Special Banana Bread

(Pictured above)

Prep: 25 min. **Bake:** 55 min. + cooling

This yummy cream cheese bread packs plenty of banana flavor and pecans. An orange glaze drizzled on top makes each slice divine—and makes you want another!
—Beverly Sprague, Baltimore, Maryland

    1 package (8 ounces) reduced-fat cream cheese
  1/2 cup butter, softened
1-1/2 cups sugar
    2 eggs
1-1/2 cups mashed ripe bananas (about 3 medium)
  1/2 teaspoon vanilla extract
    3 cups all-purpose flour
  1/2 teaspoon baking powder
  1/2 teaspoon baking soda
  1/2 teaspoon salt
    1 cup chopped pecans, *divided*
ORANGE GLAZE:
    1 cup confectioners' sugar
    3 tablespoons orange juice
    1 teaspoon grated orange peel

In a large bowl, beat the cream cheese, butter and sugar until well blended. Add the eggs, one at a time, beating well after each addition. Beat in the bananas and vanilla. Combine flour, baking powder, baking soda and salt; gradually add to creamed mixture just until moistened. Fold in 1/2 cup pecans.

Transfer to two 8-in. x 4-in. loaf pans coated with cooking spray. Sprinkle with the remaining pecans. Bake at 350° for 55-60 minutes or until a toothpick inserted near the center comes out clean.

In a small bowl, whisk the glaze ingredients; drizzle over loaves. Cool for 10 minutes before removing from the pans to wire racks to cool completely. **Yield:** 2 loaves (12 slices each).

Nutrition Facts: 1 slice equals 235 calories, 10 g fat (4 g saturated fat), 34 mg cholesterol, 157 mg sodium, 34 g carbohydrate, 1 g fiber, 4 g protein.

Tomato-Basil Bruschetta
(Pictured above)

Prep/Total Time: 25 min.

These colorful little appetizers are so good, and the recipe is easy to double for a larger crowd. Plus, you can make the tomato topping in advance to save time later.
—Marie Cosenza, Cortlandt Manor, New York

- 3 plum tomatoes, chopped
- 1/3 cup thinly sliced green onions
- 4 tablespoons olive oil, *divided*
- 1 tablespoon minced fresh basil *or* 1 teaspoon dried basil
- 1 tablespoon red wine vinegar
- 1/2 teaspoon dried oregano
- 1/4 teaspoon salt
- 1/8 teaspoon pepper
- 1 loaf (1 pound) French bread, cut into 1/2-inch slices
- 2 garlic cloves, peeled and halved

In a small bowl, combine tomatoes, onions, 2 tablespoons oil, basil, vinegar, oregano, salt and pepper; set aside.

Lightly brush both sides of bread slices with remaining oil. Arrange bread slices on ungreased baking sheets. Broil 3-4 in. from the heat for 2-3 minutes on each side or until golden brown. Rub garlic over bread slices. With a slotted spoon, top each slice with the tomato mixture. **Yield:** about 2 dozen.

Nutrition Facts: 1 appetizer equals 84 calories, 3 g fat (trace saturated fat), 0 cholesterol, 162 mg sodium, 12 g carbohydrate, 1 g fiber, 3 g protein. **Diabetic Exchange:** 1 starch.

Shrimp & Cucumber Rounds
(Pictured above)

Prep/Total Time: 25 min.

When hosting a get-together, I always serve these yummy finger foods. They're a snap to fix and a great addition to any party.   —Kelly Alaniz, Eureka, California

- 1/2 pound cooked medium shrimp, peeled, deveined and finely chopped
- 1/2 cup reduced-fat mayonnaise
- 2 green onions, thinly sliced
- 1 celery rib, finely chopped
- 1 teaspoon dill pickle relish
- Dash cayenne pepper
- 1 medium English cucumber, cut into 1/4-inch slices

In a small bowl, combine the first six ingredients. Spoon topping onto the cucumber slices. Serve immediately. **Yield:** 3 dozen.

Nutrition Facts: 1 appetizer equals 20 calories, 1 g fat (trace saturated fat), 11 mg cholesterol, 38 mg sodium, 1 g carbohydrate, trace fiber, 1 g protein. **Diabetic Exchange:** Free food.

Fresh Summer Salsa
(Pictured below)

Prep/Total Time: 25 min.

This fresh-tasting blend is fantastic alongside chips or as a condiment for grilled salmon, chicken or pork. I like the salsa so much, sometimes I just eat it with a spoon!
—Lindsay Anderson, Inman, Kansas

  4 medium tomatoes, chopped
  1 medium mango, peeled and chopped
  1 medium ripe avocado, peeled and cubed
3/4 cup fresh *or* frozen corn, thawed
1/2 cup minced fresh cilantro
1/2 cup canned black beans, rinsed and drained
1/4 cup chopped red onion
  1 jalapeno pepper, seeded and chopped
  3 tablespoons lime juice
  1 tablespoon olive oil
  2 garlic cloves, minced
1/4 teaspoon salt
Baked tortilla chip scoops

In a large bowl, combine the first 12 ingredients. Chill until serving. Serve with tortilla chips. **Yield:** 4 cups.

Editor's Note: When cutting hot peppers, disposable gloves are recommended. Avoid touching your face.

Nutrition Facts: 1/4 cup salsa (calculated without chips) equals 56 calories, 3 g fat (trace saturated fat), 0 cholesterol, 56 mg sodium, 8 g carbohydrate, 2 g fiber, 1 g protein. **Diabetic Exchange:** 1/2 starch.

Plum-Good Pork Chops
(Pictured above)

Prep/Total Time: 30 min.

Ginger and plum sauce add Asian flavor to this standout entree from our Test Kitchen staff. A big scoop of crunchy coleslaw is the perfect accompaniment.

  4 bone-in pork loin chops (7 ounces *each*)
  2 teaspoons canola oil
3/4 cup plum sauce
1/4 cup orange juice
  5 teaspoons reduced-sodium soy sauce
  2 garlic cloves, minced
  2 teaspoons Dijon mustard
  1 teaspoon minced fresh gingerroot
1/4 teaspoon pepper
  1 package (12 ounces) broccoli coleslaw mix
  1 medium carrot, grated
  2 green onions, chopped
  2 teaspoons sesame seeds, toasted

In a large skillet, brown the pork chops in oil. Combine the plum sauce, orange juice, soy sauce, garlic, mustard, ginger and pepper; pour over the chops. Bring to a boil. Reduce heat; cover and simmer for 15-20 minutes or until tender. Remove pork chops and keep warm. Set aside 1/2 cup sauce mixture.

In the same skillet, cook the coleslaw mix, carrot and onions over medium heat until crisp-tender. Serve with pork chops; drizzle with the reserved sauce and sprinkle with sesame seeds. **Yield:** 4 servings.

Nutrition Facts: 1 chop with 3/4 cup broccoli mixture equals 373 calories, 11 g fat (3 g saturated fat), 86 mg cholesterol, 685 mg sodium, 30 g carbohydrate, 3 g fiber, 33 g protein. **Diabetic Exchanges:** 4 lean meat, 1-1/2 starch, 1 vegetable, 1/2 fat.

Italian Steaks
(Pictured above)

Prep/Total Time: 25 min.

These tender Italian-style steaks topped with pizza sauce and cheese make a hearty, delicious main dish. And the amazing thing is, they're ready in under half an hour.
—*Mary Hankins, Kansas City, Missouri*

> 1 egg
> 1/2 cup seasoned bread crumbs
> 1/2 teaspoon dried basil
> 1/2 teaspoon dried oregano
> 1/8 teaspoon salt
> 1/8 teaspoon pepper
> 1 beef top sirloin steak (1 pound)
> 1 tablespoon canola oil
> 1 cup pizza sauce
> 1/4 cup shredded Italian cheese blend

In a shallow bowl, whisk egg. In another shallow bowl, combine seasoned bread crumbs, basil, oregano, salt and pepper. Cut steak into four pieces; dip each piece in egg, then coat with bread crumb mixture.

In a large skillet, cook steaks in oil over medium-high heat for 2-4 minutes on each side or until meat reaches desired doneness (for medium-rare, a meat thermometer should read 145°; medium, 160°; well-done, 170°).

Meanwhile, heat sauce in a small saucepan. Spoon over steaks; sprinkle with cheese. **Yield:** 4 servings.

Nutrition Facts: 1 steak with 1/4 cup pizza sauce and 1 tablespoon cheese equals 264 calories, 11 g fat (3 g saturated fat), 104 mg cholesterol, 435 mg sodium, 9 g carbohydrate, 1 g fiber, 29 g protein. **Diabetic Exchanges:** 4 lean meat, 1 fat, 1/2 starch.

Sauteed Squash Medley
(Pictured above)

Prep/Total Time: 25 min.

Here's a tasty combination of sauteed onion, red pepper, yellow squash, mushrooms and zucchini that disappears in a flash. It's a great side with just about any entree.
—*Kay Ayotte, Albion, Michigan*

> 1 small yellow summer squash, halved and
>   sliced
> 1 small zucchini, halved and sliced
> 1-1/2 cups sliced fresh mushrooms
> 1 medium onion, sliced
> 1 medium sweet red pepper, cut into 1/4-inch
>   strips
> 2 tablespoons butter
> 1/2 teaspoon garlic salt
> 1/4 teaspoon pepper
> 1/2 cup grated Parmesan cheese

In a large skillet, saute the squash, zucchini, mushrooms, onion and red pepper in butter for 8-10 minutes or until tender. Stir in the garlic salt and pepper; sprinkle with cheese. **Yield:** 6 servings.

Nutrition Facts: 2/3 cup equals 91 calories, 6 g fat (4 g saturated fat), 16 mg cholesterol, 285 mg sodium, 6 g carbohydrate, 2 g fiber, 4 g protein. **Diabetic Exchanges:** 1 vegetable, 1 fat.

Caribbean Four-Fruit Salsa
(Pictured below)

Prep/Total Time: 20 min.

What do you get when you blend four fruits—raspberries, blueberries, blackberries and a peach—plus jerk seasoning and a bit of lime? This bold and tangy salsa! It's a terrific way to jazz up grilled meat, fish or poultry.
—*Cheryl Perry, Hertford, North Carolina*

   1 medium peach, chopped
1/2 cup *each* fresh blackberries, blueberries and
     raspberries
1/4 cup chopped red onion
1/4 cup chopped sweet red pepper
   2 green onions, thinly sliced
1/4 cup minced fresh cilantro
   2 tablespoons lime juice
   1 jalapeno pepper, seeded and minced
1-1/2 teaspoons Caribbean jerk seasoning
   1 teaspoon minced fresh gingerroot
1/2 teaspoon grated lime peel
1/8 teaspoon salt

In a large bowl, combine all ingredients. Chill salsa until serving. Serve with grilled meat, fish or poultry. **Yield:** 12 servings.

Editor's Note: When cutting hot peppers, disposable gloves are recommended. Avoid touching your face.

Nutrition Facts: 1/4 cup equals 16 calories, trace fat (trace saturated fat), 0 cholesterol, 61 mg sodium, 4 g carbohydrate, 1 g fiber, trace protein. **Diabetic Exchange:** Free food.

Chicken with Green Chili Sauce
(Pictured above)

Prep/Total Time: 30 min.

This is such a simple way to give chicken breasts lots of flavor. Cajun seasoning adds a nice kick, and sour cream cools everything down. I like it served over rice.
—*LaDonna Reed, Ponca City, Oklahoma*

   2 boneless skinless chicken breast halves
     (5 ounces *each*)
1/2 teaspoon Cajun seasoning
2/3 cup reduced-fat reduced-sodium condensed
     cream of chicken soup, undiluted
1/4 cup water
1/4 cup canned chopped green chilies
1/2 teaspoon lemon juice
   2 tablespoons reduced-fat sour cream
   1 cup hot cooked rice

Sprinkle the chicken with the Cajun seasoning. In a large nonstick skillet coated with cooking spray, brown the chicken on both sides.

In a small bowl, combine the soup, water, chilies and lemon juice. Stir into the skillet. Bring to a boil. Reduce heat; cover and simmer for 8-10 minutes or until chicken juices run clear. Remove from the heat; stir in the sour cream. Serve with rice. **Yield:** 2 servings.

Nutrition Facts: 1 chicken breast half with 1/3 cup sauce and 1/2 cup rice equals 332 calories, 6 g fat (2 g saturated fat), 90 mg cholesterol, 634 mg sodium, 32 g carbohydrate, 1 g fiber, 33 g protein. **Diabetic Exchanges:** 4 lean meat, 2 starch.

Broccoli Mushroom Casserole

(Pictured above)

Prep: 20 min. **Bake:** 35 min.

I contribute this comforting vegetable bake to the feast at our family's Thanksgiving get-together every year...and every year, the cheesy casserole gets compliments.
—Cynthia Edmiston, Sullivan's Island, South Carolina

>   2 cups water
>   1/2 pound sliced fresh mushrooms
>   3 cups chopped fresh broccoli
>   1 small onion, chopped
>   1 can (10-3/4 ounces) reduced-fat
>   reduced-sodium condensed cream of
>   mushroom soup, undiluted
>   3/4 cup shredded Swiss cheese
>   1/2 cup reduced-fat mayonnaise
>   2 egg whites
>   1 egg
>   1 teaspoon ground mustard
>   1/4 teaspoon pepper
> 1-1/4 cups (5 ounces) shredded reduced-fat
>   cheddar cheese, *divided*
>   1 cup crushed baked potato chips

In a large saucepan, combine the water, mushrooms, broccoli and onion. Bring to a boil. Reduce heat; cover and simmer for 6-8 minutes or until the vegetables are crisp-tender.

Meanwhile, in a large bowl, combine the soup, Swiss cheese, mayonnaise, egg whites, egg, mustard, pepper and 3/4 cup cheddar cheese. Drain vegetables; stir into soup mixture.

Transfer to an 11-in. x 7-in. baking dish coated with cooking spray. Sprinkle with potato chips and remaining cheddar cheese. Bake casserole, uncovered, at 350° for 35-40 minutes or until a thermometer reads 160°. **Yield:** 6 servings.

Nutrition Facts: 1 cup equals 297 calories, 18 g fat (7 g saturated fat), 73 mg cholesterol, 631 mg sodium, 20 g carbohydrate, 3 g fiber, 16 g protein.

BEST OF THE BUNCH

When buying broccoli, choose bunches that have a deep green color, tightly closed buds and crisp leaves. Keep it in a resealable plastic bag in the refrigerator; broccoli may be stored this way for up to 4 days. Wash broccoli just before using it.

Parsnip-Carrot Medley

Prep/Total Time: 25 min.

Mixed with carrots, rosemary and just a hint of heat, the natural sweetness of parsnips shines in this easy side.
—Taryn Kuebelbeck, Plymouth, Minnesota

    2 pounds parsnips, peeled and sliced
1-1/2 pounds carrots, peeled and sliced
    3/4 cup chicken broth
      3 tablespoons butter
      2 tablespoons honey
    1/2 teaspoon salt
    1/2 teaspoon dried rosemary, crushed
Dash cayenne pepper

In a Dutch oven, bring the parsnips, carrots and chicken broth to a boil. Reduce heat; simmer, uncovered, for 6-8 minutes or until vegetables are tender. Add the remaining ingredients; heat through. **Yield:** 9 servings.

Nutrition Facts: 3/4 cup equals 152 calories, 4 g fat (2 g saturated fat), 10 mg cholesterol, 302 mg sodium, 28 g carbohydrate, 6 g fiber, 2 g protein. **Diabetic Exchanges:** 1 starch, 1 vegetable, 1 fat.

Bok Choy and Radishes
(*Pictured below*)

Prep/Total Time: 25 min.

This simple recipe capitalizes on the flavors of spring. It's a great-tasting, good-for-you dish we enjoy often.
—Ann Yarber, Goldsby, Oklahoma

     1 head bok choy
     2 tablespoons butter
     1 tablespoon olive oil
    12 radishes, thinly sliced
     1 shallot, sliced
     1 teaspoon lemon-pepper seasoning
   3/4 teaspoon salt

Cut off and discard root end of bok choy, leaving stalks with leaves. Cut green leaves from stalks. Cut leaves into 1-in. slices; set aside. Cut white stalks into 1-in. pieces.

In a large skillet, cook stalks in butter and oil for 3-5 minutes or until crisp-tender. Add the radishes, shallot, lemon-pepper, salt and reserved leaves; cook and stir for 3 minutes or until heated through. **Yield:** 8 servings.

Nutrition Facts: 3/4 cup equals 59 calories, 5 g fat (2 g saturated fat), 8 mg cholesterol, 371 mg sodium, 3 g carbohydrate, 1 g fiber, 2 g protein. **Diabetic Exchanges:** 1 vegetable, 1 fat.

Cod & Vegetable Skillet
(*Pictured above*)

Prep/Total Time: 30 min.

Our Test Kitchen staff created this satisfying dinner that combines mild cod fillets with colorful sauteed veggies. A homemade sauce pulls it all together.

   1/2 pound fresh green beans, trimmed
     1 cup fresh baby carrots, cut in half lengthwise
     1 medium onion, halved and sliced
     3 tablespoons butter
     1 tablespoon all-purpose flour
   1/2 teaspoon dried thyme
   1/2 teaspoon salt
   1/4 teaspoon pepper
     1 cup reduced-sodium chicken broth
   1/4 cup white wine *or* reduced-sodium chicken broth
     4 cod *or* haddock fillets (4 ounces *each*)

In a large skillet, saute beans, carrots and onion in butter for 2 minutes. Stir in flour and seasonings until blended; gradually add broth and wine. Bring to a boil; cook and stir for 2 minutes or until thickened.

Add fillets to the pan. Reduce heat; cover and simmer for 10-12 minutes or until fish flakes easily with a fork. **Yield:** 4 servings.

Nutrition Facts: 1 fillet with 3/4 cup vegetable mixture equals 229 calories, 9 g fat (6 g saturated fat), 88 mg cholesterol, 621 mg sodium, 12 g carbohydrate, 3 g fiber, 24 g protein. **Diabetic Exchanges:** 3 lean meat, 2 vegetable, 1-1/2 fat.

CHAPTER 18

Swift Snacks & Appetizers

When the time is right for just a bite, why settle for the same old high-priced munchies sold in stores? You don't have to when you turn to the speedy recipes in this chapter.

Make a batch of Parmesan Munch Mix in advance to keep handy for the kids after school, or thrill the gang watching the big game on TV by serving Asian Chicken Wings.

You'll even find plenty of elegant hors d'oeuvres, such as Potato-Crab Cakes with Lime Butter and Savory Tomato Tarts, for holidays and parties.

With all of these fast and scrumptious finger foods, the only hard part will be deciding which to make first! ■

CAN'T-MISS MORSELS. Thai Shrimp Appetizers (p. 277).

Crisp Cucumber Salsa
(Pictured above)

Prep/Total Time: 20 min.

Here's a fantastic way to use garden cucumbers. You'll love the creamy-crunchy texture and super-fresh flavors.
—Charlene Skjerven, Hoolpe, North Dakota

- 2 cups finely chopped seeded peeled cucumber
- 1/2 cup finely chopped seeded tomato
- 1/4 cup chopped red onion
- 2 tablespoons minced fresh parsley
- 1 jalapeno pepper, seeded and chopped
- 4-1/2 teaspoons minced fresh cilantro
- 1 garlic clove, minced
- 1/4 cup reduced-fat sour cream
- 1-1/2 teaspoons lemon juice
- 1-1/2 teaspoons lime juice
- 1/4 teaspoon ground cumin
- 1/4 teaspoon seasoned salt
- Baked tortilla chip scoops

In a small bowl, combine the first seven ingredients. In another bowl, combine the sour cream, lemon juice, lime juice, cumin and seasoned salt. Pour over cucumber mixture and toss gently to coat. Serve immediately with chips. **Yield:** 2-1/2 cups.

Editor's Note: When cutting hot peppers, disposable gloves are recommended. Avoid touching your face.

Potato-Crab Cakes with Lime Butter
(Pictured below)

Prep: 20 min. **Cook:** 5 min./batch

Want to wow guests with something extra-special? This is it! The golden patties are easy to make and boast a tangy butter topping. *—Emory Doty, Jasper, Georgia*

- 1 cup mashed potatoes (with added milk and butter)
- 1 egg, beaten
- 1 tablespoon plus 1/2 cup dry bread crumbs, *divided*
- 1 tablespoon finely chopped onion
- 1 tablespoon minced fresh parsley
- 1/2 teaspoon lime juice
- 1/8 teaspoon salt
- 1/8 teaspoon pepper
- 1 pound fresh crabmeat
- 1/4 cup all-purpose flour
- Oil for deep-fat frying
- LIME BUTTER:
- 1/2 cup butter, softened
- 4 teaspoons lime juice
- 1 teaspoon grated lime peel

In a large bowl, combine the potatoes, egg, 1 tablespoon bread crumbs, onion, parsley, lime juice, salt and pepper. Gently stir in the crab. Shape into 12 patties.

In a shallow bowl, combine the flour and remaining bread crumbs. Coat patties with crumb mixture.

In an electric skillet, heat 1/4 in. of oil to 375°. Fry crab cakes, a few at a time, for 2-3 minutes on each side or until golden brown. Drain on paper towels. Combine the butter, lime juice and peel. Serve with crab cakes. **Yield:** 1 dozen (1/2 cup butter).

Stuffed Shrimp Appetizers
(Pictured below)

Prep: 25 min. **Bake:** 10 min.

These fancy finger foods not only look impressive and taste delicious, but also are low in fat. You can indulge guilt-free! —Shirley Leasock, Rockwood, Pennsylvania

20 uncooked large shrimp (about 1 pound)
  1 egg, beaten
1/2 cup soft bread crumbs
  1 tablespoon mayonnaise
1/2 teaspoon lemon juice
1/4 teaspoon salt-free seasoning blend
1/4 teaspoon pepper
1/8 teaspoon dried oregano
Dash cayenne pepper
  1 can (6 ounces) lump crabmeat, drained
  2 tablespoons grated Parmesan cheese
  1 teaspoon paprika

Peel and devein shrimp, leaving tails on. Butterfly each shrimp along the outside curve. Open shrimp flat and place butterflied-side down in an ungreased 15-in. x 10-in. x 1-in. baking pan.

In a small bowl, combine the egg, bread crumbs, mayonnaise, lemon juice and seasonings. Stir in crab. Place 1 tablespoonful of mixture over each shrimp; sprinkle with cheese and paprika. Bake at 350° for 9-11 minutes or until shrimp turn pink. Serve warm. **Yield:** 20 appetizers.

Pimiento & Cheese Deviled Eggs
(Pictured above)

Prep/Total Time: 20 min.

If you're stuck with lots of leftover hard-cooked eggs after Easter, here's a yummy solution. These crowd-pleasing beauties are ideal for a platter at a picnic or potluck.
—Linda Foreman, Locust Grove, Oklahoma

  6 hard-cooked eggs
1/4 cup finely shredded sharp cheddar cheese
  2 tablespoons mayonnaise
  4 teaspoons diced pimientos, *divided*
  2 teaspoons Dijon mustard
  2 teaspoons finely chopped sweet onion
  1 small garlic clove, minced
Dash *each* salt and pepper

Cut eggs in half lengthwise. Remove yolks; set whites aside. In a small bowl, mash the yolks. Add the cheese, mayonnaise, 3 teaspoons pimientos, mustard, onion, garlic, salt and pepper; mix well. Stuff or pipe into egg whites. Garnish with remaining pimientos. Refrigerate until serving. **Yield:** 1 dozen.

BUTTERFLY BASICS

Attractive Stuffed Shrimp Appetizers (recipe above right) require butterflying the shrimp. It's easy to do—after the shrimp is deveined, simply cut the slit deeper into the shrimp but not all the way through, leaving the shrimp attached at the bottom.

Honey-Barbecue Chicken Wings
(Pictured above)

Prep: 20 min. **Cook:** 10 min./batch

The creative cooks in our Test Kitchen came up with these finger-licking-good wings. The slightly sweet barbecue flavor in the sauce has mass appeal.

2-1/2 pounds whole chicken wings
1/2 cup soy sauce
1/2 cup barbecue sauce
1/2 cup honey
1 cup all-purpose flour
2 teaspoons salt
2 teaspoons paprika
1/4 teaspoon pepper
Oil for deep-fat frying

Cut chicken wings into three sections; discard wing tip sections. In a small saucepan, combine the soy sauce, barbecue sauce and honey. Bring to a boil; cook until liquid is reduced to about 1 cup.

Meanwhile, in a large resealable plastic bag, combine the flour, salt, paprika and pepper; add chicken wings, a few at a time, and shake to coat.

In an electric skillet or deep-fat fryer, heat the oil to 375°. Fry the chicken wings, a few at a time, for 6-8 minutes or until no longer pink, turning once. Drain on paper towels.

Transfer the chicken wings to a large bowl; add the prepared sauce and toss to coat. Serve immediately. **Yield:** 2 dozen.

Editor's Note: Uncooked chicken wing sections (wingettes) may be substituted for the whole chicken wings.

Northwoods Chex Mix

(Pictured below)

Prep: 15 min. + cooling

Hazelnuts, dried cranberries and real maple syrup make this yummy finger food stand out from the crowd.
—Nicole Filizetti, Grand Marais, Michigan

    2 cups Cinnamon Chex
    2 cups Corn Chex
    2 cups Wheat Chex
    2 cups hazelnuts
  1/3 cup maple syrup
  1/4 cup butter, cubed
  1/4 cup packed brown sugar
1-1/2 teaspoons salt
    1 teaspoon ground nutmeg
    2 cups dried cranberries

In a large microwave-safe bowl, combine the cereals and hazelnuts; set aside. In a small microwave-safe bowl, combine the maple syrup, butter, brown sugar, salt and nutmeg. Microwave, uncovered, on high for 1 minute; stir until blended. Pour over the cereal mixture and toss to coat.

Microwave on high for 5-6 minutes or until lightly browned, stirring after each minute. Stir in cranberries. Spread onto waxed paper to cool. Store in an airtight container. **Yield:** 2-1/2 quarts.

Editor's Note: This recipe was tested in a 1,100-watt microwave.

Thai Shrimp Appetizers

(Pictured above and on page 272)

Prep: 15 min. + marinating

Your guests will love the spicy heat, garlic and tangy lime in these no-cook morsels. And you'll love how easy they are to fix! Just combine the marinade ingredients, then pop in the shrimp.　　—Edrie O'Brien, Denver, Colorado

  1/4 cup canola oil
    2 green onions, chopped
    2 tablespoons rice vinegar
    1 tablespoon minced fresh cilantro
    1 tablespoon lime juice
    1 garlic clove, minced
    1 teaspoon grated lime peel
  1/2 teaspoon crushed red pepper flakes
  1/4 teaspoon salt
  1/4 teaspoon pepper
    2 pounds cooked medium shrimp, peeled and deveined

In a large resealable plastic bag, combine the first 10 ingredients. Add the shrimp; seal bag and turn to coat. Refrigerate for 30 minutes. Drain and discard marinade; arrange shrimp on a serving plate. **Yield:** 8 servings.

A CUT ABOVE

When you need green onions for a recipe such as Thai Shrimp Appetizers (above), you don't have to dirty a cutting board. Instead of cutting them with a knife, use a kitchen scissors. Just hold the onions you need in one hand and snip away.

Spicy Sweet Potato Chips
& Cilantro Dip
(Pictured above)

Prep: 20 min. **Bake:** 25 min.

This cool dip accented with cilantro is a great partner for spicy sweet-potato chips. It's a match made in heaven!
—*Libby Walp, Chicago, Illinois*

 4 to 5 large sweet potatoes (3-1/2 pounds),
   peeled and cut into 1/8-inch slices
1/4 cup canola oil
 2 teaspoons chili powder
 1 teaspoon garlic powder
 1 teaspoon taco seasoning
3/4 teaspoon salt
1/2 teaspoon ground cumin
1/2 teaspoon pepper
1/4 teaspoon cayenne pepper
DIP:
1-1/2 cups mayonnaise
 1 cup (8 ounces) sour cream
 4 ounces cream cheese, softened
 3 tablespoons minced fresh cilantro
 1 tablespoon lemon juice
 1 teaspoon celery salt
1/4 teaspoon pepper

Place sweet potatoes in a large bowl. Combine the oil and seasonings; drizzle over potatoes and toss to coat.

Arrange potatoes in a single layer in two ungreased 15-in. x 10-in. x 1-in. baking pans. Bake at 400° for 25-30 minutes or until golden brown, turning once.

In a small bowl, beat the dip ingredients until blended. Serve the dip with sweet potato chips. **Yield:** 16 servings (3 cups dip).

Marmalade-Glazed Chicken Wings

Prep: 20 min. **Cook:** 10 min./batch

Even those who don't crave chicken wings will love this recipe from our Test Kitchen staff. Orange marmalade gives an unexpected twist to the flavor.

2-1/2 pounds whole chicken wings
 2/3 cup orange marmalade
 1/4 cup water
 1 tablespoon lemon juice
 1 tablespoon soy sauce
 1 teaspoon prepared horseradish
 1 garlic clove, minced
 1 cup all-purpose flour
 2 teaspoons salt
 2 teaspoons paprika
 1/4 teaspoon pepper
Oil for deep-fat frying

Cut wings into three sections; discard wing tip sections. In a small saucepan, combine orange marmalade, water, lemon juice, soy sauce, horseradish and garlic. Bring to a boil; cook until liquid is reduced to about 3/4 cup.

Meanwhile, in a large resealable plastic bag, combine flour, salt, paprika and pepper; add wings, a few at a time, and shake to coat. In an electric skillet or deep-fat fryer, heat oil to 375°. Fry the wings, a few at a time, 6-8 minutes or until no longer pink, turning once. Drain on paper towels. Transfer wings to a large bowl; add sauce and toss to coat. Serve immediately. **Yield:** 2 dozen.

Editor's Note: Uncooked chicken wing sections (wingettes) may be substituted for the whole chicken wings.

Savory Tomato Tarts

Prep/Total Time: 30 min.

Filled with tomatoes, bacon, herbs and cheese, these cute and creamy tarts are both refreshing and comforting.
—*Robert Frazier, Pleasant Valley, Missouri*

 1 can (14-1/2 ounces) diced tomatoes with
   basil, oregano and garlic, well drained
 4 bacon strips, cooked and crumbled
 3 green onions, chopped
 2 teaspoons minced fresh oregano *or*
   3/4 teaspoon dried oregano
 2 teaspoons minced fresh basil *or*
   3/4 teaspoon dried basil
 1 small garlic clove, minced
1/8 teaspoon salt
1/8 teaspoon pepper
 1 cup (4 ounces) shredded Italian cheese blend
1/2 cup mayonnaise
 2 packages (1.9 ounces *each*) frozen miniature
   phyllo tart shells
1/4 cup grated Parmesan cheese
Minced chives, optional

In a small bowl, combine the first eight ingredients. In another bowl, combine the Italian cheese blend and

mayonnaise. Spoon the tomato mixture into tart shells. Spread the mayonnaise mixture over tops. Place on an ungreased baking sheet; sprinkle with Parmesan cheese. Bake at 350° for 8-12 minutes or until lightly browned. Garnish with chives if desired. **Yield:** 2-1/2 dozen.

Parmesan Munch Mix
(Pictured above)

Prep: 10 min. **Bake:** 10 min. + cooling

This snack mix is irresistible! Plus, it's an easy school or work treat. Pack a few individual baggies and toss them into lunch sacks. —*Edie DeSpain, Logan, Utah*

>   8 cups popped popcorn
>   4 cups Cheerios
>   3 cups pretzel sticks
>   1 package (6.6 ounces) miniature cheddar cheese fish-shaped crackers

> 1/3 cup butter, melted
> 1/4 cup grated Parmesan cheese
> 1/2 teaspoon onion salt

In an ungreased roasting pan, combine popcorn, cereal, pretzels and crackers. Combine remaining ingredients; pour over popcorn mixture and toss to coat.

Bake, uncovered, at 350° for 10-15 minutes or until lightly browned. Cool completely. Store in airtight containers. **Yield:** 4 quarts.

POPPING UP

When I need popcorn for a recipe, I pour the popped corn into one bowl and shake it so the unpopped kernels drop to the bottom. Then it's easy to separate the unpopped kernels so they're not in my food.
—*Corrine Lance, Gold Bar, Washington*

Parmesan Asparagus Roll-Ups
(Pictured below)

Prep/Total Time: 30 min.

Fancy-looking and festive, these bites make the most of fresh-picked asparagus and crispy phyllo dough. Watch them start conversations...and rev up appetites!
—Eleanor Froehlich, Rochester, Michigan

- 12 fresh asparagus spears
- 2 sheets phyllo dough (18 inches x 14 inches)
- 4 teaspoons olive oil
- 1/4 cup grated Parmesan cheese
- Dash pepper

Cut asparagus spears into 4-in. lengths (discard stalks or save for another use). In a large saucepan, bring 1/2 in. of water to a boil. Add the asparagus; cover and boil for 2 minutes. Drain and immediately place asparagus in ice water. Drain and pat dry.

Stack both sheets of phyllo dough on a work surface. Cut the stack in half lengthwise, then widthwise into thirds. Separate pieces and brush with some of the oil. Sprinkle each with 1 teaspoon Parmesan cheese. Place one asparagus spear along one side of each piece of dough. Sprinkle lightly with pepper; roll up tightly.

Place seam side down on an ungreased baking sheet. Brush tops with oil. Bake at 400° for 7-9 minutes or until golden brown. **Yield:** 1 dozen.

Cucumber-Stuffed Cherry Tomatoes
(Pictured above)

Prep/Total Time: 25 min.

This is a wonderful appetizer you can fix ahead of time. I usually triple the recipe because the stuffed tomatoes disappear fast.   *—Christi Martin, Elko, Nevada*

- 24 cherry tomatoes
- 1 package (3 ounces) cream cheese, softened
- 2 tablespoons mayonnaise
- 1/4 cup finely chopped peeled cucumber
- 1 tablespoon finely chopped green onion
- 2 teaspoons minced fresh dill

Cut a thin slice off the top of each tomato. Scoop out and discard pulp; invert tomatoes onto paper towels to drain. In a small bowl, combine the cream cheese and mayonnaise until smooth; stir in cucumber, onion and dill. Spoon into the tomatoes. Refrigerate until serving. **Yield:** 2 dozen.

Asian Chicken Wings

Prep: 20 min. **Cook:** 10 min./batch

These Far East wings are downright addictive! Our Test Kitchen staff used creamy peanut butter to balance the sweet-savory flavors of brown sugar and soy sauce.

- 2-1/2 pounds whole chicken wings
- 1 cup all-purpose flour
- 2 teaspoons salt
- 2 teaspoons paprika
- 1/4 teaspoon pepper
- Oil for deep-fat frying

SAUCE:
- 1/4 cup creamy peanut butter
- 2 tablespoons water
- 2 teaspoons Louisiana-style hot sauce
- 1-1/2 teaspoons brown sugar
- 1-1/2 teaspoons lemon juice
- 1-1/2 teaspoons soy sauce
- 1/2 teaspoon ground ginger

Cut chicken wings into three sections; discard wing tip sections. In a large resealable plastic bag, combine flour, salt, paprika and pepper. Add wings, a few at a time, and shake to coat.

In an electric skillet or deep-fat fryer, heat oil to 375°. Fry wings, a few at a time, 6-8 minutes or until no longer pink, turning once. Drain on paper towels. Transfer the wings to a large bowl and keep warm.

In a small saucepan, combine the sauce ingredients. Cook and stir over medium heat for 1-2 minutes or until smooth. Pour over chicken wings and toss to coat. Serve immediately. **Yield:** 2 dozen.

Editor's Note: Uncooked chicken wing sections (wingettes) may be substituted for the whole chicken wings.

Mixed Olive Crostini
(Pictured below)

Prep/Total Time: 25 min.

These little toasts are always a big hit. They look like you fussed, but the ingredients are probably in your pantry.
—*Laurie LaClair, North Richland Hills, Texas*

- 1 can (4-1/4 ounces) chopped ripe olives
- 1/2 cup pimiento-stuffed olives, finely chopped
- 1/2 cup grated Parmesan cheese

- 1/4 cup butter, softened
- 1 tablespoon olive oil
- 2 garlic cloves, minced
- 3/4 cup shredded part-skim mozzarella cheese
- 1/4 cup minced fresh parsley
- 1 French bread baguette (10-1/2 ounces)

In a small bowl, combine the first six ingredients; stir in the mozzarella cheese and parsley. Cut baguette into 24 slices; place on an ungreased baking sheet. Spread with olive mixture.

Broil 3-4 in. from the heat for 2-3 minutes or until edges are lightly browned and cheese is melted. **Yield:** 2 dozen.

Bistro Beef Bites
(Pictured above)

Prep/Total Time: 25 min.

With deli roast beef and cream cheese, these zippy mini sandwiches are sure to tide everyone over until dinner.
—*Mickey Strang, Mckinleyville, California*

- 4 ounces cream cheese, softened
- 1 tablespoon prepared horseradish
- 16 slices snack rye bread
- 1/4 pound sliced deli roast beef
- 6 tablespoons sour cream
- 8 grape tomatoes, halved
- 16 sprigs fresh parsley, stems removed

Dash *each* salt and pepper

In a small bowl, combine cream cheese and horseradish. Spread over the bread slices. Top each with beef, sour cream, a tomato half and a parsley sprig.

Sprinkle with salt and pepper. **Yield:** 16 appetizers.

Warm Cranberry Spread
(Pictured above)

Prep/Total Time: 25 min.

My family loves all kinds of cranberry recipes. This one has cheeses, almonds and green onions for a wonderful mix of flavors. It's also good made with the Door County cherries we purchase on our summer trips to Wisconsin.
—Jennifer Christenson, Little Canada, Minnesota

　　1 package (8 ounces) cream cheese, softened
　　1 package (4 ounces) crumbled feta cheese
　3/4 cup whole-berry cranberry sauce
　1/3 cup slivered almonds, toasted
　1/3 cup sliced green onions
Assorted crackers

In a small bowl, combine the cream cheese and feta. Spread into an ungreased 9-in. pie plate. Spread with cranberry sauce.

　Bake, uncovered, at 350° for 15-20 minutes or until heated through. Garnish with the almonds and green onions. Serve with crackers. **Yield:** about 2-1/4 cups.

TOASTY TECHNIQUE

Toasting almonds and other nuts before using them in a recipe intensifies their flavor. Simply spread the nuts on a baking sheet and bake at 350° for 5 to 10 minutes or until they are lightly toasted. Be sure to watch them carefully so they don't burn.

Cut wings into three sections; discard wing tip sections. In a large saucepan, combine the syrup, chili sauce, lime juice and mustard. Bring to a boil; cook until liquid is reduced to about 1 cup.

Meanwhile, in a large resealable plastic bag, combine the flour, salt, paprika and pepper; add wings, a few at a time, and shake to coat.

In an electric skillet or deep-fat fryer, heat oil to 375°. Fry wings, a few at a time, 6-8 minutes or until no longer pink, turning once. Drain on paper towels. Transfer the wings to a large bowl; add sauce mixture and toss to coat. Serve immediately. **Yield:** 2 dozen.

Editor's Note: Uncooked chicken wing sections (wingettes) may be substituted for the whole chicken wings.

Cheese Rye Appetizers
(Pictured below)

Prep: 20 min. **Bake:** 10 min./batch

This topping can be mixed ahead of time and refrigerated, then spread on bread and baked at the last minute. Even kids like it! —Joyce Dykstra, Lansing, Illinois

  2 cups (8 ounces) shredded Swiss cheese
  1 cup mayonnaise
  1 can (4-1/4 ounces) chopped ripe olives
  4 bacon strips, cooked and crumbled
  1/4 cup chopped green onions
1-1/2 teaspoons minced fresh parsley *or*
  1/2 teaspoon dried parsley flakes
 30 slices snack rye bread

In a small bowl, combine the first six ingredients. Spread a rounded tablespoonful over each slice of bread. Place on an ungreased baking sheet. Bake at 450° for 6-8 minutes or until cheese is melted. **Yield:** 2-1/2 dozen.

Pineapple Salsa
(Pictured above)

Prep/Total Time: 20 min.

It's hard to beat fresh salsa on a hot summer day. This version is a great condiment for grilled fish or chicken. If you're serving it with chips, be sure you have enough—it goes fast! —Teri Rasey, Cadillac, Michigan

1-1/2 cups finely chopped fresh pineapple
  1 cup finely chopped seedless cucumber
  1/4 cup lime juice
  1/4 cup finely chopped red onion
  2 tablespoons minced fresh cilantro
4-1/2 teaspoons chopped seeded jalapeno pepper
  1 garlic clove, minced
  1 teaspoon sugar
  1 teaspoon grated lime peel
  1/4 teaspoon salt

In a large bowl, combine all ingredients. Cover salsa and refrigerate until serving. **Yield:** 2-1/2 cups.

Editor's Note: When cutting hot peppers, disposable gloves are recommended. Avoid touching your face.

Chili-Lime Chicken Wings

Prep: 20 min. **Cook:** 10 min./batch

The ingredient combination of the sauce gives these wings from our home economists a unique and delicious taste. Try them at your next football party.

2-1/2 pounds whole chicken wings
  1 cup maple syrup
  2/3 cup chili sauce
  2 tablespoons lime juice
  2 tablespoons Dijon mustard
  1 cup all-purpose flour
  2 teaspoons salt
  2 teaspoons paprika
  1/4 teaspoon pepper
Oil for deep-fat frying

CHAPTER 19

Test Kitchen Secrets

Some dishes look so impressive and sophisticated, you'd think only a professional chef could prepare them. Here, the helpful cooks in our Test Kitchen show how you can make those same gourmet-style creations right in your own home.

You'll see the techniques our staff turns to for bakery-worthy breads...delicate and elegant crepes...saucy foods that are thickened to perfection...and delicious fare featuring all sorts of favorite fruits, from peaches, plums and cherries to apples and nectarines.

We've included not only lots of scrumptious recipes, but also plenty of how-to's and hints so you can duplicate the methods of our experts—and cook like a pro in no time! ■

SIMPLY SPECIAL. Lemon-Plum Sorbet (p. 295).

BREADS THAT BEAT THE CLOCK

The aroma of baking bread simply can't be beat. Why not treat your family to some today? Whether a yeast recipe such as Garlic-Herb Braid or a bread-machine sensation such as Apricot Pecan Bread, the favorites featured here will be done in a jiffy when you use the helpful techniques from our Test Kitchen pros. ■

Blue Cheese Herb Loaf
(Pictured below)

Prep: 15 min. **Bake:** 20 min.

It's hard to believe that this special-looking, flavorful loaf starts with convenient refrigerated biscuit dough.
—Janet Allen, Sarasota, Florida

- 1 tube (12 ounces) refrigerated flaky buttermilk biscuits
- 2 tablespoons butter, melted
- 2 tablespoons crumbled blue cheese
- 1 tablespoon dried minced onion
- 2 teaspoons dried parsley flakes
- 1 garlic clove, minced
- 1 teaspoon dried tarragon
- 1 teaspoon minced chives
- 1/2 teaspoon celery seed
- 1/2 teaspoon dried oregano

Separate biscuits; cut each into quarters. Arrange into an 11-in.-long loaf on a greased baking sheet. In a small bowl, combine remaining ingredients; brush over loaf.

Bake at 375° for 18-20 minutes or until golden brown. **Yield:** 1 loaf.

Herb Bubble Bread
(Pictured above)

Prep: 20 min. + rising **Bake:** 25 min. + cooling

This is a terrific side for a soup or stew. The frozen dough is dressed up with plenty of herbs and Parmesan cheese.
—Joan Anderson, West Covina, California

- 1/2 cup grated Parmesan cheese
- 3/4 teaspoon dried parsley flakes
- 1/4 teaspoon dill weed
- 1/8 teaspoon *each* dried thyme, basil and rosemary, crushed
- 1/4 cup butter, melted
- 2 teaspoons minced garlic
- 1 loaf (1 pound) frozen bread dough, thawed

In a small bowl, combine the cheese and seasonings. In another bowl, combine butter and garlic; set aside.

Divide dough into 16 pieces. Roll into balls. Coat balls in butter mixture, then dip in cheese mixture. Place in a greased 9-in. x 5-in. loaf pan.

Cover and let rise in a warm place until doubled, about 1 hour. Bake at 350° for 22-26 minutes or until golden brown. (Cover loosely with foil if top browns too quickly.) Cool for 10 minutes before removing from pan to a wire rack. Serve warm. **Yield:** 16 servings.

Garlic-Herb Braid

Prep: 20 min. + rising **Bake:** 20 min. + cooling

The rosemary, dill, garlic and basil blend beautifully in this homey braid from our Test Kitchen home economists. Get ready for lots of oohs and aahs when you bring this tender and impressive bread to the table.

   4 to 4-1/2 cups all-purpose flour
   3 tablespoons sugar
   2 packages (1/4 ounce *each*) quick-rise
     yeast
   2 teaspoons dried basil
1-3/4 teaspoons dill weed
1-1/2 teaspoons salt
   3/4 teaspoon garlic powder
   3/4 teaspoon dried rosemary, crushed
   3/4 cup 2% milk
   1/2 cup water
   1/4 cup butter, cubed
     1 egg
     1 tablespoon butter, melted

In a large bowl, combine 1-1/2 cups flour, sugar, yeast and seasonings. In a small saucepan, heat the milk, water and cubed butter to 120°-130°. Add to the dry ingredients; beat just until moistened. Add egg; beat until smooth. Stir in enough remaining flour to form a soft dough.

Turn the dough onto a floured surface; knead until smooth and elastic, about 4-6 minutes. Cover and let rest for 10 minutes.

Divide the dough into thirds. Shape each into a 15-in. rope. Place ropes on a greased baking sheet and braid; pinch ends to seal and tuck under. Cover and let rise until doubled, about 25 minutes.

Bake at 375° for 20-25 minutes or until golden brown. Brush with melted butter. Remove from pan to a wire rack to cool. **Yield:** 1 loaf (16 slices).

Southwest Pretzels
(Pictured above right)

Prep: 30 min. + standing **Bake:** 25 min.

These fun, filling pretzels with a mild Southwestern kick are the perfect snack for watching the big game on TV or for movie night at home. They'll score just as high with grown-ups as kids! For help shaping the dough, see the tip box at right.   —Cathy Tang, Redmond, Washington

   4 cups all-purpose flour
   1 tablespoon sugar
   1 package (1/4 ounce) quick-rise yeast
1-1/2 teaspoons salt
   1 teaspoon dried minced onion
   1/2 teaspoon chili powder
   1/4 teaspoon ground cumin
   1/4 teaspoon cayenne pepper
1-1/2 cups warm water (120° to 130°)
   1 egg, beaten
Coarse salt
Salsa con queso dip

In a large bowl, combine 2 cups flour, sugar, yeast, salt, dried minced onion and spices. Add the water. Beat just until moistened. Stir in enough remaining flour to form a soft dough.

Turn the dough onto a floured surface; knead until smooth and elastic, about 4-6 minutes. Cover and let rest for 10 minutes. Divide dough into 16 equal portions; roll each portion into a 15-in. rope. Cover and let rest 10 minutes longer.

Twist into pretzel shapes. Place on greased baking sheets; brush with egg. Bake at 350° for 15 minutes. Brush again with egg; sprinkle with coarse salt. Bake 10-13 minutes longer or until golden brown. Remove to wire racks. Serve pretzels warm with salsa con queso dip. **Yield:** 16 pretzels.

PERFECT PRETZELS

1. Roll each of the 16 pieces of dough into a 15-inch rope and taper the ends.
2. Shape each rope into a circle with about 2 inches of each end overlapping.
3. Twist the ends where they overlap.
4. Flip the twisted ends over the circle; place the ends over the edge and pinch under.

Applesauce Spice Bread
(Pictured at top left in photo at right)

Prep: 15 min. **Bake:** 3 hours

Slices of this are wonderful toasted and spread with apple butter. During baking, the house smells like apple pie!
—Roger Brown, Assaria, Kansas

- 3/4 cup water (70° to 80°)
- 1/2 cup sweetened applesauce (70° to 80°)
- 2 tablespoons brown sugar
- 1 tablespoon canola oil
- 1-1/2 teaspoons apple pie spice
- 3/4 teaspoon salt
- 3 cups bread flour
- 1/3 cup quick-cooking oats
- 2 tablespoons nonfat dry milk powder
- 2-1/4 teaspoons active dry yeast

In bread machine pan, place all ingredients in the order suggested by manufacturer. Select basic bread setting. Choose crust color and loaf size if available.

Check the dough after 5 minutes of mixing; add 1 to 2 tablespoons of water or flour if needed. Bake according to bread machine directions. **Yield:** 1 loaf (1-1/2 pounds, 16 slices).

Baker's Dozen Yeast Rolls
(Pictured above)

Prep: 25 min. + rising **Bake:** 15 min.

A delicious honey-garlic topping transforms these simple rolls from our Test Kitchen cooks into something special. Whip up a batch when you're having soup or chili.

- 2 to 2-1/2 cups all-purpose flour
- 2 tablespoons sugar
- 1 package (1/4 ounce) quick-rise yeast
- 1/2 teaspoon salt
- 3/4 cup warm water (120° to 130°)
- 2 tablespoons plus 4 teaspoons butter, melted, *divided*
- 3/4 cup shredded sharp cheddar cheese
- 2 teaspoons honey
- 1/8 teaspoon garlic salt

In a large bowl, combine 1-1/2 cups flour, sugar, yeast and salt. Add the water and 2 tablespoons butter; beat on medium speed for 3 minutes or until smooth. Stir in the cheddar cheese and enough remaining flour to form a soft dough.

Turn the dough onto a lightly floured surface; knead until smooth and elastic, about 4-6 minutes. Cover and let rest for 10 minutes. Divide into 13 pieces. Shape each into a ball. Place in a greased 9-in. round baking pan. Cover and let rise in a warm place until doubled, about 30 minutes.

Bake the rolls at 375° for 11-14 minutes or until lightly browned. Combine the honey, garlic salt and remaining butter; brush over rolls. Remove to a wire rack to cool. **Yield:** 13 rolls.

Apricot Pecan Bread
(Pictured at far right in photo at right)

Prep: 20 min. **Bake:** 40 min.

Every time I serve this yummy bread, it gets rave reviews. The fruit-and-nut loaves are great for a coffee break, and they're easy to prepare using a bread machine.
—Joan Hallford, North Richland Hills, Texas

- 2-1/2 cups all-purpose flour
- 3/4 cup sugar
- 2 teaspoons baking soda
- 1 teaspoon ground cinnamon
- 1/4 teaspoon salt
- 1/4 teaspoon ground nutmeg
- 1 cup 2% milk
- 2 eggs
- 1/3 cup butter, melted
- 2 cups (8 ounces) shredded cheddar cheese
- 1 cup finely chopped dried apricots
- 3/4 cup finely chopped pecans

TOPPING:
- 3 tablespoons packed brown sugar
- 1 tablespoon butter
- 1/2 teaspoon ground cinnamon

In a large bowl, combine the first six ingredients. In a small bowl, beat the milk, eggs and butter; stir into the dry ingredients just until moistened. Fold in the cheddar cheese, apricots and pecans. Spoon into two greased 8-in. x 4-in. loaf pans. Combine the topping ingredients; sprinkle over batter.

Bake at 350° for 40-45 minutes or until a toothpick comes out clean. Cool for 10 minutes before removing from pans to wire racks. **Yield:** 2 loaves.

Sunflower Cranberry Bread
(Pictured at bottom in photo above)

Prep: 15 min. **Bake:** 3 hours

I altered this recipe from my sister-in-law by adding dried cranberries and sunflower seeds. It makes a delightful gift for friends and family during the holidays or anytime.
—Juliet Konieczny, Amsterdam, New York

    1 cup warm 2% milk (70° to 80°)
    2 eggs, lightly beaten
    2 tablespoons butter, softened
  1/2 teaspoon salt
  1/3 cup sugar
  1/3 cup dried cranberries
  1/4 cup sunflower kernels
3-1/3 cups bread flour
2-1/4 teaspoons active dry yeast

In bread machine pan, place all ingredients in the order suggested by manufacturer. Select basic bread setting. Choose crust color and loaf size if available.

Check the dough after 5 minutes of mixing; add 1 to 2 tablespoons of water or flour if needed. Bake according to the bread machine directions. **Yield:** 1 loaf (2 pounds, 16 slices).

Editor's Note: We recommend you do not use a bread machine's time-delay feature for this recipe.

BREAD MACHINE BASICS

Want to make Sunflower Cranberry Bread (recipe at left)? Check out these helpful tips:
• When using a bread machine, all of the liquid ingredients—including water, milk, yogurt, juice, cottage cheese, eggs and applesauce—should have a temperature of 70° to 80°.
• Add liquids to the bread pan first, then add all of the dry ingredients except the yeast. Adding the yeast last prevents any liquid from prematurely activating it. This is especially important if you're using the machine's "timed bake" cycle.

CAN-DO CREPES ANYTIME

Ooh-la-la...crepes bring any meal a touch of French elegance. Think they're difficult or time-consuming to make? With a little guidance from the pros in our Test Kitchen, even novice cooks will be able to whip up these culinary delights.

Try fixing scrumptious Chocolate-Fruit Crepes or savory Seafood Crepes Bearnaise following the expert techniques and tips here. You'll have an extra-special dessert or main course in no time. ■

Chocolate-Fruit Crepes
(Pictured below)

Prep: 30 min. + chilling **Cook:** 5 min./batch

These lovely, delicate treats are a wonderful addition to brunch—and can even make a sweet finale for dinner.
—Laura McDowell, Lake Villa, Illinois

1-1/2 cups buttermilk
   3 eggs
   3 tablespoons butter, melted
   1 cup all-purpose flour
   2 tablespoons sugar
   2 tablespoons baking cocoa
FILLING:
   1 can (21 ounces) cherry pie filling
   1 can (8-1/2 ounces) sliced peaches, drained and chopped
1/2 teaspoon ground cinnamon
1/8 teaspoon almond extract
1/3 cup hot fudge ice cream topping, warmed
Whipped cream, optional

In a large bowl, combine buttermilk, eggs and butter. Combine the flour, sugar and cocoa; add to buttermilk mixture and mix well. Cover and refrigerate for 1 hour.

Heat a lightly greased 8-in. nonstick skillet over medium heat; pour 2 tablespoons batter into the center of the skillet. Lift and tilt pan to coat the bottom evenly. Cook until the top appears dry; turn and cook 15-20 seconds longer. Remove to a wire rack. Repeat with the remaining batter, greasing the skillet as needed. When cool, stack the crepes with waxed paper or paper towels in between.

In a microwave-safe bowl, combine the pie filling, peaches and cinnamon. Microwave, uncovered, on high for 3-4 minutes or until heated through, stirring once. Stir in almond extract.

Spoon 2 tablespoons filling down the center of each crepe. Fold the sides of crepe over filling. Drizzle with hot fudge ice cream topping and garnish with whipped cream if desired. **Yield:** 10 servings.

Seafood Crepes Bearnaise
(Pictured above)

Prep: 30 min. + chilling **Bake:** 10 min.

This might seem like a sophisticated gourmet recipe, but prepare to be amazed at how easy it actually is to make. You'll want to fix it for your family all the time! I like to serve a tossed salad and fresh-baked rolls on the side.
—Kristy Barnes-Armstrong, Marysville, Washington

    1 cup 2% milk
    3 eggs
    3 tablespoons butter, melted
    3/4 cup all-purpose flour
    1/4 teaspoon salt
FILLING:
    2 envelopes bearnaise sauce
    1/2 pound bay scallops
    2 teaspoons butter
    1/2 pound cooked small shrimp, peeled,
        deveined and chopped
    1 cup imitation crabmeat
    1 cup (4 ounces) shredded cheddar cheese

In a small bowl, combine milk, eggs and butter. Combine flour and salt; add to milk mixture and mix well. Cover and refrigerate for 1 hour.

Heat a lightly greased 10-in. nonstick skillet over medium heat; pour 1/4 cup batter into the center of the skillet. Lift and tilt the pan to coat the bottom evenly. Cook until the top appears dry; turn and cook 15-20 seconds longer. Remove to a wire rack. Repeat with the remaining batter, greasing the skillet as needed. When cool, stack the crepes with waxed paper or paper towels in between.

Prepare the bearnaise sauce according to the package directions. Meanwhile, in a large skillet, cook scallops in butter over medium heat for 3-4 minutes or until scallops are firm and opaque. Add shrimp, crabmeat and sauce; heat through. Set aside 1/2 cup filling.

Spread 1/3 cup filling down the center of each crepe; fold sides and ends over filling and roll up. Place in a greased 13-in. x 9-in. baking dish. Spoon reserved filling over top; sprinkle with cheese. Bake, uncovered, at 350° for 10-15 minutes or until heated through and cheese is melted. **Yield:** 5 servings.

CREPE CLUES

1. When adding the crepe batter, lift the pan from the heat. This will keep the batter from cooking too quickly and allow it to coat the bottom of the skillet evenly. Tilt the pan quickly to spread the batter in a thin layer.

2. After 45-60 seconds, the crepe's surface will appear dry or cooked. To flip the crepe, slip a spatula under it. The second side will cook much faster.

3. To make crepes ahead, place waxed paper between the cooked, cooled crepes, then cover and store them in the refrigerator for up to 24 hours or in an airtight container in the freezer for up to 1 month. Thaw crepes in the fridge for 6 hours or overnight.

THINKING THICKENERS

It takes only one runny pie or lumpy sauce to ruin a meal. Here, our Test Kitchen pros share their tips for using flour, quick-cooking tapioca and cornstarch for thickening recipes without mishaps.

You'll love the scrumptious results when you try Bumbleberry Pie, Golden Peach Chicken, Pineapple Pork Stir-Fry and Spinach Manicotti with Ham. ■

Spinach Manicotti with Ham
(Pictured below)

Prep: 30 min. **Bake:** 30 min.

Everyone raves over this! It's similar to dishes served at Italian restaurants but goes together quickly in your own kitchen. Salad and bread make the perfect sides.
—Michele Nadeau, Monroe, Michigan

- 12 uncooked manicotti shells
- 1/4 cup butter, cubed
- 1/4 cup all-purpose flour
- 1/2 teaspoon pepper
- 1/4 teaspoon salt
- 1/4 teaspoon ground nutmeg
- 3 cups 2% milk
- 1 carton (15 ounces) ricotta cheese
- 1 package (10 ounces) frozen chopped spinach, thawed and squeezed dry
- 2 teaspoons dried oregano
- 1-1/2 cups cubed fully cooked ham
- 1/2 cup grated Parmesan cheese

Cook the manicotti according to the package directions. For the sauce, in a small saucepan, melt the butter. Stir in the flour, pepper, salt and nutmeg until blended. Gradually whisk in the milk. Bring to a boil. Cook and stir for 1-2 minutes or until thickened.

In a small bowl, combine the ricotta cheese, spinach and oregano. Stir in the ham; add 1/2 cup sauce. Drain the manicotti; stuff with ham mixture. Spread 1/2 cup sauce into a greased 13-in. x 9-in. baking dish. Top with the stuffed manicotti. Pour the remaining sauce over the top; sprinkle with Parmesan cheese.

Cover and bake at 350° for 25-30 minutes. Uncover and bake 5 minutes longer or until golden brown. **Yield:** 6 servings.

Pineapple Pork Stir-Fry
(Pictured above)

Prep/Total Time: 30 min.

There's no need to drive to an out-of-the-way eatery for takeout when you've got this delicious, 30-minute recipe from our Test Kitchen staff in your collection. If you'll be serving young children, omit the cayenne pepper.

- 1 can (8 ounces) unsweetened pineapple chunks, undrained
- 3 tablespoons cornstarch, *divided*
- 1 tablespoon plus 1/2 cup cold water, *divided*
- 3/4 teaspoon garlic powder
- 1 pork tenderloin (1 pound), cut into thin strips
- 1/2 cup soy sauce
- 3 tablespoons brown sugar
- 1/2 teaspoon ground ginger
- 1/4 teaspoon cayenne pepper
- 2 tablespoons canola oil, *divided*
- 4 cups fresh broccoli florets
- 1 cup fresh baby carrots, cut in half lengthwise
- 1 small onion, cut into wedges

Hot cooked rice

Drain the pineapple chunks, reserving 1/4 cup juice; set aside. In a small bowl, combine 2 tablespoons cornstarch, 1 tablespoon water, garlic powder and 1 tablespoon reserved pineapple juice. Pour into a large resealable bag; add pork. Seal bag and turn to coat.

In a small bowl, combine the soy sauce, brown sugar, ginger, cayenne and the remaining water, cornstarch and reserved pineapple juice until smooth; set aside.

In a large skillet or wok over medium-high heat, stir-fry the pork in 1 tablespoon oil until no longer pink; remove and keep warm.

Stir-fry the broccoli, carrots and onion in remaining oil until tender. Stir cornstarch mixture and add to the pan. Bring to a boil; cook and stir for 2 minutes or until thickened. Add pork and pineapple; heat through. Serve with rice. **Yield:** 6 servings.

Peach Chicken

Prep/Total Time: 30 min.

This sweet and savory entree created by our Test Kitchen cooks will appeal to the whole family. The chicken's bread crumb coating makes it especially homey.

- 1 can (15 ounces) sliced peaches in extra-light syrup
- 2 teaspoons cornstarch
- 1/4 cup peach preserves
- 1 tablespoon white wine *or* chicken broth
- 1/4 cup seasoned bread crumbs
- 1 tablespoon grated Parmesan cheese
- 1/4 teaspoon salt
- 1/4 teaspoon pepper
- 4 boneless skinless chicken breast halves (6 ounces *each*)
- 2 tablespoons butter, *divided*
- 2 green onions, chopped
- Hot cooked pasta

Drain peaches, reserving juice. In a small bowl, combine the cornstarch and reserved juice until smooth. Add the preserves and wine; set aside.

In a large resealable plastic bag, combine the bread crumbs, cheese, salt and pepper. Add the chicken, one piece at a time, and shake to coat. In a large skillet, cook the chicken in 1 tablespoon butter over medium heat for 4-6 minutes on each side or until chicken juices run clear. Remove and keep warm.

In the same skillet, melt the remaining butter. Stir the cornstarch mixture and add to pan. Bring to a boil; cook and stir for 2 minutes or until thickened. Add the chicken and peaches; heat through. Sprinkle with onions; serve with pasta. **Yield:** 4 servings.

Bumbleberry Pie

(Pictured above right)

Prep: 20 min. Bake: 55 min. + cooling

Here's a delightful ending to any meal. Apple, raspberries and rhubarb blend beautifully in this fresh-flavored pie.
—Judy Parker, Albuquerque, New Mexico

- 1-3/4 cups sugar
- 5 tablespoons quick-cooking tapioca
- 3 cups chopped fresh *or* frozen rhubarb, thawed

- 1 medium tart apple, peeled and chopped
- 1 cup fresh *or* frozen raspberries
- Pastry for double-crust pie (9 inches)

In a large bowl, combine sugar and tapioca. Stir in the rhubarb, apple and raspberries; toss gently to coat. Let stand for 15 minutes.

Line a 9-in. pie plate with bottom pastry; trim to 1 in. beyond edge of plate. Spoon filling into crust. Roll out remaining pastry to fit the top of pie. Cut slits in pastry. Place pastry over filling; trim, seal and flute edges. Cover edges loosely with foil.

Bake at 375° for 25 minutes. Remove foil and bake 30-35 minutes longer or until crust is golden brown and filling is bubbly. Cool on a wire rack. **Yield:** 8 servings.

Editor's Note: If using frozen rhubarb, measure rhubarb while still frozen, then thaw completely. Drain in a colander, but do not press liquid out.

TIPS FOR THICKENING

- Adding flour or cornstarch directly to a hot liquid causes clumps. First, combine it with the cold liquid until smooth, then gradually stir it into the pan. Stir or whisk constantly when boiling the mixture.
- Sauces and fillings thickened with all-purpose flour appear cloudy. Use it as a thickener if you want your sauce to be opaque.
- Large amounts of sugar and/or acidic ingredients (such as lemon juice) can prevent glazes and sauces from thickening.
- Quick-cooking tapioca is a great thickener for fruit pies because it withstands long cook times and gives the filling a gel-like appearance.
- Substitute 1-1/2 to 2 teaspoons of quick-cooking tapioca for each tablespoon of all-purpose flour in pies. Use 1-1/2 teaspoons for a softer filling and 2 teaspoons for a firmer set.
- When replacing flour in a recipe, use half the amount of cornstarch.
- Cornstarch and quick-cooking tapioca can be substituted for each other in equal amounts.

SECRETS OF STONE FRUITS

From peaches and plums to nectarines and cherries, stone fruits have a variety of yummy uses. The special recipes here—Lemon-Plum Sorbet, Peaches & Cream Dessert, Nectarine-Cherry Compote and Pork Chops with Chipotle Cherry Glaze—prove it's true.

Just choose your favorite dish, then follow the tips from our Test Kitchen pros to unlock the potential of these tree-ripened gems. You and your family are sure to love the orchard-fresh flavor. ■

Peaches & Cream Dessert
(Pictured below)

Prep: 30 min. + chilling

Perfect for parties and potlucks, this crowd-size treat gets raves from everyone. You'll love the contrast between the pecan crust and smooth cream cheese layer.
—Nancye Thompson, Paducah, Kentucky

- 1 package (16 ounces) pecan shortbread cookies, crushed
- 1/2 cup butter, melted
- 1 cup sugar
- 1 package (3 ounces) peach gelatin
- 2 tablespoons cornstarch
- 1 can (12 ounces) lemon-lime soda
- 1 package (8 ounces) cream cheese, softened
- 1 cup confectioners' sugar
- 1 carton (8 ounces) frozen whipped topping, thawed
- 6 cups fresh *or* frozen sliced peeled peaches, thawed
- 1/3 cup unsweetened pineapple juice

In a small bowl, combine the pecan shortbread cookie crumbs and butter; press onto bottom of an ungreased 13-in. x 9-in. dish.

In a small saucepan, combine the sugar, gelatin and cornstarch; stir in the soda until smooth. Bring to a boil. Cook and stir for 5-7 minutes or until slightly thickened. Cool to room temperature, stirring occasionally.

Meanwhile, in a large bowl, beat cream cheese and confectioners' sugar until smooth. Beat in the whipped topping until blended. Spread over the crust. Combine peaches and pineapple juice. Arrange over cream cheese layer. Pour gelatin mixture over top. Cover and refrigerate overnight. **Yield:** 15 servings.

Pork Chops with Chipotle Cherry Glaze
(Pictured above)

Prep: 15 min. **Cook:** 20 min.

Smothered with a zippy cherry sauce and sprinkled with onions and almonds, these tender chops seem fancy but are easy to make. —Roxanne Chan, Albany, California

- 1/4 teaspoon salt
- 1/4 teaspoon sugar
- 1/4 teaspoon ground cinnamon
- 4 boneless pork loin chops (5 ounces *each*)
- 1 tablespoon olive oil
- 1 cup pitted dark sweet cherries, halved
- 1/4 cup orange juice
- 2 tablespoons dried cherries

- 2 tablespoons red wine vinegar
- 1 tablespoon chopped chipotle pepper in adobo sauce
- 1 tablespoon orange marmalade
- 1 garlic clove, minced
- 2 tablespoons sliced almonds, toasted
- 1 tablespoon thinly sliced green onion

In a small bowl, combine the salt, sugar and cinnamon. Sprinkle over pork chops. In a large skillet, cook chops, uncovered, in oil over medium heat for 7-8 minutes on each side or until meat juices run clear. Remove to a serving platter and keep warm.

In the same skillet, combine sweet cherries, orange juice, dried cherries, red wine vinegar, chipotle pepper, marmalade and garlic. Cook and stir for 2-3 minutes or until heated through. Spoon over chops; sprinkle with almonds and green onion. **Yield:** 4 servings.

Nectarine-Cherry Compote

Prep: 15 min. **Bake:** 35 min.

I sometimes use half a vanilla bean in this dessert medley. Simply scrape the seeds into the baking dish and tuck the pod under the fruit. Either way, this is yummy!
—*Maria Breiner, Schwenksville, Pennsylvania*

- 6 tablespoons sugar
- 2 tablespoons rum, optional
- 1 teaspoon cornstarch
- 1 teaspoon vanilla extract
- 4 medium nectarines, halved
- 1 pound fresh sweet cherries, pitted

Vanilla ice cream

In a small bowl, combine sugar, rum if desired, cornstarch and vanilla. Transfer to a greased 13-in. x 9-in. baking dish. Place the nectarine halves cut side down over sugar mixture. Sprinkle with cherries.

Bake, uncovered, at 375° for 35-40 minutes or until bubbly and fruit is tender. Serve warm with ice cream. **Yield:** 8 servings.

Lemon-Plum Sorbet

(Pictured above right and on page 284)

Prep: 25 min. + freezing

This gorgeous sorbet is a refreshing delight on hot summer days. Enjoy it by itself or with a slice of angel food cake.
—*Eirianedd Simpson, Pahrump, Nevada*

- 8 medium plums
- 2 cups sugar
- 1 cup water
- 1/3 cup lemon juice
- 2 teaspoons grated lemon peel

In a large saucepan, bring 8 cups water to a boil. Add the plums; cover and boil for 30-45 seconds. Drain and immediately place the plums in ice water. Drain and pat dry. When cool enough to handle, remove the skins. Cut in half; remove the pits.

In a small saucepan, bring sugar and water to a boil. Cook and stir until sugar is dissolved. Add lemon juice and peel; set aside to cool.

Place the plums in a food processor; add sugar syrup. Cover and process for 2-3 minutes or until smooth. Transfer puree to an 8-in. square dish. Freeze for 1 hour or until edges begin to firm; stir. Freeze 2 hours longer or until firm.

Just before serving, transfer sorbet to a food processor; cover and process for 2-3 minutes or until smooth. **Yield:** 6 servings.

BEST BLANCHING

Use this technique when blanching plums, peaches or nectarines:

1. Place plums in a covered saucepan of boiling water for 30-45 seconds or until the skin splits. Use tongs or a slotted spoon to remove the fruit from the boiling water.

2. Immediately place plums in an ice-water bath to cool the fruit and stop the cooking process.

3. Use a paring knife to easily peel the skin. If stubborn areas of the skin won't peel off, return the fruit to the boiling water for a few more seconds.

EASY IDEAS FOR APPLES

"A" is for apple...and you'll have those fresh-picked favorites down from A to Z when you rely on these appealing dishes and expert tips.

Our Test Kitchen home economists got to the core of this popular fruit, choosing recipes that showcase common varieties deliciously. After one bite, they're sure to become the apple of your eye! ∎

Spinach Almond Salad
(Pictured below)

Prep/Total Time: 15 min.

I hear raves whenever I serve this refreshing medley. Dried cranberries add an extra burst of color and flavor.
—*Jennie Richards, Riverton, Utah*

- 1 package (6 ounces) fresh baby spinach
- 2 large tart apples, thinly sliced
- 10 bacon strips, cooked and crumbled
- 1 cup dried cranberries
- 3/4 cup slivered almonds, toasted

VINAIGRETTE:
- 1/4 cup sugar
- 3 tablespoons cider vinegar
- 2 teaspoons finely chopped onion
- 1/4 teaspoon salt
- 1/3 cup olive oil

In a large bowl, combine the first five ingredients. In a blender, combine sugar, vinegar, onion and salt; cover and process until blended. While processing, gradually add oil in a steady stream. Pour over salad; toss to coat. Serve immediately. **Yield:** 8 servings.

Apple Pork Chops
(Pictured above)

Prep/Total Time: 30 min.

With sweet-tart apple slices, onion, thyme and mustard, this entree is great and takes just 30 minutes to fix.
—*Deb Williams, Peoria, Arizona*

- 2 teaspoons cornstarch
- 3/4 cup chicken broth
- 4 boneless pork loin chops (4 ounces *each*)
- 2 teaspoons canola oil
- 1 large apple, peeled and thinly sliced
- 1 small onion, finely chopped
- 1/3 cup unsweetened apple juice
- 2 teaspoons Dijon mustard
- 1/4 teaspoon dried thyme

In a small bowl, combine the cornstarch and broth; set aside. In a large skillet, brown pork chops in oil. Remove and keep warm.

In the same skillet, saute apple and onion until apple is crisp-tender. Stir in broth mixture, apple juice, mustard and thyme; bring to a boil. Add the pork chops. Reduce heat; cover and simmer for 8-10 minutes or until a meat thermometer reads 160°. **Yield:** 4 servings.

Apple Crisp

Prep: 25 min. **Bake:** 45 min.

A package of yellow cake mix sets this yummy crisp apart from others. Serve it a la mode for an extra-special treat.
—Ruby Hodge, Richland Center, Wisconsin

- 7 cups thinly sliced peeled tart apples (about 7 medium)
- 1 cup sugar
- 1 tablespoon all-purpose flour
- 1 teaspoon ground cinnamon
- Dash salt
- 1/4 cup water
- 1 package (9 ounces) yellow cake mix
- 3/4 cup quick-cooking oats
- 1/3 cup butter, softened
- 1/4 cup packed brown sugar
- 1/4 teaspoon baking powder
- 1/4 teaspoon baking soda
- Vanilla ice cream

Place the apples in a greased 2-1/2-qt. shallow baking dish. In a small bowl, combine the sugar, flour, cinnamon and salt; sprinkle over the apples. Drizzle with the water. In a large bowl, combine yellow cake mix, oats, butter, brown sugar, baking powder and baking soda. Sprinkle over apples.

Bake, uncovered, at 350° for 45-50 minutes or until apples are tender and topping is golden brown. Serve warm with ice cream. **Yield:** 8 servings.

Caramel Apple Strata

(Pictured above right)

Prep: 20 min. + chilling **Bake:** 50 min. + standing

When you're craving a warm, comforting breakfast on a chilly autumn or winter morning, this is it! The oven-baked strata prepared with day-old cinnamon bread is ooey, gooey and oh-so-good. You'll want to serve it for brunch buffets, too.
—Kelly Boe, Whiteland, Indiana

- 2 cups packed brown sugar
- 1/2 cup butter, cubed
- 1/4 cup corn syrup
- 3 large apples, peeled and chopped
- 2 tablespoons lemon juice
- 1 tablespoon sugar
- 1 teaspoon apple pie spice
- 1 loaf (1 pound) day-old cinnamon bread
- 1/2 cup chopped pecans
- 10 eggs
- 1 cup 2% milk
- 1 teaspoon salt
- 1 teaspoon vanilla extract

In a small saucepan, combine the brown sugar, butter and corn syrup. Bring to a boil over medium heat, stirring constantly. Cook and stir for 2 minutes or until thickened. Set aside.

In a small bowl, combine the apples, lemon juice, sugar and pie spice. Arrange half of the bread slices in a greased 13-in. x 9-in. baking dish. Spoon apples over bread; drizzle with half of the caramel sauce. Sprinkle with pecans; top with remaining bread.

In a large bowl, combine eggs, milk, salt and vanilla. Pour over top. Cover and refrigerate overnight. Cover and refrigerate remaining caramel sauce.

Remove strata from the refrigerator 30 minutes before baking. Bake, uncovered, at 350° for 50-55 minutes or until a knife inserted near the center comes out clean. Let stand for 10 minutes before cutting.

In a small microwave-safe dish, microwave reserved sauce, uncovered, for 1-2 minutes or until heated through. Drizzle over strata. **Yield:** 12 servings.

PICKING AN APPLE

Want to know what variety of apple our Test Kitchen staff would use in each of these recipes? Here's what they selected:

- **Spinach Apple Salad.** Its sweet, slightly tangy dressing pairs well with any apple that's good for snacking. Our staff chose Granny Smith because of its full flavor and light green skin, which contrasts nicely with the dark green spinach.
- **Apple Pork Chops.** Braeburn apples hold their shape when sliced and sauteed, and their sweet-tart flavor complements the savory ingredients.
- **Apple Crisp.** Granny Smith apples are ideal for crisps because their tartness balances the dessert's sweetness. Jonathans would also work well.
- **Caramel Apple Strata.** The tartness of Granny Smith apples complements the caramel in the strata. Sweet-tart apples such as Braeburn, Empire or Pink Lady would also work but may add sweetness.

CHAPTER 20

Easy Odds & Ends

If you want recipes that go on the grill, serve two people, use leftovers or give you the perfect party dessert, look no further. You get it all in this chapter!

We've featured five different sections to suit your needs. Just turn the page to find BBQ Bacon Burgers for your cookout...or see page 304 for a sized-for-two sensation—Sweet Onion Slaw Pork Wraps.

Need a treat for a youngster's birthday? Check out cute and colorful Ocean Cake on page 306. Have extra food from your Thanksgiving feast or another meal? Dig into Cheddar Turkey Casserole and other next-day delights on pages 308-311.

Just choose whatever fits your meal plan—then enjoy! ■

THRILLING GRILLING. Marinated Sirloin Steak (p. 302).

GREATS TO GO ON THE GRILL

Want to really fire up the crowd at your next backyard barbecue? Replace plain burgers and hot dogs with the sensational new recipes here. They're sure to give your cookout plenty of spark!

Mouthwatering entrees such as Portobello Lamb Chops, Shrimp and Scallop Kabobs, Sweet and Spicy Grilled Chicken and Marinated Sirloin Steak come off the grill with fantastic flavor. Best of all, they don't require lots of time and effort to prepare. ▪

Spicy Paprika Herb Rub
(Pictured below)
Prep/Total Time: 5 min.

Rub this tongue-tingling blend on your chicken or roast. The meat will turn golden brown and taste terrific.
—Marian Platt, Sequim, Washington

    1 tablespoon garlic powder
    1 tablespoon brown sugar
    1 tablespoon ground mustard
    1 tablespoon paprika
    1 teaspoon onion salt
    1 teaspoon dried rosemary, crushed
    1 teaspoon ground cumin
    1 teaspoon dried thyme
    1 teaspoon pepper
  1/2 teaspoon cayenne pepper

In a small bowl, combine all ingredients; store herb rub in a covered container. Rub over meat or poultry before grilling or broiling. **Yield:** 1/2 cup.

Sweet and Spicy Grilled Chicken
(Pictured above)
Prep/Total Time: 20 min.

This simple recipe has become one of my family's grilled favorites. The combination of sweet and spicy is perfect.
—Melissa Ball, Pearisburg, Virginia

    2 tablespoons brown sugar
    1 tablespoon paprika
    2 teaspoons onion powder
1-1/2 teaspoons salt
    1 teaspoon chili powder
    6 boneless skinless chicken breast halves
      (6 ounces *each*)

Combine the first five ingredients; rub over the chicken. If grilling chicken, use long-handled tongs to dip a paper towel in cooking oil and lightly coat the grill rack. Grill chicken, covered, over medium heat or broil 4-6 in. from the heat for 4-5 minutes on each side or until a meat thermometer reads 170°. **Yield:** 6 servings.

Sausage & Chicken Kabobs
Prep: 15 min. + marinating **Grill:** 10 min.

While experimenting in the kitchen, my husband created a delicious marinade that's so good on these skewers.
—Diane Mateer, Florence, Kentucky

  1/4 cup soy sauce
    1 tablespoon Worcestershire sauce
    1 teaspoon garlic powder
  1/4 teaspoon pepper
  1/8 teaspoon seasoned salt
    1 pound boneless skinless chicken breasts,
      cut into 1-1/2-inch cubes
    1 pound fully cooked kielbasa *or* Polish
      sausage, cut into 3/4-inch slices
    4 medium red potatoes, cut into 1-1/2-inch
      cubes
    2 cups cubed fresh pineapple
Ranch salad dressing

In a large resealable plastic bag, combine the first five ingredients; add the chicken and sausage. Seal bag and turn to coat; refrigerate for 1 hour.

Meanwhile, place potatoes in a large microwave-safe bowl. Cover and microwave on high for 6-8 minutes or until almost tender, stirring twice.

Drain and discard the marinade. On metal or soaked wooden skewers, alternately thread chicken, potatoes, sausage and pineapple. Grill, covered, over medium heat for 10-15 minutes or until chicken juices run clear, turning frequently. Serve with ranch dressing. **Yield:** 8 servings.

BBQ Bacon Burgers
(Pictured below)

Prep/Total Time: 30 min.

With bacon bits inside and a tangy barbecue-mayo sauce spread on top, these are definitely not your ordinary beef burgers. I like to add Swiss cheese, lettuce and tomato.
—Joan Schoenherr, Eastpointe, Michigan

   1/4 **cup mayonnaise**
   1/4 **cup barbecue sauce**
     4 **bacon strips, cooked and crumbled**
1-1/2 **teaspoons dried minced onion**
1-1/2 **teaspoons steak seasoning**
     1 **pound ground beef**
     4 **slices Swiss cheese**
     4 **hamburger buns, split**
Lettuce leaves and tomato slices

In a small bowl, combine the mayonnaise and barbecue sauce. In another bowl, combine bacon, 2 tablespoons mayonnaise mixture, dried onion and steak seasoning; crumble the beef over the mixture and mix well. Shape into four patties.

Grill the burgers, covered, over medium heat for 5-7 minutes on each side or until a meat thermometer reads 160° and juices run clear. Top with cheese. Cover and cook 1-2 minutes longer or until the cheese is melted. Spread the remaining mayonnaise mixture over the buns; top each with a burger, lettuce and tomato. **Yield:** 4 servings.

Shrimp and Scallop Kabobs
(Pictured above)

Prep/Total Time: 30 min.

These seafood kabobs go over big with everyone who likes spicy food. Don't forget to use the extra seasoned butter for dipping!   *—Mitzi Sentiff, Annapolis, Maryland*

   3/4 **cup butter, cubed**
     3 **teaspoons Cajun seasoning**
1-1/2 **teaspoons hot pepper sauce**
   3/4 **teaspoon garlic powder**
   3/4 **teaspoon onion powder**
  12 **uncooked large shrimp (about 1/2 pound)**
  16 **sea scallops (about 2 pounds)**

In a microwave-safe bowl, melt butter. Stir in the Cajun seasoning, hot pepper sauce, garlic powder and onion powder; set aside 1/2 cup butter mixture for serving and keep warm.

Use long-handled tongs to dip a paper towel in cooking oil and lightly coat grill rack. Peel and devein shrimp, leaving tails on. On four metal or soaked wooden skewers, alternately thread shrimp and scallops.

Grill, covered, over medium heat for 3-5 minutes on each side or until shrimp turn pink and scallops are firm and opaque, basting occasionally with butter mixture. Serve with reserved butter. **Yield:** 4 servings.

Honey-Glazed Chicken Kabobs

(Pictured below)

Prep: 20 min. + marinating **Grill:** 10 min.

My husband always requests these fun, colorful chicken skewers for our "special day" meals. I usually serve rice pilaf, a tossed salad and garlic bread as sides.
—*Tracey Miller, Aiken, South Carolina*

- 2/3 cup reduced-sodium soy sauce
- 2/3 cup honey
- 1/2 cup canola oil
- 1 tablespoon prepared horseradish
- 2 teaspoons steak seasoning
- 2 garlic cloves, minced
- 2 pounds boneless skinless chicken breasts, cut into 1-1/2-inches cubes
- 1 large sweet red pepper, cut into 1-1/2-inch chunks
- 1 large green pepper, cut into 1-1/2-inch chunks
- 1 large onion, cut into 1-1/2-inch wedges

In a small bowl, combine the first six ingredients. Pour 1 cup marinade into a large resealable plastic bag; add chicken. Seal the bag and turn to coat; refrigerate for 5-6 hours. Cover and refrigerate remaining marinade.

Drain and discard marinade. On six metal or soaked wooden skewers, alternately thread the chicken and vegetables. Grill, covered, over medium heat for 5-7 minutes on each side or until chicken juices run clear, basting frequently with the reserved marinade. **Yield:** 6 servings.

Editor's Note: This recipe was tested with McCormick's Montreal Steak Seasoning. Look for it in the spice aisle.

Marinated Sirloin Steak

(Pictured above and on page 298)

Prep: 10 min. + marinating **Grill:** 20 min.

The recipe for this marinade came from my brother, and we rarely grill without it. You'll want to try it on chicken and pork, too. —*Terrie Sowders, Carthage, Indiana*

- 3/4 cup apple juice
- 3/4 cup soy sauce
- 1/4 cup olive oil
- 1 tablespoon *each* minced fresh oregano, rosemary and thyme
- 3 garlic cloves, minced
- 1 teaspoon ground ginger
- 1 beef top sirloin steak (1-1/2 pounds)

In a large resealable plastic bag, combine apple juice, soy sauce, oil and seasonings. Add beef; seal bag and turn to coat. Refrigerate for at least 1 hour.

Drain and discard the marinade. Grill steak, covered, over medium heat for 8-10 minutes on each side or until the meat reaches desired doneness (for medium-rare, a meat thermometer should read 145°; medium, 160°; well-done, 170°).

To serve, thinly slice the meat against the grain. **Yield:** 4 servings.

Barbecue Grilling Sauce

Prep/Total Time: 5 min.

This lip-smacking, slightly sweet basting sauce requires only five simple ingredients. It's fantastic on nearly any grilled entree. —*Kathryn Dunn, Axton, Virginia*

- 1 bottle (12 ounces) chili sauce
- 1 jar (10 ounces) orange marmalade
- 1/4 cup cider vinegar
- 1 tablespoon Worcestershire sauce
- 1-1/2 teaspoons celery seed

In a small bowl, combine all of the ingredients. Store the sauce in an airtight container in the refrigerator for up to 1 month. Use as a basting sauce for grilled meats. **Yield:** 2-1/2 cups.

Portobello Lamb Chops
(Pictured above)

Prep: 10 min. + marinating **Grill:** 20 min.

The fast-to-make marinade that flavors these lamb chops has a subtle hint of mellow peach preserves and the tang of balsamic vinegar. The sliced portobello mushrooms are jazzed up with rosemary, too. It's a great summer treat.
—Diane Barr, Louisville, Kentucky

3/4 cup peach preserves
1 tablespoon balsamic vinegar
1/4 teaspoon pepper
1/8 teaspoon salt
4 lamb loin chops (5 ounces *each* and
   2 inches thick)
1/4 cup olive oil
1 teaspoon dried rosemary, crushed
4 large portobello mushrooms

Combine the first four ingredients. Pour 1/3 cup marinade into a large resealable plastic bag; add lamb chops. Seal bag and turn to coat; refrigerate for 1-4 hours. Cover and refrigerate remaining marinade.

Use long-handled tongs to dip a paper towel in cooking oil and lightly coat grill rack. Combine 1/4 cup olive oil and rosemary; brush over mushrooms.

Grill the lamb chops and portobello mushrooms, uncovered, over medium heat 8-10 minutes on each side or until the meat reaches the desired doneness (for medium-rare, a meat thermometer should read 145°; medium, 160°; well-done, 170°), basting frequently with the reserved marinade.

Slice the mushrooms and serve with the lamb chops.
Yield: 4 servings.

QUICK COOKING FOR TWO

If it's just the pair of you at the table, why prepare a lot of extra food—and end up with lots of leftovers—when you can savor a meal that's sized right?

From scrumptious wrap sandwiches to jazzed-up chicken salad and a chock-full vegetable omelet, the recipes here give you the smaller yield you're looking for without sacrificing great flavor. ■

Southwest Chicken Wraps

(Pictured below)

Prep/Total Time: 25 min.

My husband can't get enough of these zippy roll-ups and enjoys them for both lunch and supper. Sometimes I use grilled chicken in place of the frozen popcorn variety.
—Sarah Rodefeld, Maud, Oklahoma

- 16 pieces frozen popcorn chicken
- 2 tablespoons prepared ranch salad dressing
- 2 tablespoons picante sauce
- 2 flour tortillas (10 inches), warmed
- 1/4 cup shredded lettuce
- 1/4 cup chopped tomato
- 1/4 cup shredded Mexican cheese blend

Prepare the chicken according to package directions. Meanwhile, spread 1 tablespoon each salad dressing and picante sauce over each tortilla. Place chicken down the center of each tortilla. Layer with lettuce, tomato and cheese. Roll up tortillas. **Yield:** 2 servings.

Sweet Onion Slaw Pork Wraps

(Pictured above)

Prep/Total Time: 20 min.

The strips of pork and sweet onion coleslaw go wonderfully together in these 20-minute wraps. They're so hearty, you might want to eat them with a knife and fork!
—Nancy Roth, Saint Joseph, Illinois

- 2/3 cup coleslaw mix
- 4 teaspoons finely chopped sweet onion
- 1 tablespoon mayonnaise
- 2 teaspoons sugar
- 1/2 teaspoon rice vinegar
- 1/2 teaspoon lemon juice
- Dash celery seed
- Dash pepper
- Dash salt
- 1 boneless pork loin chop (6 ounces), cut into 2-inch strips
- 1 teaspoon olive oil
- 2 flour tortillas (8 inches), warmed

In a large bowl, combine the first nine ingredients; set mixture aside.

In a small skillet, cook the pork in oil until pork is no longer pink. Spoon coleslaw mixture and pork down the center of each tortilla; roll up. **Yield:** 2 servings.

▌ TORTILLA TRICK ▐

To prevent your tortillas from tearing when rolling them up for wrap sandwiches or other recipes, just warm them slightly in a nonstick skillet before filling them. The warm tortillas are more pliable.
—Connie Deck, Springfield, Missouri

Mushroom Pepper Omelet

Prep/Total Time: 20 min.

Here's a delicious, home-style omelet for two that's ready in a jiffy and will keep you satisfied all morning long.
—Diana Howard, Ava, Illinois

- 1/4 cup chopped green onions
- 1/4 cup sliced fresh mushrooms
- 1/4 cup chopped green pepper
- 2 tablespoons butter, *divided*
- 5 eggs
- 1/2 teaspoon salt
- 1/4 teaspoon pepper
- 1/4 cup shredded cheddar cheese
- 1/4 cup shredded Monterey Jack cheese

In a large nonstick skillet, saute the onions, mushrooms and green pepper in 1 tablespoon butter until tender. Remove and keep warm.

In the same skillet, melt the remaining butter over medium-high heat. Whisk eggs, salt and pepper. Add the egg mixture to the skillet (the mixture should set immediately at edges).

As eggs set, push cooked edges toward the center, letting the uncooked portion flow underneath. When the eggs are set, spoon the vegetable mixture on one side and sprinkle with the cheeses; fold the other side over the filling. Cut in half. **Yield:** 2 servings.

Honey-Mustard Chicken Salad

(Pictured below)

Prep/Total Time: 15 min.

This is a twist on a recipe I found for those with diabetes. It makes a great cool meal on a hot summer's day.
—Mary Beth Bond, Washington, Kansas

- 1 cup cubed cooked chicken breast
- 3/4 cup seedless red grapes, halved
- 1/2 cup chopped water chestnuts
- 1/2 teaspoon grated lemon peel
- Dash pepper
- 1/4 cup fat-free honey Dijon salad dressing
- 3 cups fresh baby spinach
- 1/4 cup shredded smoked Swiss cheese
- 2 tablespoons coarsely chopped walnuts

In a small bowl, combine the chicken, red grapes, water chestnuts, lemon peel and pepper. Drizzle with dressing; toss to coat. Divide the spinach between two plates; top with chicken mixture. Sprinkle with cheese and walnuts. **Yield:** 2 servings.

Yes, you can have your cake and eat it, too—these recipes prove it! Each one is both easy to prepare and a wow-the-crowd dessert.

Created in our Test Kitchen, these surprising treats start with a mix. From there, fun decorations lead to party-worthy sensations sure to impress guests. ■

Flowers and Vines Cake
(Pictured below)

Prep: 30 min. **Bake:** 25 min. + cooling

This beautifully blooming delight may look complicated, but it's really a snap to make. Serve it for a bridal shower, ladies' luncheon or any occasion at all.

  1 package (18-1/4 ounces) white cake mix
  1 can (16 ounces) vanilla frosting
Shoestring licorice
Jelly beans
Nonpareils

Prepare and bake the cake according to the package directions, using two greased 9-in. round baking pans. Cool for 10 minutes before removing from pans to wire racks to cool completely.

Spread the frosting between layers and over top and sides of cake. Lightly press licorice and candies into cake forming flower and vine designs. **Yield:** 12 servings.

Ocean Cake
(Pictured above)

Prep: 30 min. **Bake:** 25 min. + cooling

Whether it's for a pool or birthday party, this sea-themed creation is guaranteed to snag smiles! Our Test Kitchen staff spread frosting on top of the two-layer cake using the back of a spoon to produce "waves." Bright candies and Fruit Roll-Ups form the colorful ocean.

  1 package (18-1/4 ounces) white cake mix
 2-2/3 cups canned vanilla frosting
Blue and green Fruit Roll-Ups
Fish candies
Black shoestring licorice
Candy stick

Prepare and bake the cake according to the package directions, using two greased 9-in. round baking pans. Cool for 10 minutes before removing from pans to wire racks to cool completely.

Spread 1-2/3 cups frosting between layers and over top and sides of cake. Using the back of a spoon, make waves on the top of cake with remaining frosting.

Cut wave shapes out of Fruit Roll-Ups; gently press along the bottom of the cake. Arrange additional wave shapes and fish candies on the top of the cake as desired. Tie licorice on one end of candy stick to create a fishing pole. **Yield:** 12 servings.

Chocolate Fruit Basket Cake
(Pictured below)

Prep: 30 min. **Bake:** 25 min. + cooling

Wow! Your friends and family will be amazed when they see this bountiful basket...and you'll be amazed at how simple it is to assemble! Kit Kat bars surround the cake, which features fresh berries on top.

- 1 package (18-1/4 ounces) chocolate cake mix
- 1 can (16 ounces) chocolate frosting
- 11 Kit Kat candy bars (1-1/2 ounces *each*)
- 2 pounds fresh strawberries
- 1 pint fresh blueberries
- 1 pint fresh raspberries
- 2 tablespoons apricot preserves, warmed

Fresh mint leaves, optional

Prepare and bake the cake according to the package directions, using two greased 9-in. round baking pans. Cool for 10 minutes before removing from pans to wire racks to cool completely.

Spread the frosting between the layers and over the top and sides of cake. Separate candy bars; lightly press into sides of cake.

Arrange the berries on top of the cake; brush with the apricot preserves. Garnish with mint leaves if desired. **Yield:** 12 servings.

Rocky Road Cake
(Pictured above)

Prep: 30 min. **Bake:** 25 min. + cooling

This creative take on classic rocky road flavor gives you a real showstopper for any event. Sweet tooths will come running as soon as you start slicing.

- 1 package (18-1/4 ounces) chocolate cake mix
- 1 can (16 ounces) chocolate frosting
- 1-3/4 cups dry roasted peanuts, *divided*
- 1-1/2 cups miniature milk chocolate kisses
- 1-1/2 cups miniature marshmallows, *divided*

Prepare and bake the cake according to the package directions, using two greased 9-in. round baking pans. Cool for 10 minutes before removing from pans to wire racks to cool completely.

Spread the chocolate frosting between the layers and over the top and sides of cake. In a large bowl, combine 1-1/2 cups peanuts, the chocolate kisses and 1 cup marshmallows; set aside.

Arrange remaining marshmallows to form the border of a road across the top of cake. Coarsely chop remaining peanuts and sprinkle inside marshmallow border. Lightly press chocolate mixture over sides and remaining top of cake. **Yield:** 12 servings.

DECORATING TIPS

After the Rocky Road Cake (recipe above) is frosted, use 1/2 cup mini marshmallows to outline a 2-inch wide "road" on top of cake.

Lightly press on the marshmallows, peanuts and chocolate kisses to evenly distribute the topping on frosting.

LIVELY LEFTOVERS BY DESIGN

If extra food at the end of a meal is something you try to avoid, you might have a change of heart when you see the recipes here!

Two of them—German-Style Beef Roast and Pork Roast with Plum Sauce—give you a mouthwatering dinner for your family, plus plenty of leftovers. Both recipes yield a whopping 10 servings.

The next day, use the extra meat to fix a deliciously different entree. The beef is perfect for making Roast Beef with Chive Roasted Potatoes, and the pork is ideal for Pork & Vegetable Stir-Fry. ■

Pork Roast with Plum Sauce
(Pictured below)

Prep: 20 min. **Cook:** 5 hours

Flavors blend to create a subtle hint of Asian flair in this juicy entree. The recipe lends itself to variation—feel free to replace the plum jam with apricot preserves.
—Jeannie Klugh, Lancaster, Pennsylvania

   1 boneless whole pork loin roast (4 pounds)
   2 tablespoons canola oil
   1 cup sherry
   2 tablespoons dried thyme
   2 tablespoons soy sauce
   4 garlic cloves, minced
   1 tablespoon ground mustard
1-1/2 teaspoons ground ginger
   1 teaspoon garlic salt
1/2 teaspoon salt
1/2 teaspoon pepper

1/2 cup plum jam
  2 tablespoons cornstarch
1/4 cup cold water

Cut roast in half. In a large skillet, brown roast in oil on all sides; drain. Transfer to a 4-qt. slow cooker. In a small bowl, combine sherry, thyme, soy sauce, garlic, mustard, ginger, garlic salt, salt and pepper; pour over the pork. Cover and cook on low for 5 to 6 hours or until a meat thermometer reads 160°.

Remove meat to a serving platter; keep warm. Skim the fat from cooking juices; transfer to a small saucepan. Add jam. Bring to a boil. Combine cornstarch and cold water until smooth. Gradually stir into the pan. Bring to a boil; cook and stir for 2 minutes or until thickened. Slice roast and serve with gravy. **Yield:** 10 servings.

Pork & Vegetable Stir-Fry
(Pictured above)

Prep/Total Time: 20 min.

I love using leftovers from my pork roast this way! The colorful, hearty dish served over rice is a family-pleasing meal-in-one for busy weeknights or any time at all. With frozen veggies, it comes together in just 20 minutes.
—Jeannie Klugh, Lancaster, Pennsylvania

  1 tablespoon cornstarch
1/4 cup unsweetened apple juice
  2 tablespoons sherry *or* additional
     unsweetened apple juice
  2 tablespoons soy sauce
  1 package (16 ounces) frozen stir-fry
     vegetable blend, thawed
  1 garlic clove, minced
  1 tablespoon canola oil
  2 cups cubed cooked pork

1/4 cup slivered almonds, toasted
Hot cooked rice

In a small bowl, combine cornstarch, apple juice, sherry and soy sauce until smooth; set aside.

Stir-fry the vegetable blend and garlic in oil for 1-2 minutes or until the vegetables are crisp-tender. Stir the cornstarch mixture and add to the pan. Bring to a boil; cook and stir for 1-2 minutes or until thickened. Add pork; heat through. Sprinkle with almonds. Serve with rice. **Yield:** 4 servings.

German-Style Beef Roast
(Pictured below)

Prep: 10 min. **Cook:** 8 hours

My grandmother used to fix this, and I adapted it for a slow cooker. If you like, serve mashed potatoes to soak up the gravy. —Lois Stanley, Myrtle Beach, South Carolina

    1 boneless beef chuck roast (4 pounds),
      trimmed
    1 teaspoon pepper
    1 large onion, thinly sliced
    1 bottle (12 ounces) beer *or* nonalcoholic beer
    1 cup ketchup
  1/4 cup packed brown sugar
  1/4 cup all-purpose flour
  1/4 cup cold water

Cut roast in half; sprinkle with pepper. Place onion and roast in a 5-qt. slow cooker. In a small bowl, combine the beer, ketchup and brown sugar; pour over the top. Cover and cook on low for 8 to 10 hours or until meat is tender.

Remove meat to a serving platter; keep warm. Skim the fat from cooking juices; transfer to a small saucepan. Bring the liquid to a boil. Combine flour and cold water

until smooth; gradually stir into the pan. Bring to a boil; cook and stir for 2 minutes or until thickened. Serve with the roast. **Yield:** 10 servings.

Roast Beef with Chive Roasted Potatoes
(Pictured above)

Prep: 20 min. **Bake:** 25 min.

It's hard to believe that last night's beef roast could get any better, but that second-day meat will really shine in this heartwarming bake from our Test Kitchen.

    2 pounds red potatoes, cut into 1-inch cubes
    2 tablespoons olive oil
    2 teaspoons minced chives
  3/4 teaspoon salt, *divided*
    2 medium onions, halved and thinly sliced
    1 pound sliced fresh mushrooms
  1/4 cup butter, cubed
    1 garlic clove, minced
    1 teaspoon dried rosemary, crushed
  1/4 teaspoon pepper
  1/3 cup dry red wine *or* beef broth
    2 cups cubed cooked roast beef
    1 cup beef gravy

Place potatoes in a greased 15-in. x 10-in. x 1-in. baking pan. Drizzle with the oil and sprinkle with the chives and 1/4 teaspoon salt; toss to coat. Bake, uncovered, at 425° for 25-30 minutes or until tender, stirring occasionally.

Meanwhile, in a large skillet, saute the onions and mushrooms in butter until tender. Add garlic, rosemary, pepper and remaining salt; cook 1 minute longer. Stir in wine. Add beef and gravy; heat through. Serve with potatoes. **Yield:** 6 servings.

EXTRAS FROM TURKEY DAY

Holiday cooking is just too good to limit to one day's feast. When your fridge is filled with leftover turkey from Thanksgiving, put it to delicious use with one of the creative entrees here.

From Greek-style wraps and a Southwest-flavored casserole to a fruitful salad and cheesy baked pasta, these second-day delights will let you enjoy every bit of your special-occasion fare. ■

Mediterranean Turkey Wraps
(Pictured below)

Prep/Total Time: 15 min.

Here's a fresh, fun option when you need a filling lunch or fast weekday dinner. I serve these yummy roll-ups with a side salad or soup. —Donna Noel, Gray, Maine

- 1/3 cup mayonnaise
- 1/4 cup pitted Greek olives
- 2-1/2 teaspoons capers, drained
- 1 teaspoon lemon juice
- 1 small garlic clove
- 4 flour tortillas (10 inches), room temperature
- 4 lettuce leaves
- 3/4 pound thinly sliced cooked turkey
- 2 medium tomatoes, sliced
- 1/2 cup crumbled feta cheese

Place the first five ingredients in a food processor; cover and process until blended. Spread over tortillas. Layer with lettuce, turkey, tomatoes and cheese. Roll up and secure with toothpicks. **Yield:** 4 servings.

Southwest Turkey Casserole
(Pictured above)

Prep: 20 min. **Bake:** 25 min.

This creamy bake gets my family members to happily eat their veggies! They like the crunchy chips, too.
—Crystal Kolady, Henrietta, New York

- 2 large onions, chopped
- 2 jalapeno peppers, seeded and chopped
- 2 tablespoons butter
- 6 cups cubed cooked turkey
- 2 cans (10-3/4 ounces *each*) condensed cream of chicken soup, undiluted
- 2 cups (16 ounces) sour cream
- 1 package (10 ounces) frozen chopped spinach, thawed and squeezed dry
- 2 cups (8 ounces) shredded Monterey Jack cheese
- 1 package (12-1/2 ounces) nacho tortilla chips, crushed
- 4 green onions, sliced

In a Dutch oven, saute the onions and jalapeno peppers in butter until tender. Stir in the turkey, cream of chicken soup, sour cream and spinach. In a greased 13-in. x 9-in. baking dish, layer half of the turkey mixture, cheese and tortilla chips. Repeat layers.

Bake, uncovered, at 350° for 25-30 minutes or until bubbly. Let stand for 5 minutes before serving. Sprinkle with green onions. **Yield:** 12 servings.

Editor's Note: When cutting hot peppers, disposable gloves are recommended. Avoid touching your face.

Cheddar Turkey Casserole
(Pictured below)

Prep: 20 min. **Bake:** 35 min.

Please all ages at your table with this oven-baked supper. Featuring an ooey-gooey cheese sauce, pasta, chunks of turkey and mixed vegetables, the casserole is a satisfying meal-in-one everyone will gobble up and request again.
—*Steve Foy, Kirkwood, Missouri*

    4 cups uncooked spiral pasta
    1 garlic clove, minced
    3 tablespoons butter
    3 tablespoons all-purpose flour
    1 teaspoon salt
  1/4 teaspoon prepared mustard
  1/4 teaspoon dried thyme
  1/4 teaspoon pepper
    2 cups 2% milk
1-1/2 cups (6 ounces) shredded cheddar cheese
    2 cups cubed cooked turkey
    2 cups frozen mixed vegetables, thawed
  1/2 cup slivered almonds

Cook the pasta according to the package directions.

Meanwhile, in a large saucepan, saute the garlic in butter until tender. Stir in the flour, salt, mustard, thyme and pepper. Gradually stir in milk. Bring to a boil; cook and stir for 2 minutes or until thickened. Remove from the heat; stir in the cheese until melted. Drain the pasta; place in a large bowl. Toss with turkey, vegetables and cheese sauce.

Transfer the mixture to a greased 13-in. x 9-in. baking dish. Sprinkle with the slivered almonds. Bake, uncovered, at 350° for 35-40 minutes or until the casserole is heated through. **Yield:** 6 servings.

Fruited Curry Turkey Salad
(Pictured above)

Prep/Total Time: 15 min.

You'll love the well-balanced flavors in this quick salad. Have extra chicken from last night's dinner? Feel free to use those leftovers in place of the turkey in this recipe.
—*Suzanne Kesel, Cohocton, New York*

  1/2 cup plain yogurt
  1/2 cup mayonnaise
    1 tablespoon honey
1-1/2 teaspoons curry powder
  1/4 teaspoon salt
Dash pepper
    4 cups cubed cooked turkey
  1/2 cup chopped apple
  1/3 cup chopped celery
  1/3 cup chopped walnuts, toasted
  1/3 cup dried cranberries
    5 cups torn mixed salad greens

In a large bowl, combine the first six ingredients. Stir in the turkey, apple, celery, walnuts and cranberries. Divide salad greens among five serving plates; top with turkey mixture. **Yield:** 5 servings.

SAUCY SOLUTION

I put leftover turkey in a slow cooker and add some minced garlic, barbecue sauce and a little hot sauce. I serve the warmed meat on buns. My family looks forward to these sandwiches every year.
—*Stacy Anderson, Twin Falls, Idaho*

Substitutions & Equivalents

EQUIVALENT MEASURES

3 teaspoons	= 1 tablespoon	16 tablespoons	= 1 cup
4 tablespoons	= 1/4 cup	2 cups	= 1 pint
5-1/3 tablespoons	= 1/3 cup	4 cups	= 1 quart
8 tablespoons	= 1/2 cup	4 quarts	= 1 gallon

FOOD EQUIVALENTS

GRAINS

Macaroni	1 cup (3-1/2 ounces) uncooked	= 2-1/2 cups cooked
Noodles, Medium	3 cups (4 ounces) uncooked	= 4 cups cooked
Popcorn	1/3 to 1/2 cup unpopped	= 8 cups popped
Rice, Long Grain	1 cup uncooked	= 3 cups cooked
Rice, Quick-Cooking	1 cup uncooked	= 2 cups cooked
Spaghetti	8 ounces uncooked	= 4 cups cooked

CRUMBS

Bread	1 slice	= 3/4 cup soft crumbs, 1/4 cup fine dry crumbs
Graham Crackers	7 squares	= 1/2 cup finely crushed
Buttery Round Crackers	12 crackers	= 1/2 cup finely crushed
Saltine Crackers	14 crackers	= 1/2 cup finely crushed

FRUITS

Bananas	1 medium	= 1/3 cup mashed
Lemons	1 medium	= 3 tablespoons juice, 2 teaspoons grated peel
Limes	1 medium	= 2 tablespoons juice, 1-1/2 teaspoons grated peel
Oranges	1 medium	= 1/4 to 1/3 cup juice, 4 teaspoons grated peel

VEGETABLES

Cabbage	1 head	= 5 cups shredded	Green Pepper	1 large	= 1 cup chopped
Carrots	1 pound	= 3 cups shredded	Mushrooms	1/2 pound	= 3 cups sliced
Celery	1 rib	= 1/2 cup chopped	Onions	1 medium	= 1/2 cup chopped
Corn	1 ear fresh	= 2/3 cup kernels	Potatoes	3 medium	= 2 cups cubed

NUTS

Almonds	1 pound	= 3 cups chopped	Pecan Halves	1 pound	= 4-1/2 cups chopped
Ground Nuts	3-3/4 ounces	= 1 cup	Walnuts	1 pound	= 3-3/4 cups chopped

EASY SUBSTITUTIONS

When you need... / Use...

When you need...		Use...
Baking Powder	1 teaspoon	1/2 teaspoon cream of tartar + 1/4 teaspoon baking soda
Buttermilk	1 cup	1 tablespoon lemon juice or vinegar + enough milk to measure 1 cup (let stand 5 minutes before using)
Cornstarch	1 tablespoon	2 tablespoons all-purpose flour
Honey	1 cup	1-1/4 cups sugar + 1/4 cup water
Half-and-Half Cream	1 cup	1 tablespoon melted butter + enough whole milk to measure 1 cup
Onion	1 small, chopped (1/3 cup)	1 teaspoon onion powder or 1 tablespoon dried minced onion
Tomato Juice	1 cup	1/2 cup tomato sauce + 1/2 cup water
Tomato Sauce	2 cups	3/4 cup tomato paste + 1 cup water
Unsweetened Chocolate	1 square (1 ounce)	3 tablespoons baking cocoa + 1 tablespoon shortening or oil
Whole Milk	1 cup	1/2 cup evaporated milk + 1/2 cup water

COOKING TERMS

Here's a quick reference for some of the cooking terms used in *Taste of Home* recipes:

BASTE—To moisten food with melted butter, pan drippings, marinades or other liquid to add more flavor and juiciness.

BEAT—A rapid movement to combine ingredients using a fork, spoon, wire whisk or electric mixer.

BLEND—To combine ingredients until just mixed.

BOIL—To heat liquids until bubbles form that cannot be "stirred down." In the case of water, the temperature will reach 212°.

BONE—To remove all meat from the bone before cooking.

CREAM—To beat ingredients together to a smooth consistency, usually in the case of butter and sugar for baking.

DASH—A small amount of seasoning, less than 1/8 teaspoon. If using a shaker, a dash would comprise a quick flip of the container.

DREDGE—To coat foods with flour or other dry ingredients. Most often done with pot roasts and stew meat before browning.

FOLD—To incorporate several ingredients by careful and gentle turning with a spatula. Used generally with beaten egg whites or whipped cream when mixing into the rest of the ingredients to keep the batter light.

JULIENNE—To cut foods into long thin strips much like matchsticks. Used most often for salads and stir-fry dishes.

MINCE—To cut into very fine pieces. Used often for garlic or fresh herbs.

PARBOIL—To cook partially, usually used in the case of chicken, sausages and vegetables.

PARTIALLY SET—Describes the consistency of gelatin after it has been chilled for a small amount of time. Mixture should resemble the consistency of egg whites.

PUREE—To process foods to a smooth mixture. Can be prepared in an electric blender, food processor, food mill or sieve.

SAUTE—To fry quickly in a small amount of fat, stirring almost constantly. Most often done with onions, mushrooms and other chopped vegetables.

SCORE—To cut slits partway through the outer surface of foods. Often used with ham or flank steak.

STIR-FRY—To cook meats and/or vegetables with a constant stirring motion in a small amount of oil in a wok or skillet over high heat.

General Recipe Index

This handy index lists every recipe by food category, major ingredient and/or cooking method, so you can easily locate recipes to suit your needs.

✓ Recipe Includes Nutrition Facts and Diabetic Exchanges

✓ Recipe Includes Nutrition Facts and Diabetic Exchanges

✓ Recipe Includes Nutrition Facts and Diabetic Exchanges

✓ Recipe Includes Nutrition Facts and Diabetic Exchanges

✓ Recipe Includes Nutrition Facts and Diabetic Exchanges

✓ Recipe Includes Nutrition Facts and Diabetic Exchanges

✓ Recipe Includes Nutrition Facts and Diabetic Exchanges

✓ Recipe Includes Nutrition Facts and Diabetic Exchanges

✓ *Recipe Includes Nutrition Facts and Diabetic Exchanges*

✓ Recipe Includes Nutrition Facts and Diabetic Exchanges

✓ *Recipe Includes Nutrition Facts and Diabetic Exchanges*

✓ Recipe Includes Nutrition Facts and Diabetic Exchanges

✓ Recipe Includes Nutrition Facts and Diabetic Exchanges

✓ Recipe Includes Nutrition Facts and Diabetic Exchanges

✓ Recipe Includes Nutrition Facts and Diabetic Exchanges

✓ Recipe Includes Nutrition Facts and Diabetic Exchanges

✓ Recipe Includes Nutrition Facts and Diabetic Exchanges

Alphabetical Index

*This handy index lists every recipe in alphabetical order,
so you can easily locate recipes to suit your needs.*

✓ Recipe Includes Nutrition Facts and Diabetic Exchanges

✓ Recipe Includes Nutrition Facts and Diabetic Exchanges

✓ Recipe Includes Nutrition Facts and Diabetic Exchanges

✓ Recipe Includes Nutrition Facts and Diabetic Exchanges

✓ Recipe Includes Nutrition Facts and Diabetic Exchanges

✓ Recipe Includes Nutrition Facts and Diabetic Exchanges